خرج و لم يعد

Sometimes You Have
To Go A Long Way
To Come Back
A Short Distance

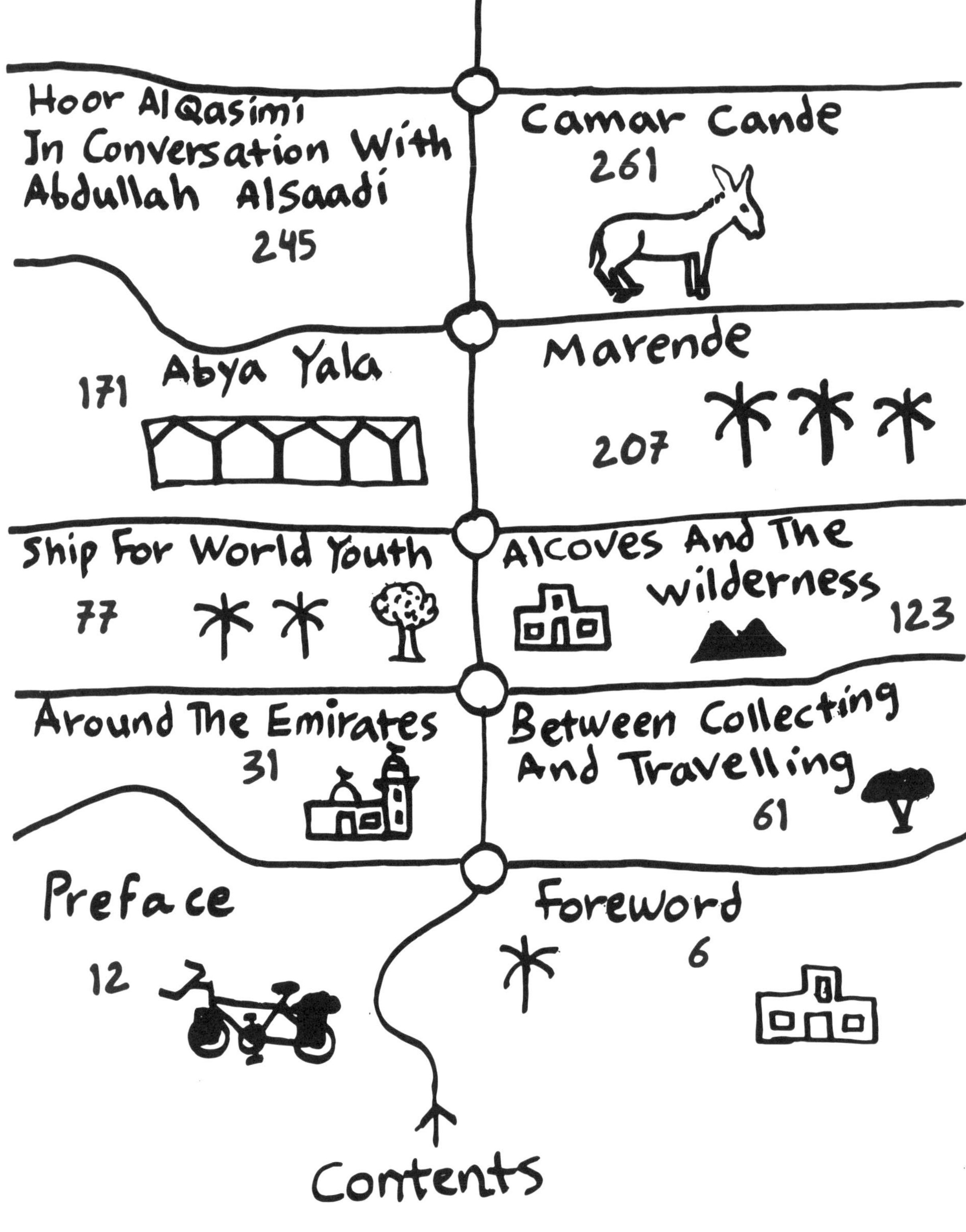

Contents

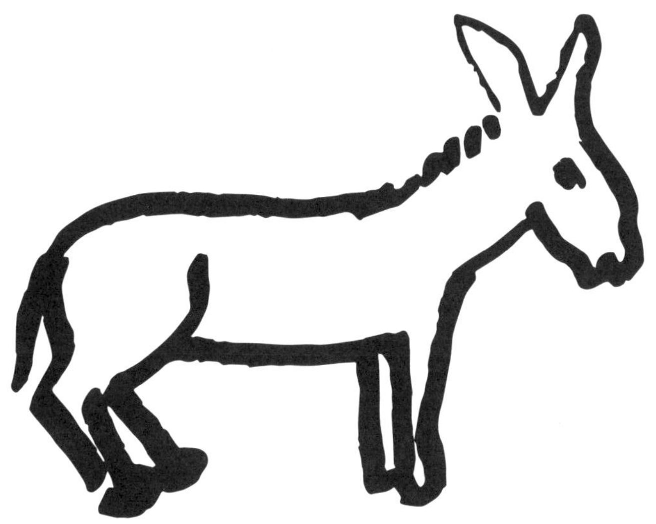

Abdullah Alsaadi

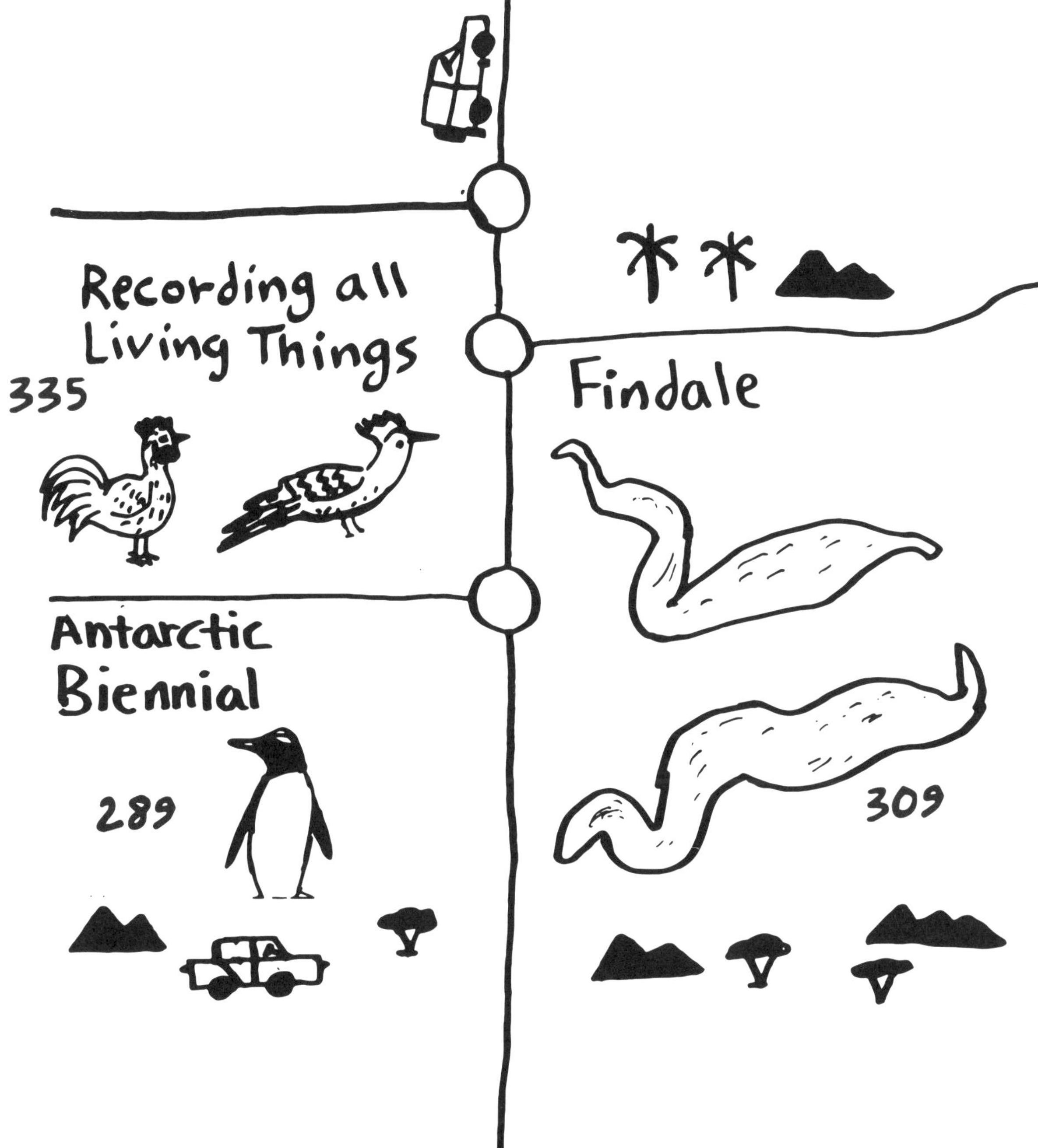
Recording all Living Things
335
Antarctic Biennial
289
Findale
309

FOREWORD

Abdullah Al Saadi has a long and storied relationship with the Emirate of Sharjah, starting with high school and later being the collection point for mail from his penpals. He is among its best-travelled residents and most extensive chroniclers, particularly of the Emirate's landscapes beyond its metropolitan centres. He is also one of its most prolific cultural figures. Hailing from the valley settlements of the east coast, known locally for germinating poets, actors, artists and practitioners of traditional crafts, Al Saadi was an integral part of the pioneering 'Five' – the generation of conceptual artists who emerged in the 1980s and reshaped the cultural landscape, ushering in a new philosophical and conceptual turn in the local arts scene.

Much of this movement unfolded in Sharjah against the backdrop of the educational and cultural reforms that emerged from the modernisation efforts between the 1960s and 1970s. Even before his rise to prominence with the pioneering Five, Al Saadi made his presence felt in Sharjah's cultural spaces, cutting his teeth at the Emirates Fine Arts Society (EFAS) and being one of the main artists to use their artist studios in Khorfakkan and Sharjah. The EFAS also staged some of his earliest exhibitions, such as *I am in Japan* (1997), and introduced him to key contemporaries such as Hassan Sharif.

His imprint on the local scene in the early 1990s was enduring, especially with EFAS, which coordinated the Sharjah Biennial from 1993 to 2001. Attending the biennial in the formative stages of his career expanded his understanding of art. After I took charge of the biennial in 2003 and shifted its curation towards a more global and deterritorialised direction, Al Saadi's practice remained among the most sought-after by the curators of subsequent editions. That his work continuously emerged as a source of engagement across different iterations reflected its capacity to traverse boundaries, generations and lines of inquiry while speaking to both Sharjah's ancestral past and its contemporaneity.

Our long-standing working relationship has evolved over five editions of the Sharjah Biennial, spanning 20 years beginning with the 2003 edition. At Sharjah Biennial 8: *Still Life – Art, Ecology and the Politics of Change* (2007), Al Saadi exhibited ink and watercolour scrolls depicting his home in Madha as well as the landscape of the Emirate's eastern coast. Sharjah Biennial 10: *Plot for a Biennial* (2011), Sharjah Biennial 12: *The past, the present, the possible* (2015) and Sharjah Biennial 13: *Tamawuj* (2017) all commissioned works arising from journeys undertaken by the artist the Emirate's eastern region.

When I curated the UAE National Pavilion at the 56th International Art Exhibition of La Biennale di Venezia in 2015, I spotlighted his indelible impact on the local art scene alongside the work of 14 other Emirati artists, many of whom, in contrast to Al Saadi, emerged from practising within metropolitan contexts of the Emirates. I also curated Al Saadi's first institutional solo show, *Al Toubay* (2014), at the Sharjah Art Foundation. This major retrospective not only brought together and synthesised many of his previous works but also foregrounded *Camar Cande's Journey* (2010–2011) as one of the first major 'journeys' commissioned by the Sharjah Art Foundation for Sharjah Biennial 10, an approach for which his practice is now well-known. The transference of these journeys into diverse bodies of work emerged from this exhibition and continues to inform the central role of travelling in his practice.

From working together for many years, the idea for this monograph was seeded and incubated. In keeping with the ambition of the exhibition to evoke the far-ranging scope and unique vantage point of his work, خرج ولم يعد / *Sometimes You Have to Go a Long Way to Come Back a Short Distance* aims to present an important cross-section of his prolific and inimitable practice. Generated from the efforts and archives of Sharjah Art Foundation in collaboration with the artist and local cultural organisations, it is by no means an attempt at a definitive or exhaustive volume; instead, it intends to crystallise and ground the human and environmental narratives at the core of Al Saadi's work. Featuring extracts from the artist's sketchbooks and journals, as well as his installations and live documentation of his travels, the monograph is an initiation into Al Saadi's life and art, and we hope, a catalyst for further research into artistic practices beyond the canon and an initiation into environmental and land art from the region on its own terms.

—Hoor Al Qasimi
President and Director, Sharjah Art Foundation

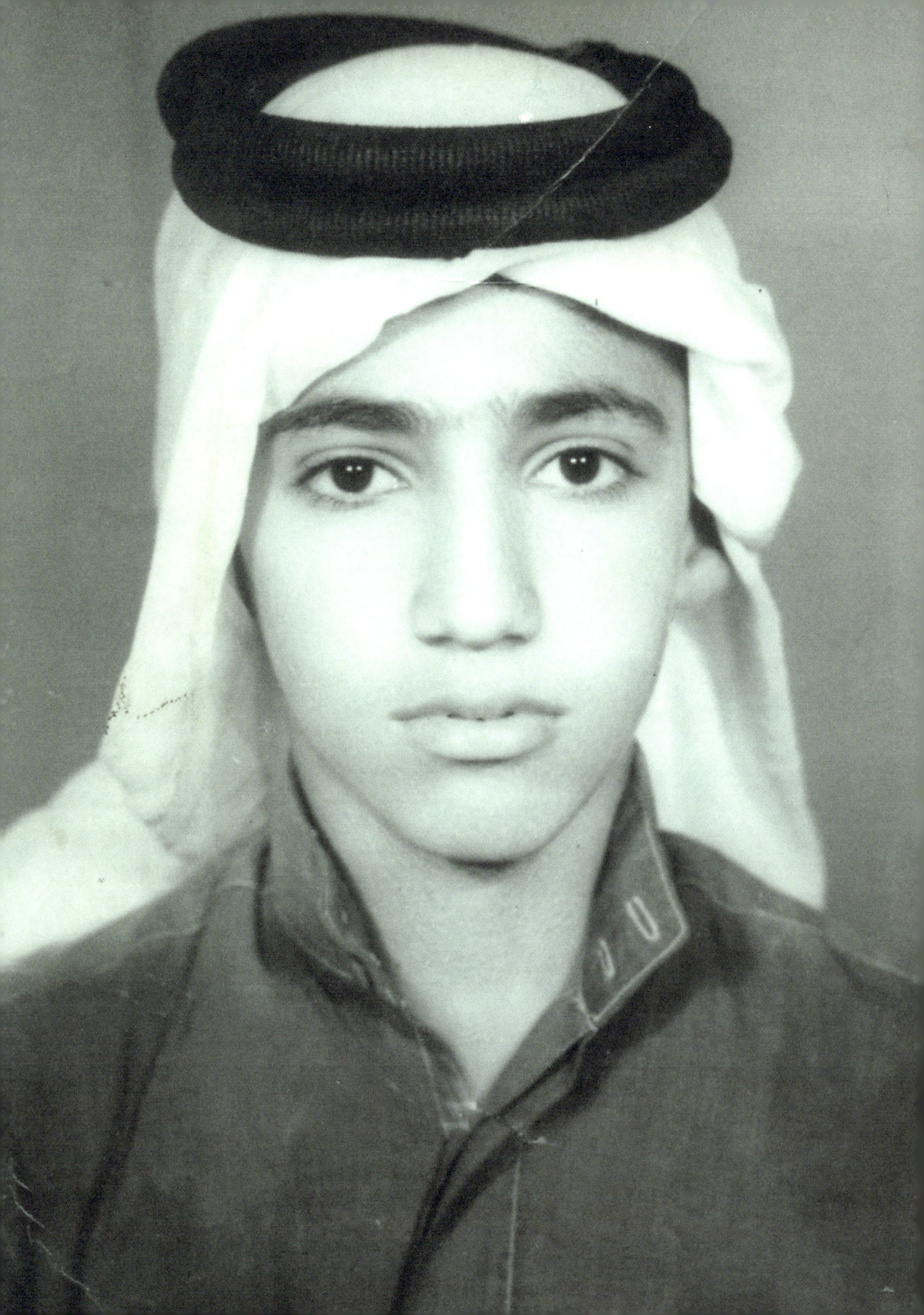

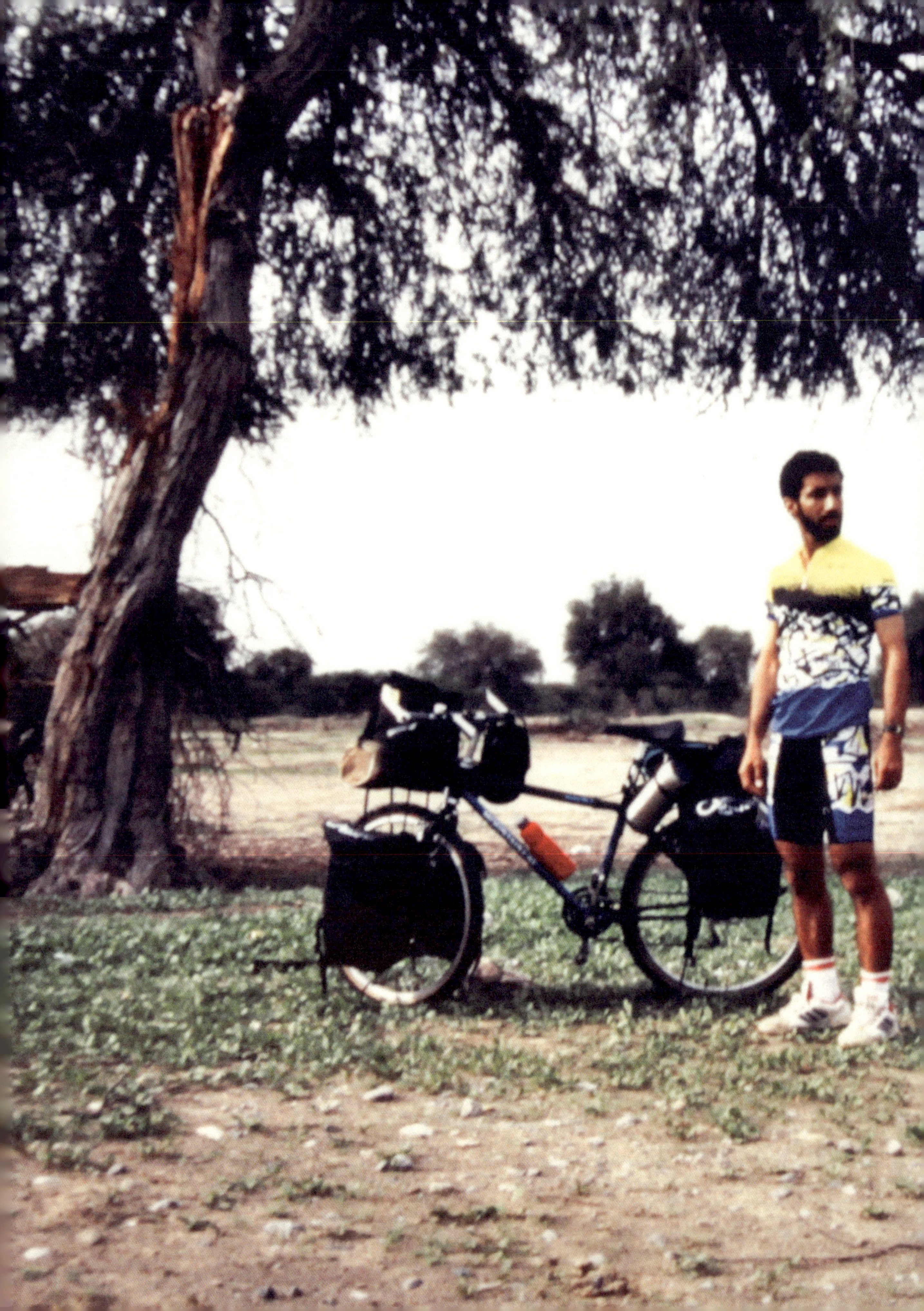

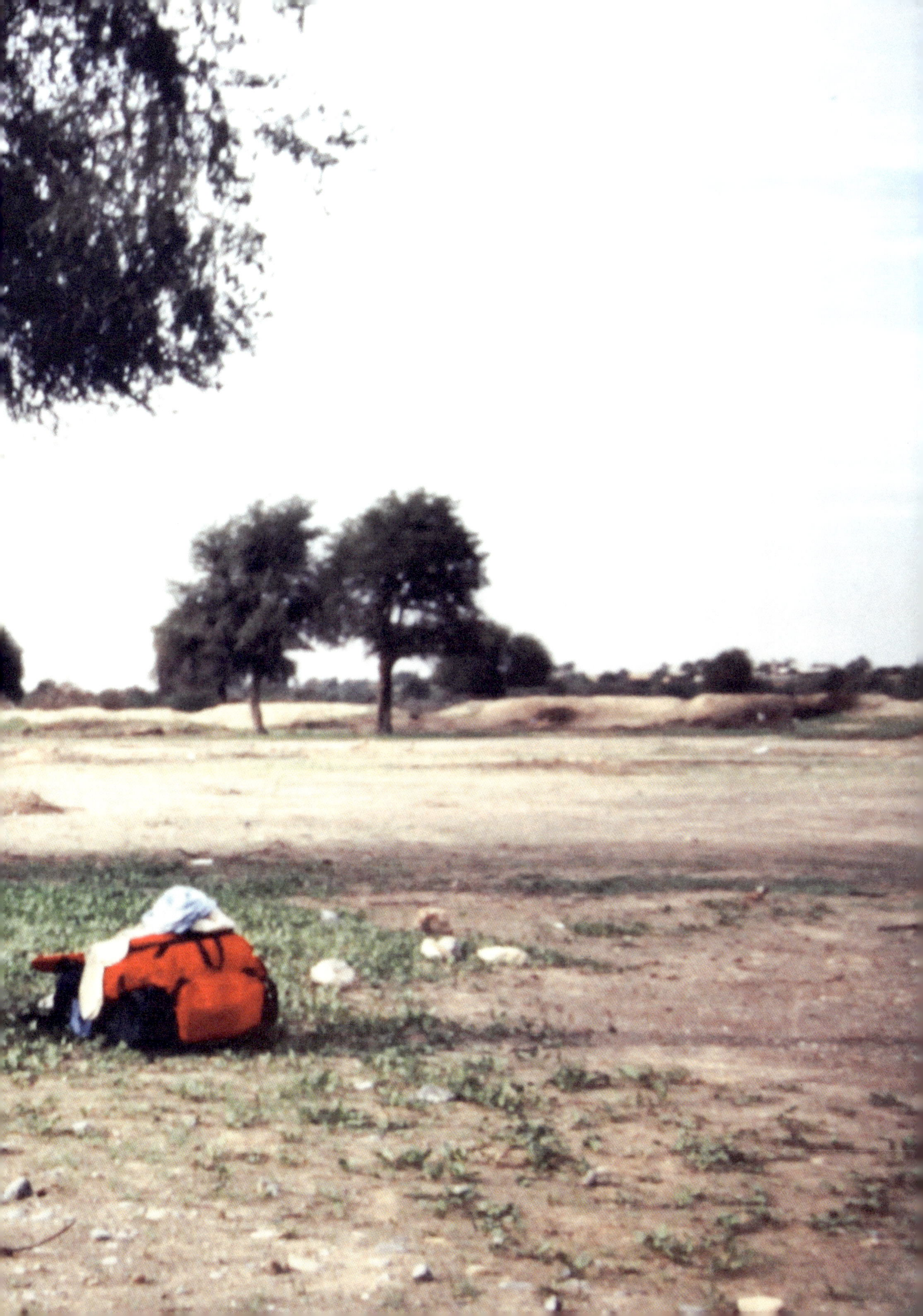

PREFACE

When his mother bought her first mobile phone, Abdullah Al Saadi felt a wistful ambivalence. For years she had left mementoes at the doorstep of his studio – small stones, fragments of wood, bits of detritus – to signal her presence when she paid him a visit but he was out or asleep. His mother could not read or write, and in his absence, this was her idiolect of care, a private language shared between them which he cherished. This system of communication was a tradition in Madha, their *dhahiya*, meaning suburb or exurb, located near the northeastern coast of the Emirates, slightly south of the Musandam Peninsula and east of the Hajar Mountains. The advent of the mobile portended its obsolescence and the inevitable stamp of modernity on such traditions. As is his nature, Al Saadi collected these intimate traces of the everyday, which may escape the notice of anyone not already attuned to their signifying power. Keeping every one of the messages his mother left for him – labelling, inventorying, categorising and sketching them one after the next – he transmuted them into a language of universal poetic force. From the contours of these line drawings and assemblages of found objects and materials, Al Saadi abstracted an alphabetic system informed by his knowledge of the Japanese hiragana and katakana scripts, which he had learnt in Kyoto as an exchange student, that would become the basis of the project *My Mother's Letters* (1998–2013).

In many ways, the work epitomises the scales at which his artistic practice operates, translating the hyperspecificity of his local context, from its traditions and rituals to its topography, into a form that speaks to the universal qualities of his wandering soul. Everywhere he goes he carries with him the cultural signature of his *dhahiya*'s geomorphologies, and wherever he finds himself in turn imprints upon his perception of his own context. In *My Mother's Letters*, like so many of Al Saadi's artistic ventures, viewers encounter the collision of a hyperlocal sensitivity to place with a peripatetic curiosity for the world beyond it. From the cross-pollination of these scales emerges a luminous way of seeing and capturing the seemingly utilitarian coordinates and textures of the everyday, not as reflections of the political and social but of the geologic and intergenerational transmission of knowledge outside canonical reading and writing systems. Al Saadi's projects often take morphological and environmental phenomena as source material for the creation of alphabets, lattices and scrolls as well as sculptures and assemblages. Many of his works are devised from found objects, both industrial or 'human-made' and naturally-occurring. Al Saadi is an astute and non-judgmental observer of human-natural kinships, which he collates, archives and sketches, then extrapolates to various material ends. 'Over time', Al Saadi tells Hoor Al Qasimi in an interview published in this volume, "I began to think that every work creates its own unique alphabet." These alphabets, or *Abjadiya* as Al Saadi calls them, embody the regimented and globalised form, refined into visual and pictorial typographic expression, of his unique approach to language-making. Reflecting the broader calls of his hyper-practice, Al Saadi's *Abjadiya* series encapsulates and echos early sapien cave drawings, civilisational scripts and contemporary lettering and typography alphabets which revive ancestral and idiosyncratic communicative forms.

Another of Al Saadi's best-known works, *Findale*, or sweet potato, project, positions the local variety of the root vegetable as an ideogrammatic animating force. When Al Saadi was a child, growing up in the mountainous *dhahiya* of Madha as the Emirates modernised in the wake of unification in the 1970s and 1980s, his father cultivated sweet potatoes. From a young age, he gravitated to their oblong, tapering silhouettes and irregular forms. Drawn to the diversity of its distinctive shapes and enamoured with its resemblance to the human figure, Al Saadi collected and catalogued sweet potatoes of varying sizes, unearthed and denuded, and used his sketchbook as a conduit to translate and refine their curves into a set of glyphs. With this sweet potato alphabet, he made stone engravings, oil-on-canvas works, clay and metal sculptures and even gold jewellery, alluding to his own family history, the non-metropolitan and settled agrarian heritage of the region and transnational affinities with the Neolithic Peruvian cultures for whom the tuber was a staple crop.

Aboard the *Akademik Ioffe*, the research vessel that hosted the inaugural Antarctic Biennale expedition in 2017, Al Saadi encountered a newfound object of morphological fascination. Amid the glaciated expanse of the world's most far-flung continent, he found parallels between its landforms and those of his native topography a hemisphere away. Evoking the mountains of the Musandam Peninsula, across which he had travelled all his life, the polar icebergs inspired his *Antarctic Alphabet* (2017). In keeping with his methodology for *My Mother's Letters* and the sweet potato project, Al Saadi sketched these floating spires of ice and composed a typography comprising 26 letters, corresponding to those of the English alphabet, derived from their sculptural essence.

What manifests in the rigours of this methodology is a certain zeal for collecting, preserving, organising and systemising experience that Al Saadi shares with the cartographer, the taxonomist and the archaeologist. Channelling the spirit of an explorer and the mind of a linguist, his artistic practice becomes a perennial act of translation across contexts through acts of visual communication using environmental shapes and phenomena. The central axis orienting his work, as the late writer Ahmed Rashid Thani observes in a 1994 essay translated and reprinted in this book, is between collecting and journeying. 'Al Saadi leans towards a unique, elusive and impossible dream,' Thani writes. 'It is none other than the intense desire to possess everything, to capture each moment in a relentless grasp, defying death itself.' From the flat files and shelves of his studio, the texture of material experience and the residues of existence threaten to spill over: from preserved insect specimens, animal bones and carcasses, to rock engravings, journals and scrolls documenting his visual impressions of notable landscapes. The accretion of sensory and physical data from a decades-long daily commitment to travelling, recording and gathering. Herein lies one of the tensions of Al Saadi's practice: in order to collect, one must travel, but always with ample storage space to return to. The book takes its inspiration and its title from this notion of leaving for new places and returning to known ones.

Do we travel to understand where we are from? Does Al Saadi return to a known place? Or does each departure, journey and adventure return with him, not only imprinting itself through memory and embodiment but also manifesting spatially in his studio, in the materials he gathers and in situ at the places he encounters? Ranging from excursions on foot and by bicycle across the rocks and mountainous terrain of the eastern Arabian Peninsula, retracing the interregional cultures of the Strait of Hormuz, to exchanges as far afield as Europe, Japan, South America and Antarctica, his travels, and the subtle restlessness they evoke, echo the continuous movement of the region's hill tribes and agriculturalists as well as the preachers who settled the Arabian Peninsula, traversing the globe after the *fateh* of Mecca in the year 630 to disseminate the message of Islam.

Yet, Al Saadi traces this peripatetic impulse to his youth and his hometown: 'It has something to do with an inherited obsession with moving and travelling across a landscape', as he tells Al Qasimi. 'These are problems that have troubled me since childhood.' Born in 1967, shortly before the unification of the Emirates, Al Saadi moved every year between his family's date palm farm in Al Ghouna, a village in the Omani exclave of Madha, and the coastal cities of Khorfakkan, Masafi and Fujairah. 'I found such upheavals stressful,' he says. 'They continue to haunt me in my current life.' Whatever residual ambivalence Al Saadi feels towards these early seasonal migrations, the wanderlust and sense of uprootedness, gave rise and remained the basis of both his artistic practice and way of being,

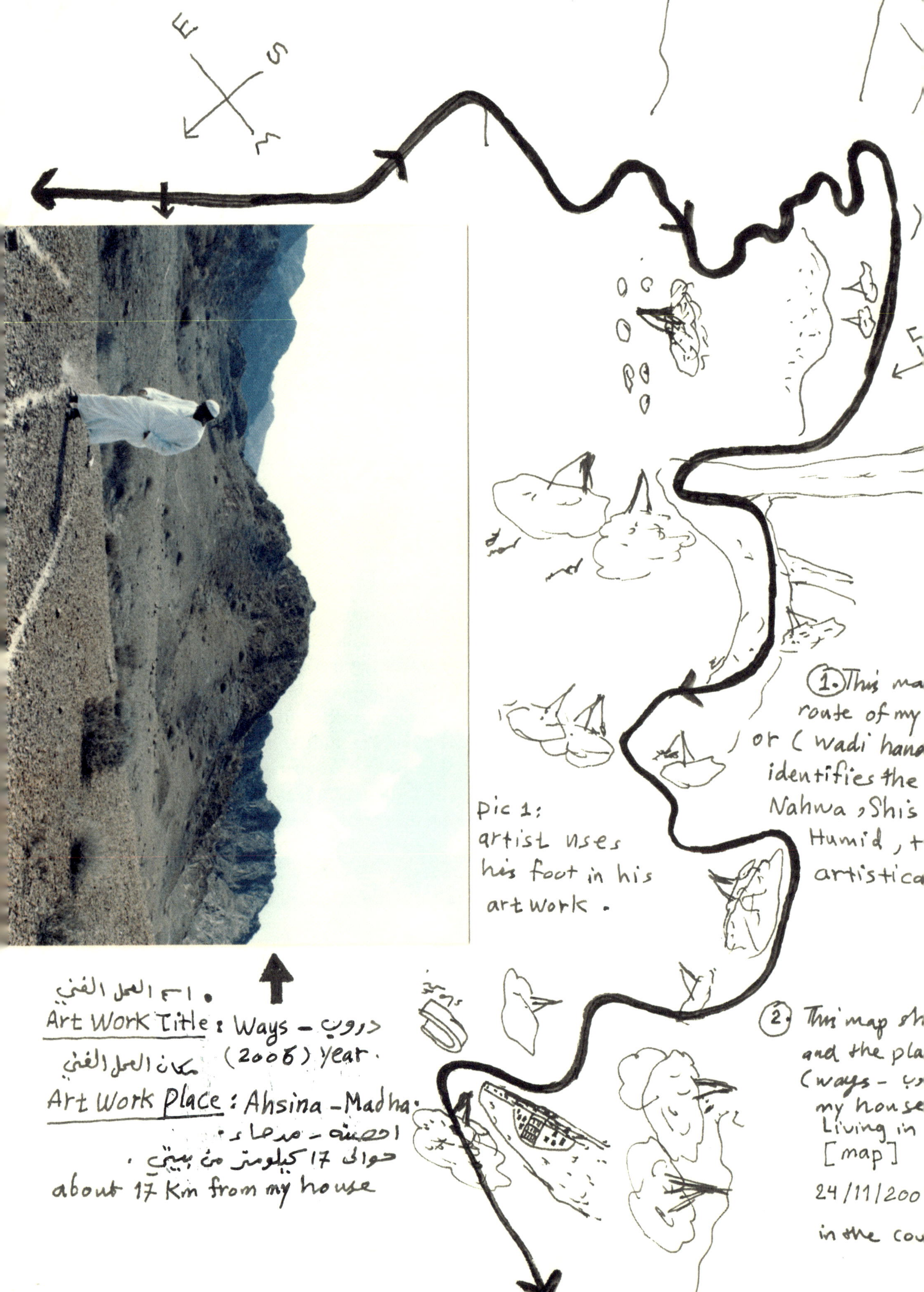

.١−العمل الفني

Art Work Title: Ways − دروب
(2006) Year.

مكان العمل الفني

Art Work Place: Ahsina − Madha.

احصنه − مدحاء

حوالي ١٧ كيلومتر من بيتي.

about 17 Km from my house

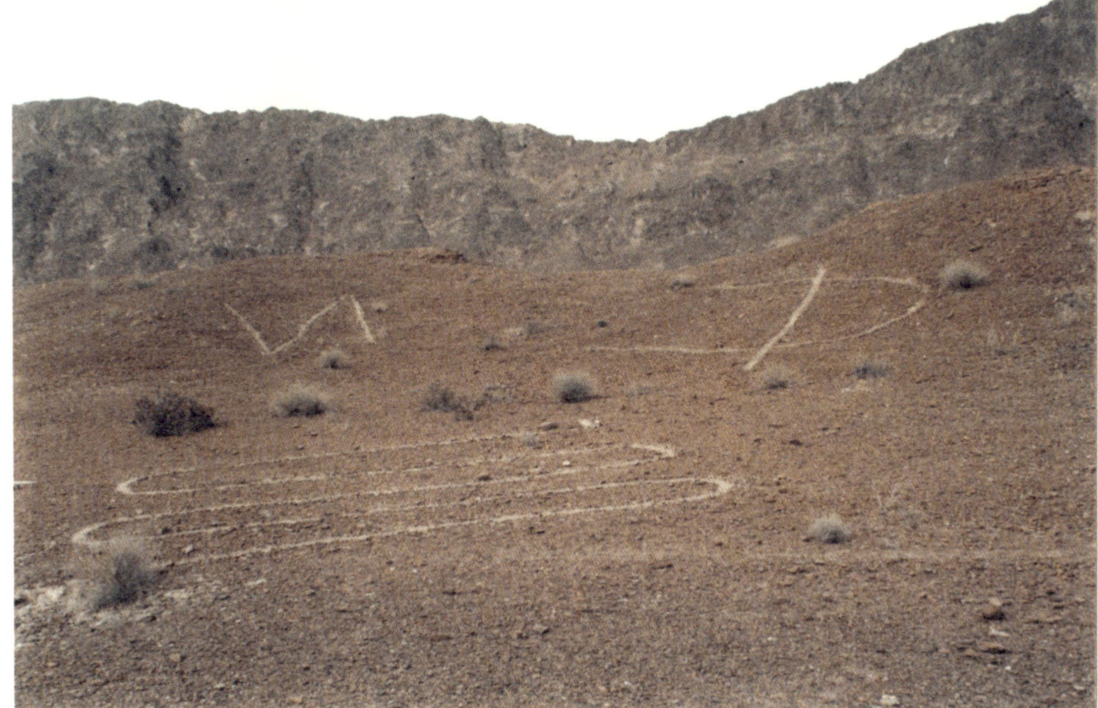

pic 2: These signs were derived from my art work,
my mother's letters [98 - 2000]. See the printed book [2003].
И means C or ☺ . Ɖ = J or ﺝ . ⧣ = ﺱ

fallon

us the
ork: Valley
ll) and
ges, Madha,
Hajer Bani
united

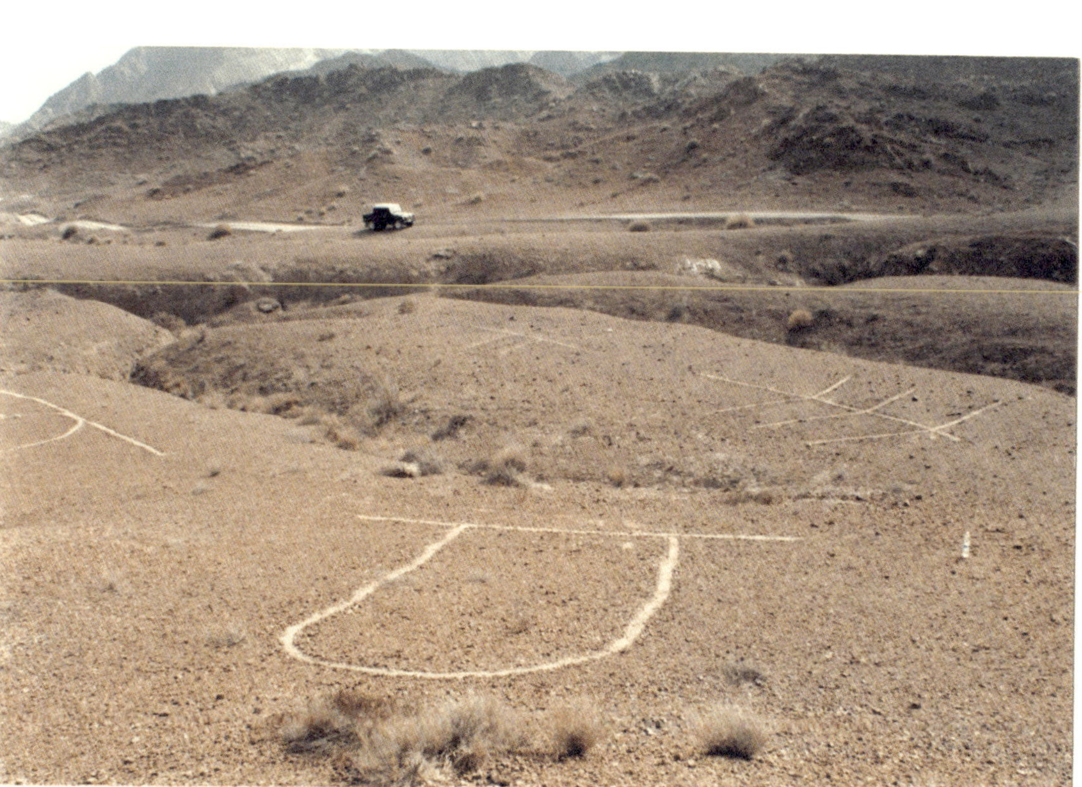

the **title**
my artwork
om - to
e I have been
n house

at

sicle in Madha.

pic 3: ⟱ means Y or ☺ . ⟰ = V or ﺡ
⊥ and ⟂ have no equal letters as in Arabic or in
the English language. I have about 40 letters (signs)
28 letters I use them in writing

if the two are even separable. His travels across the surrounding domestic landscapes evoke a sense of topographical memory, of the strata of ancestral wisdom embedded within the geological landscapes he traverses, accumulated through generations of reciprocity between indigenous culture and the terrain, reiterating its localised land-based practices such as rock stacking, trail blazing and camping. His journeys have also explored the dynamics of interspecies companionship and centred non-human experiences of trekking. In 2010, Al Saadi embarked on a 20-day expedition across the Hajar Mountains, accompanied by his dog, the donkey Camar Cande, and his friend, Abdulrahman Al Muaini, who drove a pick-up truck alongside them. Throughout the trip, he documented their exploits on camera, composed watercolour landscapes and chronicled his emotional responses in a journal. For Al Saadi, journalling is a ritual as inextricable from his artistic practice as time spent in the studio. In these records of the everyday and the offbeat, he collects and preserves the outputs of his own consciousness – memories of funny moments and banal encounters, sense-impressions, feelings – as he would an insect specimen or animal skull retrieved along the path. *Camar Cande's Journey* (2010–2011), the multimedia installation Al Saadi produced in the aftermath of the trek and exhibited as part of Sharjah Biennial 10, presented his non-human companions as co-authors and performers on equal footing with the artist.

There are resonances, too, between the site specificity of his interventions and those espoused by the American land-art movement of the 1970s. Defying the architectural and exhibitionary logic of viewing art in spaces sanctioned for its appreciation, Al Saadi's *Mobile Exhibition* (2003) displayed his work against the backdrop of the 'nature' sites he frequents on his camping trips. In this unadvertised and informal showcase, he draped scrollworks on his jeep and hung paintings from tree branches using camping ropes and poles. It was staged for passersby and hikers, perhaps even for the landscape itself, for the rocks, trees and surfaces he encounters on his travels. While the pioneers of land art in the United States conceived of the landscapes of the American Southwest as a depopulated, vacant canvas to project themselves onto, Al Saadi seeks continuity and communion with the cultures and histories that have unfolded across these topographies long before him and with the people who continue to use them. For Al Saadi, 'natural' landscapes are not voids awaiting artistic intervention or elaboration but sites of connectivity and intimacy. His practice augments their cyclical ancestral memories rather than signalling a confrontation or presumed opposition between 'nature' and humanity.

Collectively, his work is better understood through the lens of the intergenerational, transgeographic ways of living arising from the region's environmental landscapes, particularly seasonal nomadism and the transmission of experience and narratives via petroglyphs, geoglyphs and other forms of rock and boulder art. Like the geologic artefacts and preserved rock heritage sites of the Arabian Peninsula, Al Saadi's bodies of work extend far beyond the nation and its modern interpretations of territorial inscription, or even medieval histories. Transporting us back anywhere from five to even 10,000 years ago, he contemplates the genealogies of rocks, feathers and bones, gesturing perhaps towards a post-natural trans-fusion of 'organic' and synthetic materials. Many of his projects, *My Mother's Letters* among them, have an affinity with, and perhaps transpire from, ancient Babylonian and Assyrian spiritual cultures that proselytise stones as vessels containing ancestral knowledge and stories, and believe that by burying them in the ground their wisdom can sprout again.

This monograph positions Al Saadi's works as possible resur-rections of these mythologies. His practice eludes the visual culture of the Islamic canon usually tied to the region, which espouses the non-representational and the search for symmetry, entropy and the immaterial. Echoing instead what may be considered Jahaliyaa or pre-Islamic traditions of the region, Al Saadi's work expresses mate-rial and visible forms, and daily interfaces, as opposed to the solaces found in meditation and the otherworldly.

Against the backdrop of the Emirates' rapid modernisation, Al Saadi has navigated the tension between this historical tendency towards movement, on the one hand, and societal pressures towards sedentism and rootedness, on the other. His coming of age and coming into his own as an artist during this transition dovetailed with the region's development but was not dictated by it. Though he reaped the benefit of educational and artistic exchanges intro-duced in an era of unprecedented cross-cultural diplomacy – among them the Ship for World Youth (SWY) programme, elaborated on pp. 77-121 – Al Saadi always remained grounded in his beginnings. His experience in the Emirates' art scene was enriching, particularly the relationships he built and the early exhibitions he staged as part of the Emirates Fine Arts Society, but his trajectory wasn't a rapid ascent incubated in a metropolitan context, as it was for so many of his contemporaries, such as Hassan Sharif and Mohammed Kazem. Al Saadi remains the rare, true outsider artist: as content to mount his work on his car by the side of the road as he is to exhibit in a white cube space, a peripatetic soul in a sedentist world of visas and (often arbitrary) borders that police and restrict movement. The urban landscape Al Saadi posits aligns with how some contemporary urbanists conceive of development today, with no real divide between the urban and the rural. He presents urbanity beyond its usual markers of verticality, superficiality, commercialism and density. Instead of the fast-paced, digitised and modelled world, ushered in by the large-scale migrations typifying the 21st-century city, Al Saadi brings forth the institutionalisation of space into national and global orders, the imposition of new vectors of relation between cities and their surroundings. His spaces of familiarity are inundated with quarries, highways, electrical lines and mobile networks. Coexisting rather than sitting at odds with his supposed 'rural' or 'natural' spaces, they lay bare a neglected undercurrent of the contemporary urban landscape, mapping the interconnectedness of worldwide spaces.

This monograph celebrates journeying as a methodology, a ritual practice and a way of life for Al Saadi. It centres his affinity for movement and exploration as generative of his artistic output but not reducible to it. What comes into focus from its panoramic view of Al Saadi's life on the road and his creative practice is the impression that perhaps the two are inextricable. That, at least for Al Saadi, journeying and art making are reciprocal endeavours. That, in other words, movement and creation are mutually enriching and parallel expressions of a broader pursuit: to engage his curiosity for the textures and traces of experience, not only those felt today, but also in the residues of the geologic and intergenerational. Rather than instrumentalising the peripatetic within his oeuvre, this book positions his prolific body of work, ranging from figurative painting and scrolls to found-object sculpture, assemblages and installations, as one component of a ritualistic way of being in the world, not its definitive result.

The book chapters are envisioned as constellations of somewhat chronological travels and periods spanning nearly 40 years of Al Saadi's practice, and the resultant bodies of work produced therein, comprising not only art but also documentation and paraphernalia. Each constellation presents a description of a different trip accompanied by images of the work it gave rise to, along with photographs, sketches and journal entries excerpted from Al Saadi's personal archives. These vignettes are punctuated by an archival essay from Emirati writer Ahmed Rashid Thani, on journeying and collecting in Al Saadi's early artistic practice; an intimate and far-ranging interview with the artist, conducted by President and Director of the Sharjah Art Foundation Hoor Al Qasimi;

and a newly commissioned essay by architect and thinker Meitha Almazrooei on Al Saadi's documentary drawings of fruits from nearby farms and how they relate to his self-authored environmental wisdom and topographical memories.

The first of these constellations recounts Al Saadi's childhood seasonal migrations between Madha and Khorfakkan, bicycle trips from Al Ain to Sharjah during his cash-strapped college years and early-career wanderings across landscapes of decay, such as a slaughterhouse dumping grounds in Khorfakkan. Alongside images of preserved insect specimens and animal skeletons collected during these excursions, the chapter reflects on Al Saadi's abiding interest in found materials and human-animal kinships, both of which manifested in the sculptural series *The Cavity Room* and *Bones* (1991).

The second constellation turns to Al Saadi's formative pedagogic experiences and early cultural exchanges, most notably his voyage aboard the *Nippon Maru* cruise liner as a representative of the Emirates in the 1992 iteration of the Ship for World Youth programme. This educational diplomacy initiative of the Japanese government, which occasioned Al Saadi's first trip beyond the Emirates, brought the artist into contact with the skylines of Tokyo and Singapore, the forests of Sri Lanka and the shores of Muscat, the pyramids of Egypt and the churches of Barcelona. He would return to Japan the following year as a research student, studying traditional story scrolls and calligraphy in Kyoto as well as bicycling to and camping at Biwa Lake.

The third constellation explores Al Saadi's penchant for the self-directed exhibition of his work in unorthodox settings. At Sharm Cafe in Fujairah, a favourite way station for journaling, sketching and conversation after his return from Japan, he staged his own solo show of illustrations, paintings, assemblages and miscellanea from his journeys, revisiting his preoccupations with found material and the natural world. In 2003, against the scenic backdrop of Fujairah and Khorfakkan, Al Saadi held a series of roving exhibitions, parking his Nissan Defender by the roadside and draping it with mountain and desert sketches, land scrolls, surrealist landscape paintings and self-portraiture.

The fourth revisits Al Saadi's several trips to Abya Yala, namely Brazil and Argentina, where he exhibited *My Mother's Letters* at the São Paulo Biennial in 2005 and returned for an artist residency in 2009. Of all his excursions abroad, Brazil felt the most familiar and intuitive to him. Its landscapes and culture conjured parallels to

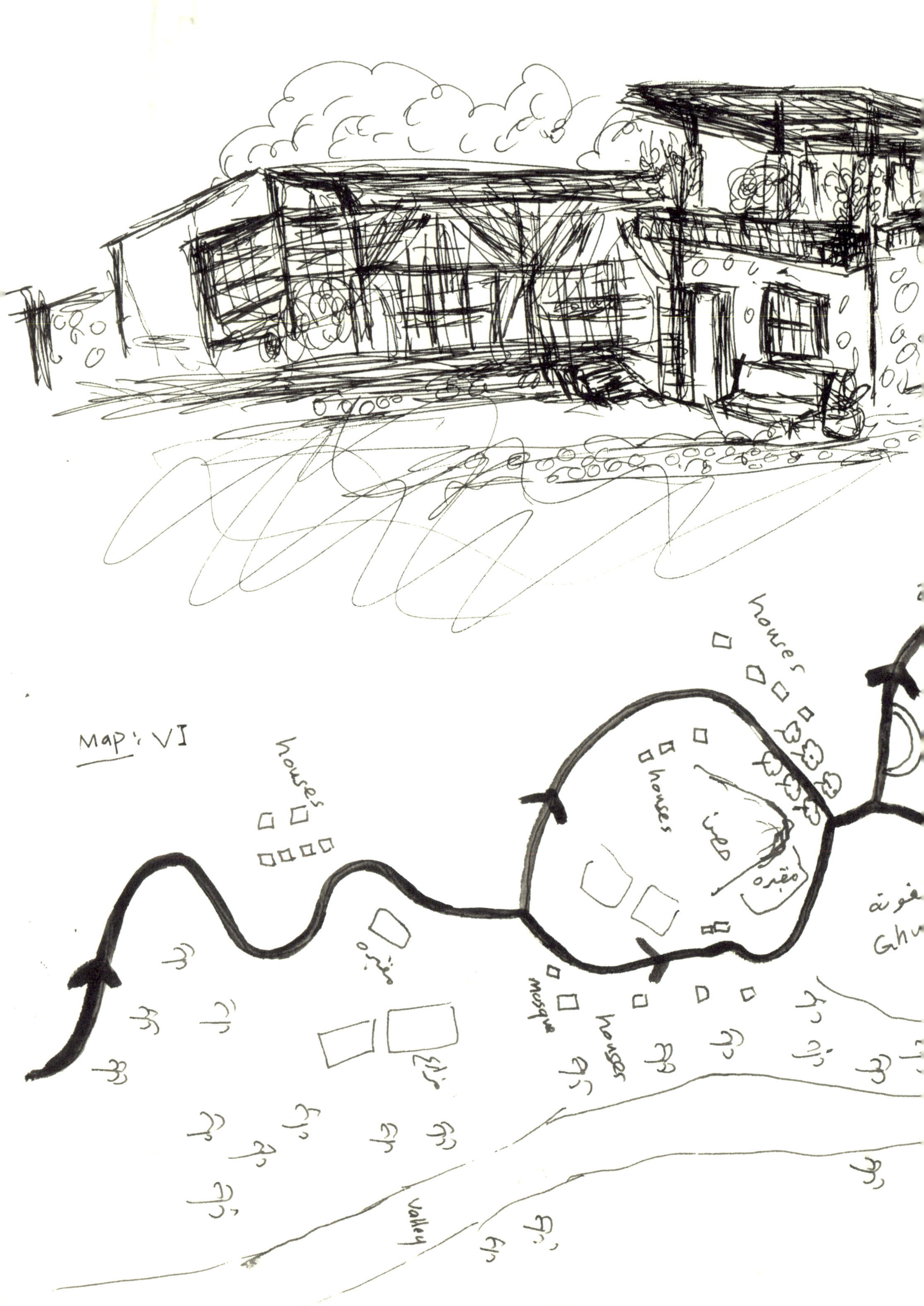

Map: VI
houses
houses
houses
houses
mosque
valley
Ghu

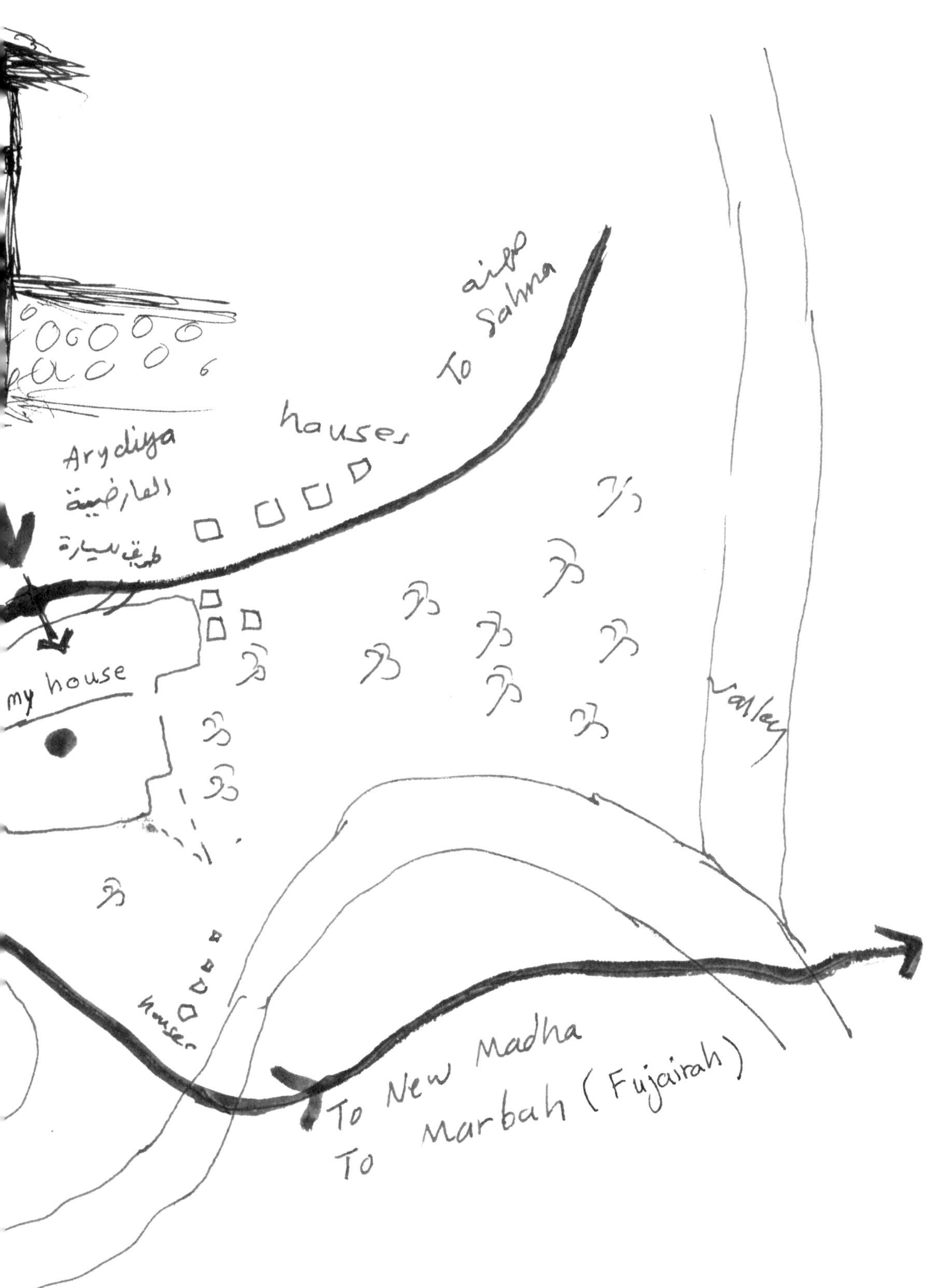
Arydiya
العريضية
طبيعة للسيارة
hauses
To Sahna
صحم
To
my house
houses
valley
To New Madha
To Marbah (Fujairah)

his own context, the close observation of which would form the basis of *The Comparative Journey* (2013), a cultural and geographic reading of the Emirates through the lens of his experiences in Abya Yala.

The fifth constellation examines Al Saadi's summer in Austria and Italy during a three-month artist exchange programme in 2008. Sketching and journalling in riverfront cafes and parks, he was swept up by the festive musical atmosphere of Salzburg and the storied coffeehouse culture of Vienna. At a symposium hosted by the International Academy of Ceramics in the Austrian state of Tyrol, he moulded a series of clay sweet potatoes. Across the Italian border in Bolzano, he found a sense of kinship with Ötzi, a famous Copper Age natural mummy and fellow wayfarer. His sketches and diaries documenting these experiences became the artist book *Marende* (2008), the title of which invokes a hearty meal served after a day of physical labour, traditional to the Tyrol region.

The sixth circles back to the familiar topography of the Emirates, detailing Al Saadi's excursions through the Hajar Mountain range between 2009 and 2017, several of which were represented in *Al Toubay*, his 2014 solo show at Sharjah Art Foundation. Epitomising his non-anthropocentric perspective, with its emphasis on interspecies companionship and the ancestral knowledge embedded in the land, these journeys were transmuted into watercolour compositions, photographs, video and stone engravings.

The seventh constellation recounts Al Saadi's voyage from Ushuaia, the southernmost port of Argentina, to the Antarctic Archipelago with the Antarctic Biennale in 2017. Captained by artist Alexander Ponomarev, a nautical engineer by training, this 12-day odyssey convened 100 artists, scientists and academics aboard the *Akademik Ioffe*, envisioning the uninhabited continent and its environs as a stage for interdisciplinary dialogue and research.

The eighth constellation is devoted to tracing the transcontinental journey of the sweet potato, from its earliest known cultivation in the caverns of coastal Peru to the manure-rich soil of Madha. Juxtaposing the glyphs of Al Saadi's sweet potato alphabet with the research photos from which they were abstracted, this final section occasions reflection on one of the central motifs of his work and its 'amorphous, polyphonic nature.'

The overarching design concept of the book pays homage to the accumulative and reiterative processes of Al Saadi's practice. Braiding together various folios, its stitching is inspired by the artist's approach to gathering, preserving and organising the textures and residues of experience, mirroring the taxonomic logic of the flat files in his studio. The book's cover design evokes the geomorphological qualities of a rock embedded with ancestral wisdom and knowledge. As in the ancient spiritual cultures of Babylon and Assyria alluded to above, it opens up to seeds of regrowth, germinating fresh interpretations of Al Saadi's work rather than prescribing a finite or definitive reading.

Neither of its titles, either in Arabic or in English, literally translates the other. Instead of attempting a one-to-one approximation, they aim to evoke similar sentiments within the respective poetics of each language, honouring Al Saadi's multilingualism and longstanding profession as an English language teacher. Drawing on a popular Arab expression and referencing the fictional media about the phrase, it signifies a wanderer who leaves their village and doesn't look back, forsaking the familiar in the unwavering pursuit of meaning in the world. An early painting of Al Saadi's, in which we see him running away from his hometown, takes its title from the same phrase. In the wake of his travels, Al Saadi, of course, always returns to his village, but never unaltered. Journeying invariably furnishes him with new impressions, memories and materials; the land, conversely, never remains unaltered by his presence either, bearing his traces as a form of geologic memory. The English title, meanwhile, alludes to Edward Albee's one-act play *The Zoo Story*, connoting one who must travel far and wide to arrive at insights near and intimate. This is Al Saadi's peripatetic essence twice distilled: the alchemy of experiencing parts unknown leaves its reciprocal imprint on both the wanderer and the land wandered across.

—Ahmad Makia

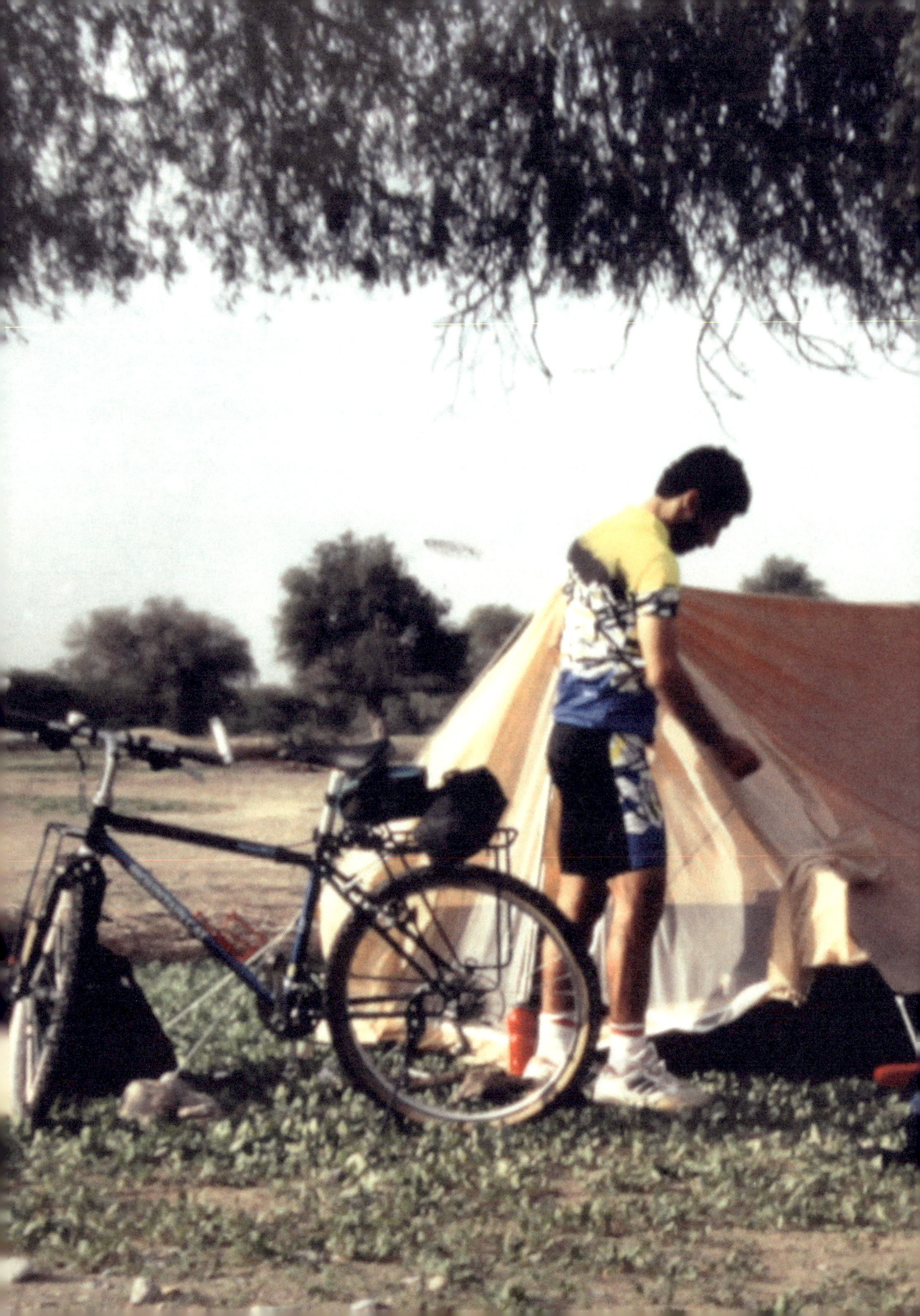

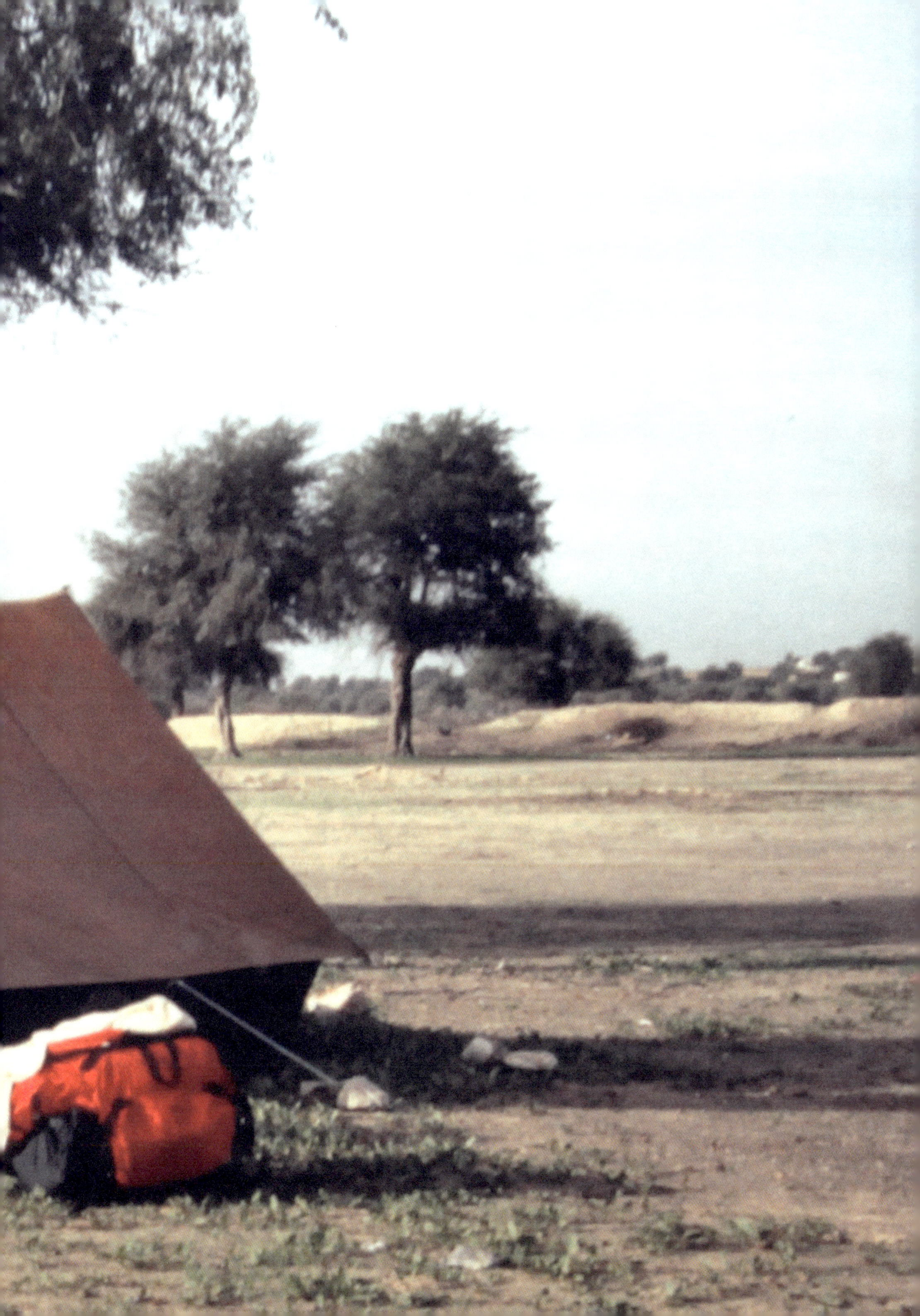

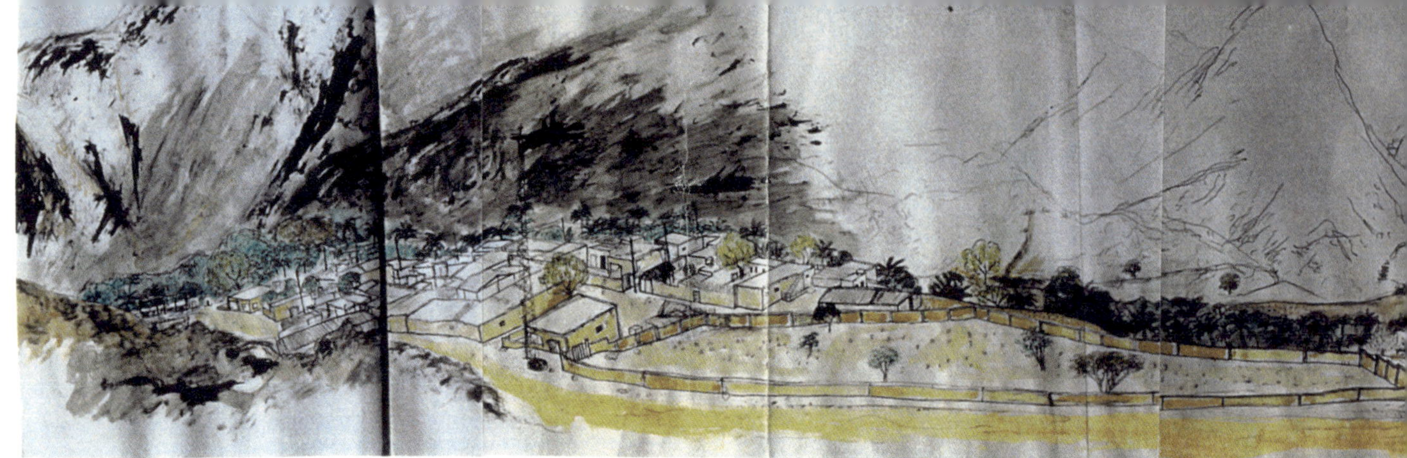

Wadi Scroll : water color on paper . 2002 . 42 X   cm . place : Old Nahwa.

Map : IV

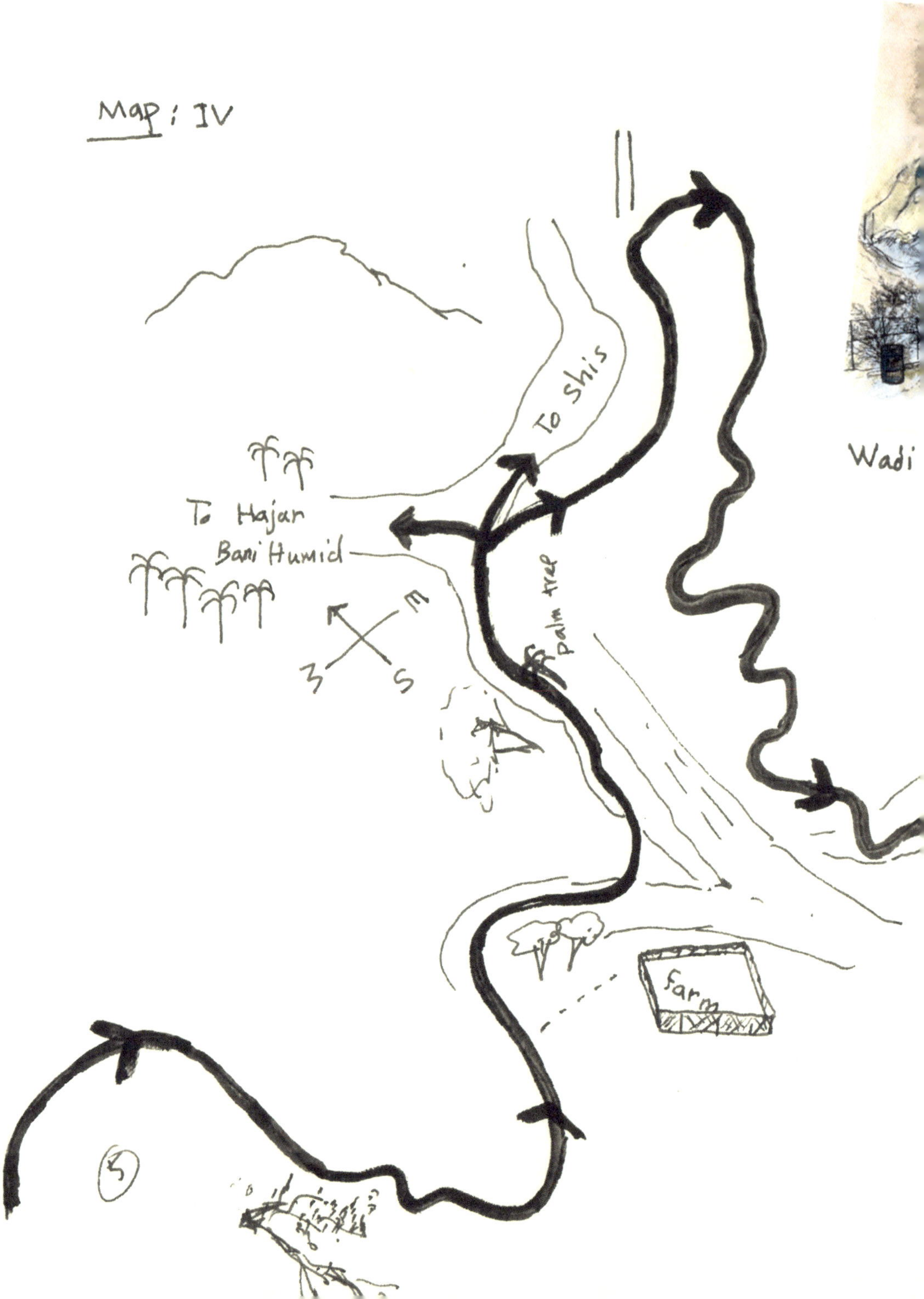

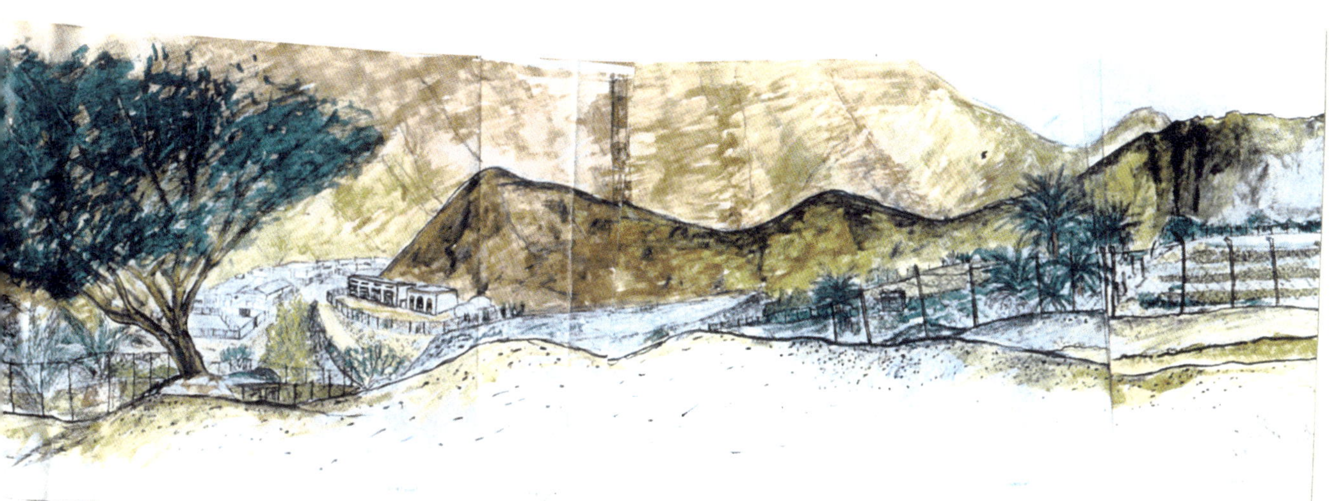

: water color on paper . 2002 . 42 X   cm . place : New Nahwa .

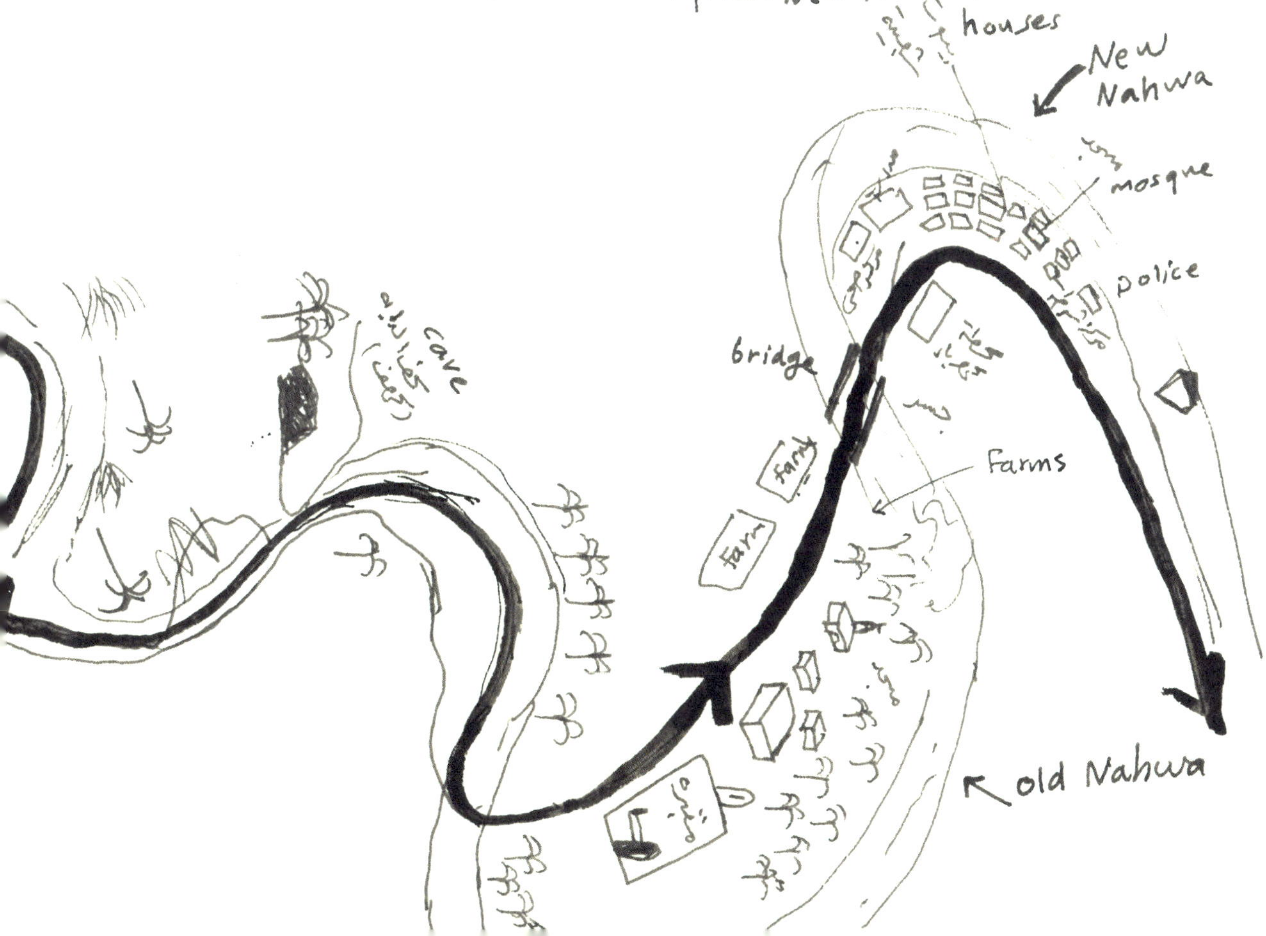

houses

New Nahwa

mosque

Police

bridge

Farms

Farm

Farm

cave

old Nahwa

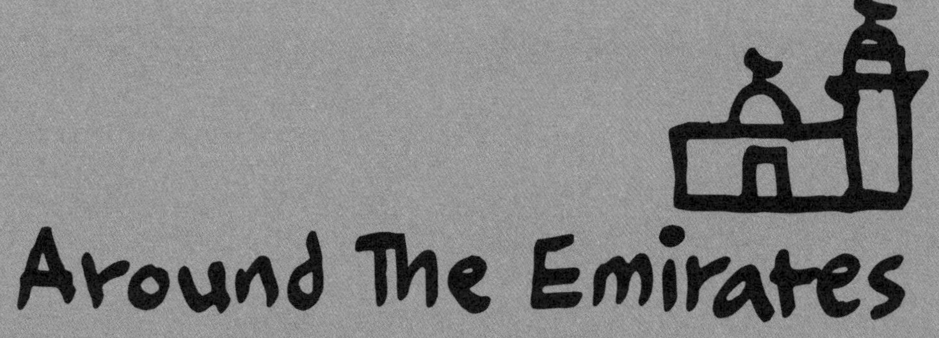

Around The Emirates

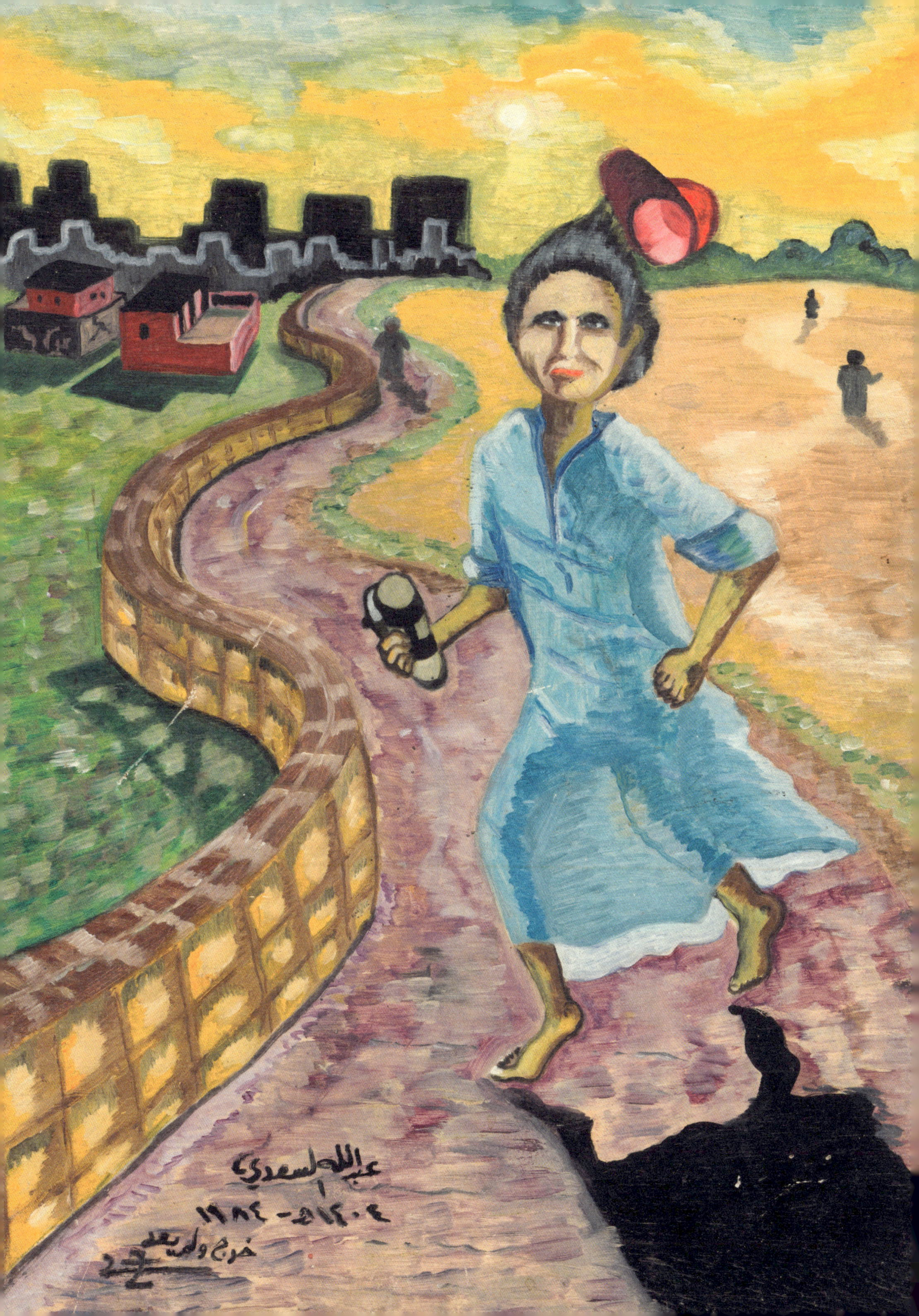

عبد الله صدي
٢٠١٥.٢ - ١٩٨٤
خروف

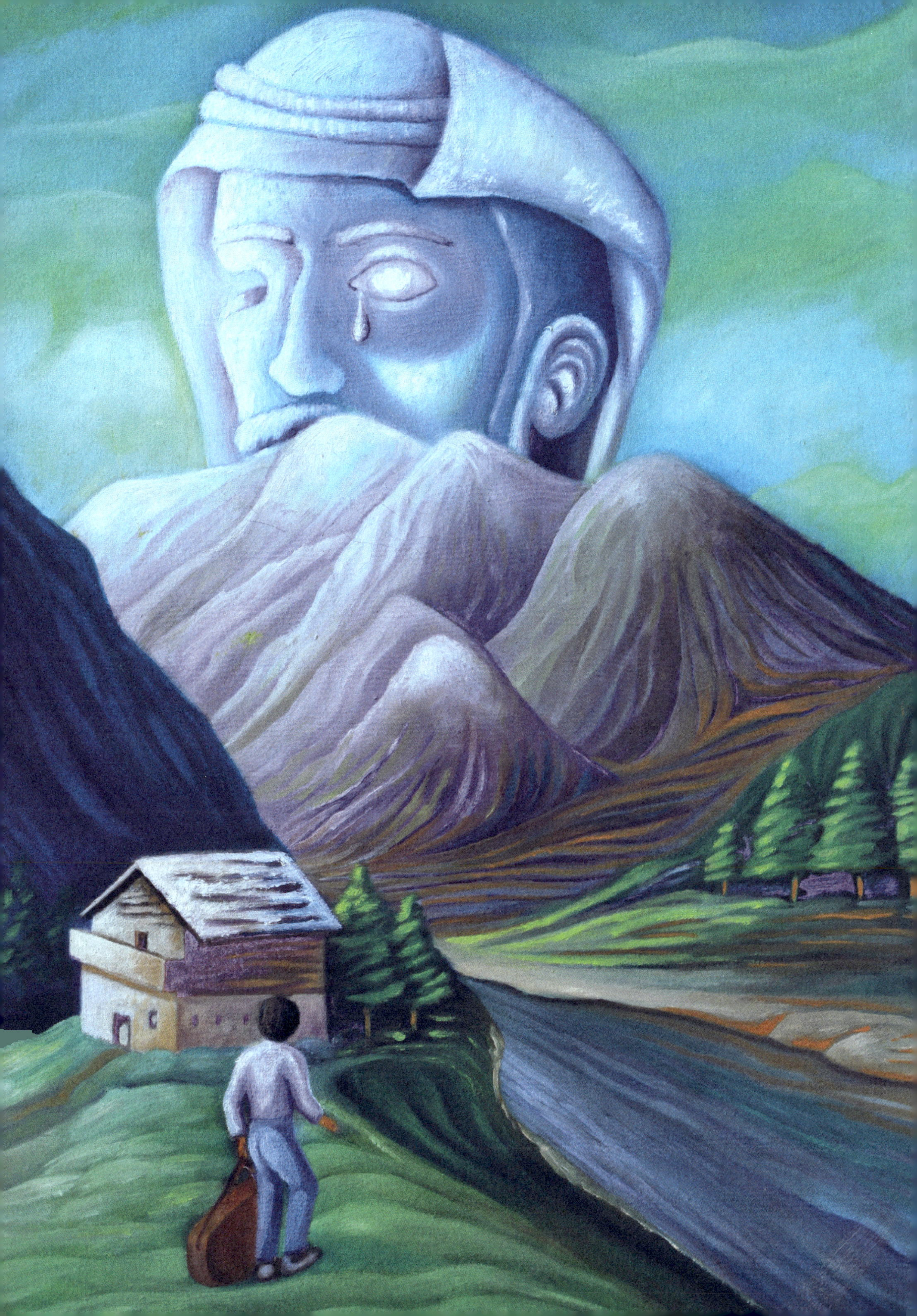

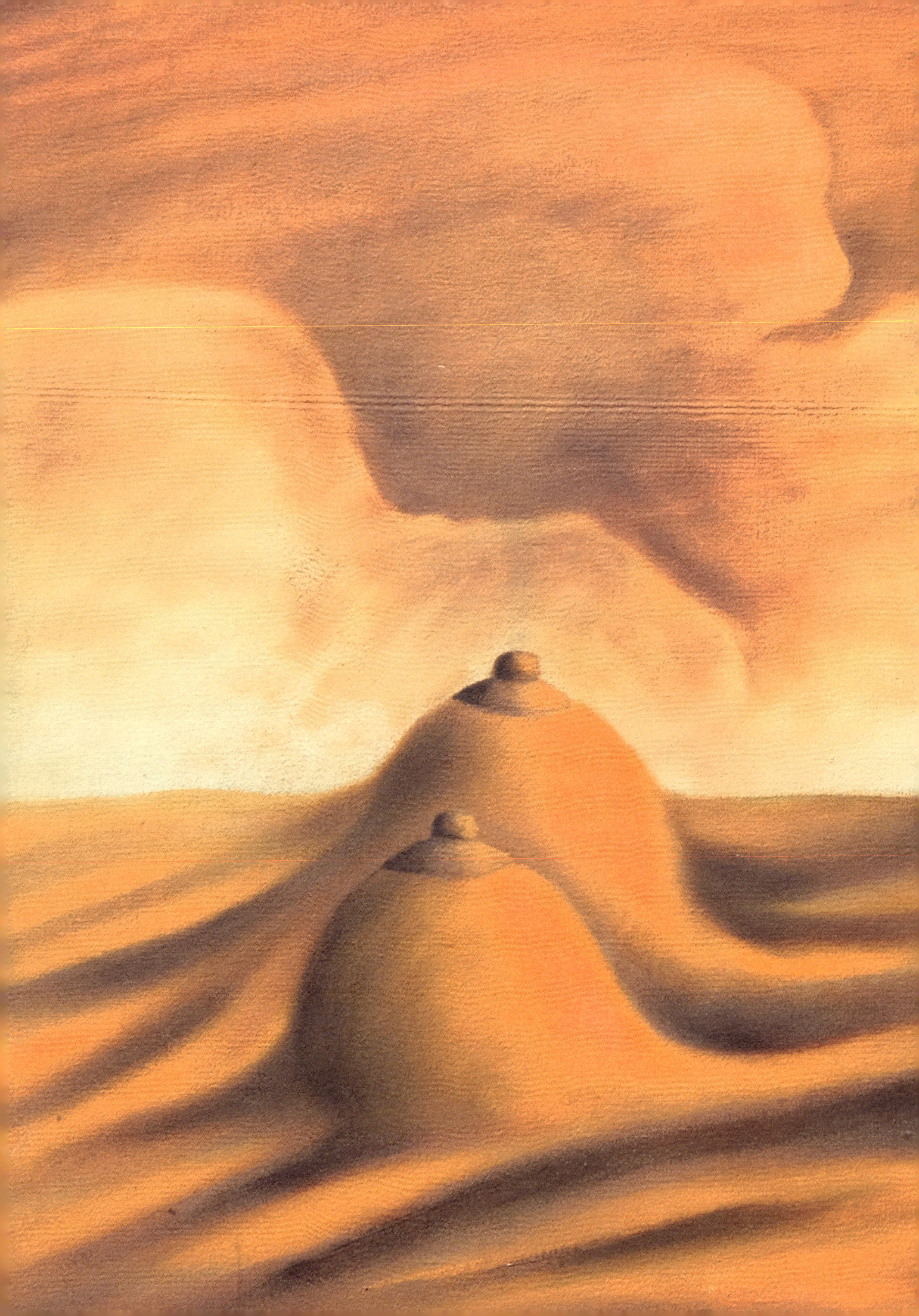

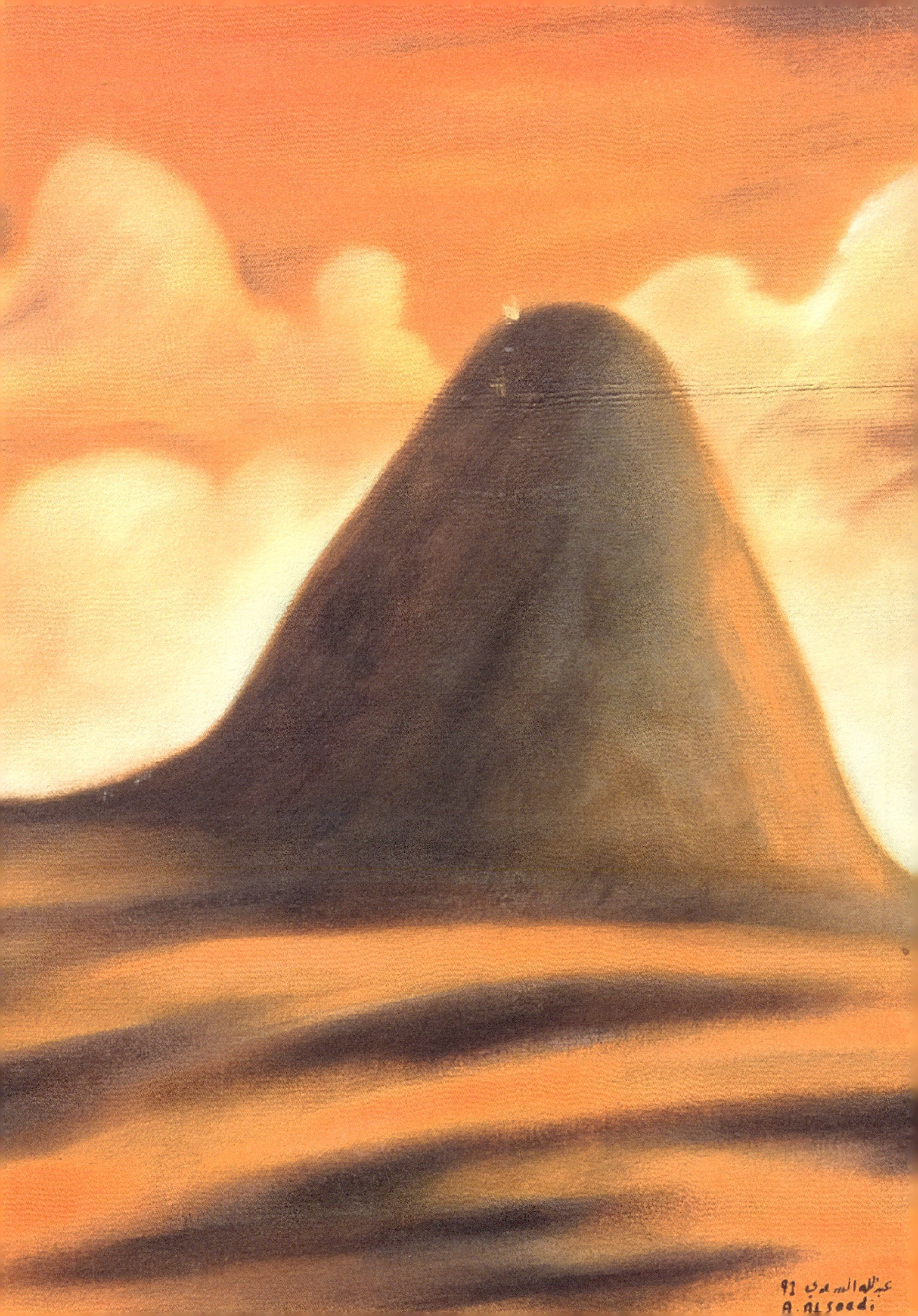
عبدالله السعدي ٩١
A. ALSoadi

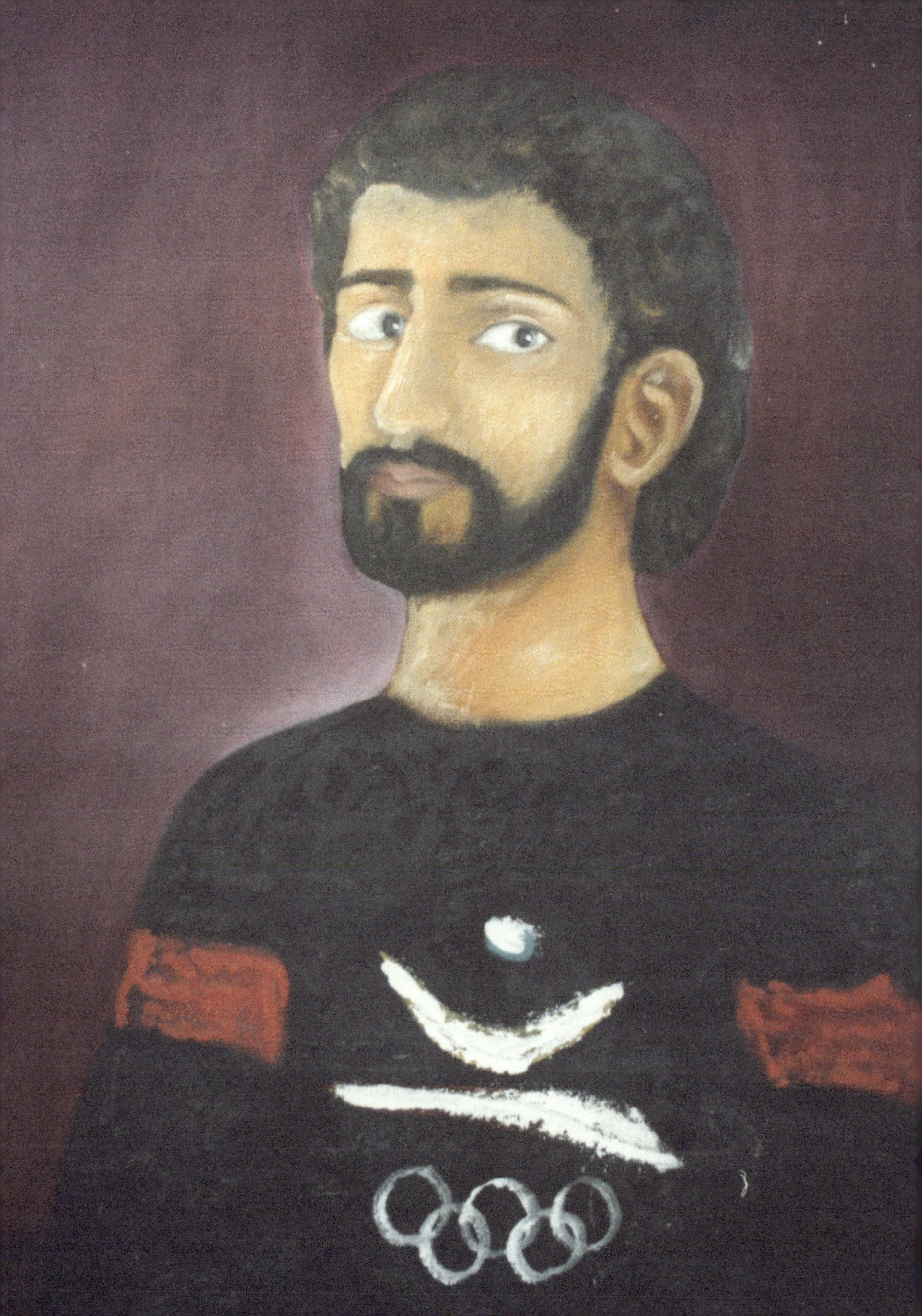

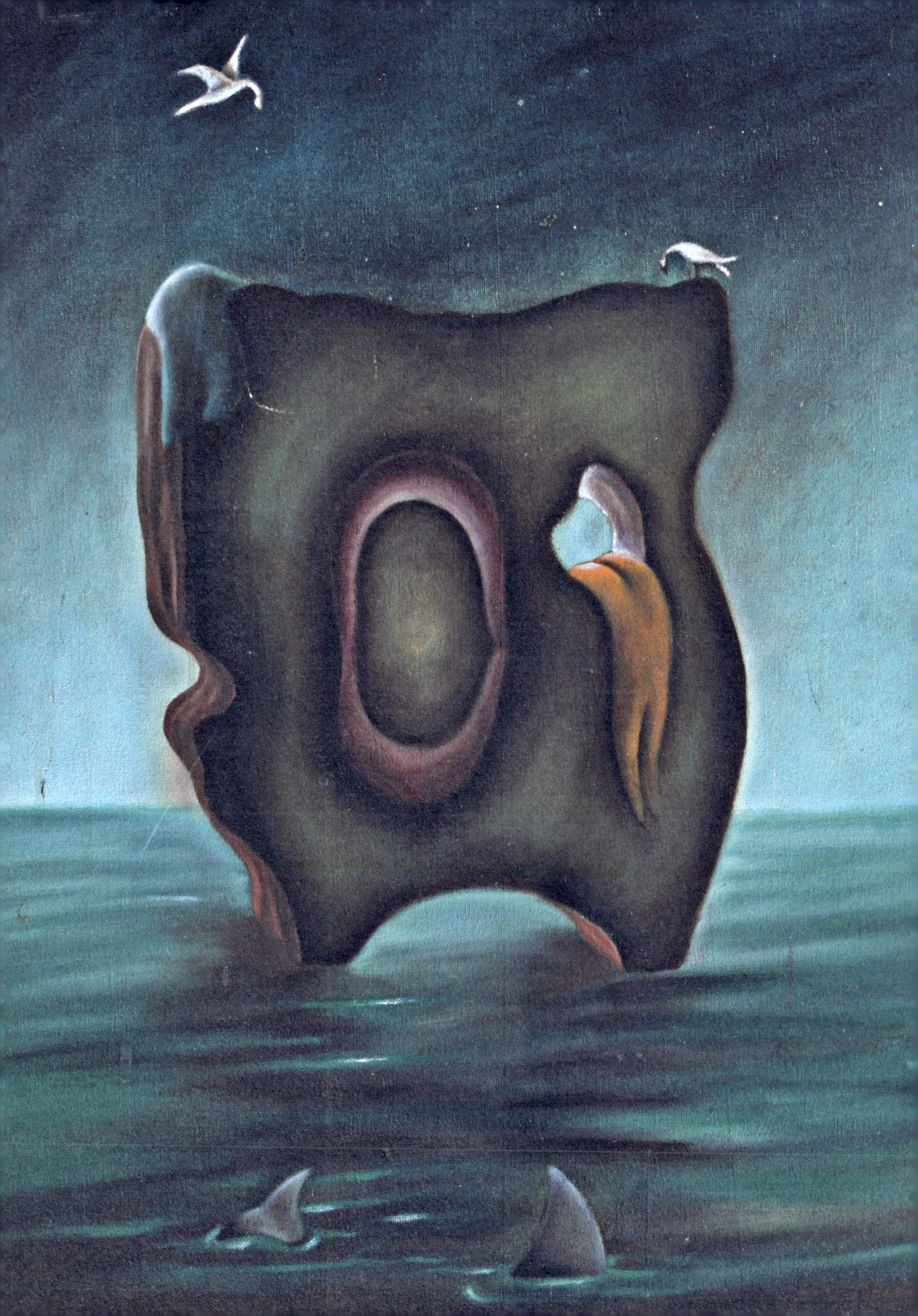

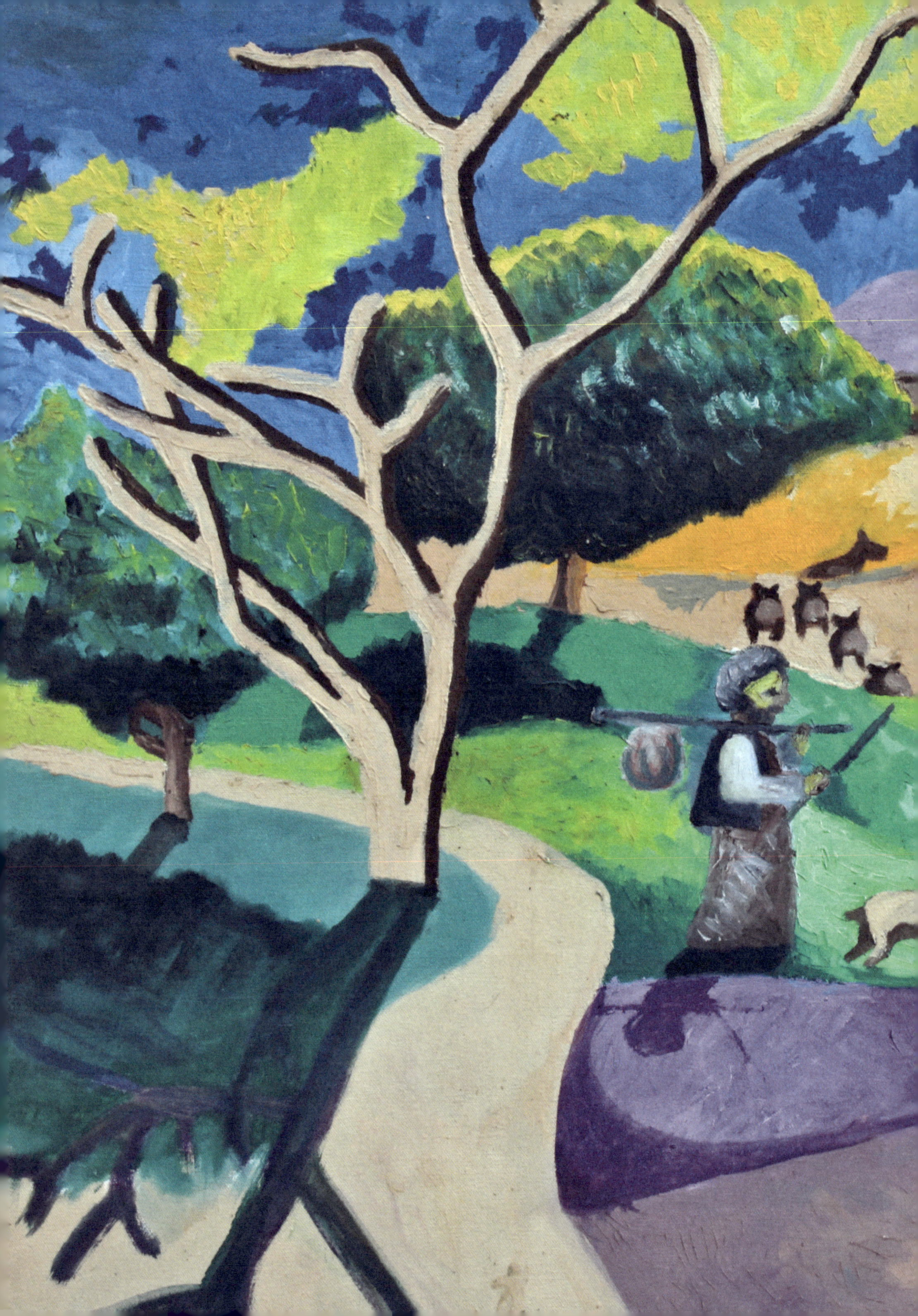

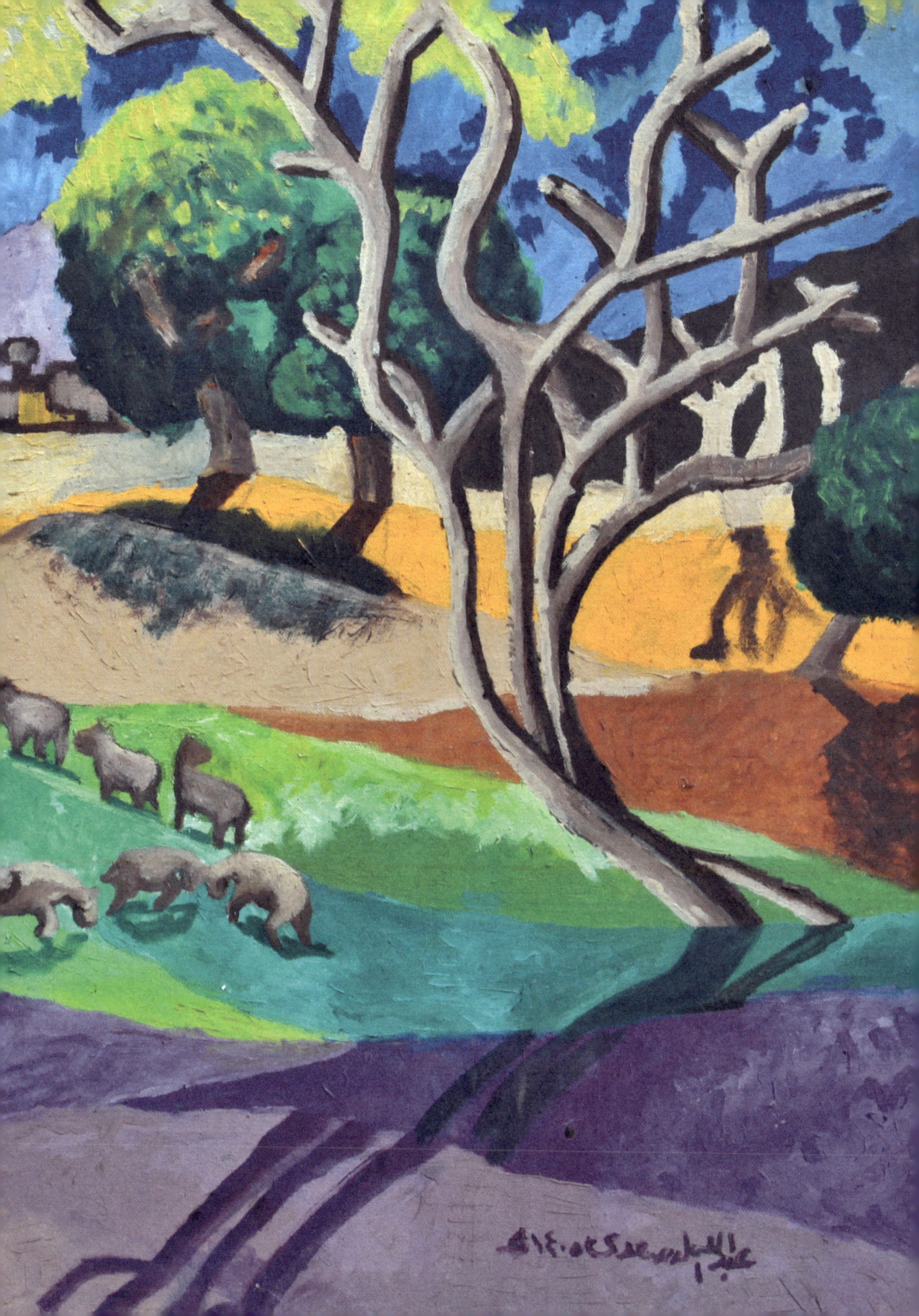

عبدالله ... ١٩٨٧

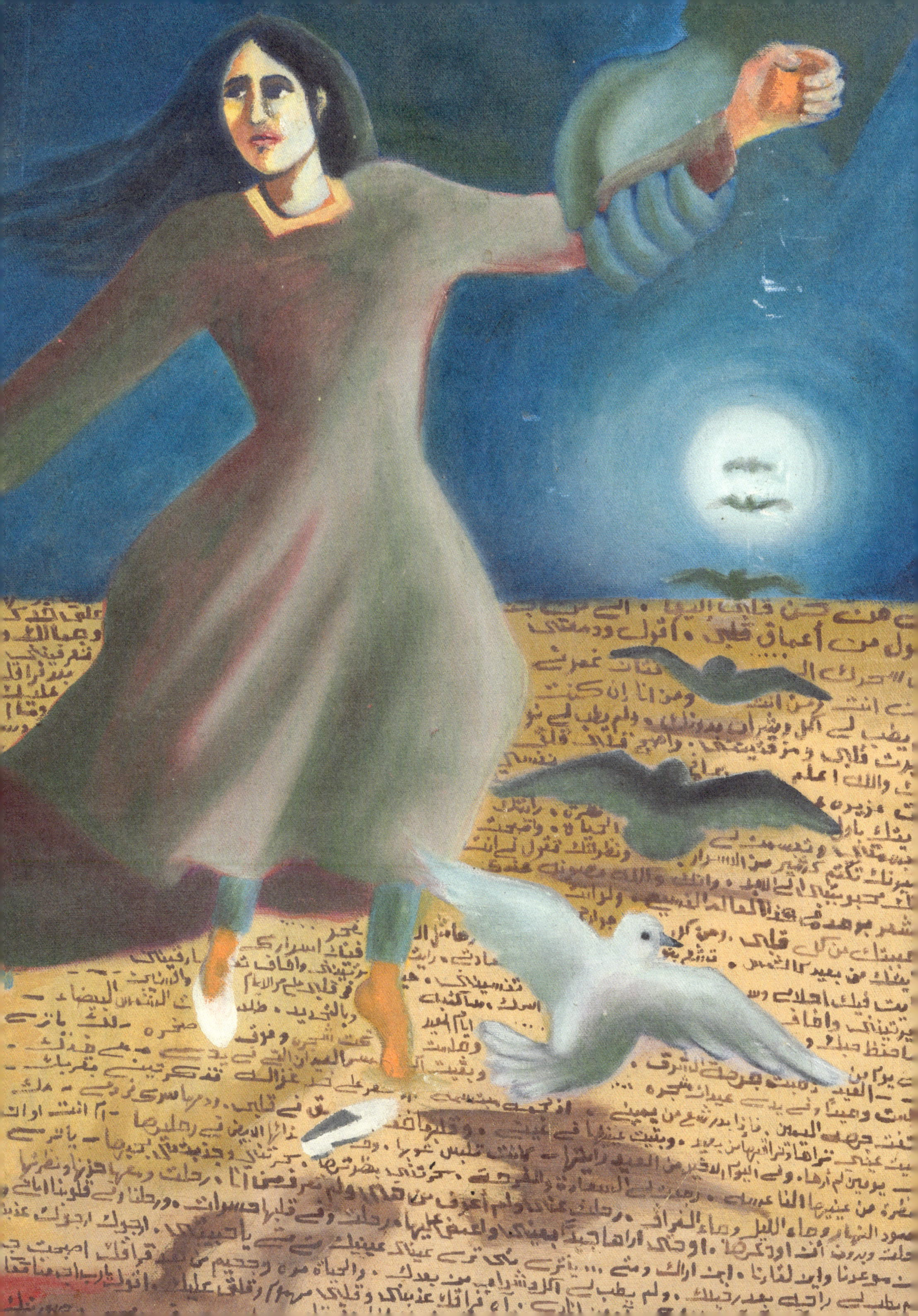

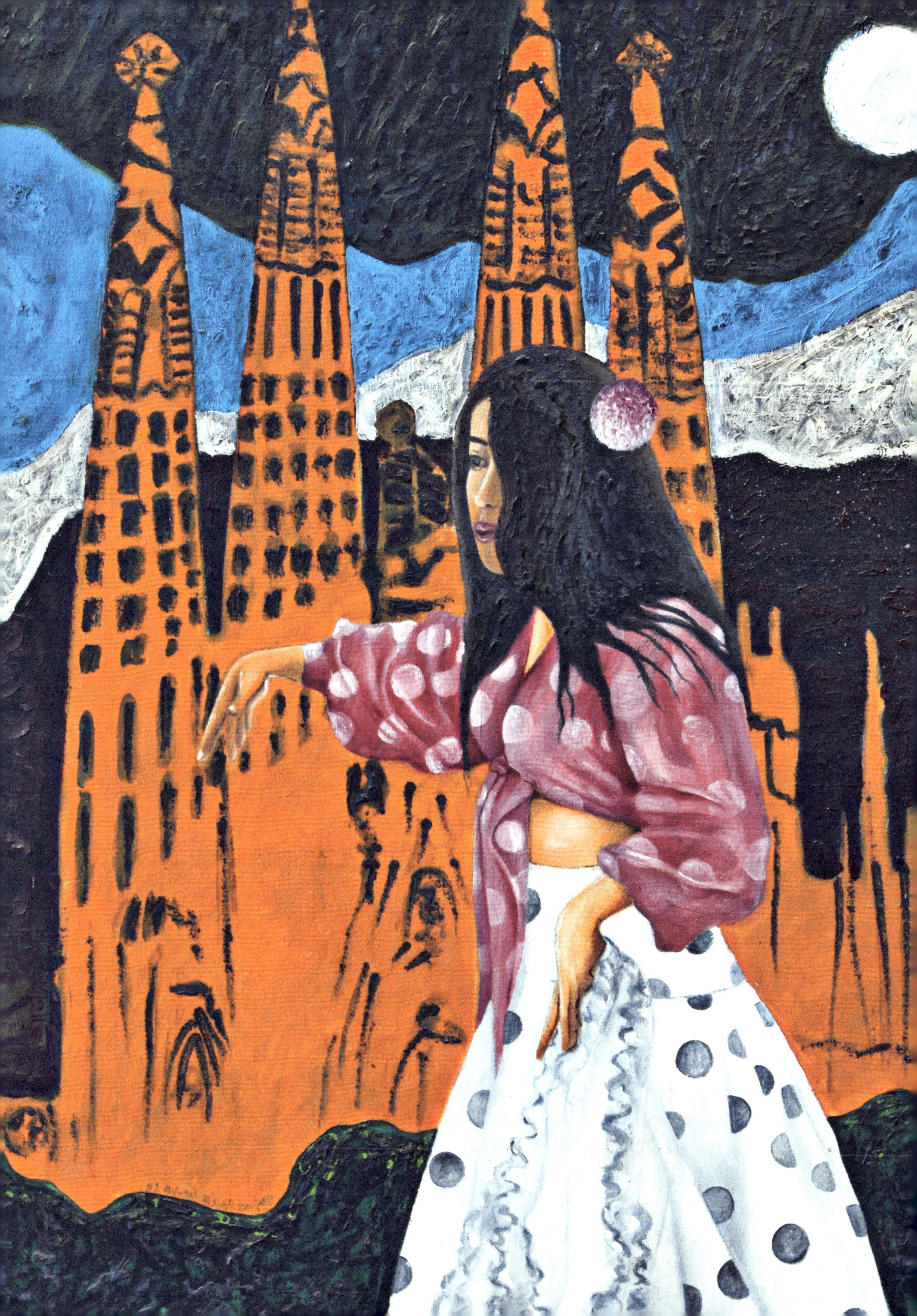

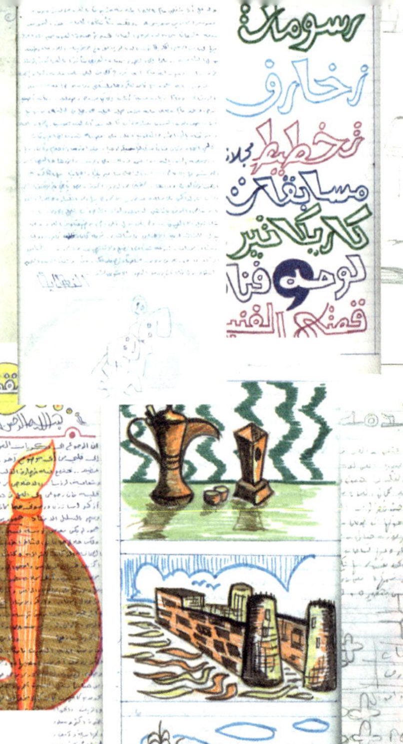

رسومات
زخارف
خطوط
مسابقة
لوحة فنية
قصة الفن

رسومات

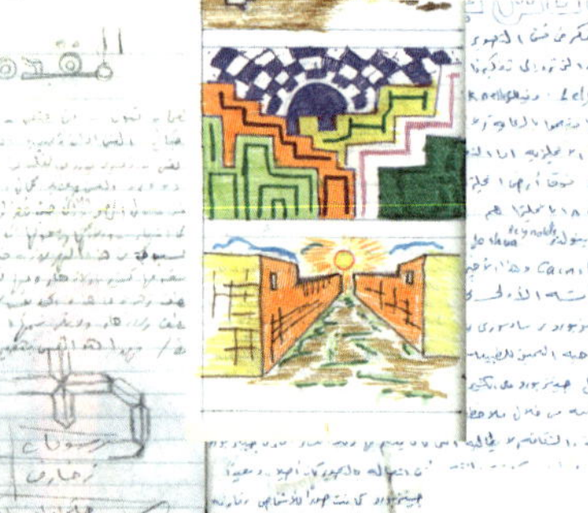
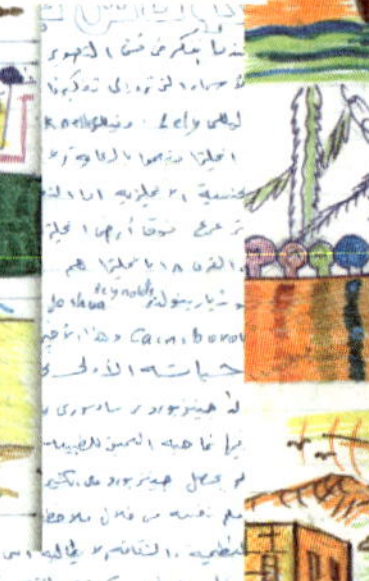
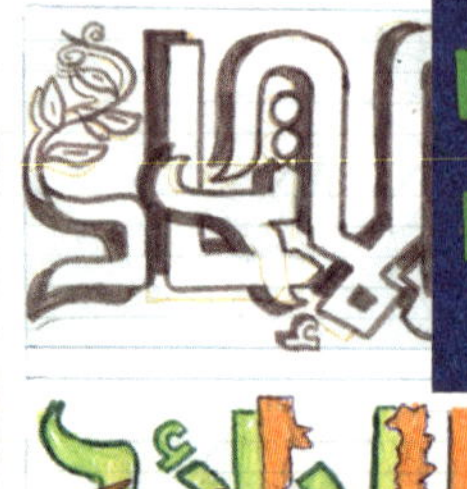
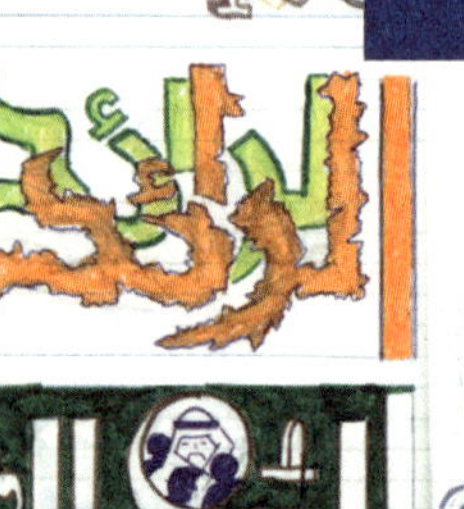
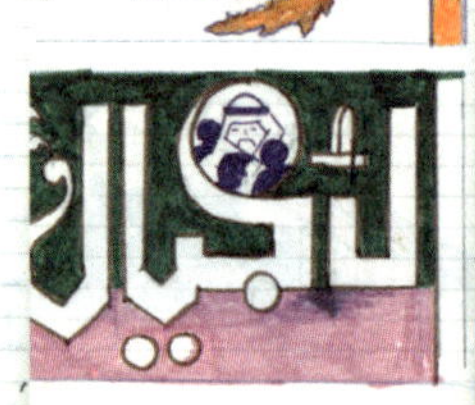
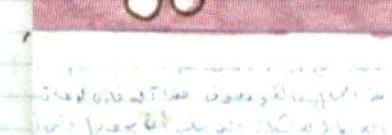
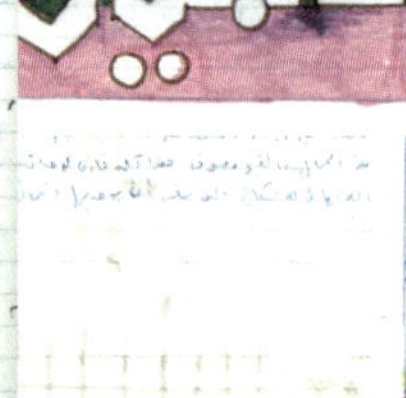
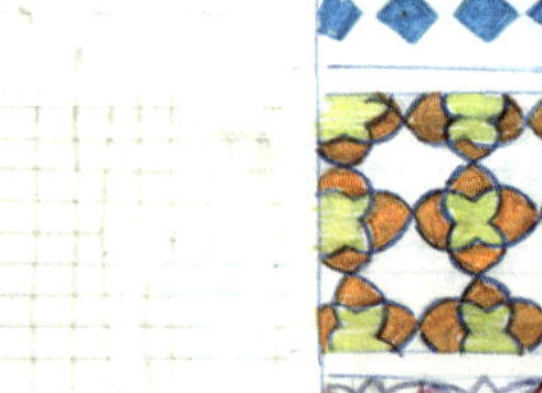
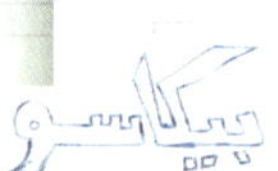
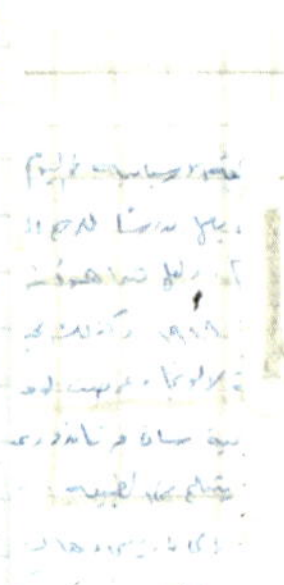
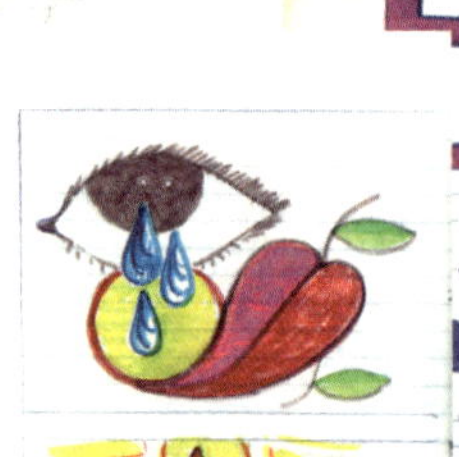
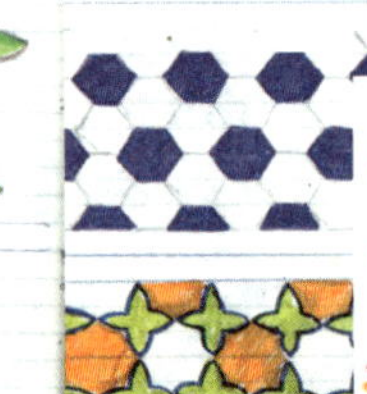
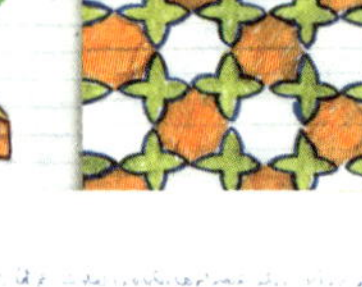
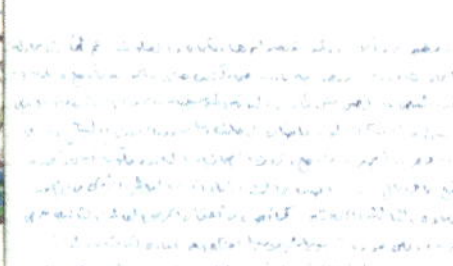

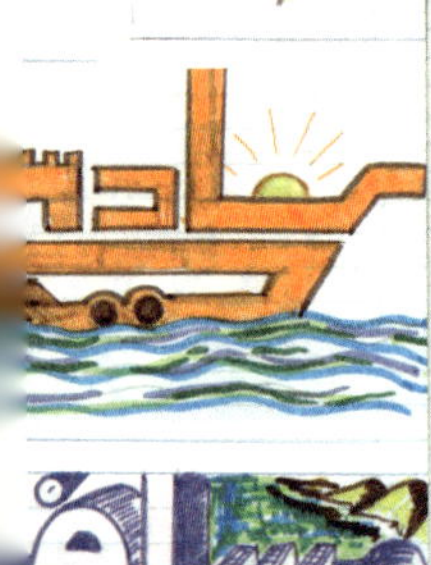
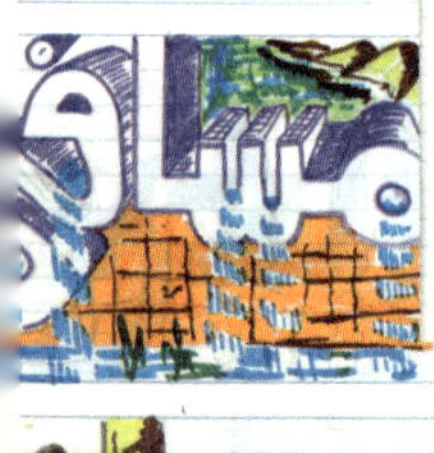
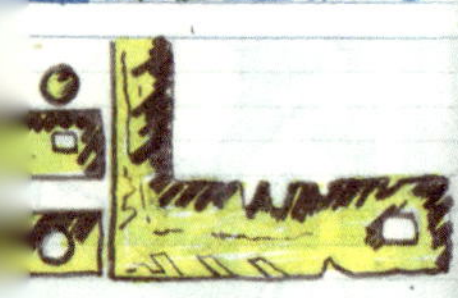
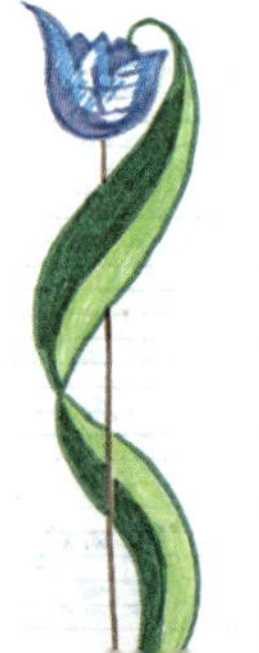
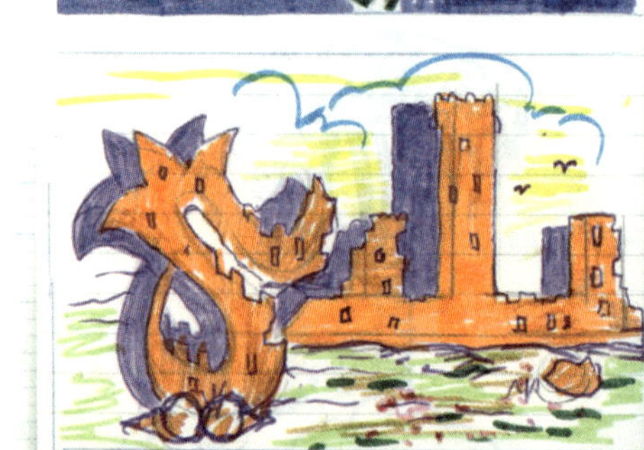
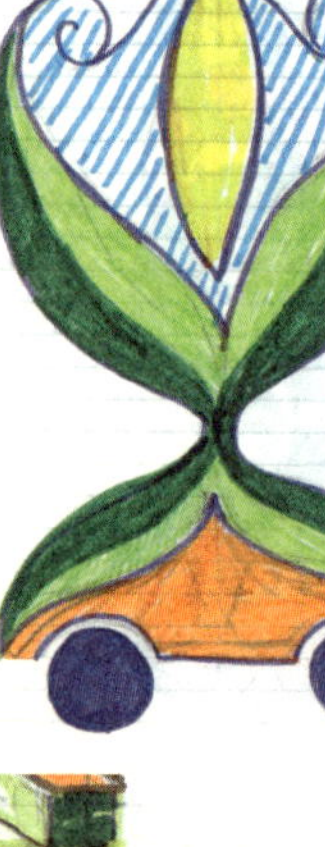
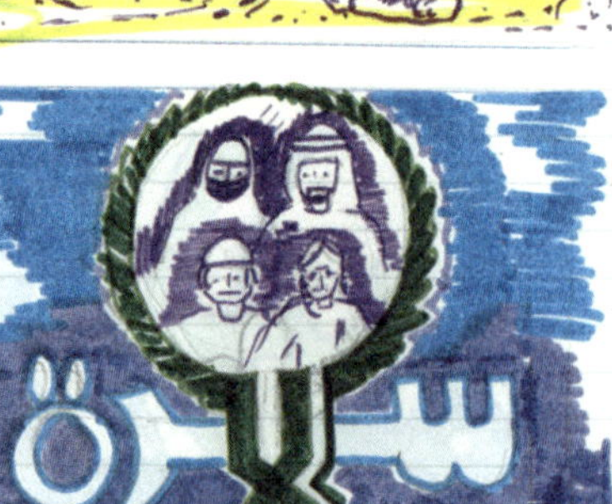
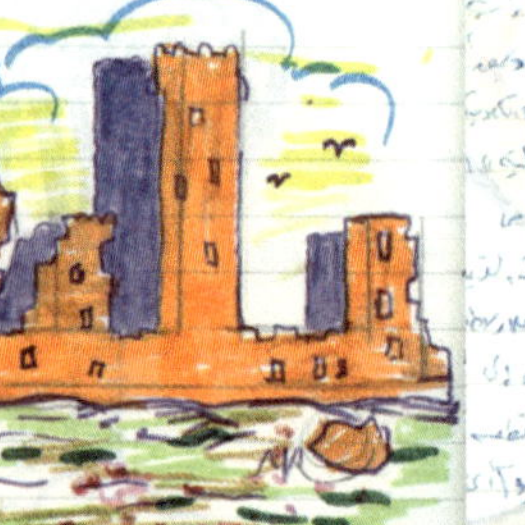

سيرة

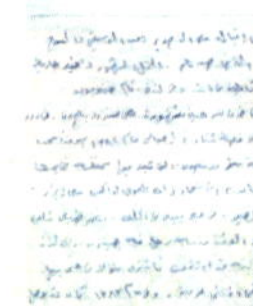

Kharaj Walam Ya'ud [Left and never returned] (1984), an oil-on-wood work by then 17-year-old Abdullah Al Saadi, depicts a boy racing down a winding dirt path, about to disappear out of frame. His *kandoora* flaps around him, slippers sandwiched together in one fist, a red baseball cap taking flight from his head. Far off loom metropolitan silhouettes, dwindling into a pair of traditional houses. He's glad to be getting ahead or simply away. This ethos carries over to an untitled painting from 1991, in which a boy sits atop an earthen pillar punctuating a sparse, green clearing framed by rolling hills. Hundreds of ruminators mill and graze around its base. His arms are raised above his head triumphantly, like a modern-day Hayy Ibn Yaqzan discovering some universal truth.

In a conceptual art community only a few decades old, one that is already being defined by the activities of a tight-knit circle of collaborators, Al Saadi's proclivity for escape and isolation has been evident from the start. For Al Saadi, born in 1967 near the eastern foothills of the Hajar Mountains, several years before the federal unification of the Emirates, childhood and adolescence were marked by constant movement and abrupt upheavals. Seasonal migrations to Khorfakkan from his family's date palm farm in Al Ghouna, a village in the Madha enclave, instilled in him a sense of compulsory nomadism that was already fading from the collective memory of his generation.

Al Saadi left home early on for a boarding school in Masafi, nearly an hour away, returning to Al Ghouna only on weekends. It was there, as far back as the second grade, that he began to draw. Years later, after relocating to Sharjah for his last two years of secondary school, he developed a zealous journaling habit. The parallels and intersections of these practices would prime Al Saadi for his entry into the Emirates Fine Arts Society (EFAS) in the early 1990s. For Al Saadi, EFAS was a crossroads of artistic currents spanning the Arab world, a form of travel far exceeding anything he was capable of on his student stipend.

Then less than a decade old, the organisation had already attracted a regular rotation of nascent plastic artists to its annual exhibitions. During its 1988 showcase, Al Saadi exhibited an assemblage of found objects at the Sharjah Expo Centre alongside one of Hassan Sharif's early installations, as well as a landscape by the Khorfakkan-born Mohamed Ahmed Ibrahim, two major figures of the Emirates' conceptual arts scene. Unbeknown to Al Saadi, he was contributing to a collective body of work of which he would himself eventually become a key figure.

The Sharjah of Al Saadi's youth was then reaping the benefits of almost two decades of modernisation following the discovery of oil in the Mubarak offshore field. Port Khalid, established in 1976 as Sharjah's first deepwater port, helped centralise maritime commerce and breathe new life into this historic trade centre, accelerating its infrastructure and real estate development. Nearby these modern projects was the area's historic quarter restoration of several 19th-century buildings and former residences, including the home of pearl merchant Obaid bin Hamad Al Shamsi and that of British commissioner for the Arabian Gulf Issa Bin Abdul Latif Alserkal, which had been converted into the Sharjah's first maternity ward in the 1960s. Khorfakkan as Al Saadi knew it was also transforming, thanks in part to its own port. Established a decade after Port Khalid, Khorfakkan Container Terminal was located outside the Strait of Hormuz, making it an ideal intermediate shipping destination as well as a conduit for the international market into the Emirates itself.

After completing secondary school in 1986, Al Saadi relocated to Al Ain to pursue his bachelor's in English at the University of the United Arab Emirates (UAEU), the country's first higher education institute. During these cash-strapped college years, Al Saadi maintained a distant connection to the happenings in Sharjah, journeying there by bike and sleeping in mosques along the way.

With no independent source of income or readily available art supplies, Al Saadi looked closer to home for his materials. Discarded doors, wood both scavenged and purchased, and other detritus all became artistic mediums that helped steer his focus from the figurative and abstract painting of his early years to assemblage and installation.

Al Saadi's interest in modern-day cycles of production and consumption also extended to the natural world. In 1991, he gravitated towards a local dumping ground for slaughterhouse waste in Khorfakkan. Once plucked clean of their remaining flesh, skin and connective tissue by scavengers, these skeletons were left to bleach and disintegrate under the sun.

Photographs from the time document Al Saadi's descent into, and communion with, the animal realm, shirtless near a mound of bones with a cow skull over his head. They echo and complicate the Islamic postulation of creation as hierarchical: minerals evolved into plants and plants into animals. Animals, however, could never transmigrate to a higher form of creation than themselves. Defying this notion, Al Saadi spent hours cleaning and disinfecting bones to preserve the vitality that had carried their proprietors through their short lives. Their next incarnation would be painless and eternal.

The new forms Al Saadi conjured in *The Cavity Room* (1991), a sculpture series culled from these remains, were no longer animal, though nowhere near human either. Instead, they perhaps recast more-than-human dissolutions. Assembled in a studio at the Khorfakkan Library, where Mohamed Ahmed Ibrahim and poet Ahmed Rashid Thani were also in residence, the works were exhibited in 1994 at Al Saadi's second EFAS solo show. In a dim, lamp-lit room, the sculptures were accompanied by live animal recordings and shadowed by the movement of a ceiling fan. Developed in parallel with *The Cavity Room* and shown at the same exhibition was an assortment of preserved insect specimens. In an accompanying text denouncing the growing use of pesticides, Al Saadi also vowed never to deliberately kill an insect. Transcending simple taxidermy, both works epitomise his post-naturalist approach to art making.

These early works reveal how he thrived off of his connection to the environment, one that could only be sustained through excursions allowing him to reflect on his place in the world and his obligations towards it. Life was after all, in Al Saadi's own words, an endless bicycle ride.

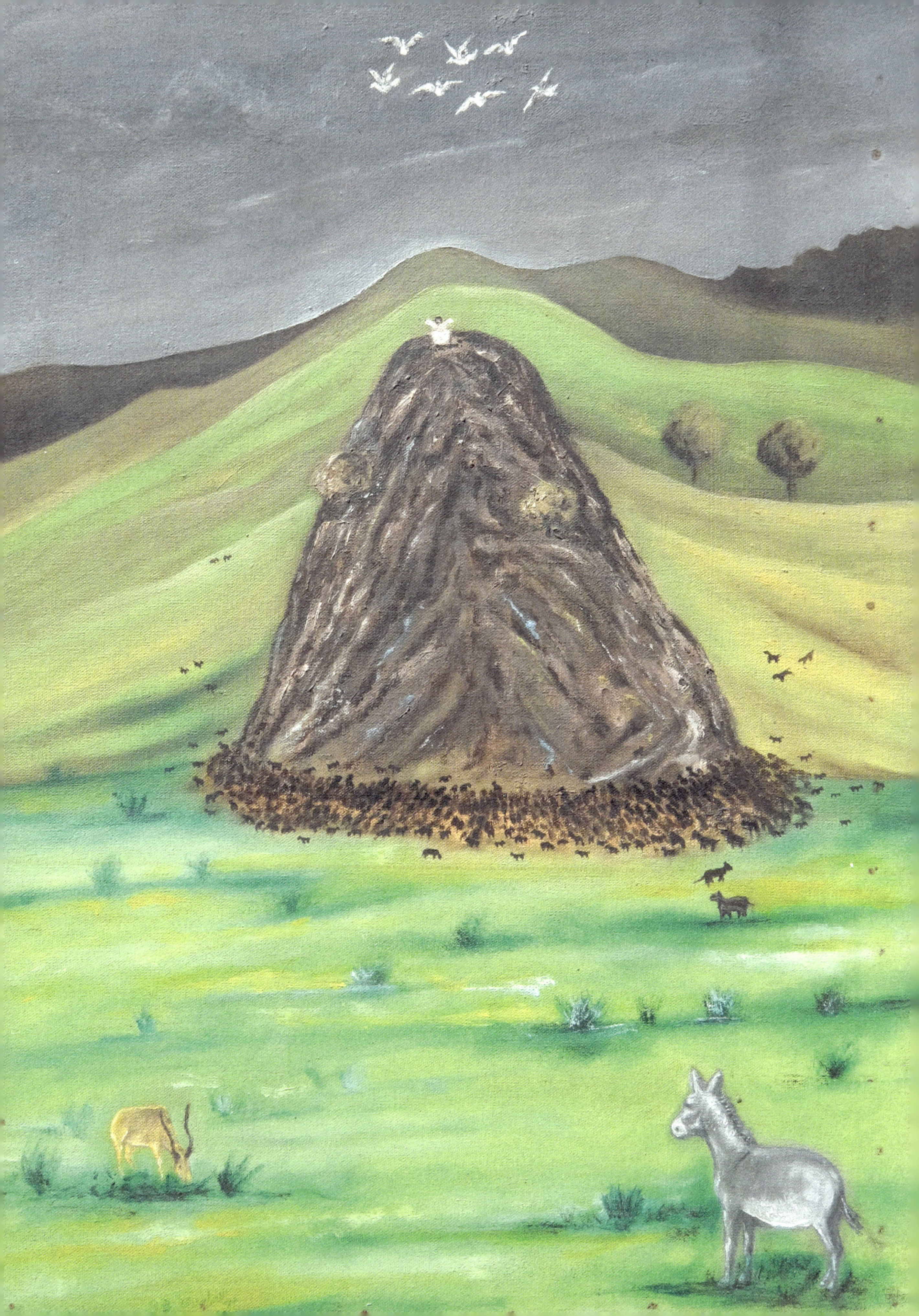

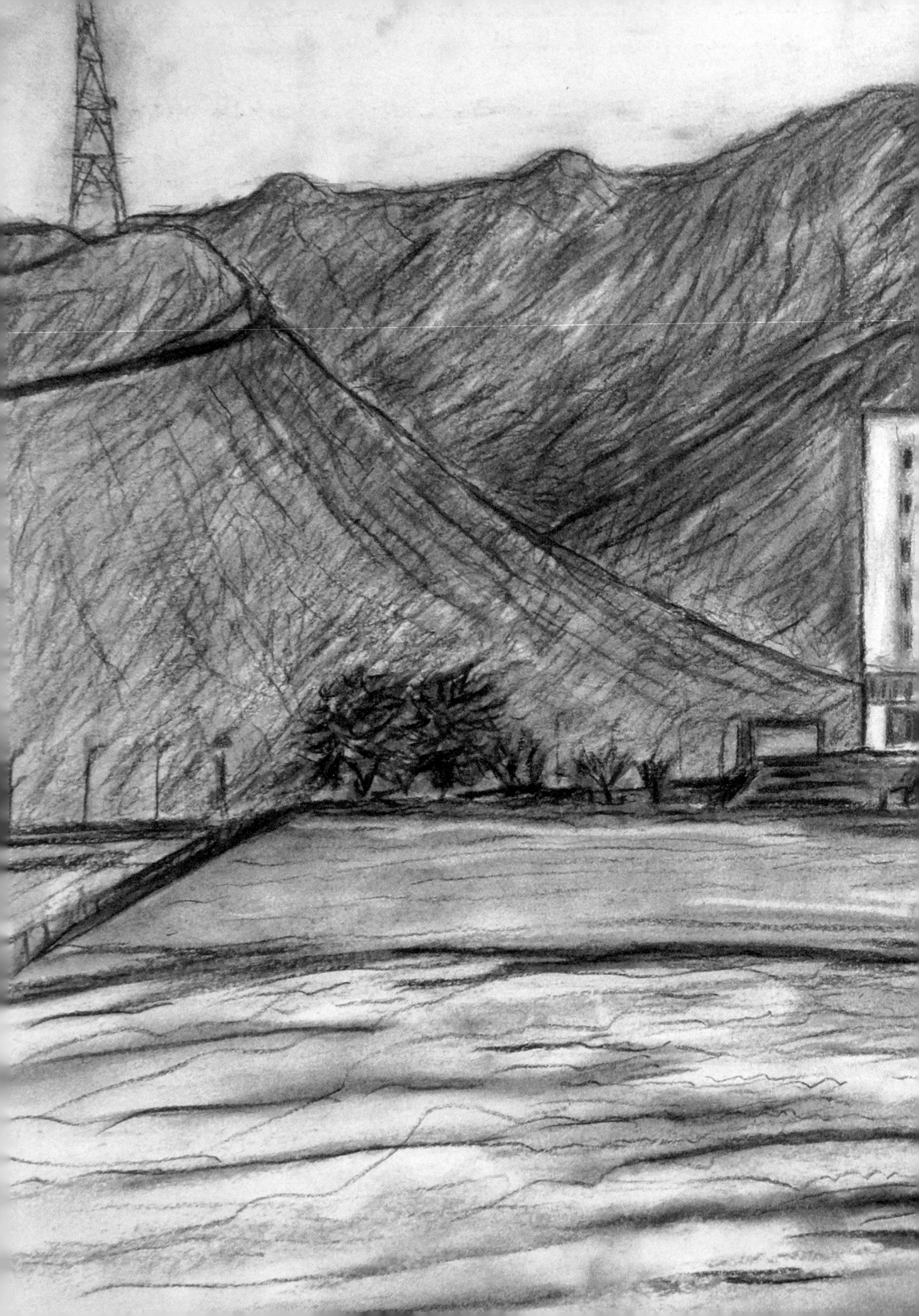

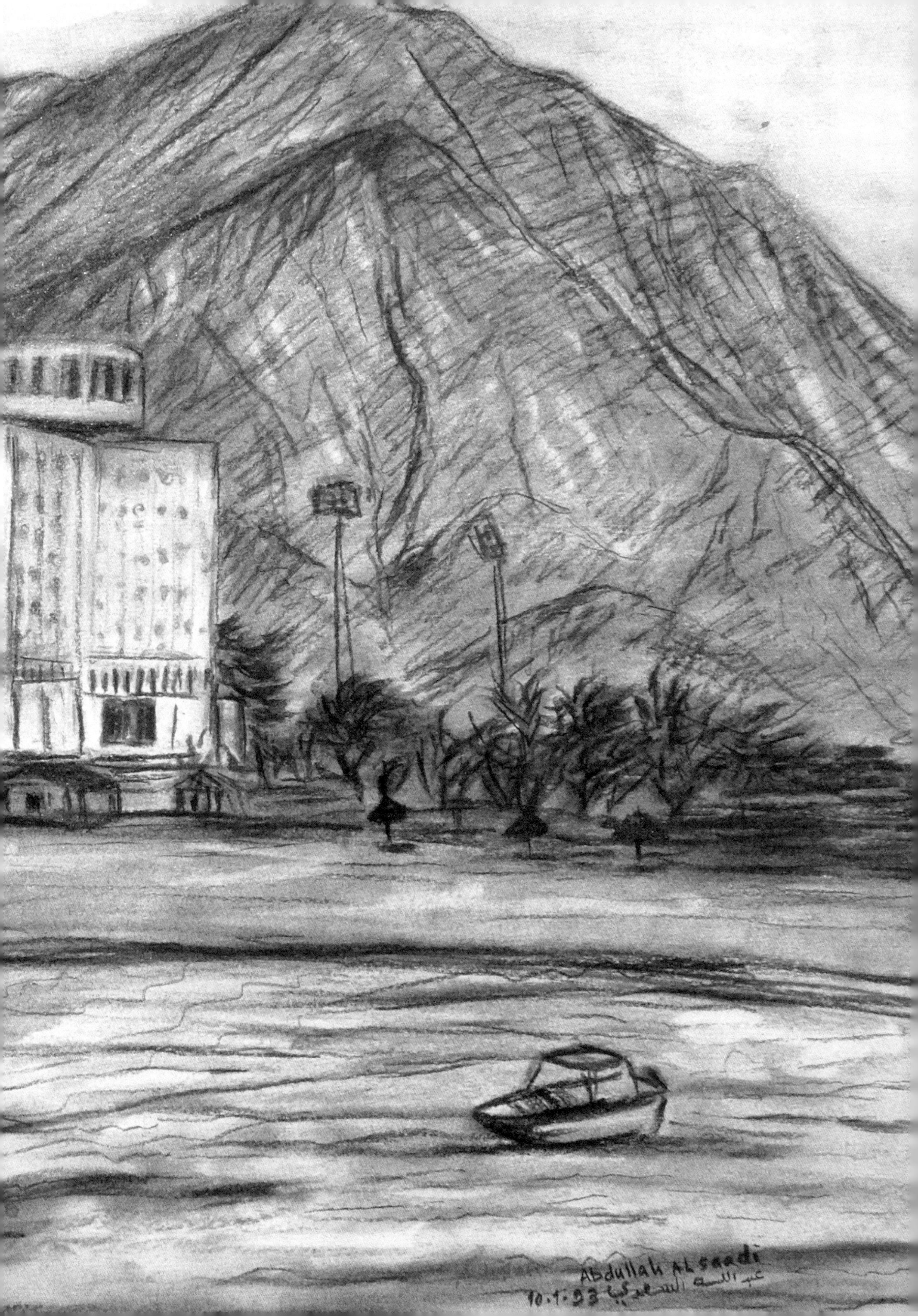

Abdullah Al saadi
10.1.93 عبد الله السعدي

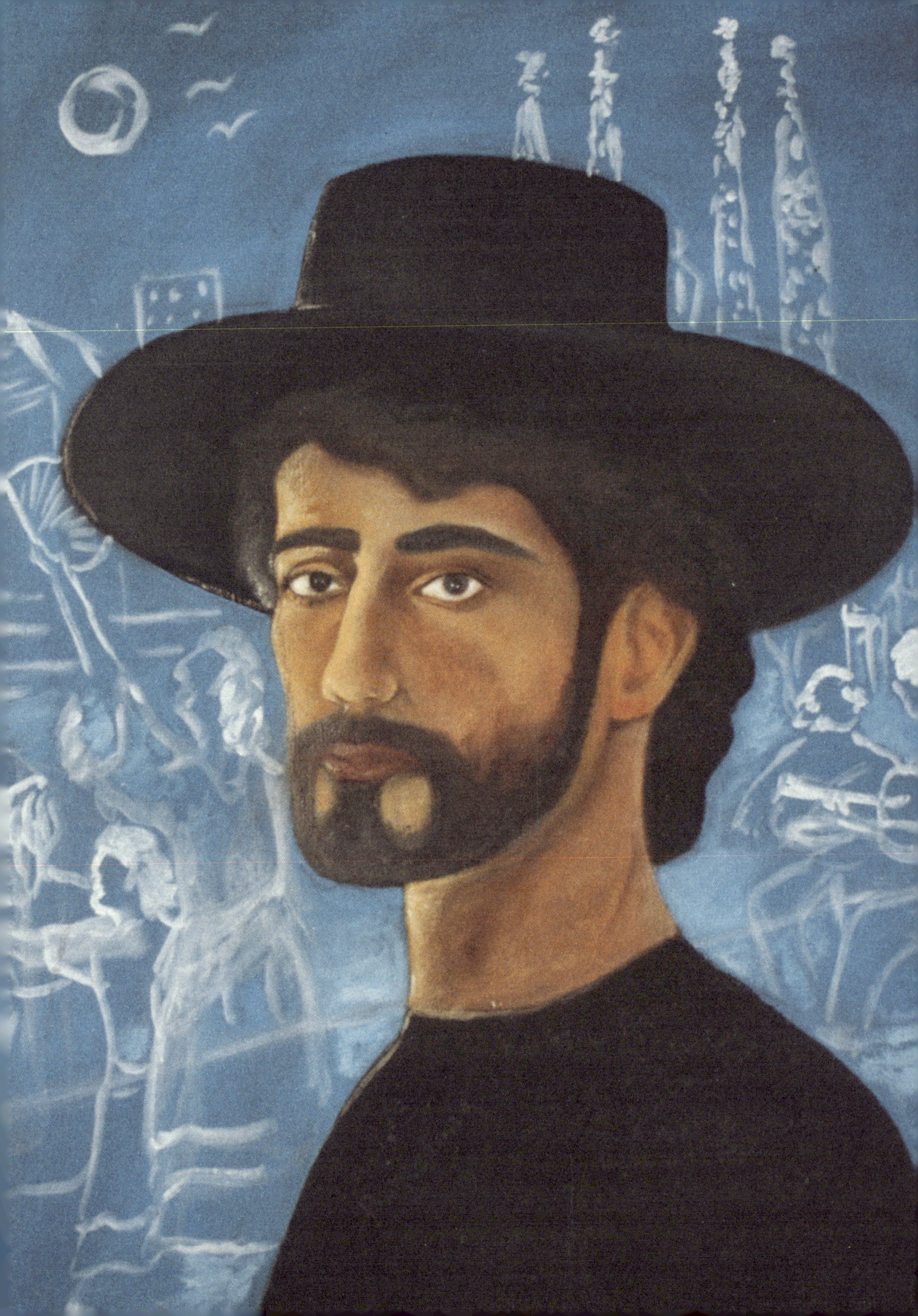

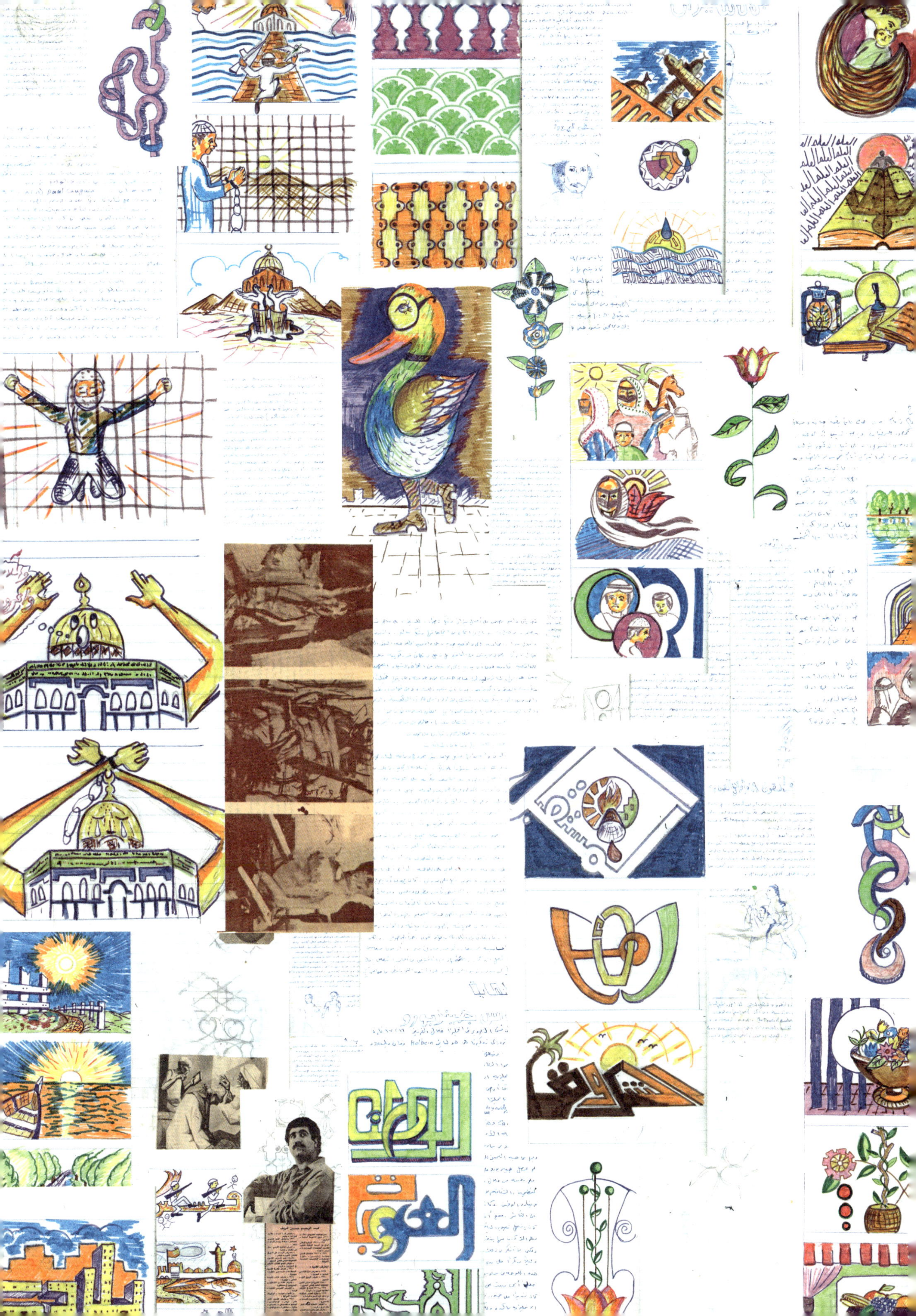

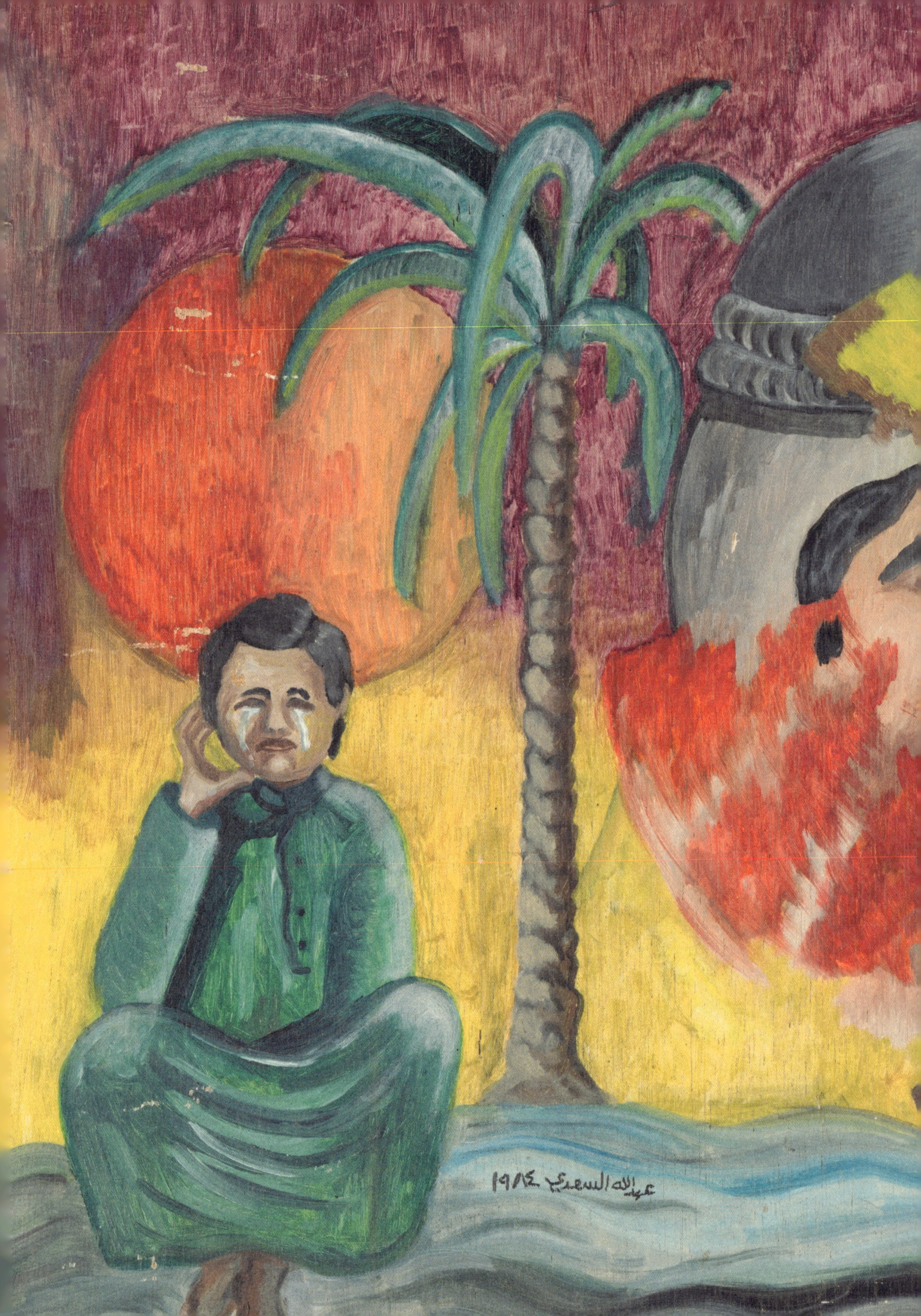
عبد الله السبتي ١٩٨٤

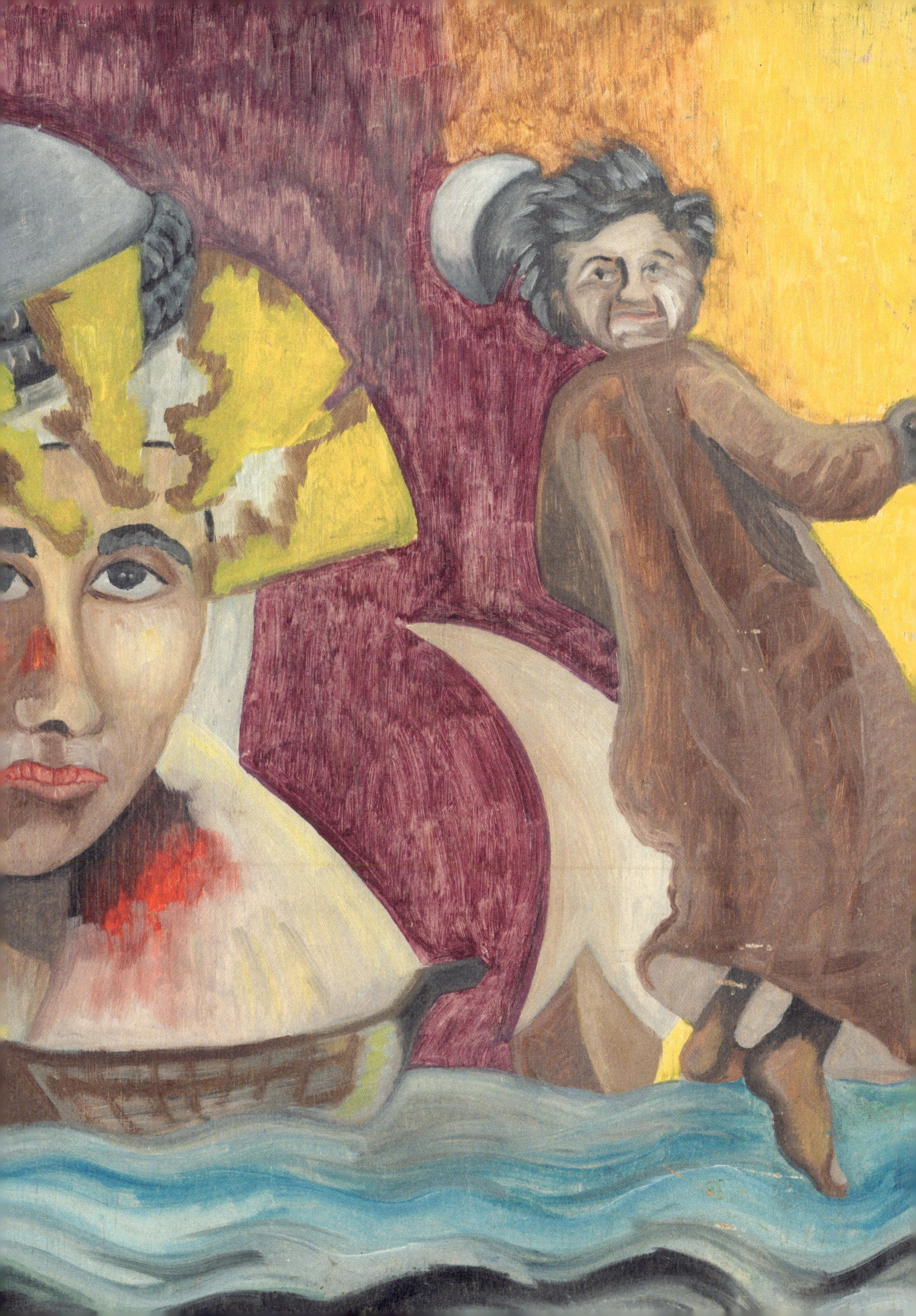

Between Collecting
And Travelling

Abdullah Al Saadi left his village, Al Ghouna, nestled within the mountains of the Eastern Region, with his family and moved to Khorfakkan. Since childhood, however, he has been independent and lived apart from his family. He lived as a boarding student, first in Masafi, during his elementary school studies, then in Sharjah for high school. Later he lived in the university dormitories in Al Ain. He then settled in his first studio, which was located near the old market in Khorfakkan. In this studio, one could hear the echo of the sea penetrating the walls. Eventually, he moved to another studio opened by the Emirates Fine Arts Society in Al Khor, which was later closed down. Now, Abdullah Al Saadi, the young painter, is heading to Japan.

Al Saadi was always silent, lonely, eerie and peculiar. Before he had the opportunity to buy a bicycle, he never left a spot in Khorfakkan, be it beaches, mountains, or valleys, unexplored on foot. Al Saadi was born on a rock. When he first connected and interacted with his world, it was within the mountain villages embedded in the valleys: Al Ghouna, Nahwa, Madha and their surroundings. This world was very close to nature and the environment, to insects, water and darkness. It was a world of magic, where the book of Al-Ghazali opens and unfolds, and where mythology awakens those ancient bones. This solitude, separation and ruggedness that encompass the inner self are nurtured by fertile soil and deep clay, shaping his unique artistic identity: the imprint of his soul. Upon exploring his second solo exhibition (held at Emirates Fine Arts Society, Sharjah, from 27 January to 1 February 1994), it becomes evident that Al Saadi leans towards a unique, elusive and impossible dream. It is none other than the intense desire to possess everything, to capture each moment in a relentless grasp, defying death itself.

Al Saadi collects insects, freezes them and places them in small boxes, which are then nested within larger ones. He also collects the bones of deceased animals. He meticulously cleans, sterilises, preserves and displays them in various forms (such as the room-shaped installation in the Emirates Fine Arts Society exhibition). Additionally, for over a decade, Al Saadi has been documenting his daily experiences – if we may use that expression. Whatever he sees, hears or unexpectedly encounters, he consistently returns to his solitude, detachment and longing, recording and capturing them on paper. It is as if Al Saadi, when documenting himself, unveils the silence of others and the world, exposing his own silence and the silence of the universe within and around him.

What truly captivates are the photographic images presented by Al Saadi in the aforementioned exhibition. The photographs displayed by Al Saadi were not presented for their artistic aesthetics as photographic images. It can be said, without much risk, that Al Saadi is not truly preoccupied with aesthetics.

The photographs exhibited by Al Saadi serve as records, confirming his journeys here in the Emirates or around the world. As a traveller and migrant by nature, he documents his experiences through his photographs. Al Saadi presents these photographs to 'validate,' for others, that he has indeed roamed, travelled, walked, migrated and experienced solitude, detachment and uniqueness. He also presents them because when he sees a particular scene – a mountain, a river, a valley or a woman – he fears that once it is witnessed, it will separate and depart from him. Al Saadi fears solitude, so he preserves such scenes in a photographic image that, ironically, only preserves its own captured and fixed moment.

As for the fleeting and ephemeral passerby, whom Al Saadi cannot capture, freeze and sterilise like he can the insects and the bones, and whom he cannot photographically capture (and fix) in a single frame, he hastens to the whiteness of the paper to record it in his journal. If not a story, he writes it as a poem in Arabic. If that fails, he attempts it in English. If the poem cannot fully preserve what Al Saadi experienced, he then tries to capture it through a sketch or a painting. Al Saadi is not preoccupied with writing as a mere act of writing, not in the form of journals, poems or stories. Likewise, he does not find meaning in drawing as a mere act of drawing, whether in sketches or paintings. When he collects insects, bones or boxes, he pays no heed to the internal logic of the collection. Al Saadi collects, preserves and records in order to possess the world. In this world, he incessantly expresses, separates from and dissects it.

Did I not mention that Al Saadi was born on a rock?!

The overwhelming sense of detachment and the desire for collection, preservation and recording, alongside the experience of migration and travel, which is life as Al Saadi has lived it and found himself in, together form the fundamental inspirations of his young artistic journey. The experience that, in one way or another, intersects with what the artist Hassan Sharif refers to as 'the experience of art with the new in the Emirates.'

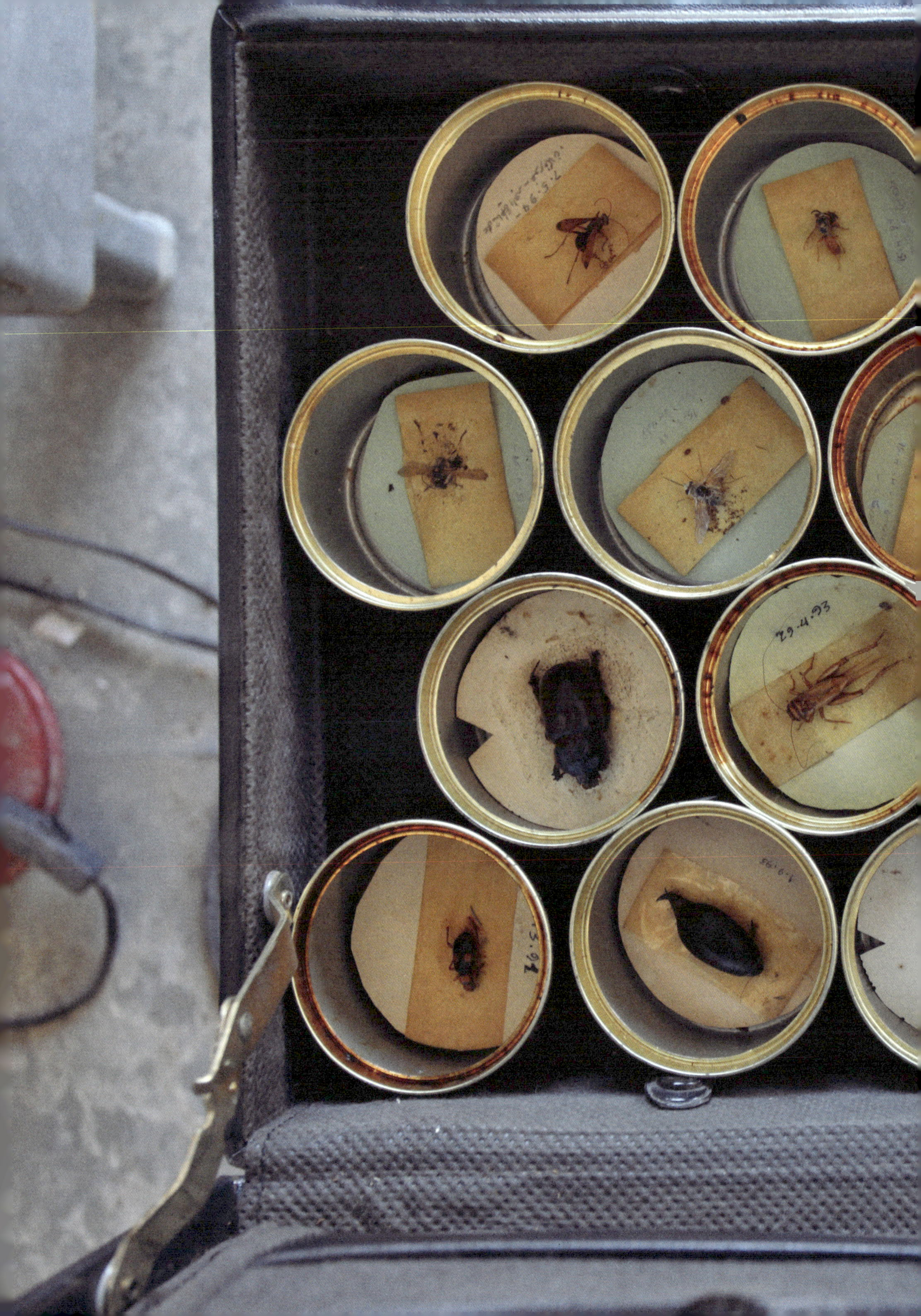

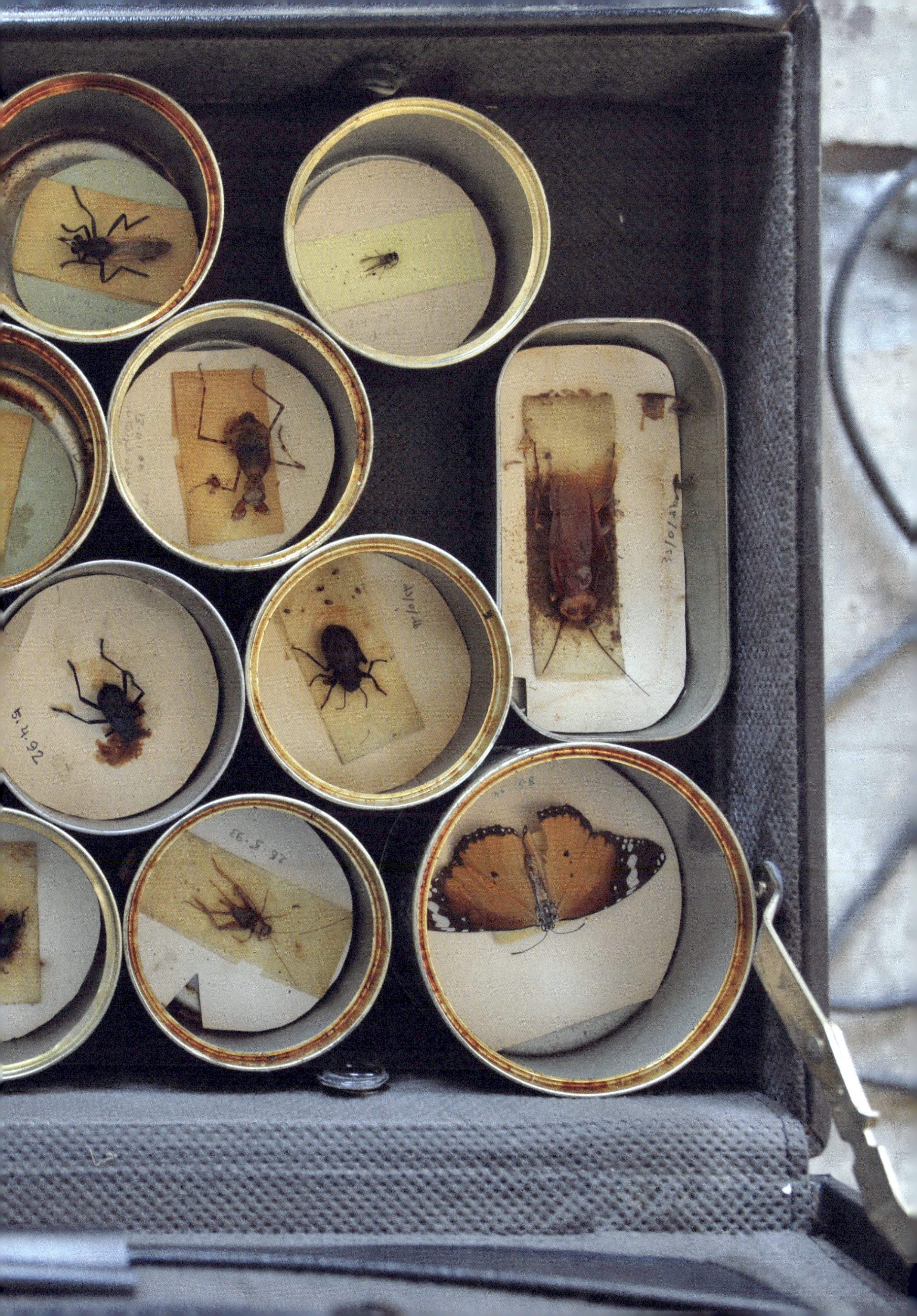

Al Saadi's experience, to the same extent that it possesses confidence and courage, also possesses insecurity and a deep-seated desire for validation from others – the audience. As much as it feels internally complete, it is an experience that does not engage in dialogue or conversation with others, as its external deficiencies and continuous failure to grasp everything remain glaringly evident.

In the end, it is the experience that encompasses all that can be gathered, yet it remains both deprived and perceptive, even violent in its deprivation and detachment.

A journey of collecting and preserving to travel and travelling to collect and preserve: this is the essence of Al Saadi's spirit, as I perceive it. Al Saadi possesses the capacity to remain within the confines of his own being (in quietude) or within the sanctuary of his chamber (in solitude) for extended hours and even days. Yet, when he ventures forth on meticulously planned expeditions to mountains, valleys, distant villages or foreign lands, he harbours no inclination to extend invitations for others to partake in his sojourns.

Al Saadi's impulse to collect what he finds in his voyages is a manifestation of his inward odyssey, where he embarks upon a solitary pilgrimage to assemble and commune with his own essence. It is within this singular, detached and evocative expedition that he endeavours to amass and coalesce.

The profound silence, as perceived by Al Saadi, assumes an imposing demeanour. Whenever he takes a seat and seals the portal of his chamber, a profound reverie takes hold of him, wherein he amasses the mosaic of his past voyages, meditates upon the vistas he has beheld and artfully inscribes his emotions and insights. Furthermore, he is visited by reveries, flights of fancy and an inexorable yearning towards realms uncharted, beckoning him to embark on journeys yet untaken.

When he shares his journey, he unveils a treasure trove of travel-induced artefacts: a curated assortment of insects, skeletal remains, photographic mementoes, artistry, Arabic and English poems, and an anthology of exploratory tales and diaries, culminating in an ethereal collection of folklore. When Al Saadi showcases all or part of this in an exhibition, it is intended for a wide audience, and the exhibition is open for anyone who wishes to view, contemplate and observe. Al Saadi, as an artist, does not aim to become the central focus – a focus that seeks personal recognition. This is a personal and non-referential preoccupation. Al Saadi, perhaps owing to a profound sense of detachment and singularity, aspires to serve as an exemplar.

I believe what Al Saadi lacks now is the creation, weaving and deepening of his 'cultural mask' to defend the exemplar he desires and seeks to present. Moreover, what he lacks is the intense tension between his yearning to travel and his yearning to collect (collecting that represents home, dwelling and stability).

The 'cultural mask' is essential in such a soul, for psychological illness, or rather, psychological inclinations alone, are not sufficient to declare someone an artist. When the artist proclaims himself and asserts his ideals, he becomes the very embodiment of the transmuting of his psychological inclinations from the realm of the unconscious (where dominant inclinations reside) to the realm of consciousness (where governed inclinations prevail). 'Cultural mask': it is that truth, devoid of countenance and abode, which is none other than this heart and this transformation. Travel is not merely geographical displacement (separated from history) or vice versa, just as collecting is not merely a dwelling and retreat within oneself (separated from the world) or vice versa; however, it is indeed the passage and transformation from this realm to that one. Above this and beyond that. Indeed, the Japanese Embassy in the Emirates acted commendably by finally providing Abdullah Al Saadi with a seat at one of its universities. In his new journey, migration and separation, Al Saadi shall return a renewed scholar, particularly as he immerses himself in the fertile atmosphere of travel, migration and the collective spirit for which Japan is renowned. And from what I hear, Japan boasts a wealth of diverse climates to nurture his intellectual pursuits. We cannot let this commendation for the actions of the Japanese Embassy pass us by without emphasising the importance of the Emirates Fine Arts Society and cultural institutions here, collaborating to support artists, especially the talented youth and the exceptionally gifted individuals. It is crucial to encourage them to embark on journeys, travel and engage with artistic communities worldwide, as this can lead to significant development and a deepening of awareness and artistic output.

—Ahmed Rashid Thani

Originally published in Arabic in *Al Khaleej* newspaper (Sharjah), 26 September 1994.
Translated into English by Torjoman.

ولا تبقى الا العظام

الشـــاة

مسكينة أيتها الشاة

عندما حضرتك الوفاة

رموك بعيدا عن بيوتهم

وبعيدا عن أعين الناس

لتكوني في القفراء

حيث الجبال والصخور

والأشجار والسكون

وحيث تعيش الثعالب

والذئاب والطيور

أنا كنت هذا اليوم

هناك

أبحث عن عظام

لما رأيت جسد شاة

جلست على صخرة

أراقب كيف للرمة

أن تأكل اللحم

ولا تبقى الا العظام

فتساءلت عن اسم تلك الشاة

وهل لها حملان صغار

ما زالوا على قيد الحياة

وتساءلت عن الحياة والموت

الذي يأتي للانسان

والحيوان على السواء

وكيف للحيوان أن يرمى

وللانسان أن يدفن في التراب

فمهلا يا شاة

سأرجع اليك بعد أن

تأكل الرمة اللحم

سأشكل من عظامك

هيكلا خرافيا

سيطير في السماء

فان كان لحمك قد فنى

فان عظامك ستبقى

سرمدية بلا فناء.

Bones العظـــــام

أذكر في يوما مـا كنت أمشي عند سفح الجبل استوقفني منظر تلك العظام المبعثرة على الأرض من هنا وهناك، فجلست على صخرة أتأمل تلك العظام بعد أن أكلت الرمة اللحم فحدثت نفسي قائلا:

هذه العظام كانت في يوم ما عظام شاة ولدت على هذه الأرض وكانت عبدة لأحد الناس، كـان عندها الأصدقاء والصديقات يشاركوها فرحـة الحيـاة في تلك الحظيرة التي تقضي فيها ليلتها الدافئة كل يـوم. وعند الصباح تنطلق مـع القطيع فرحة وسط الجبال والتلال، ترى العشب الأخضـر، وعنـد المسـاء تعود الـى بيت مالكها حزينة، فما تزال السكين تلاحقها.

لقد جلست أفكر في تلك العظـام طويـلا، وبعد أيام رجعت اليهـا وحملتها في كيسا، كنت أحاول أن أحفظ تلك العظام معي الى الأبـد لأنها عظـام شاة مـا زلت أحس انها تتحرك، لا يهمنـي اللحم بقدر مـا تهمنـي العظـام التي يجب أن تصان وتحفظ كما تحفظ جثة الانسان عندما يدفن في القبر.

كنت أقضي الساعات في تنظيف تلك العظام بالماء المغلي والمبيدات الكيماويـة وتهويتها تحت الشمس وعرضها، وأخيرا تبين لي ان العظام والكائنات الاسطورية التي شكلتها يجب أن تعيش في بيئة معينة، هي تلك البيئة التي صنعتها لها، عبـارة عن غرفة مظلمة وفيها نور خافت وموسيقى، في تلك الغرفة كل شيء يتحرك أحس وكأن العظام عادت اليهـا الـروح من جديد، وأسـمع أيضـا أصـوات الأغنام وهي ترعى عند سفح الجبل.

ما زلت أتذكر تلك الحكاية الشعبية التي روتها لـي أمي في أن أغـراب حطوا رحـالهم عند سيدة لا تملك الا شاة واحدة، ذبحتهـا لهم، فلمـا أكل الضيوف اللحم، رموا العظام في الذرب قبل رحيلهم، وفي الغد استفاقت تلك السيدة العجوز على أصوات أغنام في زربها بعد أن تحولت تلك العظام الى أغنام حية.

ملاحظة : الى أرواح كل الأغنام والحيوانـات أقدم عزائـي وأقول ان عظامكم في الحفظ والصون وستبقى سرمدية بلا فناء، عظامكم أداة أحتج بها أمـام وجوه آكلي اللحم ومصاصي العظام..

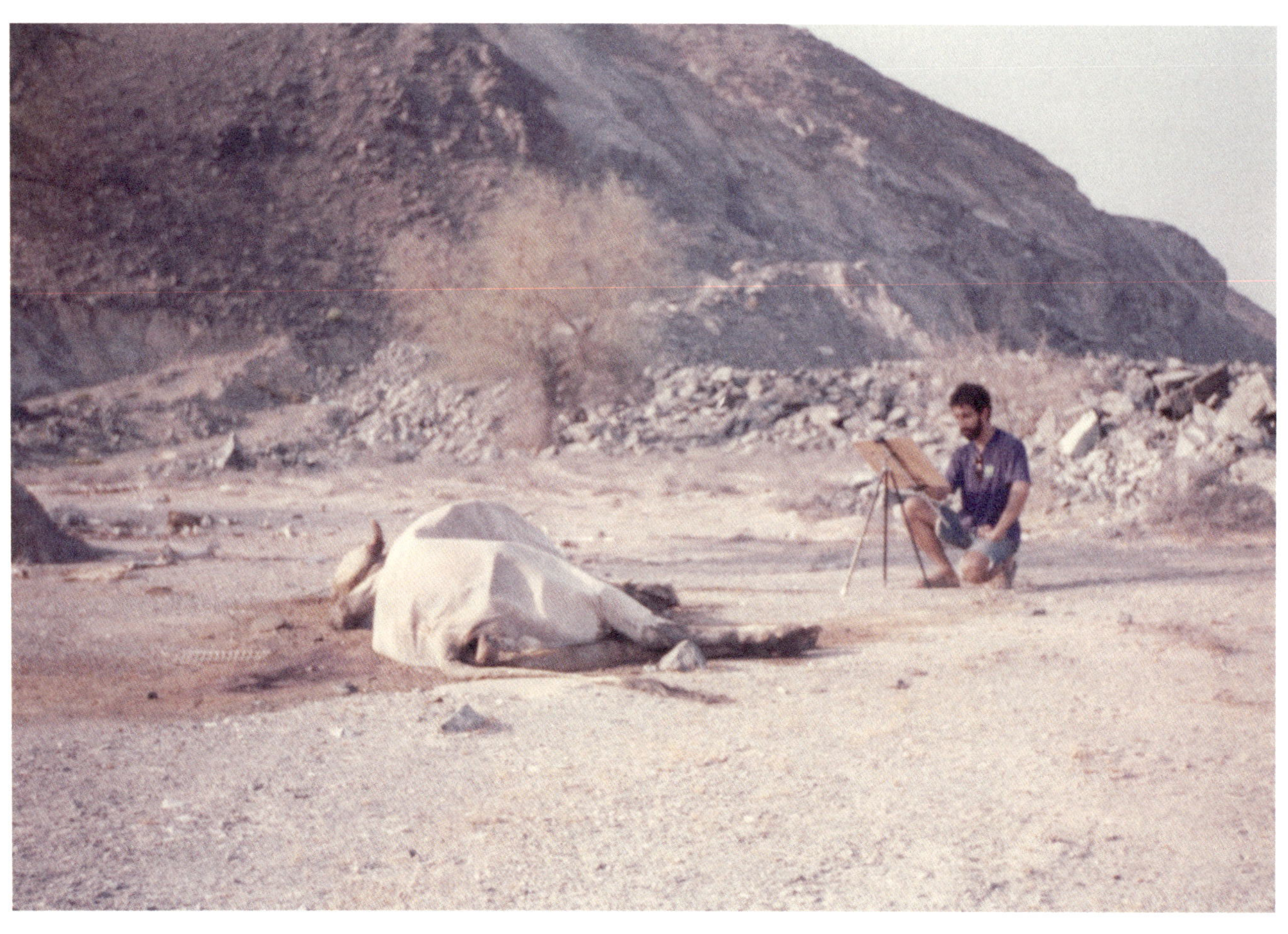

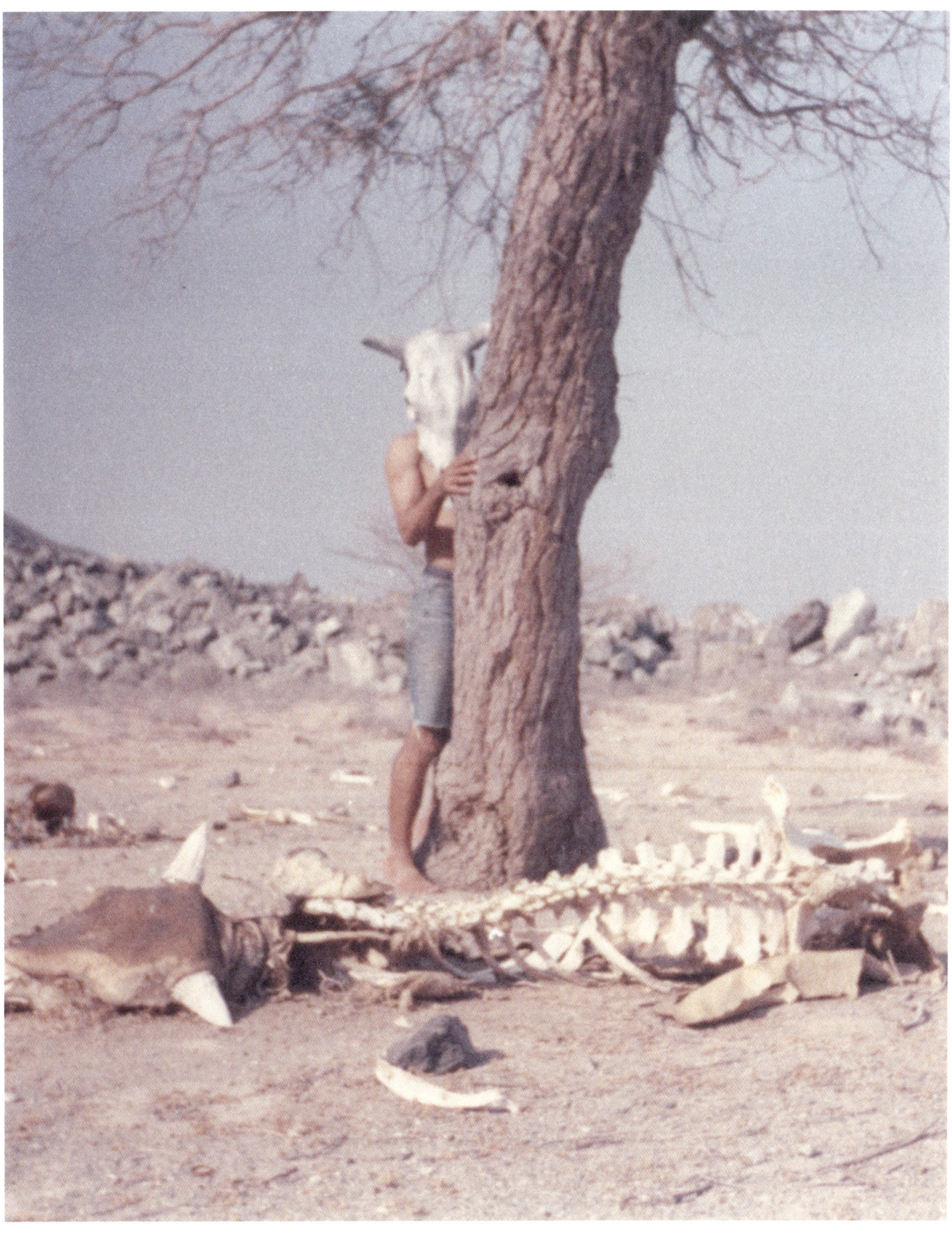

قدر ما تمتلك من اللائقة ومن السعي الدفين إلى تصديق آخرين _ الجمهور _ لها، وهي التجربة التي بقدر ما شعر باكتمالها التام داخليا، هي أيضا التي لا تسمع ولا نحاور كتجربة مع الآخر لأن نقصها الخارجي وفشل نقبض على كل شيء مستمر، على المرأى وفادح .

وهي في الأخير _ التجربة التي تجمع كل ما يمكن جمعه، إلا أنها الفاقدة والحاسة، حتى العنف، بالفقدان الفصل .

سفر يجمع ويثبت ليسافر ويجمع ويثبت ويسافر: هذه هي الروح من السعدي كما أراها. بإمكان السعدي ألا يخرج من ذاته (يتكلم) أو من غرفته (يجتمع) لساعات طوال لأيام، ولكن السعدي كذلك وحينما يذهب في رحلات مخططة إلى الجبال والوديان والقرى البعيدة أو إلى البلدان أخرى، فأنه بالطبع لا يدعو، وليس من هاجسه أن يدعو حدا لمرافقته .

والجمع الذي يسكن إليه السعدي من السفر، هو السفر لذي يذهب إليه السعدي كي يجمع ويجتمع في جمعه مع نفسه، كما هو في سفره الوحيد، المنفصل والمستوحش .

السكون مرعب عند السعدي هو الساكن هيئة، وكلما قعد وأغلق عليه باب غرفته انتابه جمع ما سافره والتفكير في ما مشاه وكتابة ما عبر عنه، كما انتابته أحلام وخيالات ونوازع نحو ما لم يسافر ويهاجر إليه بعد.

وهو حين يعلن تجربته عن السفر وعن جمع ما أسفر عن السفر في مثبتات من حشرات وعظام وصور فوتوغرافية ولوحات واستكشافات وقصائد بالعربية وأخرى بالإنجليزية ، ومن قصص ويوميات وحتى جمع "فولكلوري". وحين يعرض السعدي كل هذا أو بعضه في معرض يقصده جمهور عام ويكون العرض متاحا لكل من يريد أن يرى ويطلع ويتفرج، فإن الفنان في السعدي لا يريد أن يكون الهاجس. هاجس السفر والجمع عنده. هاجسا شخصيا وغير معبر ولا دال، فالسعدي يريد _ نظرا ربما لإحساس عميق بالانفصال والتفرد _ أن يكون أمثولة .

واعتقد أن ما ينقص السعدي الآن هو خلق ونسج وتعميق قناعه الثقافي الخاص به للدفاع عن الأمثولة التي يرغب ويسعى في عرضها. كما أن ما ينقصه هو التوتير الأشد ما بين هاجسه للسفر وهاجسه للجمع (الجمع الذي هو سكن ومنزل وتثبيت) .

"القناع الثقافي" أساس في روح كهذه، فالمرض النفسي . أو بمعنى أصح الميول السيكولوجية وحدها لا تكفي للإعلان عن

فنان. فالفنان حين يعلن عن نفسه ويدعي أمثولته، فأنه أيضا ذلك الذي يقلب ميوله السيكولوجية من اللاوعي إلى الوعي (ميول حاكمة) (ميول محكومة). والقناع الثقافي: تلك الحقيقة التي بلا وجه ولا مستقر هي هذا القلب وهذا التحويل. أن السفر ليس سفرا في الجغرافيا (وفصلها) عن التاريخ (أو العكس) فحسب، كما أن الجمع ليس سكنا وركونا إلى النفس (وفصلها) عن العالم (أو العكس). إن السفر هو العبور والتحول من هذا إلى ذلك. فوق هذا وفوق تلك وحسنا فعلت السفارة اليابانية في الدولة حين وفرت أخيرا لعبدالله السعدي مقعدا في إحدى جامعاتها، لأن السعدي في سفره وهجرته وانفصاله الجديد هذا، سيعود جامعا جديدا، خاصة حين يكون المناخ المسافر والمهاجر إليه والمجموعة منه الروح، مناخا ثريا، وكما أسمع فان اليابان ثرية في أكثر من مناخ. لن يفوت علينا هذا الاستحسان لما فعلته السفارة اليابانية فرصة التأكد على جمعية الإمارات للفنون التشكيلية والمؤسسات الثقافية هنا لأن تتعاون في دفع الفنانين والشبان خصوصا والمتميزين على الأخص إلى الذهاب والسفر والاختلاط بالمجتمعات الفنية في العالم لما يمكن أن يؤرثه هذا من تطوير وتعميق للوعي والنتاج الفني

أحمد راشد ثاني

جريدة الخليج ٩٤/٩/٢٦

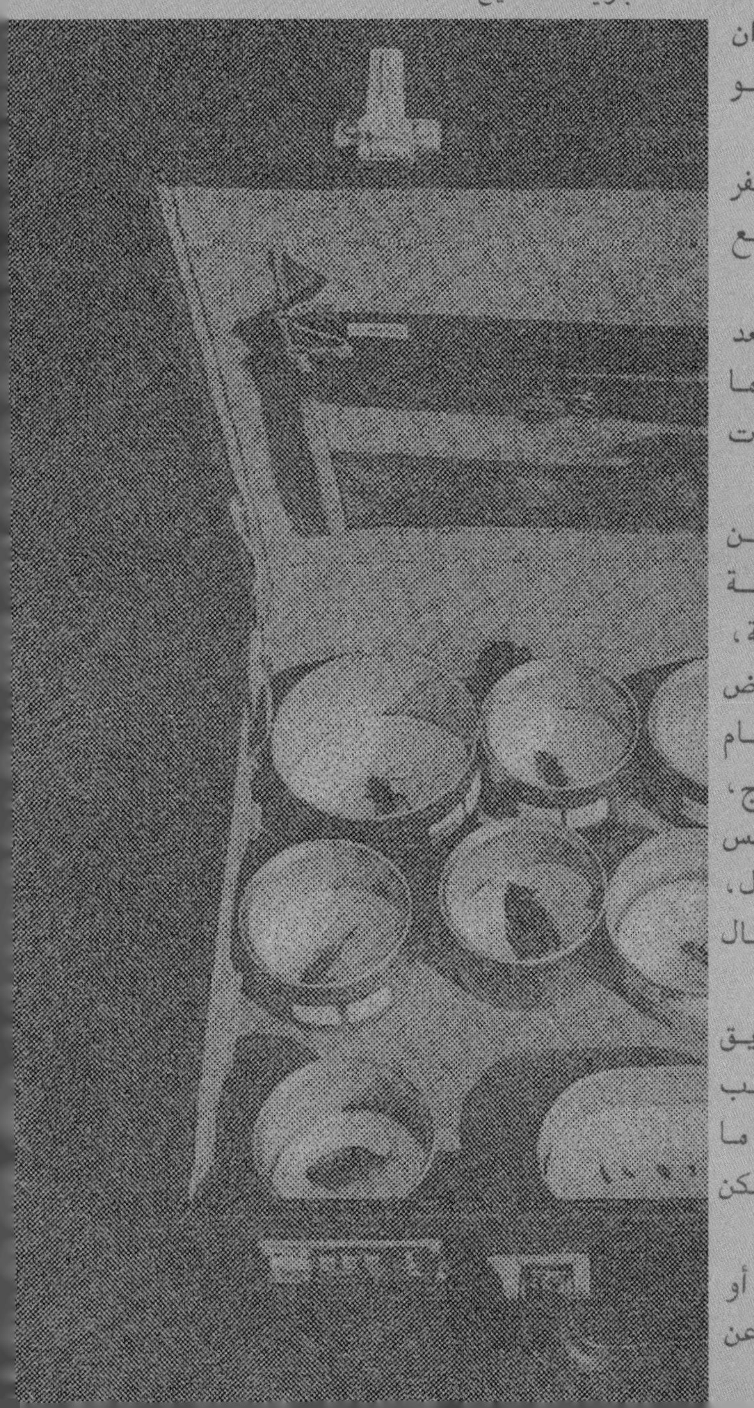

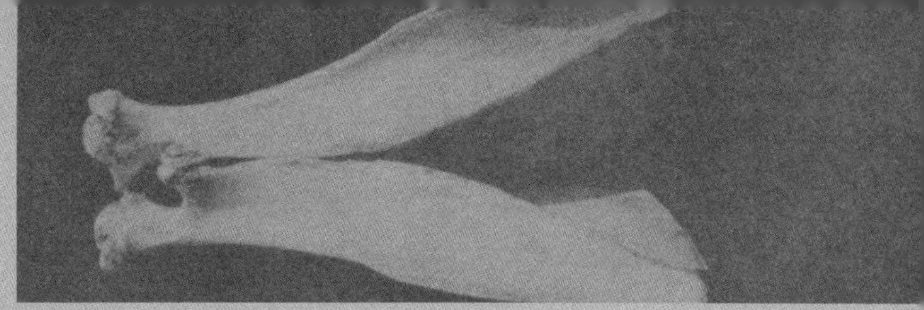

عبدالله السعدي بين الجمع والسفر

أحمد راشد ثاني

نزل عبدالله السعدي من قريته "الغونة" المدسوسة في رؤوس الجبال من المنطقة الشرقية مع أهله إلى خورفكان، إلا أنه ومنذ الطفولة انفرد وانفصل عن العائلة، فمن سكن الطلاب الداخلي "ساقي" عند دراسته للابتدائية، إلى السكن الداخلي في الشارقة حين الثانوية، إلى السكن الجامعي في العين، ومن ثم سكنه في مرسمه الأول قريباً من السوق القديم في خورفكان (حيث في هذا المرسم كان بإمكانك أن تسمع صدى البحر وهو يخترق الجدران) إلى سكنه في المرسم الذي افتتحته جمعية الإمارات للفنون التشكيلية في "الخور" وبعد ذلك أغلقته، وها هو الآن السعدي، الشاب الرسام، ذاهب إلى اليابان.

على الدوام كان السعدي صامتاً ووحيداً ومستوحشاً وغريباً. فهو وقت أن تتوفر له الفرصة لشراء دراجة، لم يترك بقعة في خورفكان من شواطئ أو جبال أو أودية إلا قطعها على قدميه. لقد ولد السعدي على صخرة، وحين تلمس وتلامس مع عالمه الأول، كان هذا العالم فإلقرى الجبلية المعلقة على الوديان: "الغونة"، "النحوة"، "مدحا" وما جاورها. كان هذا العالم قريباً جداً من الطبيعة والبيئة، من الحشرات والماء والظلام، من السحر حيث يفتح ويتفتح كتاب "الغزالي"، وحيث الخرافة تلك التي توقظ العظام الرميمة هذه الوحشة والانفصال والجبلية التي ينطوي عليها الداخل هي ما تهبه التربة الخصبة والطمي العميق لما قد يكون لاحقاً فنيته الخاصة وخصوصيته الفنية: بصمة روحه. أن السعدي ومن قراءة لمعرضه الشخصي الثاني (صالة جمعية التشكيل – الشارقة – ٢٧ يناير / ١ فبراير ١٩٩٤م) يجنح إلى وهم فريد وأشقر ومستحيل، ألا وهو الرغبة العارمة في امتلاك كل شيء؛ تثبيت كل لحظة، القبض على الموت.

فغير جمع السعدي للحشرات وتجميدها ووضعها فيناديق صغيرة ووضع الصناديق الصغيرة في أخرى أكبر، وغير جمعه للعظام، عظام الحيوانات النافقة، وتنظيفها وتعقيمها وحفظها أو عرضها بأشكال مختلفة (كشكل الغرفة في المعرض)، فإن السعدي يكتب يومياته كل يوم – إذا صح التعبير – ومنذ ما يزيد على عشر سنوات، فالذي يراه أو يظن أنه يسمعه أو ما يصادفه ويفاجئه، يعود السعدي كل مــ رة وحدته وانفصاله ووحشته ليسجله ويثبته ويجمعه على الورق، كأنما السعدي حين يسجل نفسه مع الآخرين والعالم، ويفضح صمته وصمت الكون فيه وعنه.

بل أن ما يلفت حقاً هو الصور الفوتوغرافية التي قدمها السعدي في معرضه المذكور. فالصور المعروضة لم يعرضها السعدي نظراً لجمالياتها الفنية كصور فوتوغرافية، إذ نستطيع القول وبلا مجازفة كبيرة أن السعدي ليس مشغولاً شغلاً حقا بالجماليات على الأرجح. أن الصور التي يعرضها السعدي لتسجل (أي لتؤكد) أسفاره هنا في الإمارات أو في العالم (فهو من المسافرين والمهاجرين طبعا وطبيعة). ويعرض السعدي الصور ليصدق (نضع خط تحت يصدق) الآخرون أنه جال وسافر ومشى وهاجر واغترب وتوحش وانفصل وتفرد. ويعرض السعدي هذه الصور أيضاً لأنه إذا ما رأى مشهداً ما: جبلا أو نهراً أو وادياً أو امرأة، فأنه يخشى عند رؤيته أن يمر المرئي ويفترق عنه يخشى السعدي .. الوحشة فيحتفظ بهذا المشهد فيصورة فوتوغرافية – للمفارقة – لا تحتفظ إلا بمشهدها هي، بما التقطت وتثبت هي وحوت.

والعابر الآني الزائل الذي لا يستطيع السعدي القبض عليه وتجميده وتعقيمه كالحشرات والعظام، والذي لا يستطيع تصويره فوتوغرافيا (وتثبيته) في لقطة فإنه يهرع إلى بياض الورق ليسجله في يومياته، فإن لم تستطع "القصة" عنده يكتبه كقصيدة بالعربية، فإن لم تستطع فبالإنجليزية، فإن لم تستطع "القصيدة" أن تحفظ كليا ما عبر عن السعدي، يحاول عبدالله القبض على ما عبر عنه وذهب على هيئة "اسكتش" أو "لوحة". السعدي ليس معنياً بالكتابة ككتابة، لا كيوميات ولا كقصيدة ولا كقصة، كما أنه ليس معنياً بالرسم كرسم، لا "كاسكتش" ولا كلوحة. وهو حين يجمع الحشرات أو العظام أو العلب، فإنه لا يعتني بالمنطق الداخلي للجمع. السعدي يجمع ويثبت ويسجل ليمتلك العالم. هذا العالم الذي لا ينفك يعبر عنه وينفصل عنه ويفصله.

ألم أقل أن السعدي ولد على صخرة؟!

الإحساس الجارف بالانفصال وشهوة الجمع والتثبيت والتسجيل، وتلك الهجرة والسفر التي هي الحياة كما عاشها ووجد فيها السعدي تشكل البواعث الأساس من تجربته الفنية الشابة، هذه التجربة التي تتلامس بشكل أو بآخر مع ما يسميه الفنان حسن شريف "تجربة الفن الجديد في الإمارات".

كما أن تجربة السعدي هي التجربة التي تمتلك من الثقة والشجاعة

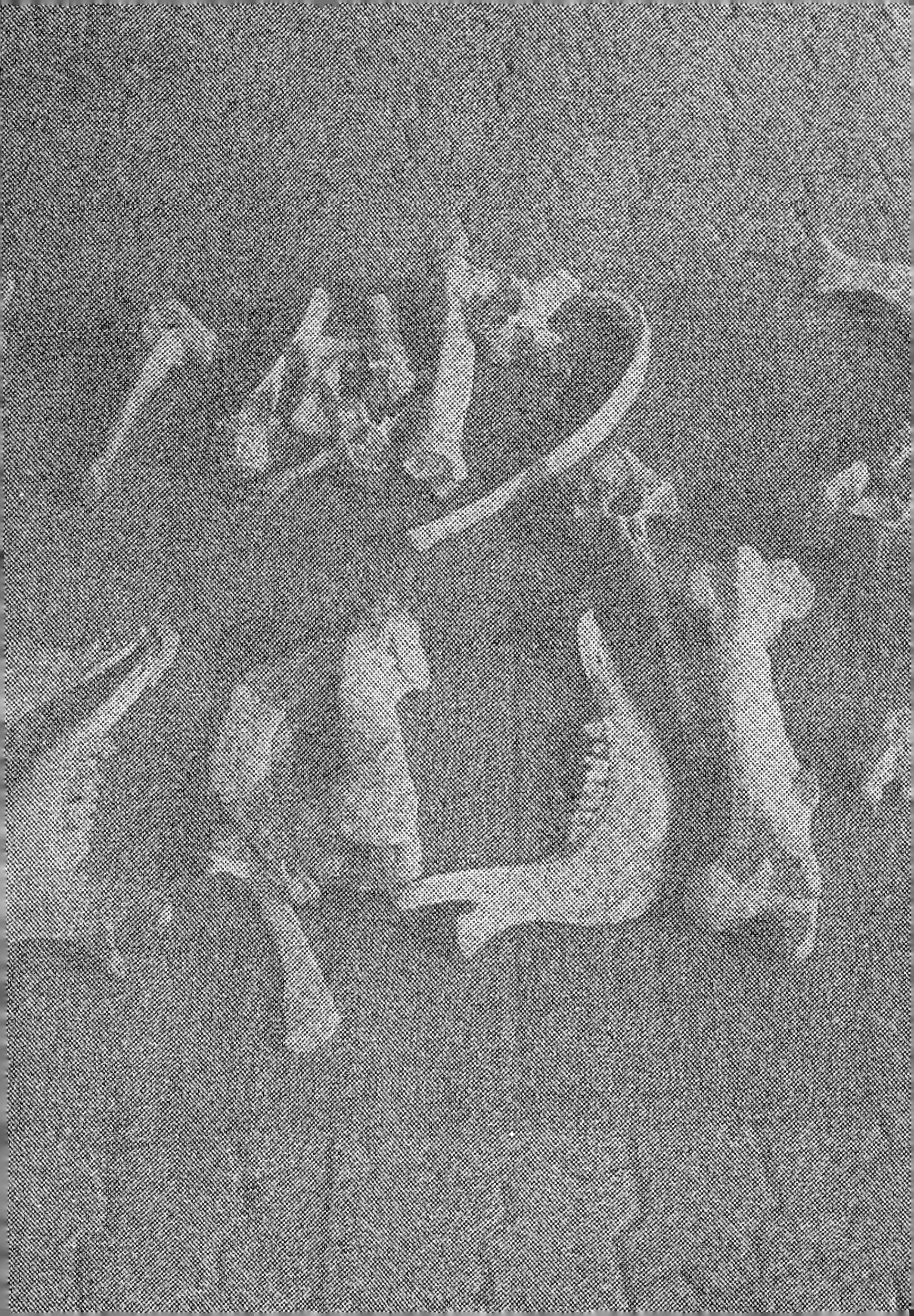

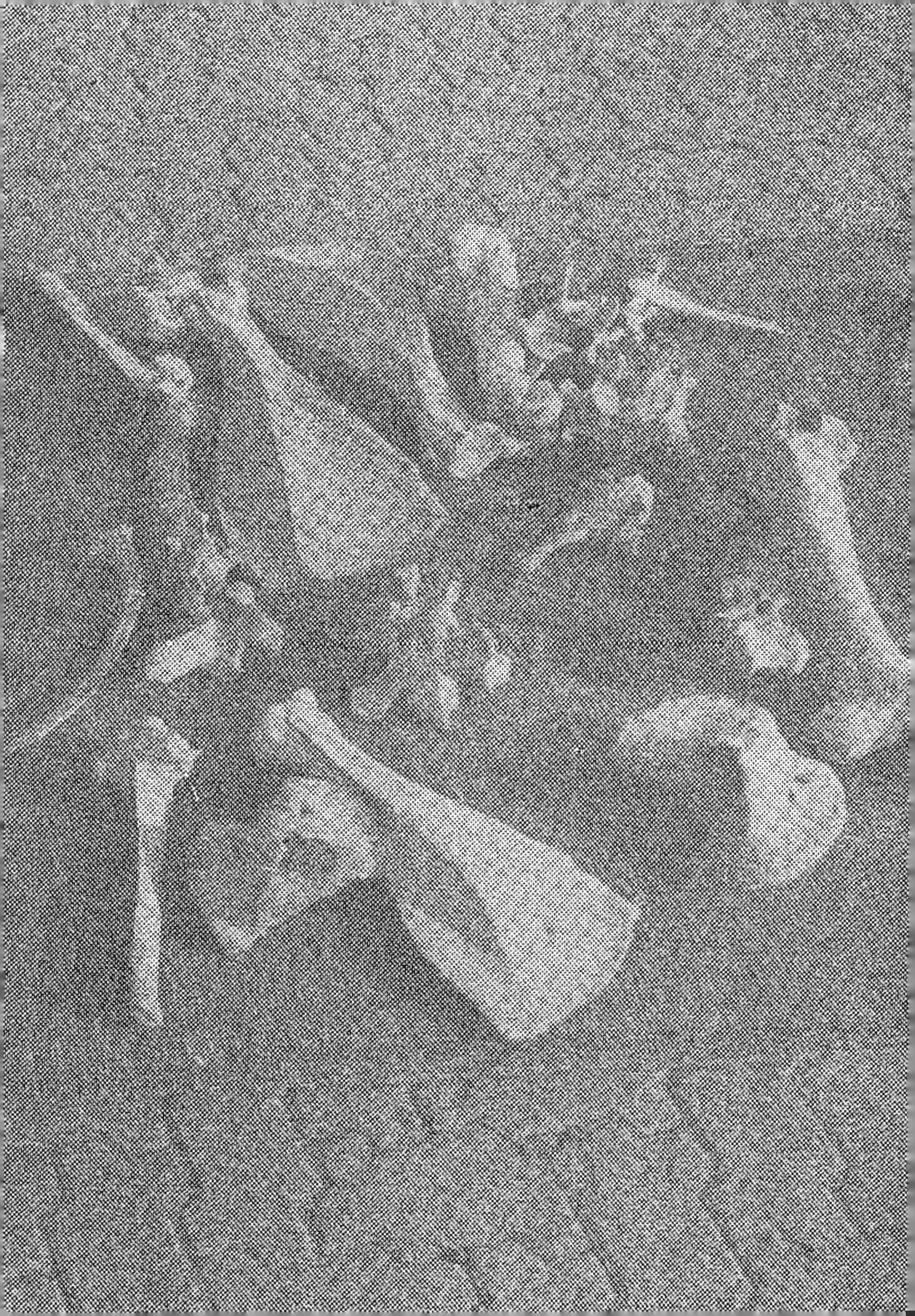

Ship For World Youth

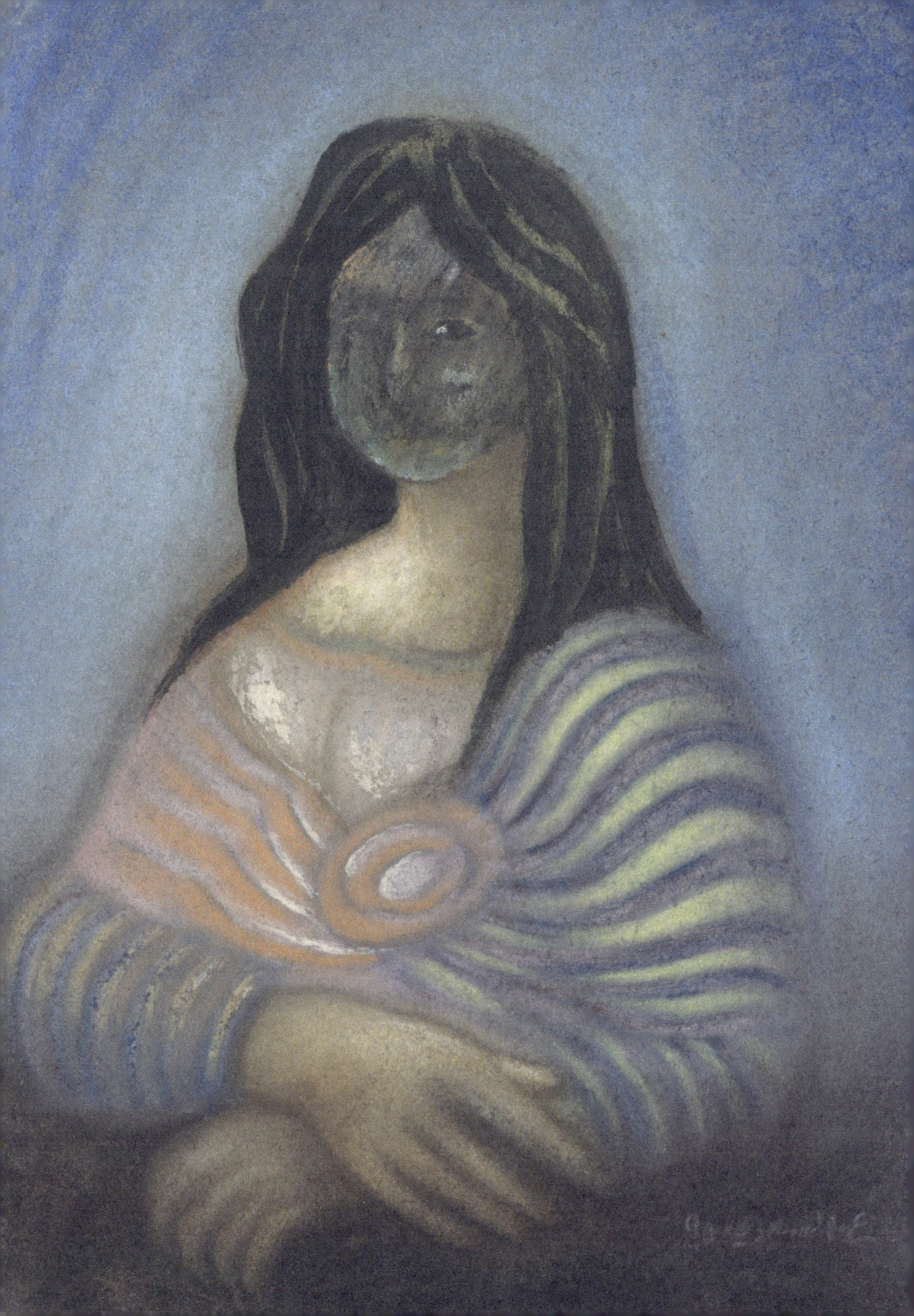

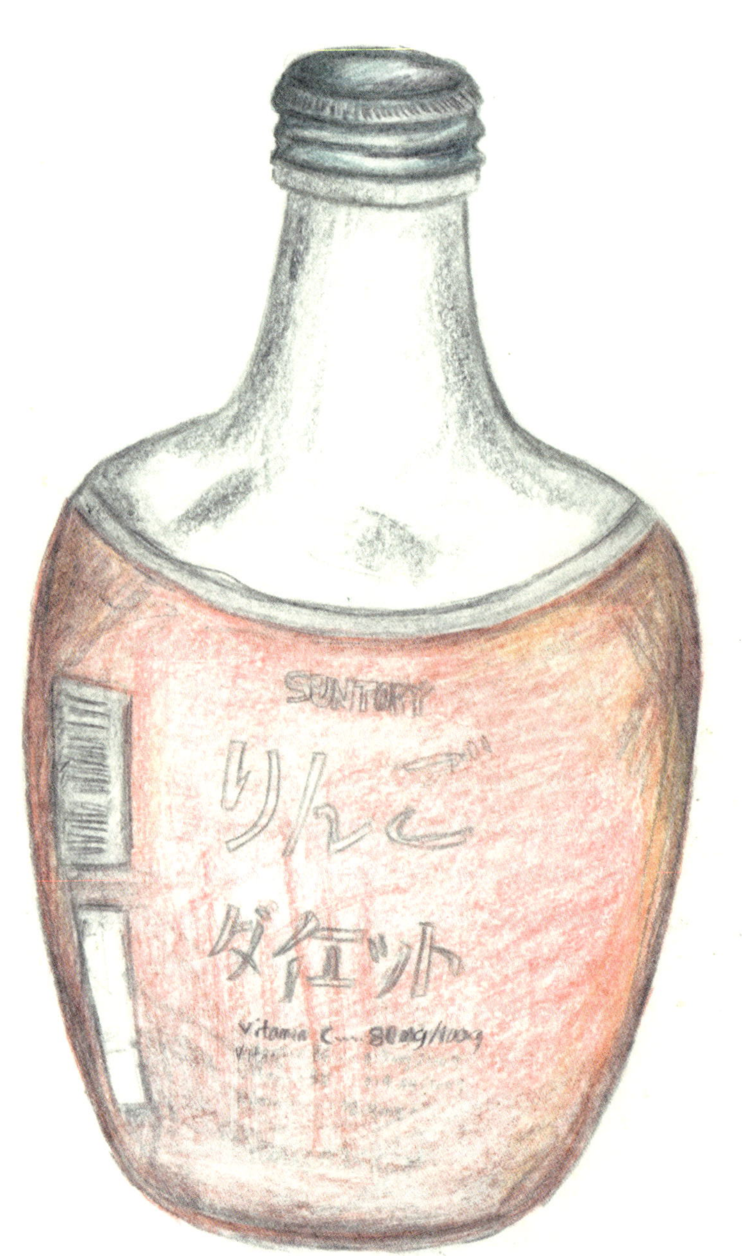

SUNTORY
りんご
ダイエット
Vitamin C...80mg/100g
Suntory
apple juice
250 g
100g   35kcal

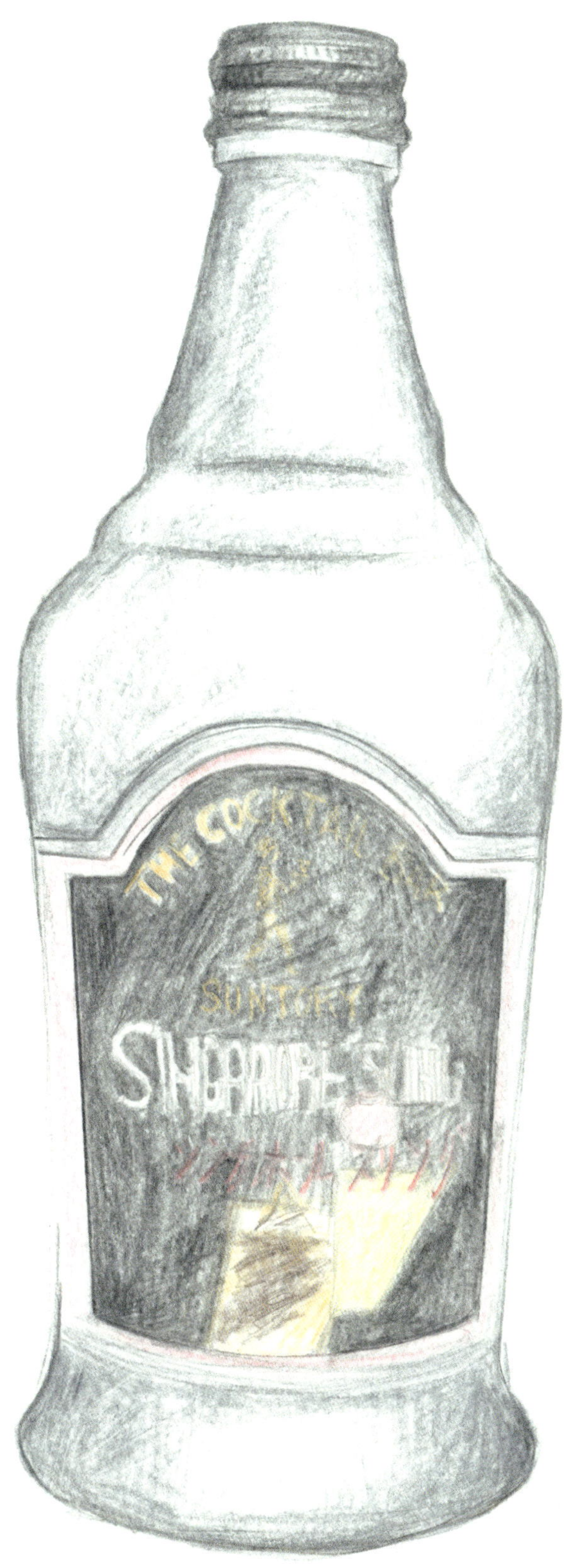

The Cocktail Bar
Suntory
Singapore Sling

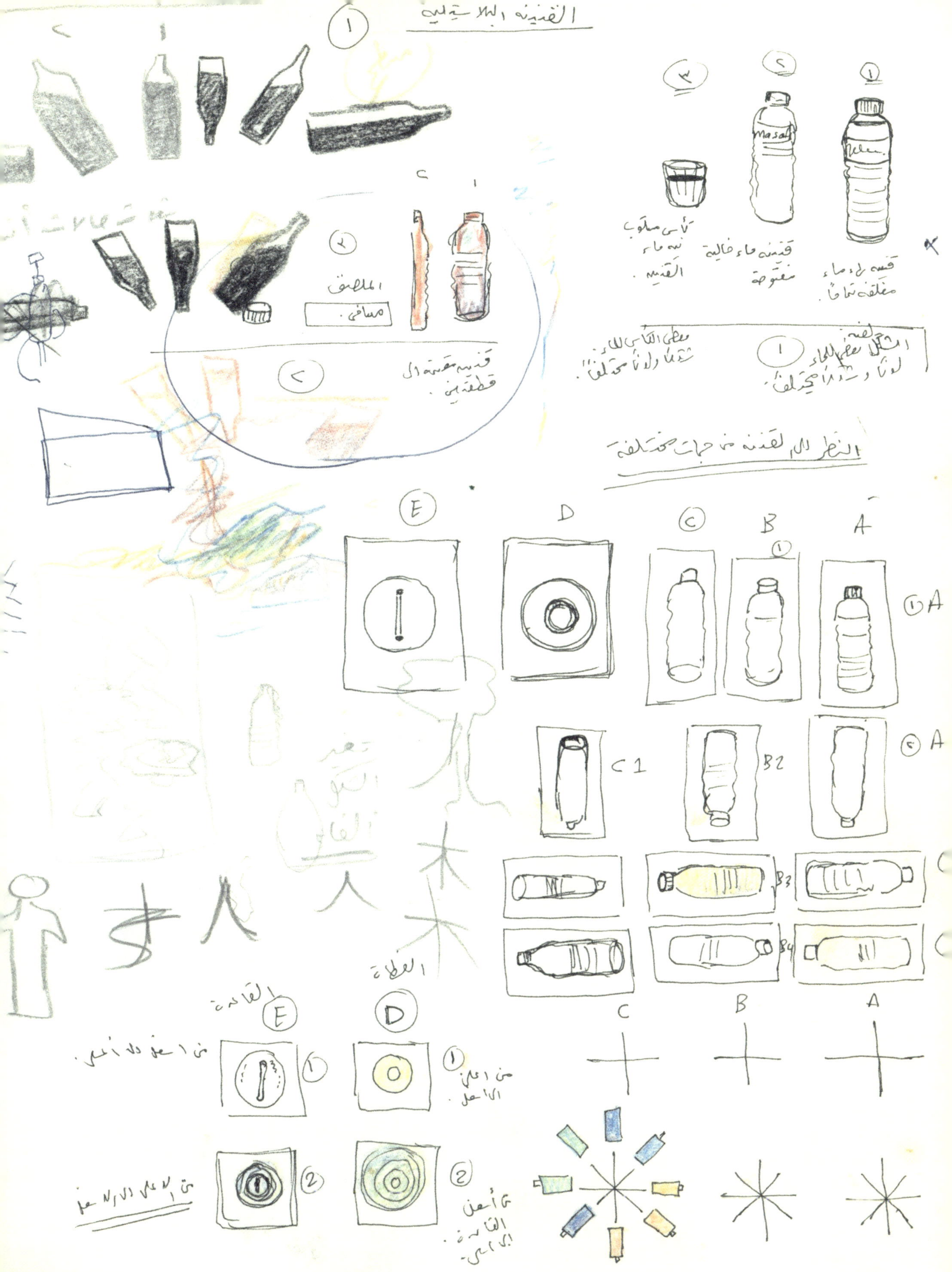
القنينه البلاستيكيه
قنينة ماء مغلقة تماما.
قنينة ماء خالية مفتوحة
كأس مقلوب فيه ماء القنينة.
الملصق
مسافي.
قنينة مقسمة الى قطعتين.
النظر الى القنينة من جهات مختلفة
A
B
C
D
E
C1
B2
B3
B4
الغطاء
القاعدة

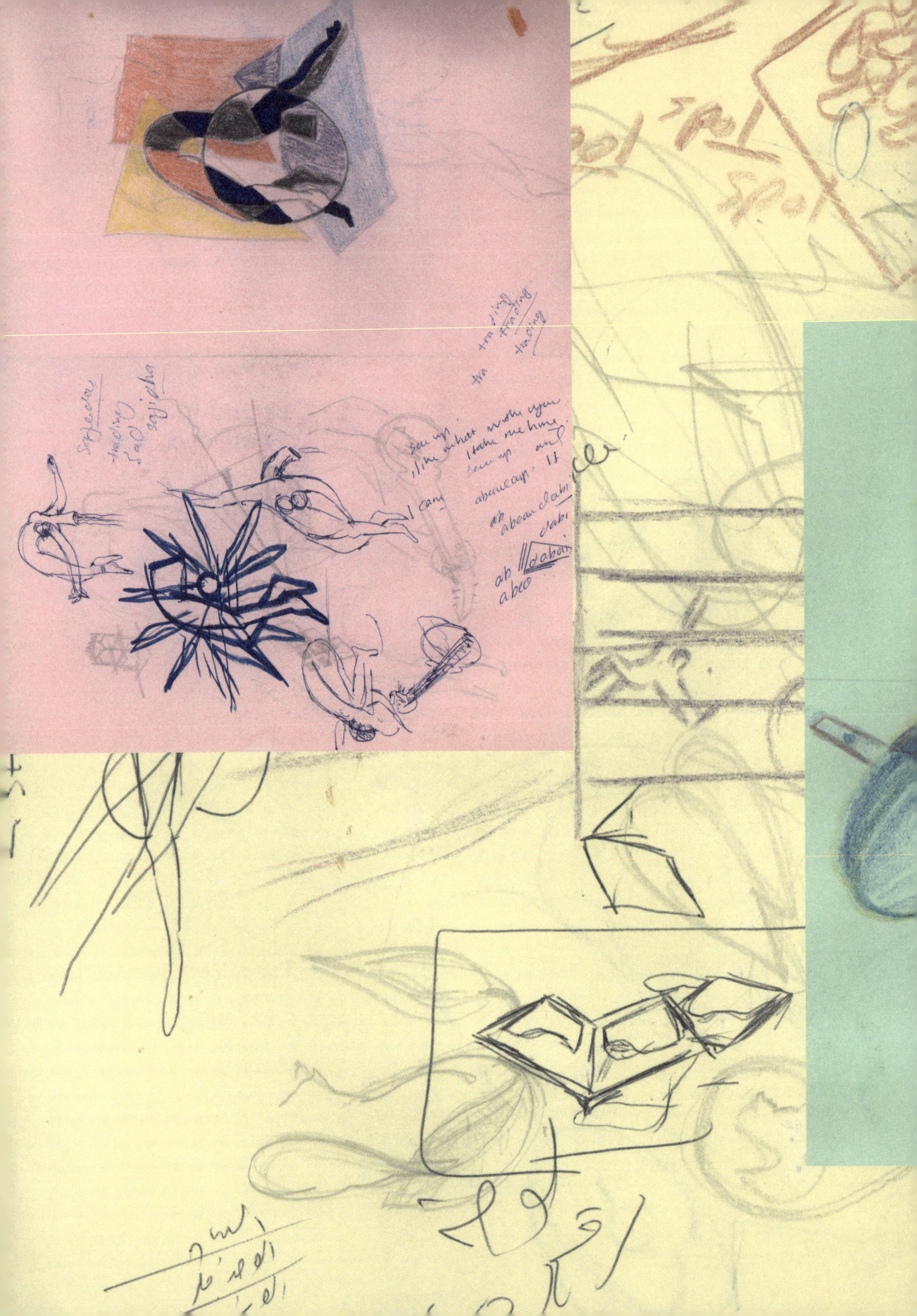

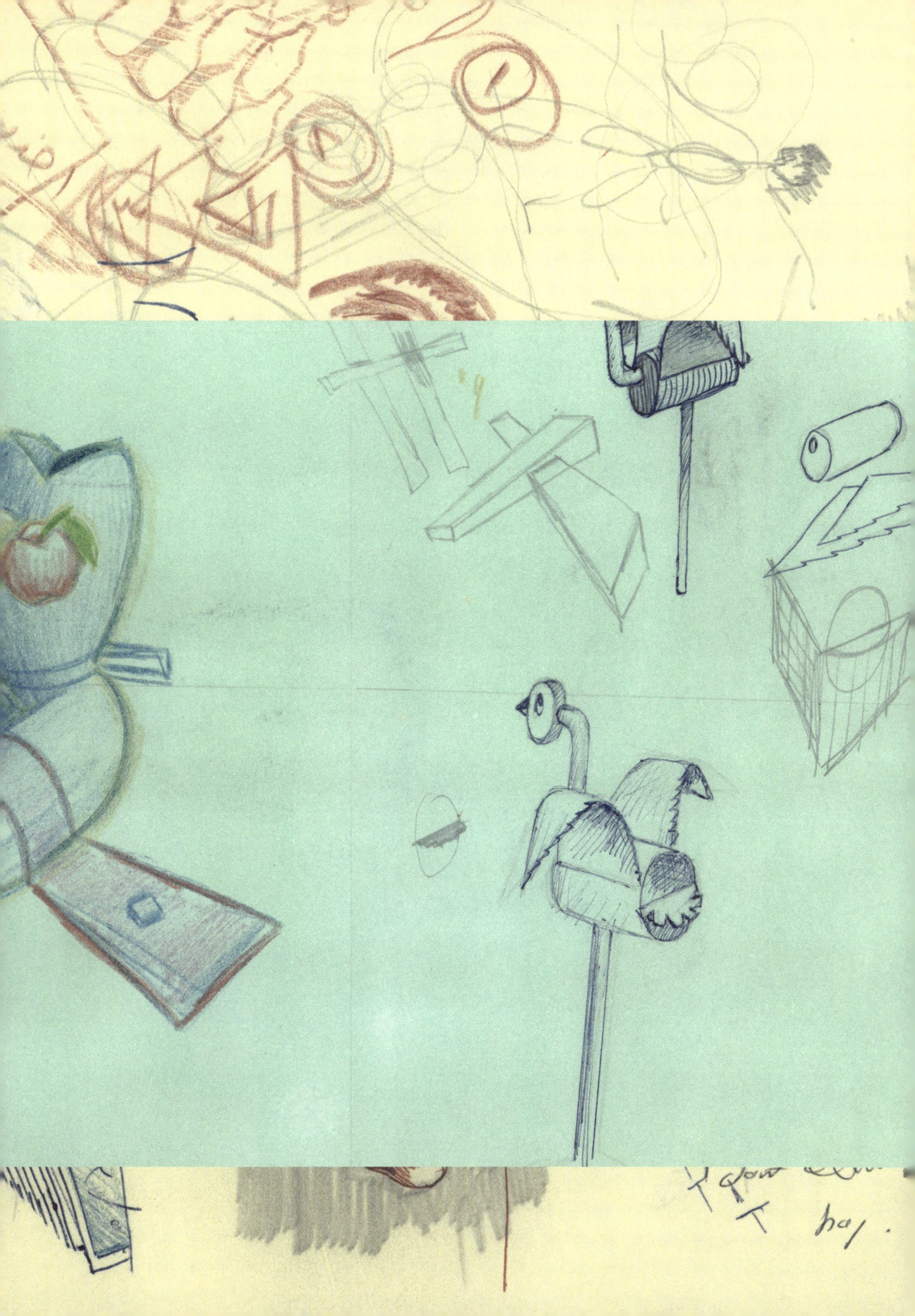

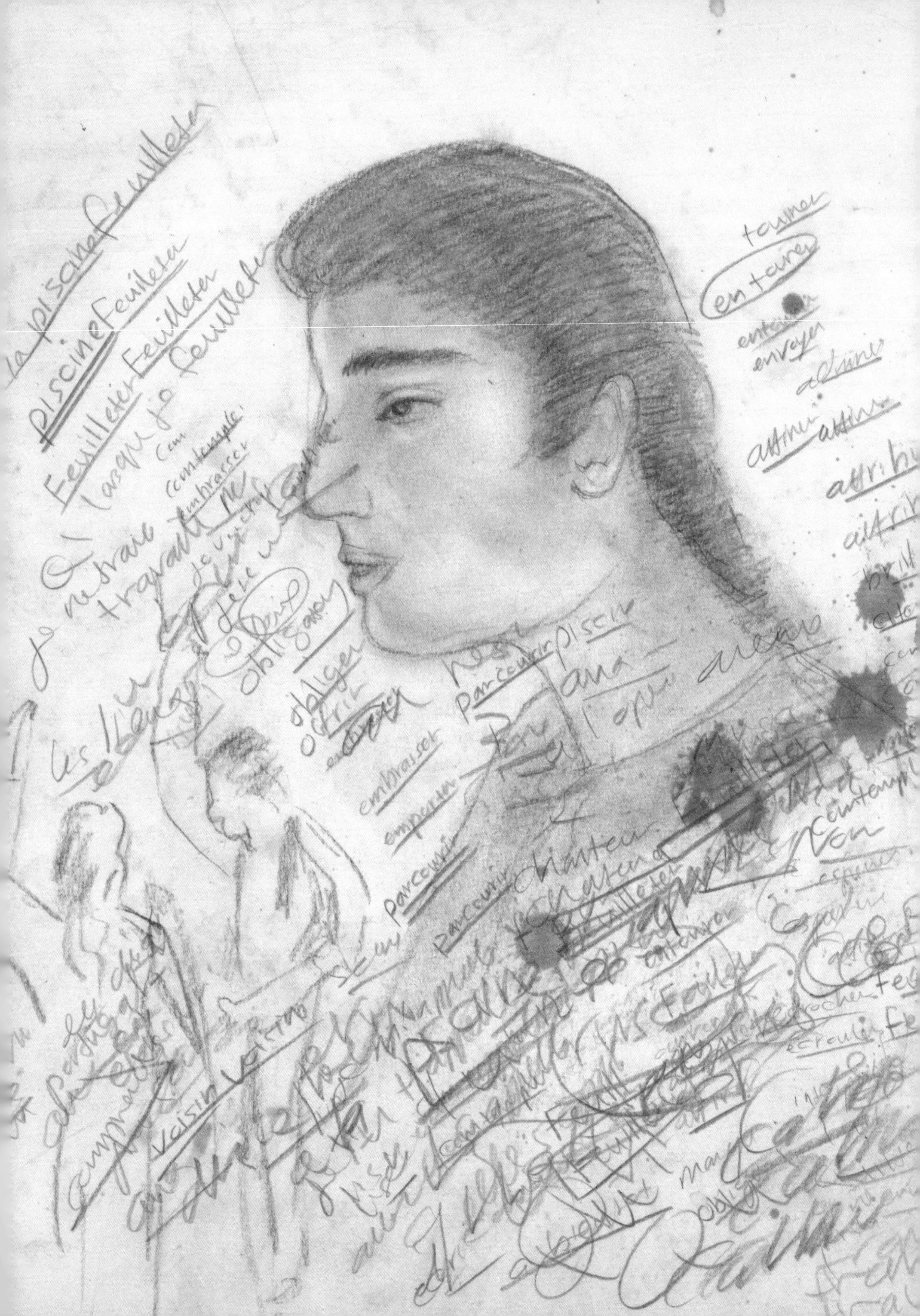

La piscine Feuilleter
Piscine Feuilleter
Feuilleter Feuilleter
Feuilleter Feuilleter
tourner
enrouler
envoyer
attirer
attirer
attribuer
attribuer

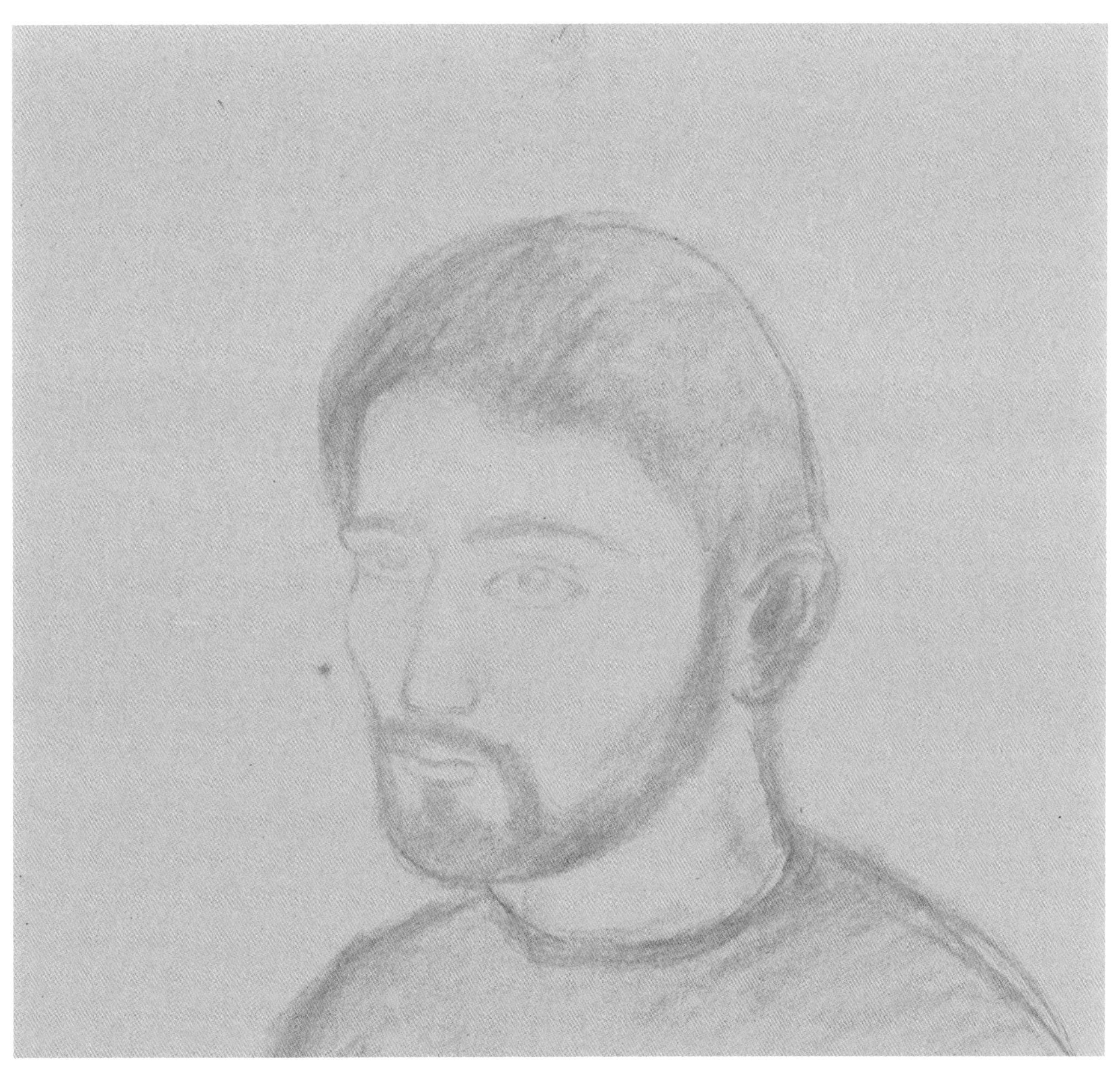

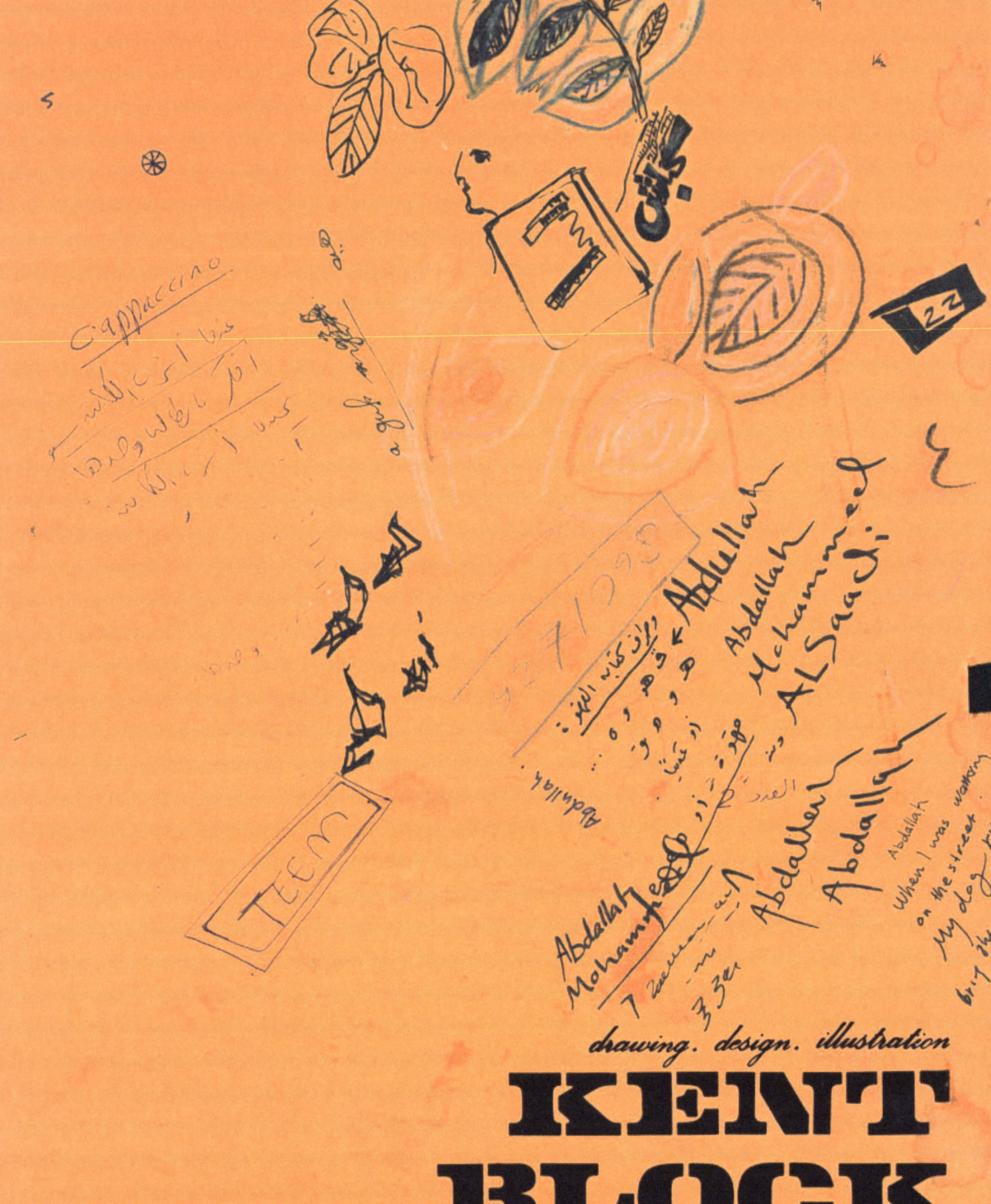

drawing. design. illustration
KENT
BLOCK
maruman / NO. 21

On a chilly January morning in 1992, Abdullah Al Saadi looked out over a very different mountain range than the one he had grown up with. After a connecting flight from Dubai to Tokyo's Narita International Airport and an hour or more transiting by car, he had arrived at the home of a Japanese family, where he would spend the next 10 days. This stay, Al Saadi's first time outside the Emirates, marked the beginning of a long, fruitful association with the country that would come to texturise the growth of his voice as an artist. His longing for world travel, however, truly took root back in Tokyo, at the docks of the Harumi Passenger Ship Terminal.

The *Nippon Maru* cruise liner departed from Harumi on 17 January 1992, its decks already teeming with the barely contained energy of over 100 young delegates from 13 different countries. Over the next 62 days, participants in the fourth Ship for World Youth (SWY) programme would visit the shores of Singapore, Sri Lanka, Egypt, Spain and the Sultanate of Oman. Then a senior at United Arab Emirates University, Al Saadi was one of 10 Emirati representatives.

Sponsored by the Japanese government's Cabinet Office, SWY began in 1967 as the Japanese Youth Goodwill Cruise Program (JYGC). Founded to commemorate the centennial of the 1868 Meiji Restoration and the beginning of the modern era, this earlier iteration emerged at a time when international travel was still extremely difficult for the majority of Japan's young adult population.

Knot tying and safety drills, tours of the quarterdeck and engine room, cultural awareness presentations, sari-wrapping tutorials, tai chi lessons, karate and kendo showcases, flamenco and Japanese folk performances kept Al Saadi and his fellow passengers occupied during their time at sea. Offshore, they planted trees in rural Colombo, took the well-worn Giza pyramid excursion via Alexandria and craned their necks at the gothic spires of Barcelona's unfinished Sagrada Família Church, ending their journey in early March on the shores of Muscat.

Each leg of the SWY programme was bookmarked by a careful curation of traditional song and dance recitals, museum visits, team-building activities and bus tours through crowded city centres. Marked by more arrivals and departures than Al Saadi could adequately capture in his sketches and poetry, the trip was a fortunate stroke of educational diplomacy that would also influence the next leg of his pedagogic journey.

Less than a year after his college graduation in 1993, Al Saadi's grant application to Kyoto Seika University was accepted, sponsored by the UAE Ministry of Culture. Aside from occasioning his first encounters with snowfall and earthquakes as well as the wonders of Japanese vending machines, his time as a research student introduced him to *emaki*, traditional story scrolls that he would emulate in later landscape works. Towards the end of his time in Kyoto, Al Saadi biked several hours to the shores of Biwa Lake, where he camped for a week. As the largest freshwater body in Japan, this lake has been the subject of paintings, woodblock prints, prose and poetry throughout the nation's history.

Following citizen-led efforts to curb harmful algae blooms, the endangered reed colonies emblematic of Biwa Lake had begun a slow recovery by the mid-1990s. The water pollution had brought a once-vibrant and cultured pearl industry, whose cultivation method originated in the area, to a standstill. Al Saadi, himself some three generations removed from the demise of the Gulf's own pearling economy, depicted this recovering landscape in his field notes with great affection.

In doing so, he may have also unwittingly retraced the steps of the famed 17th-century Edo poet and travel essayist Matsuo Bashō. Thought to have studied in Kyoto as well, he spent much of his formative literary years in and around the region, developing a special fondness for the lake. As with Al Saadi, it was Bashō's peripatetic tendencies that drove a lifetime of creative output.

Germinating during his stay in Japan was a sensationalist desire to crystalise the everyday through plodding, continuous self-narrativisation. His two-year sojourn, marked by a sense of mobility and freedom renewed via the country's extensive network of bike routes, lent itself greatly to this purpose.

Al Saadi's time in Kyoto was cut short, however, and he returned to the Emirates in 1995 after failing to sit for the language exam that would have granted him a seat as a full-time student. *I am in Japan* (1997), a solo exhibition at the Emirates Fine Arts Society that served as his senior capstone project, reconstructed Al Saadi's living space: books and clothing, spoons and saucers, palette and brushes, were interspersed with diary pages and artworks from his stay. It illustrated the daily life of a young man who, for a few semesters, stacked empty beverage containers in his kitchen, made himself heard across the city's cafes in English and Japanese and dreamt of a cycling tour across Asia.

Another formative collegiate experience of his would come later, in August 1998, at a painting workshop at The University of Edinburgh's College of Art, one of Scotland's oldest higher learning institutions, alongside Mohammed Kazem. During the monthlong course, he created 20 charcoal-on-paper entries in a notebook, simply titled *Julia* after the eponymous class model. This was Al Saadi's first encounter with live anatomy drawing.

Suggestions of the female nude, however, had appeared across earlier works from his high school and college years. An untitled oil-on-canvas work from 1987, for example, depicts an anthropomorphised vase, legs kneeling, arms clasped at its side like the loop of a handle, with two green apples dotting its chest. In another work from 1991, the silhouette of a woman emerges, the ripples of her form-fitting ensemble accentuated by moonlight overhead. In the absence of such a class during his formative years, Al Saadi had explored form and expression, traditionally within the domain of figurative art, through a vaguely surrealist lens.

Al Saadi's workshops and transnational exchanges point to new mobilities offered by the Emirates' early years of economic consolidation and identity building, characterised by widespread educational subsidisation and global relationship building. Al Saadi was part of a wave of creatives who benefitted from this support and later shaped the local contemporary art scene through diplomatic cross-cultural policies. It speaks to the development of his work from a self-initiated and autonomous practice into one also endorsed and supported by formal institutions, inflected by the need to negotiate and think about the boundaries between his independent voice and the platforms which texturise and enable it.

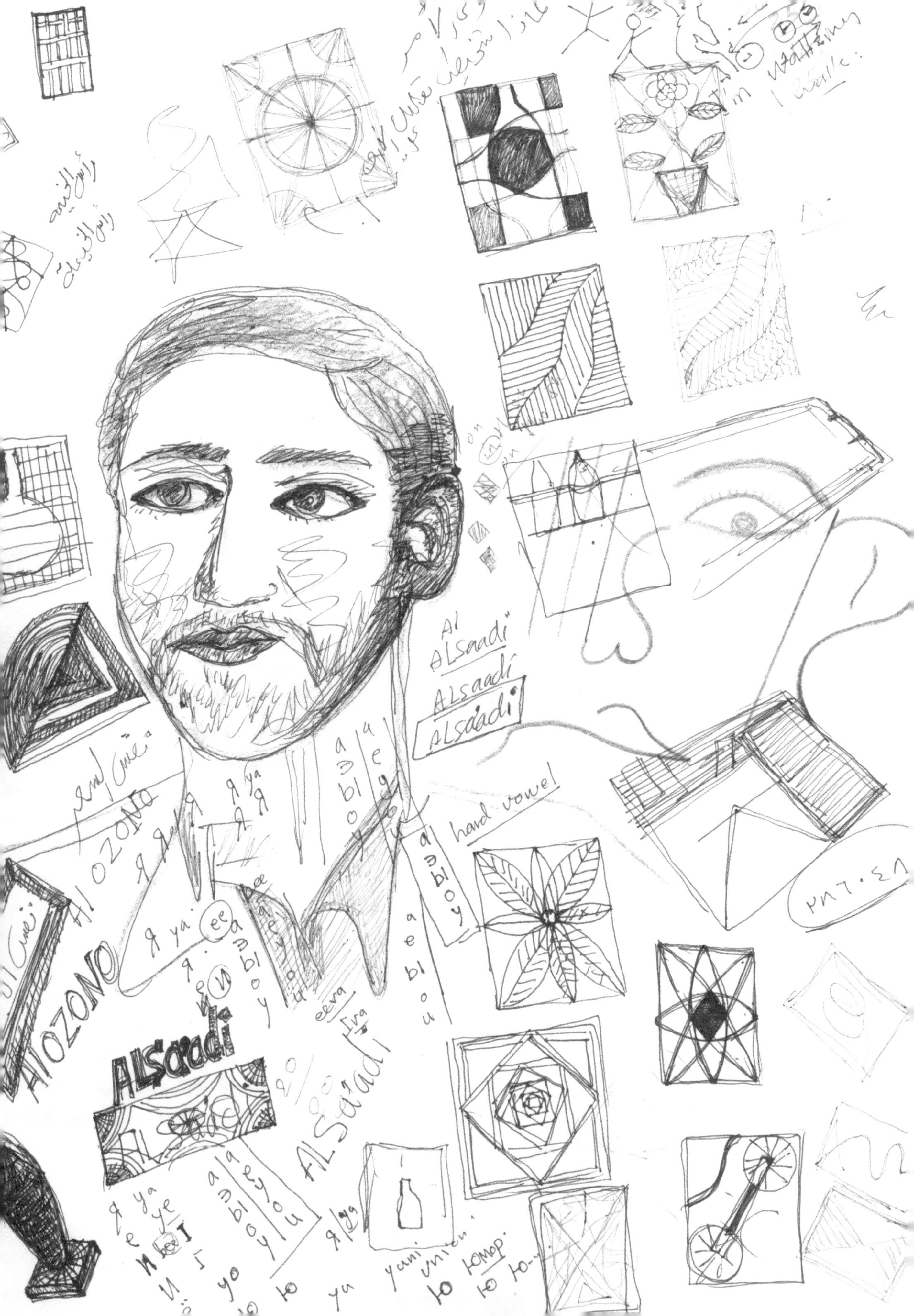

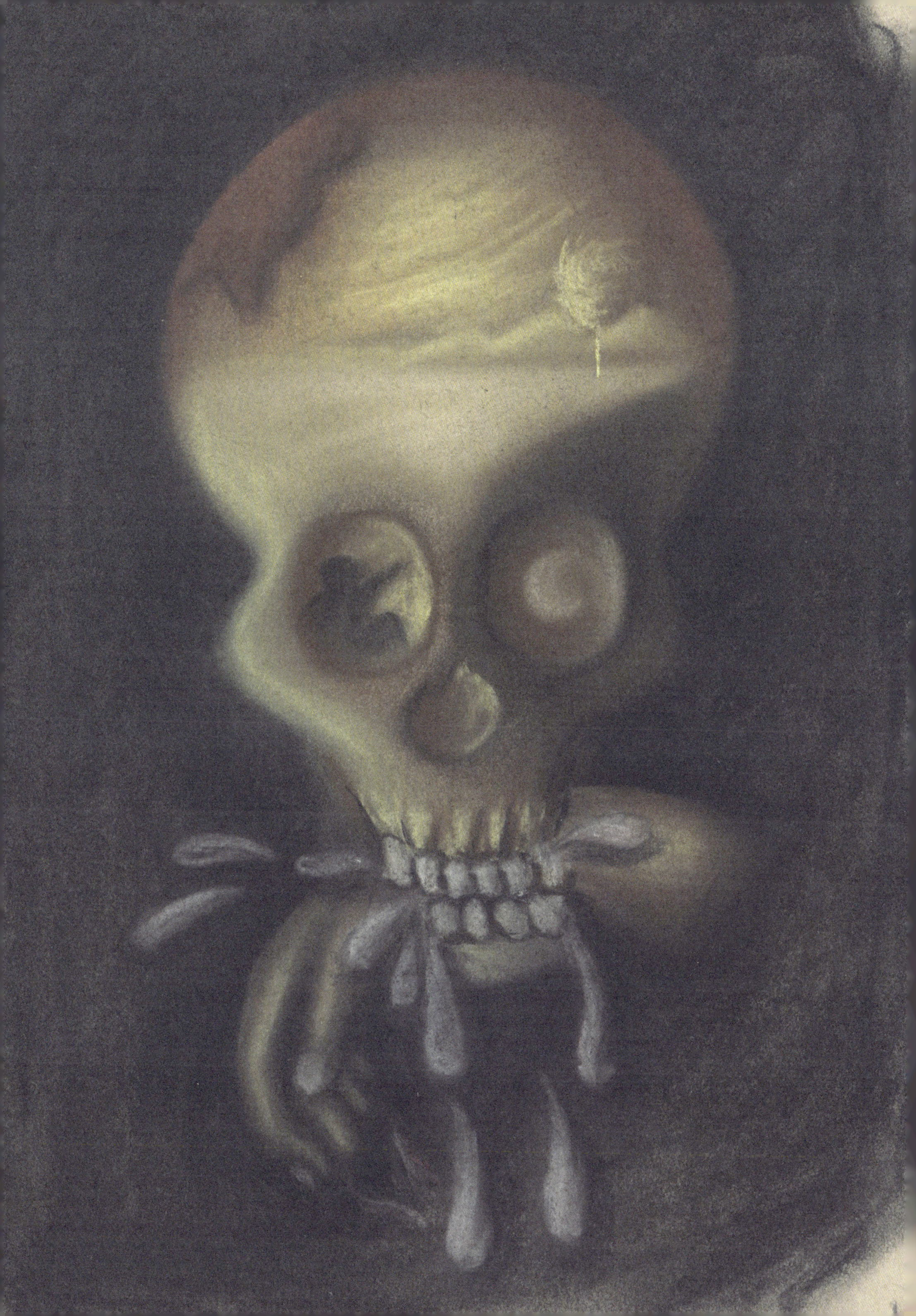

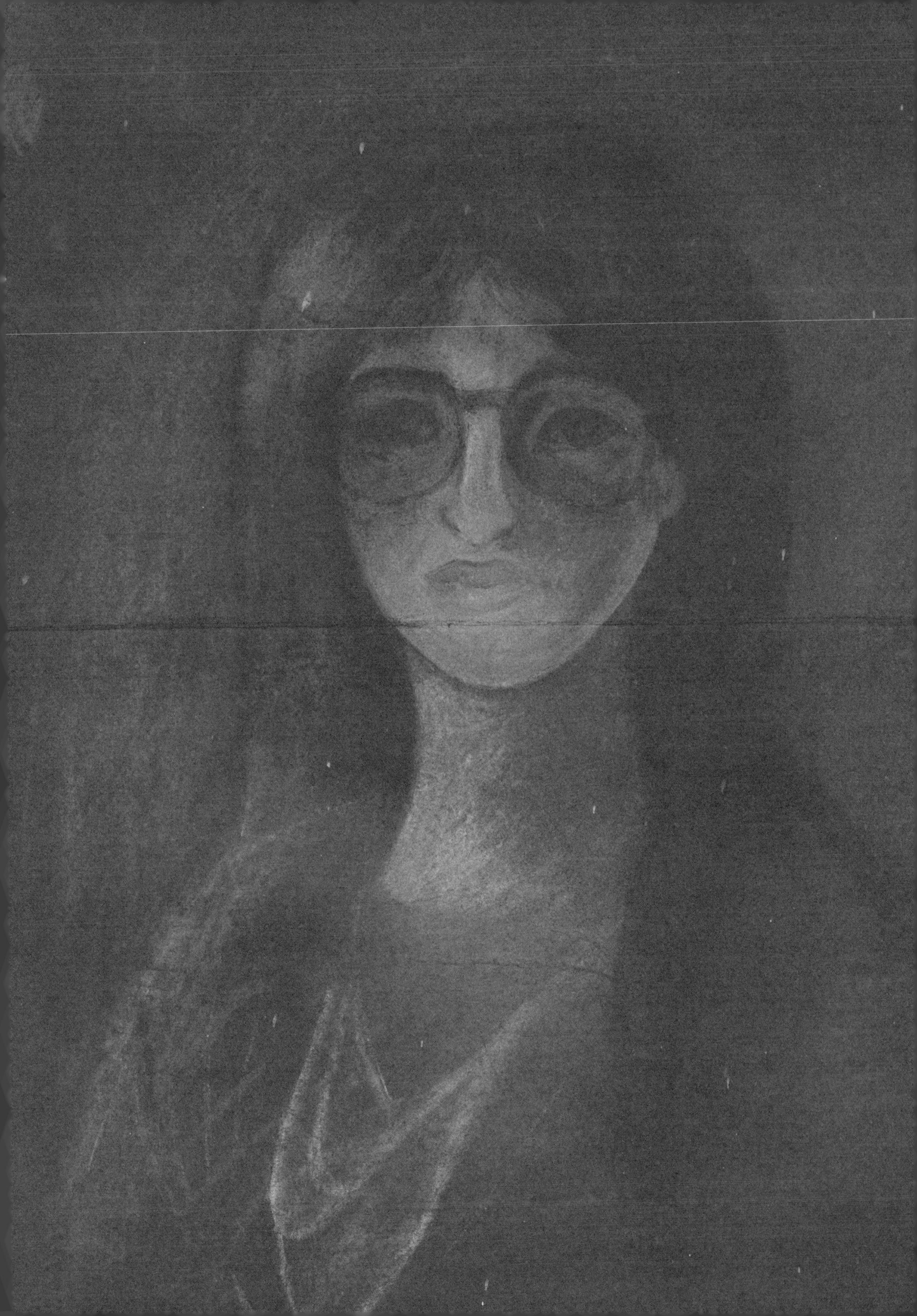

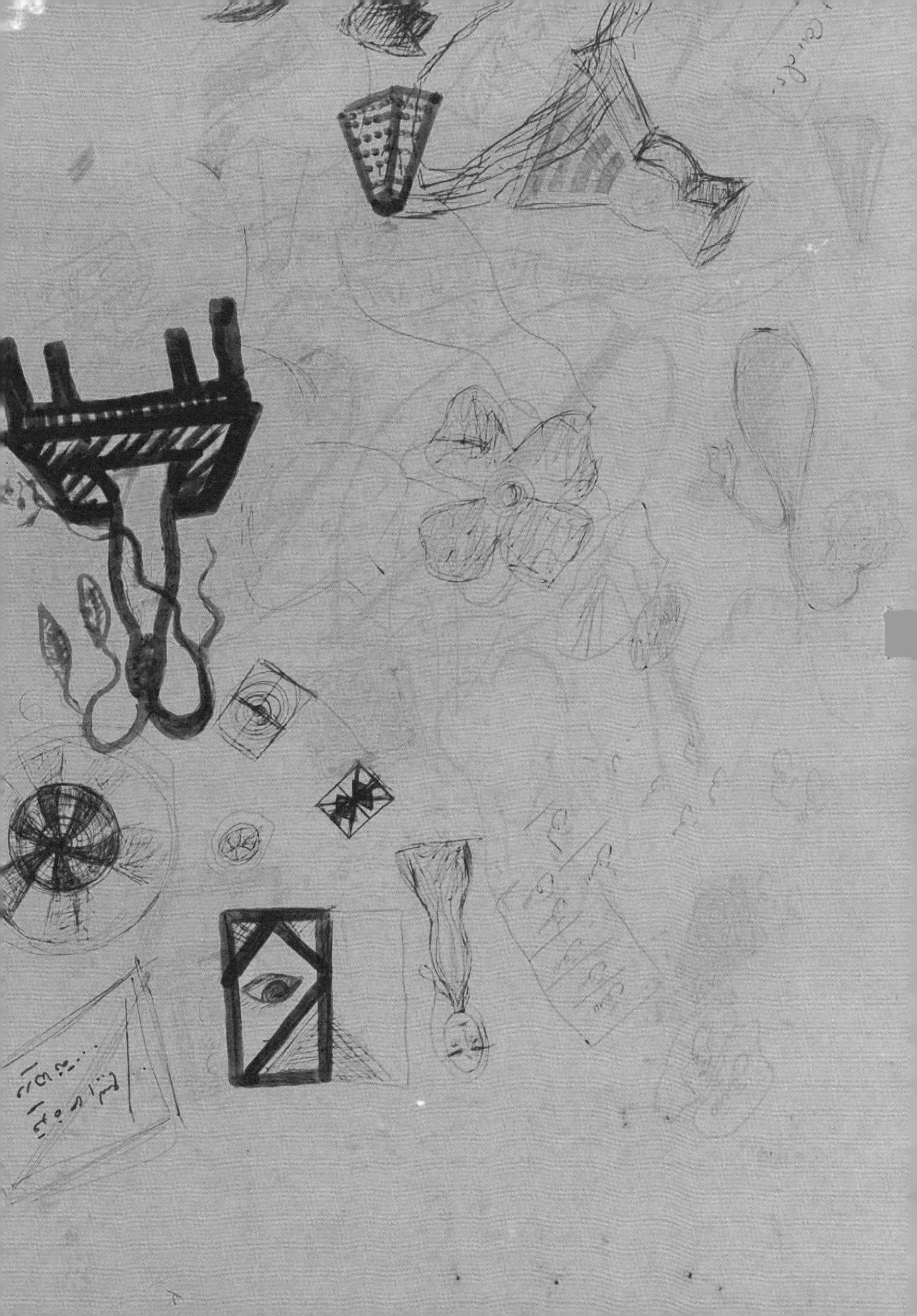

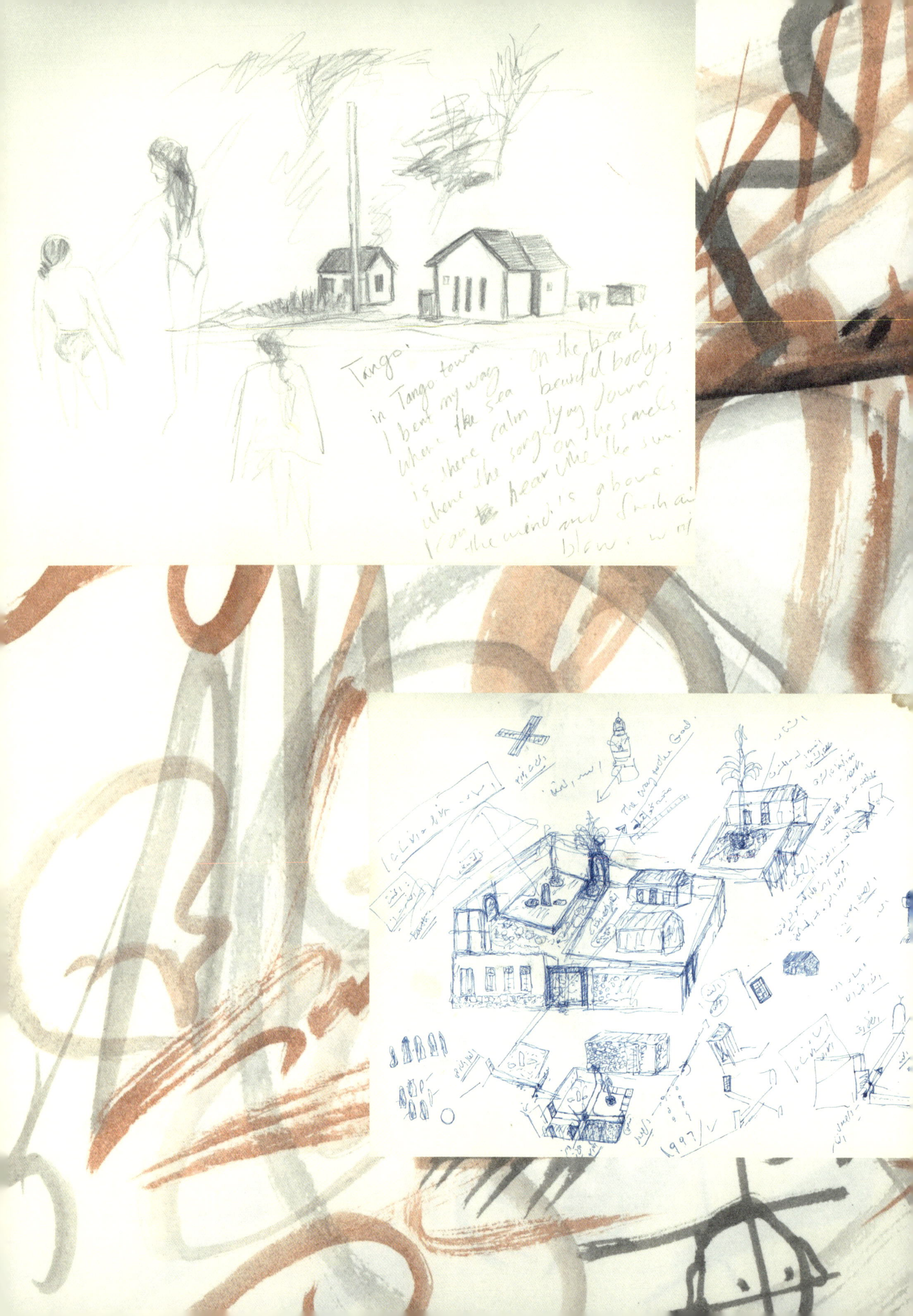

Tango.
in Tango town
I bent my way
where the sea
is there calm lying down
where the songs on the sands
hear the the sun.
On the beach
beautiful bodys
the mind is above
and such a
blow. w m

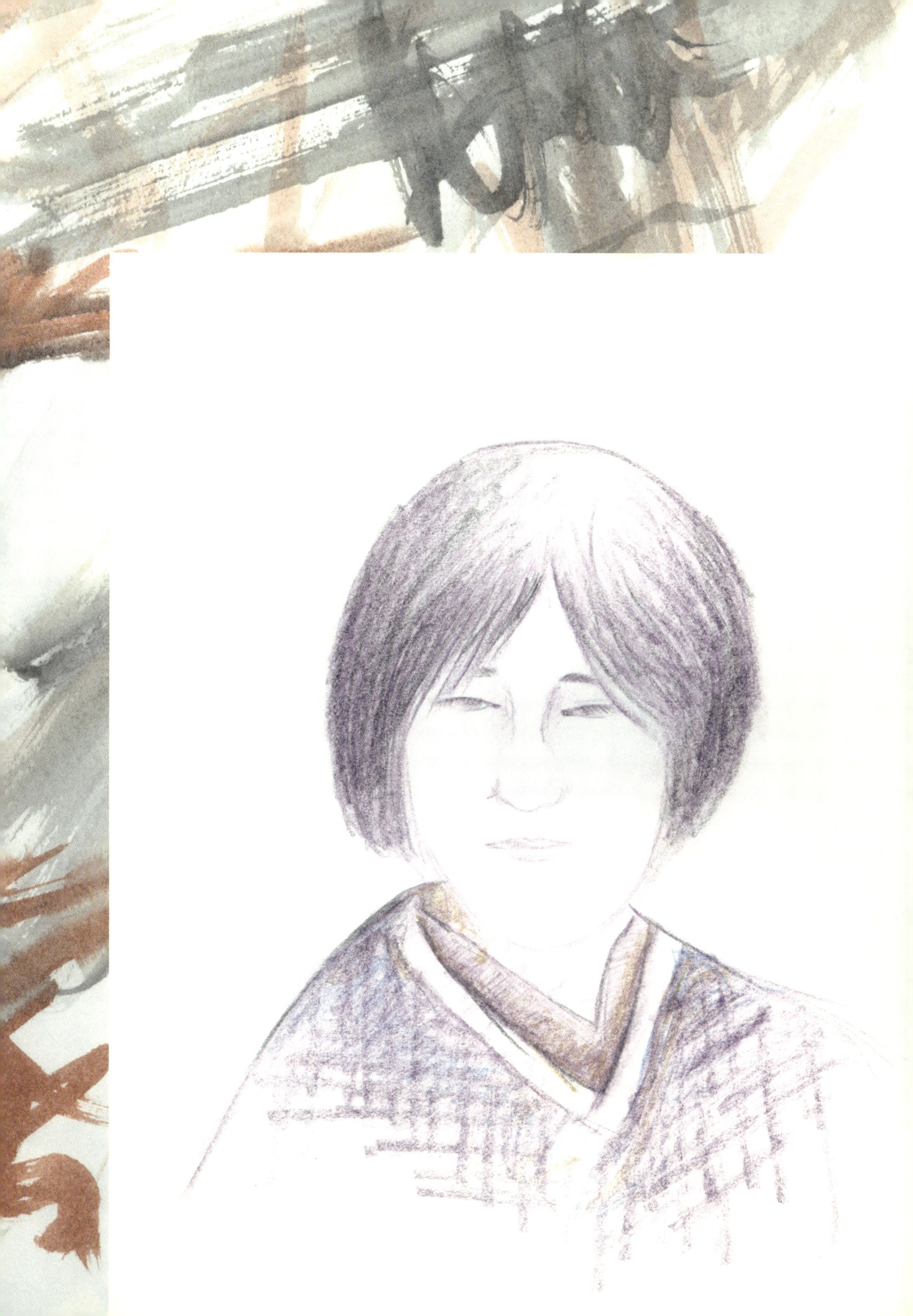

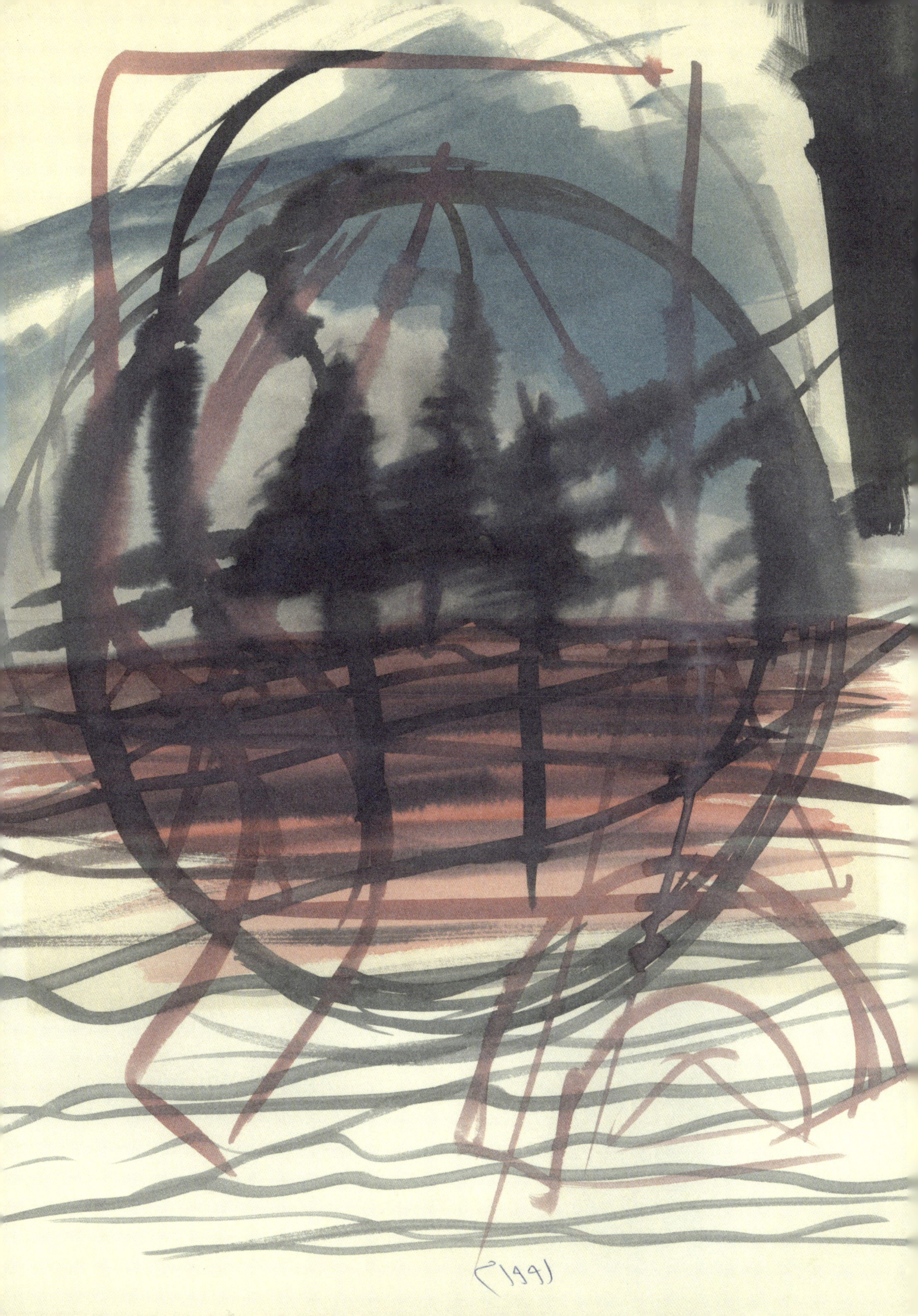

1991

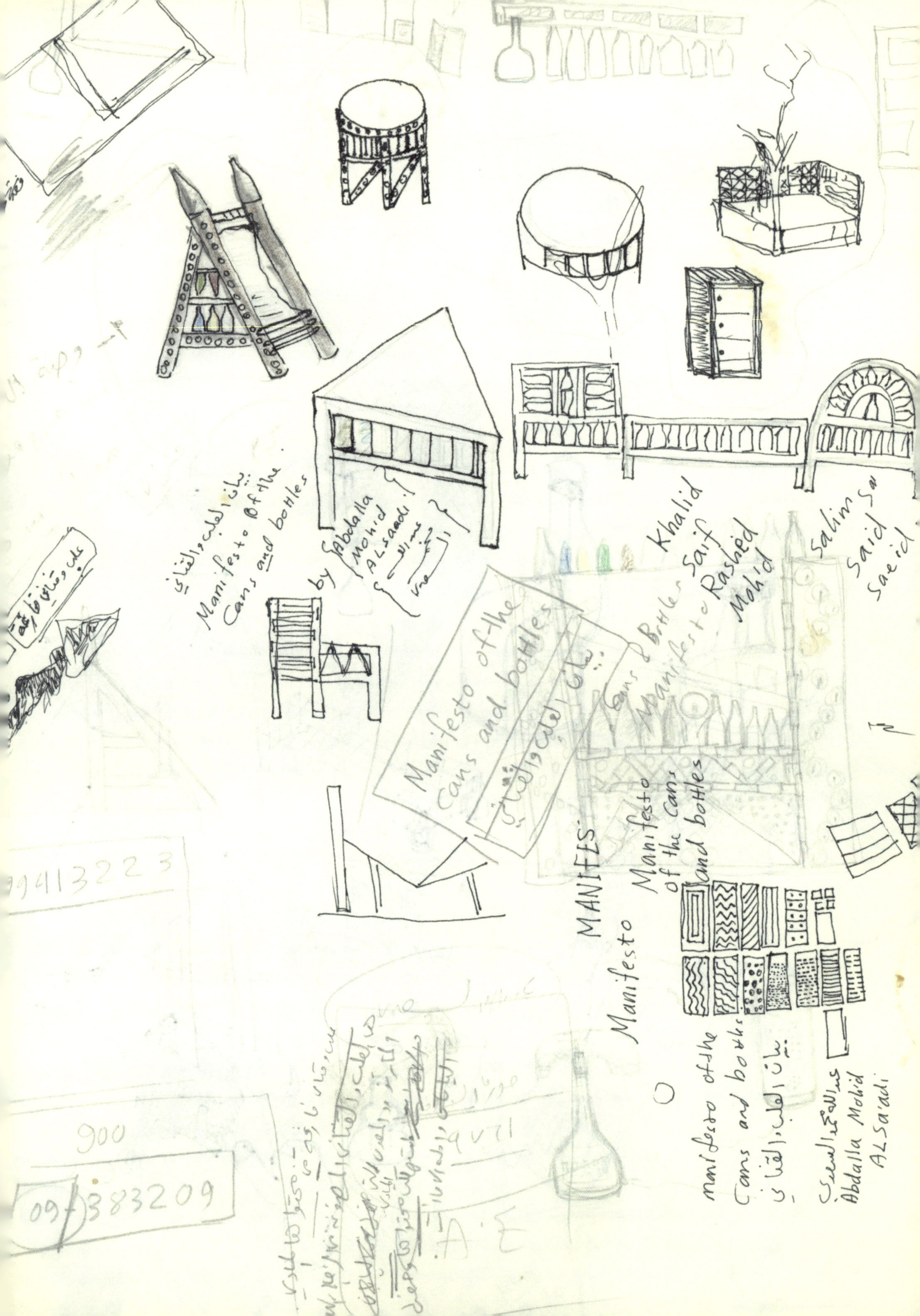

Manifesto Of the Cans and bottles
by Sabdalla Mohid ALsaadi
Manifesto of the Cans and bottles
MANIFES
Manifesto
Manifesto of the Cans and bottles
Khalid
Saif
Rashed Mohid
Salim Sa
Said Saeid
Cans & Bottles Manifesto
manifesto of the Cans and bottles
Abdalla Mohid ALsaadi
1941322 3
900
09 383209

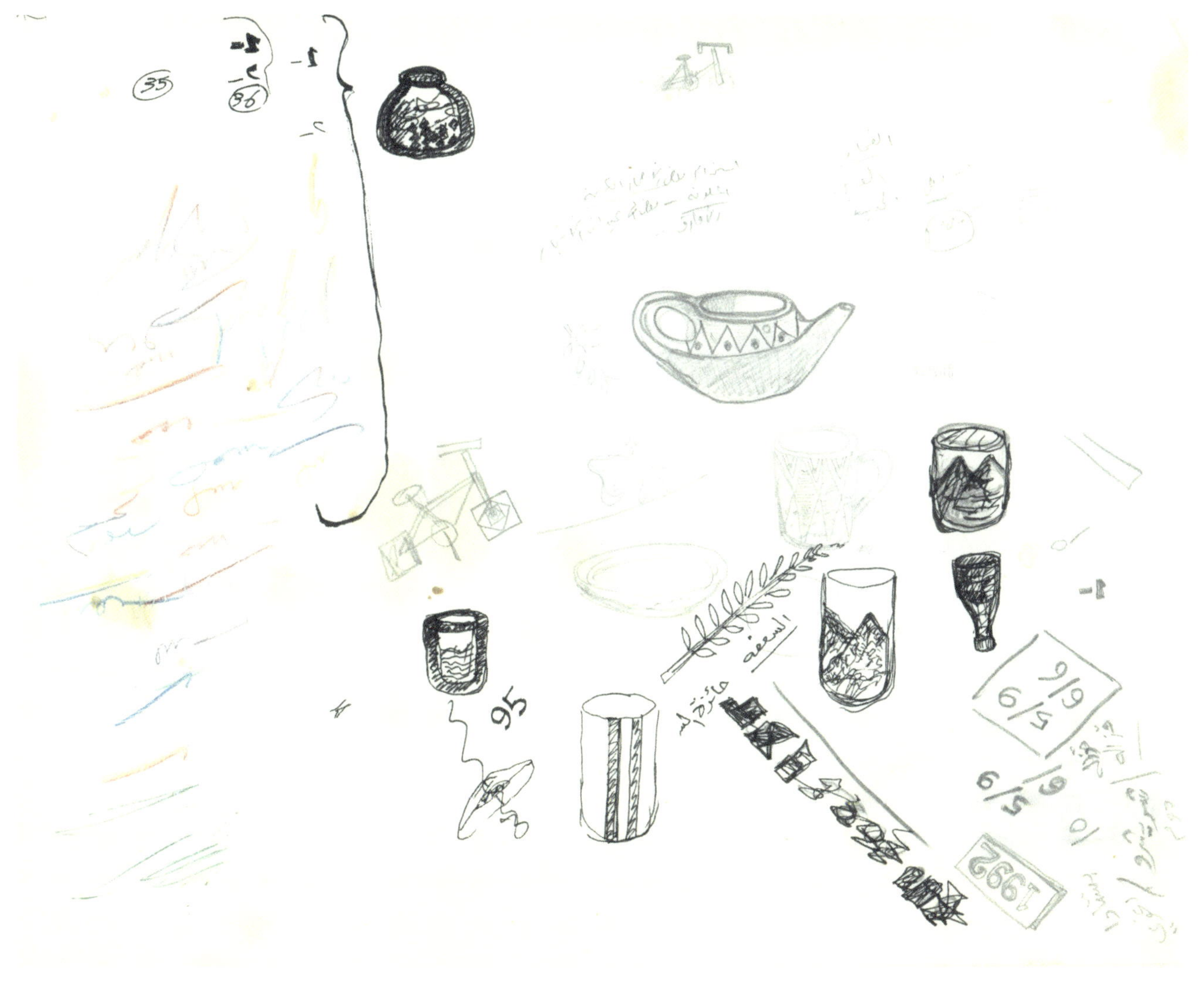

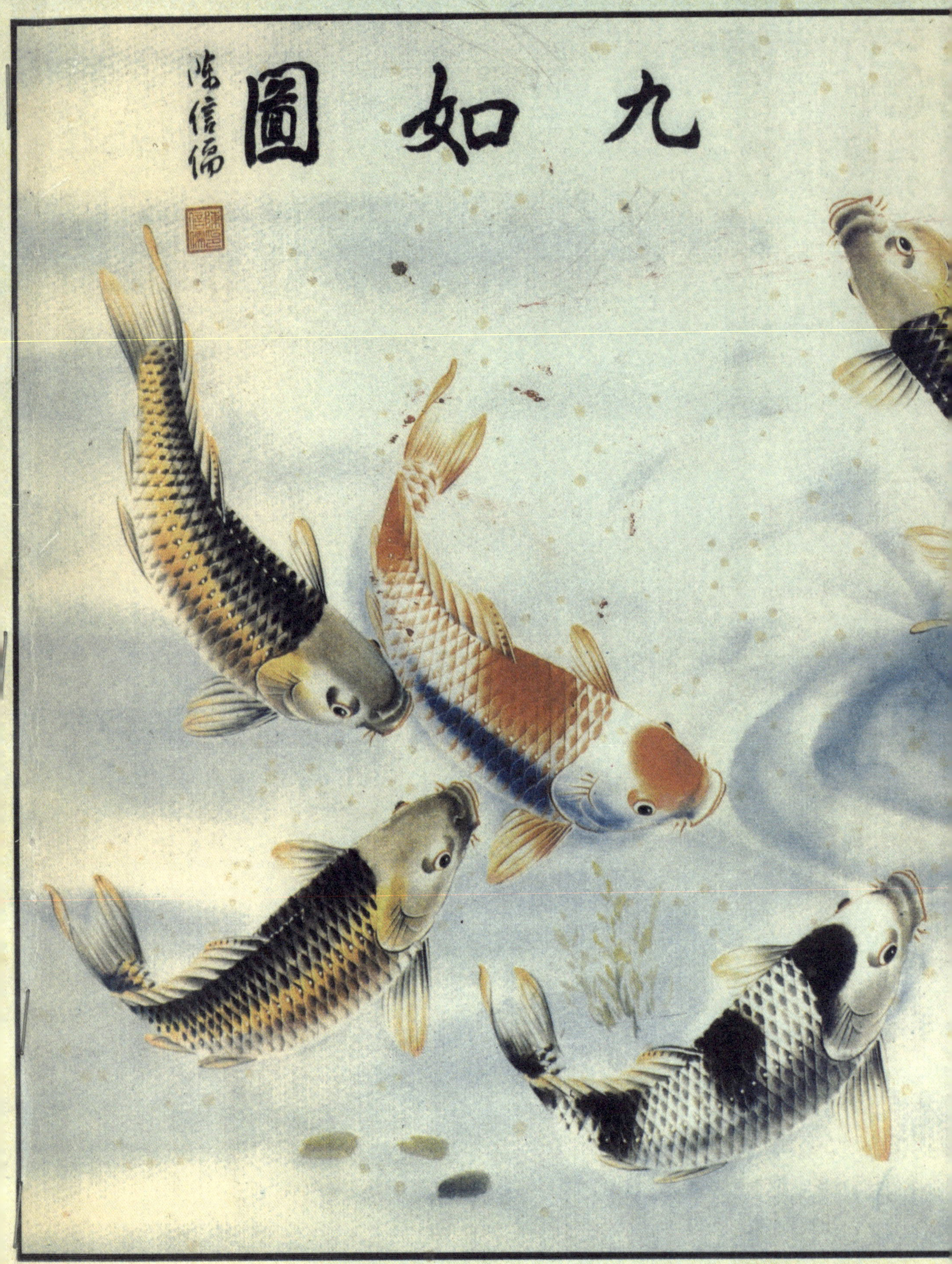

PRODUCED BY

MAD

أنا في اليابان
I am In Japan
私 は 日本 に います

Watashi Wa Nihon ni imasu

عبد الله محمد السعدي
Abdalla . M . ALSa'adi
アルサダ・アブドゥーラ・モハメッド
1996

أنا في اليابان

Iam In Japan

私 は 日本 に います

Watashi Wa Nihon ni imasu

عبدالله محمد السعدي

Abdalla . M . ALSa'adi

アルサダ・アブドゥーラ・モハメッド

1996

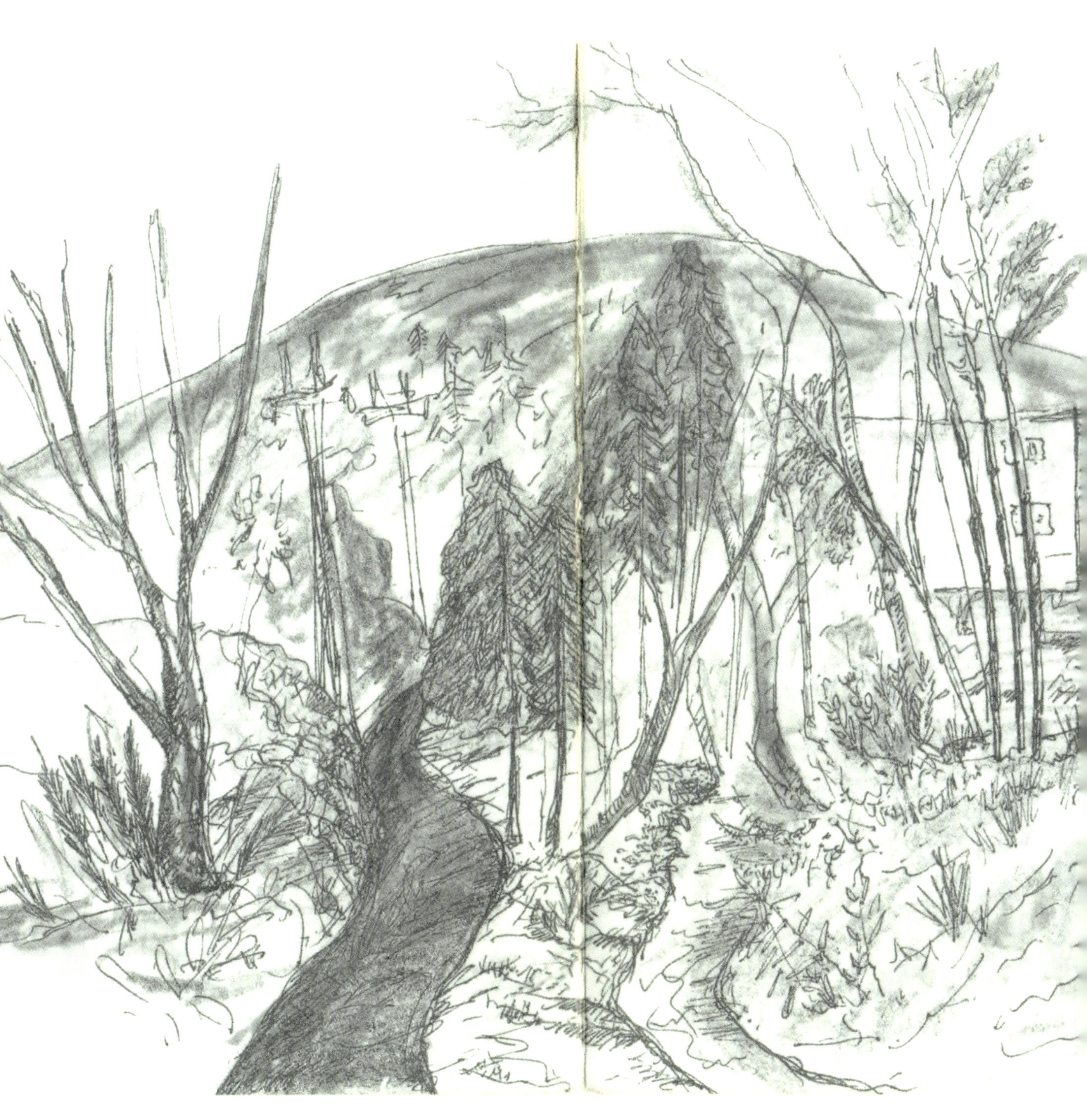

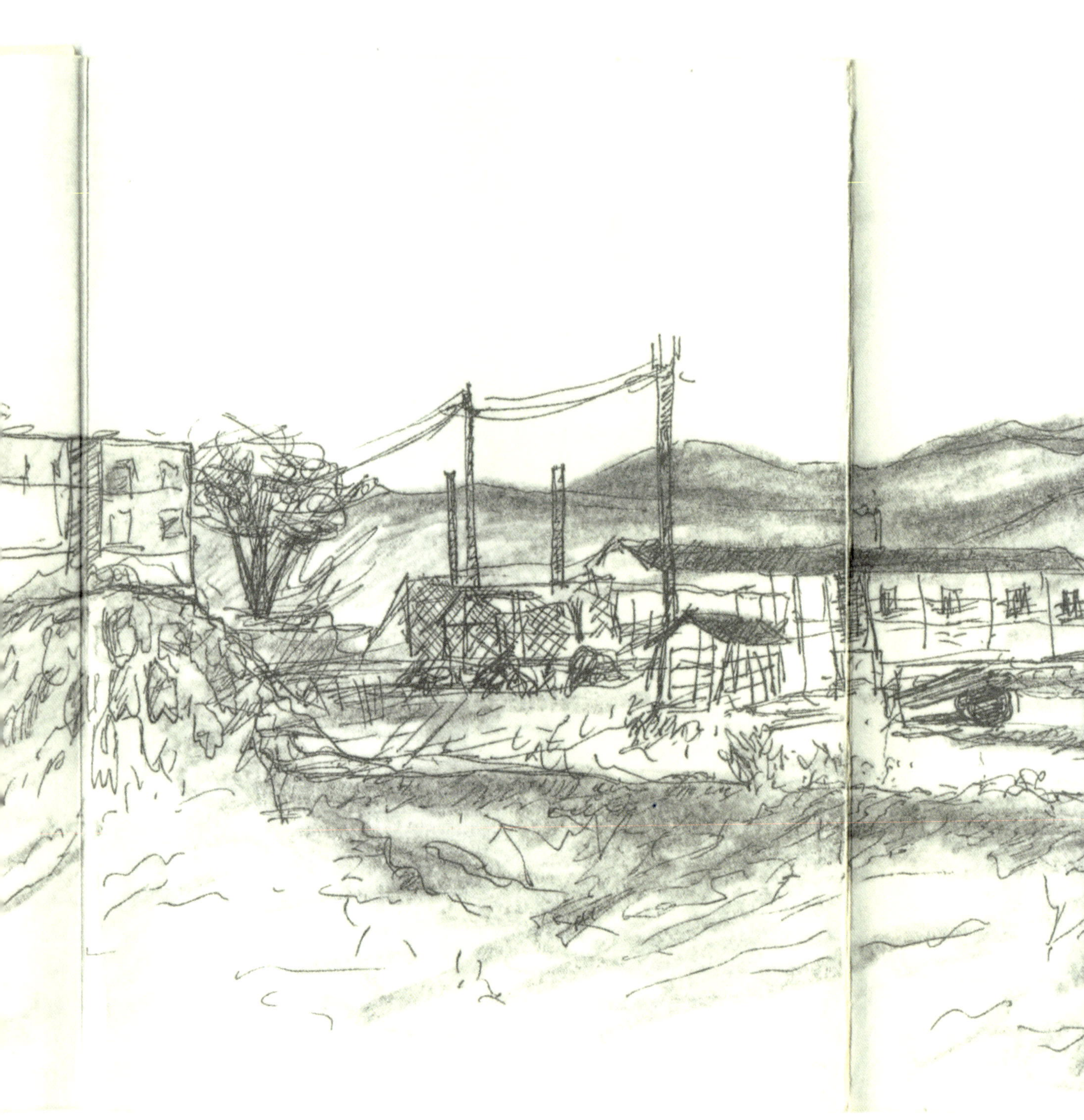

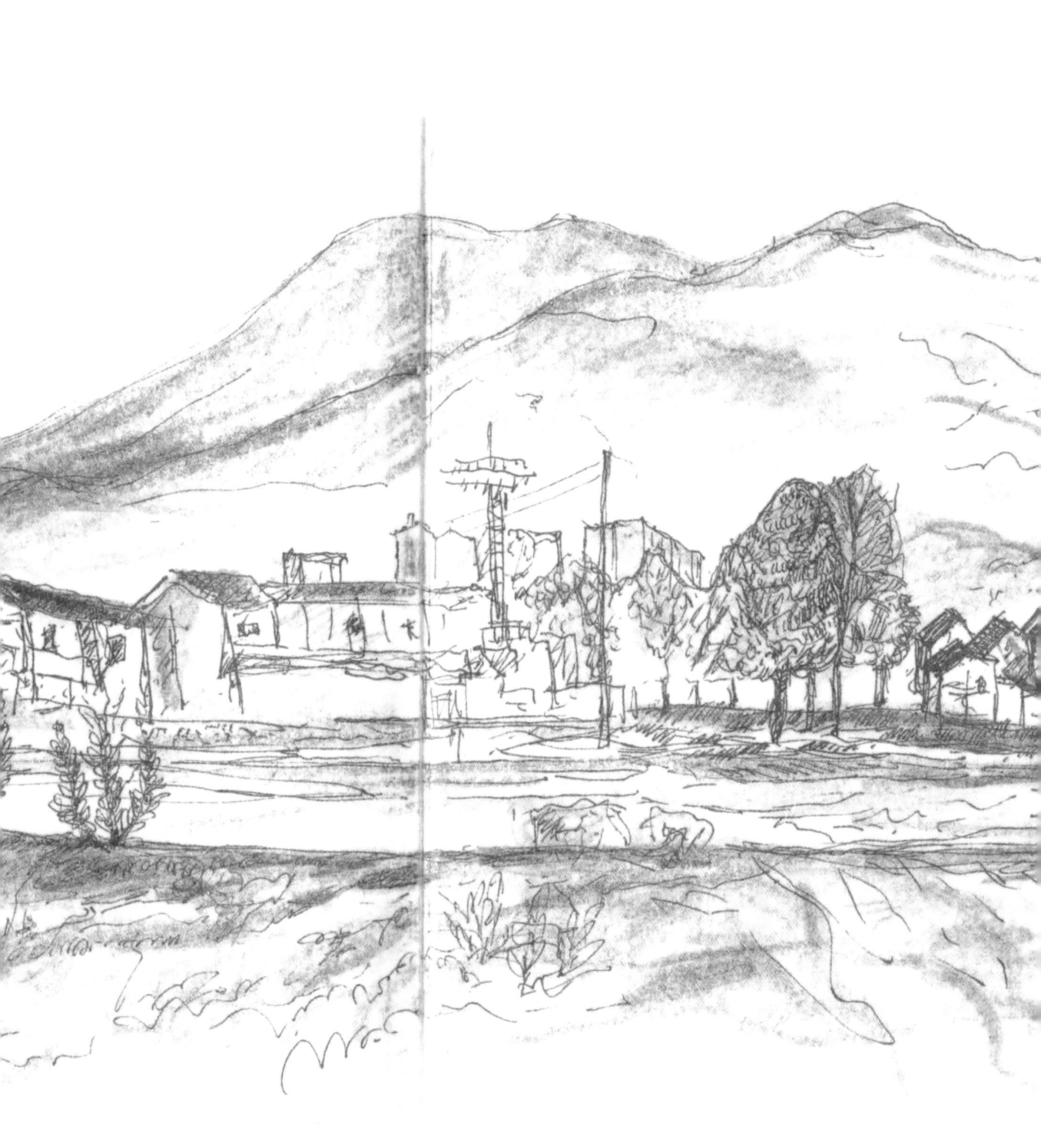

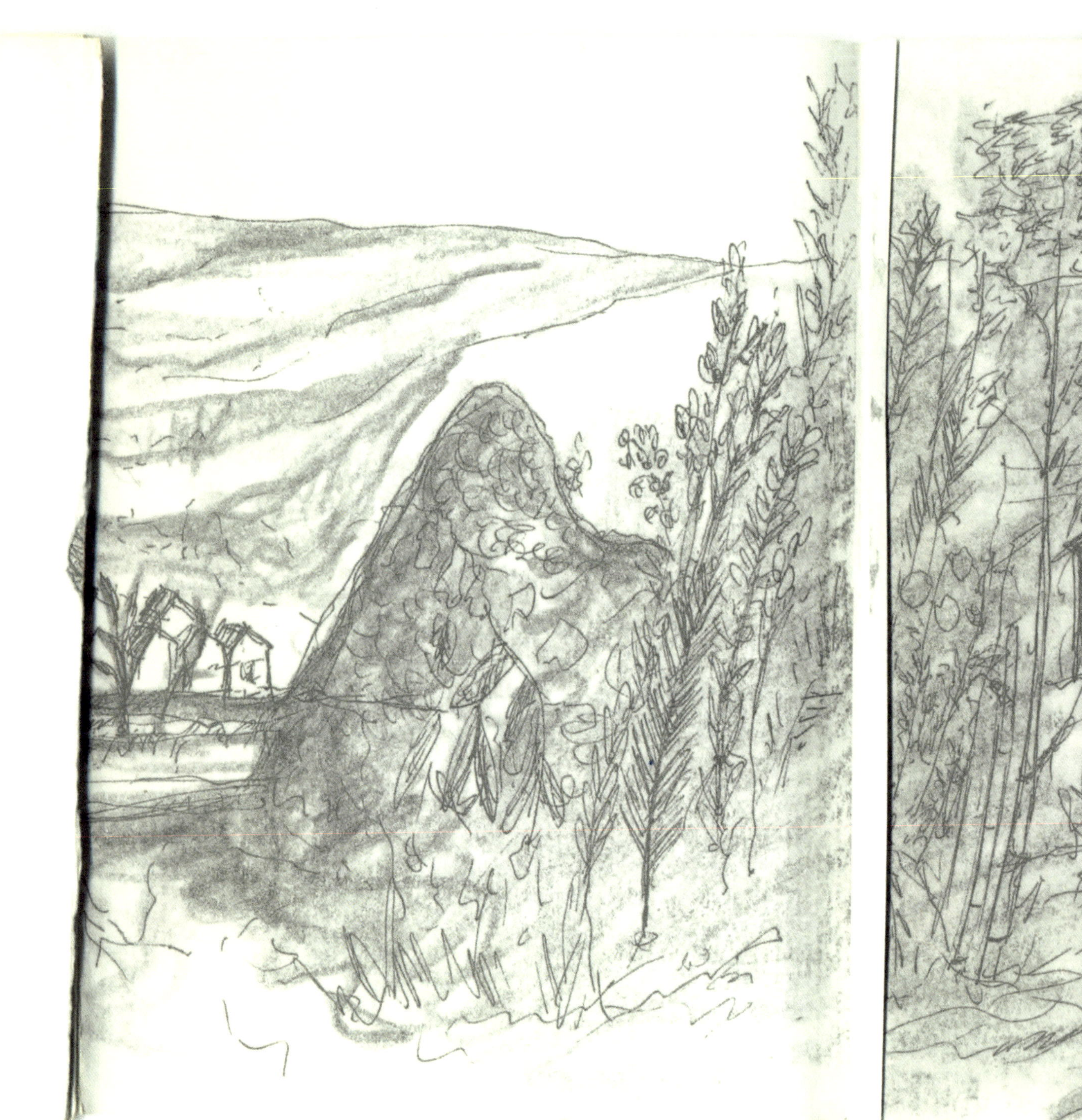

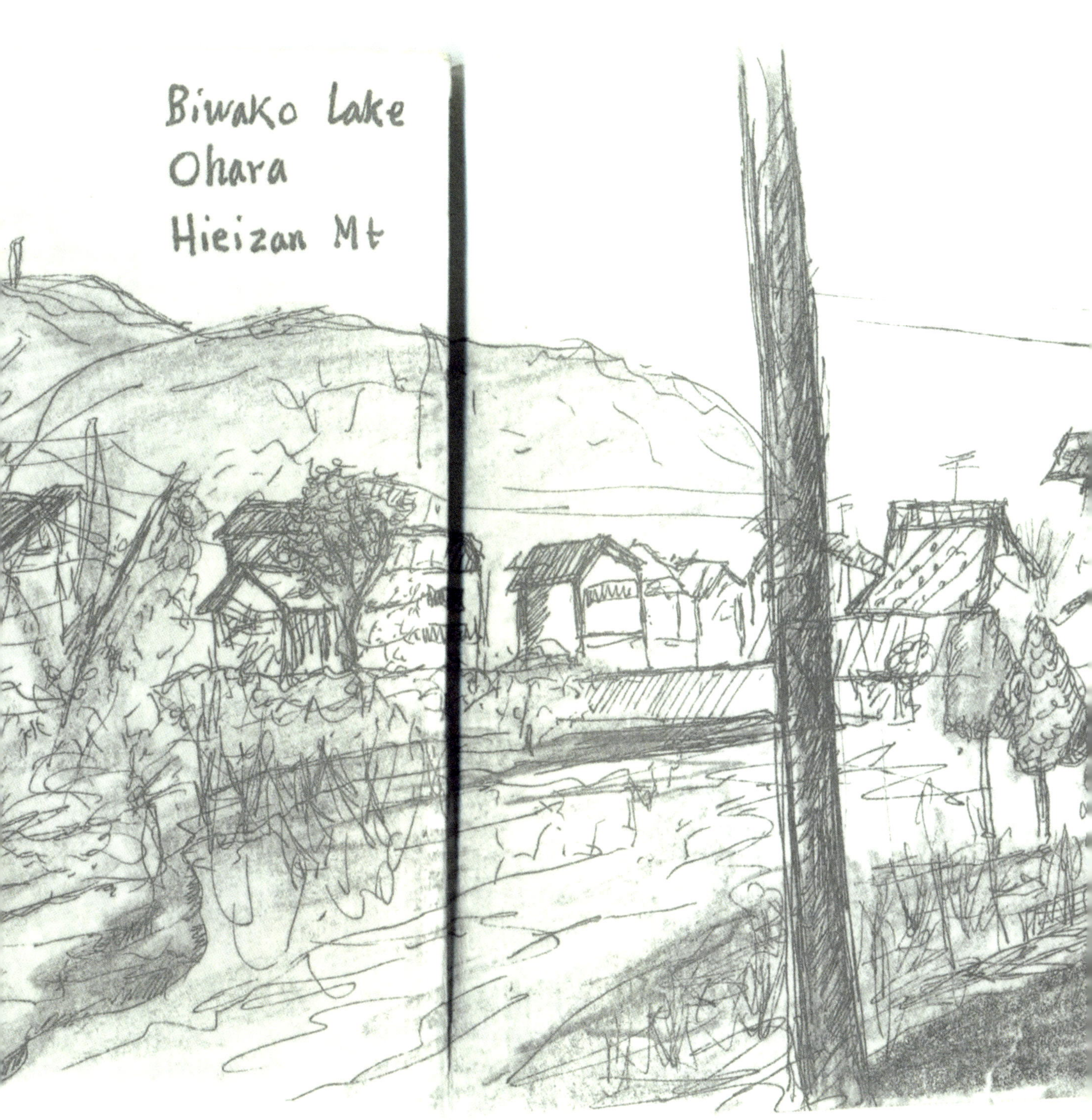

Biwako Lake
Ohara
Hieizan Mt

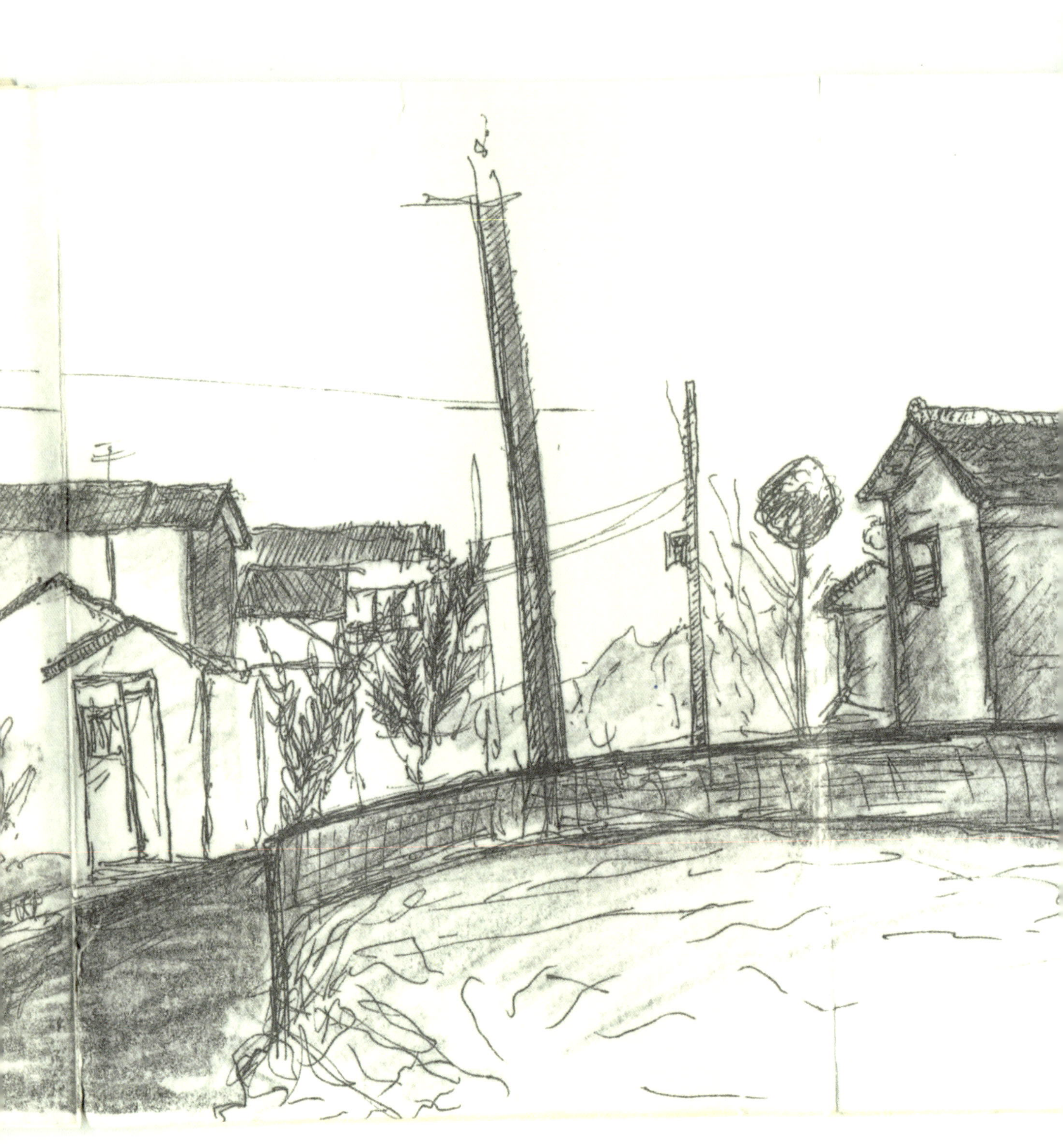

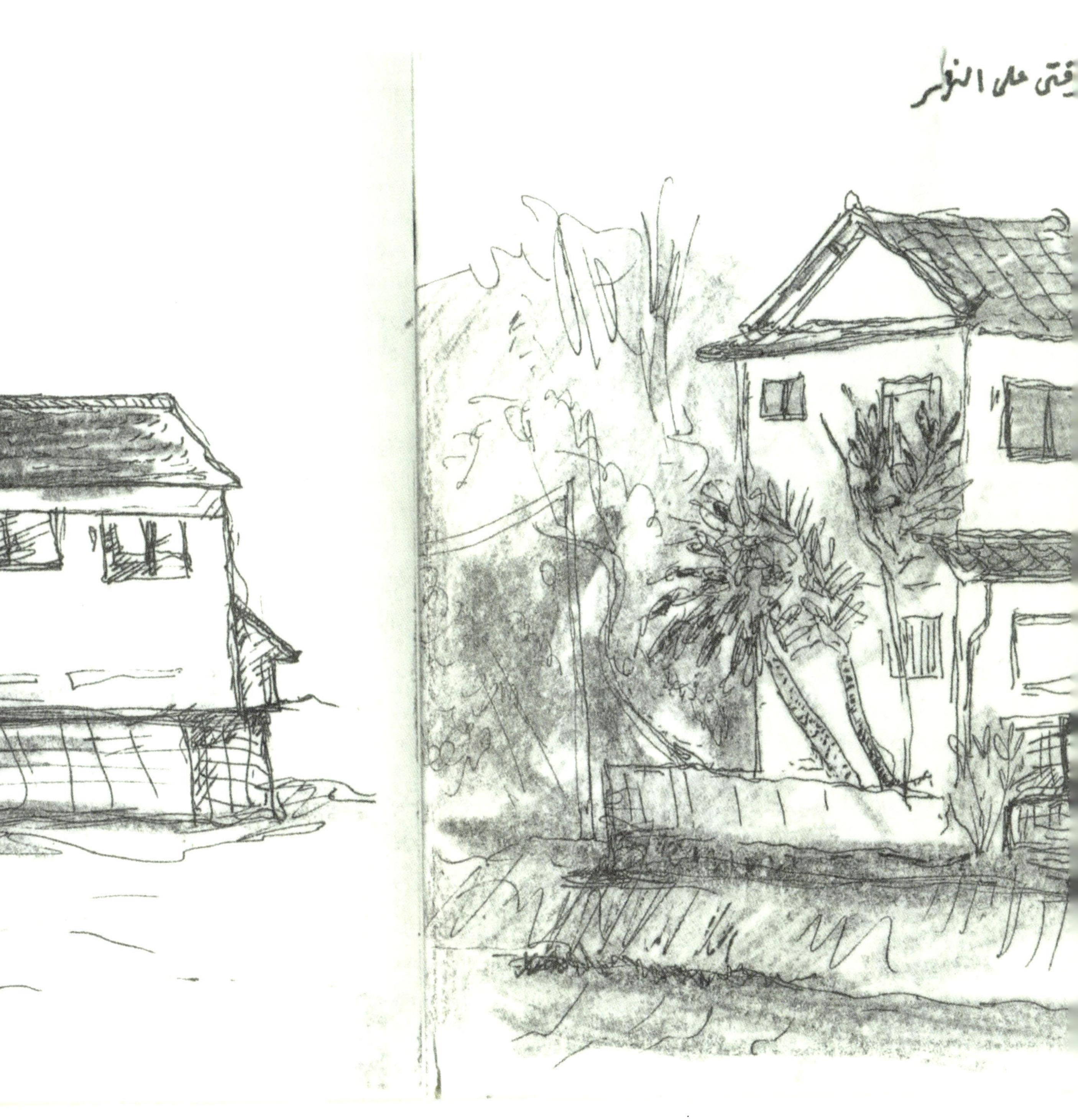
قتى على المنازل

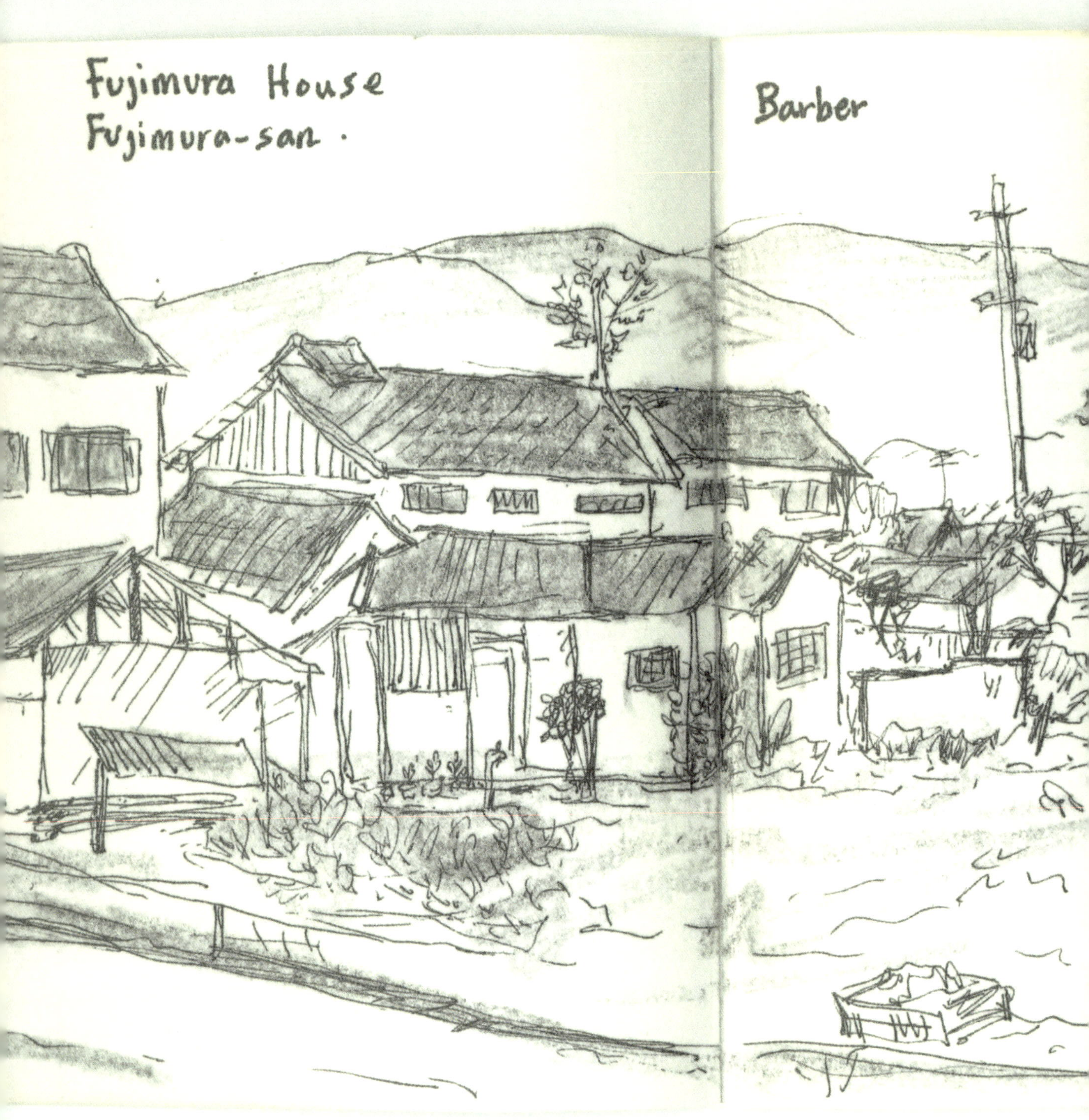
Fujimura House
Fujimura-san.
Barber

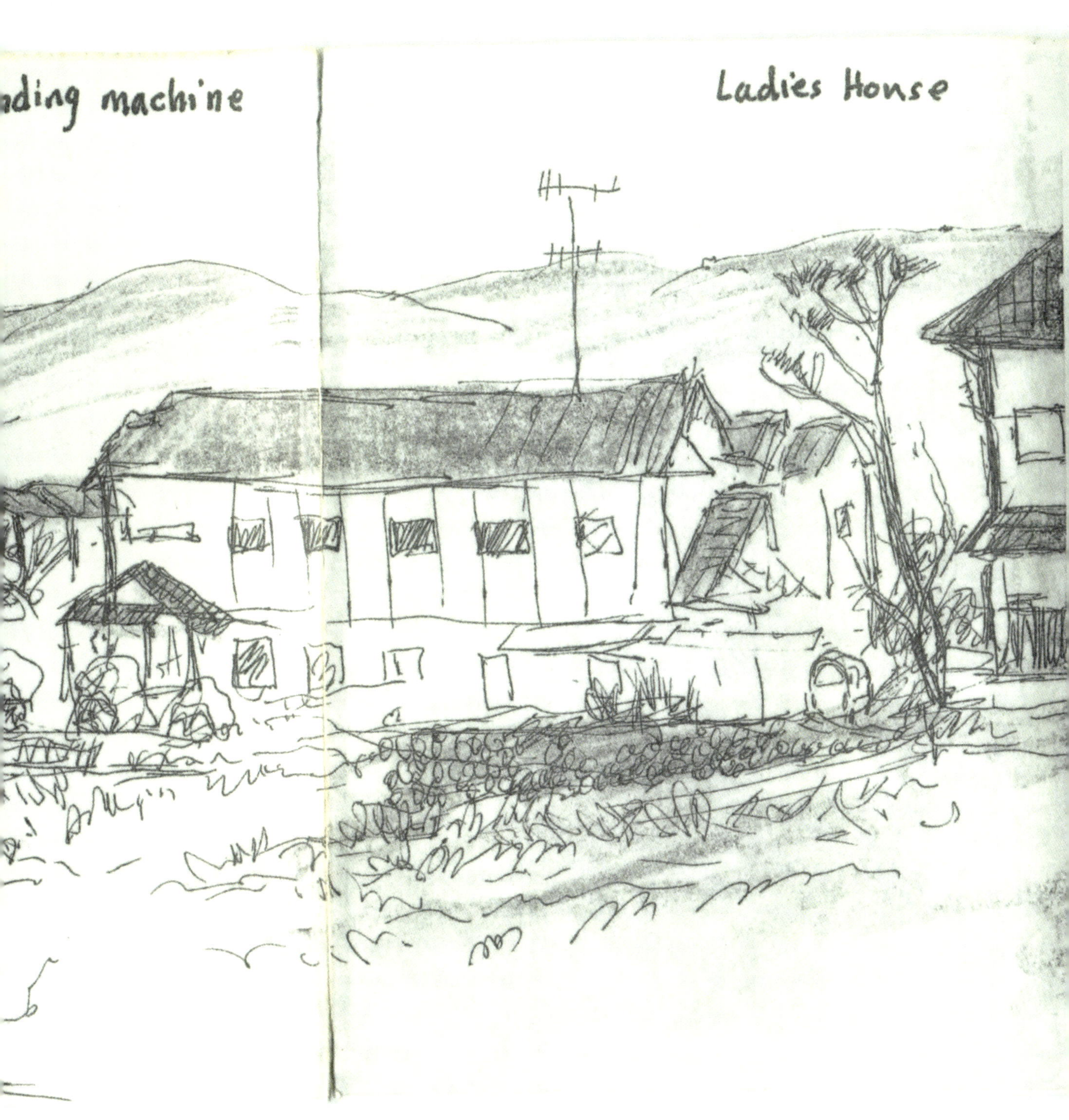
ding machine
Ladies House

Café de Lark
صديقم القديم الدرك
الذي كنت أذهب دائماً لشاطئ، القهوة
your's
super market

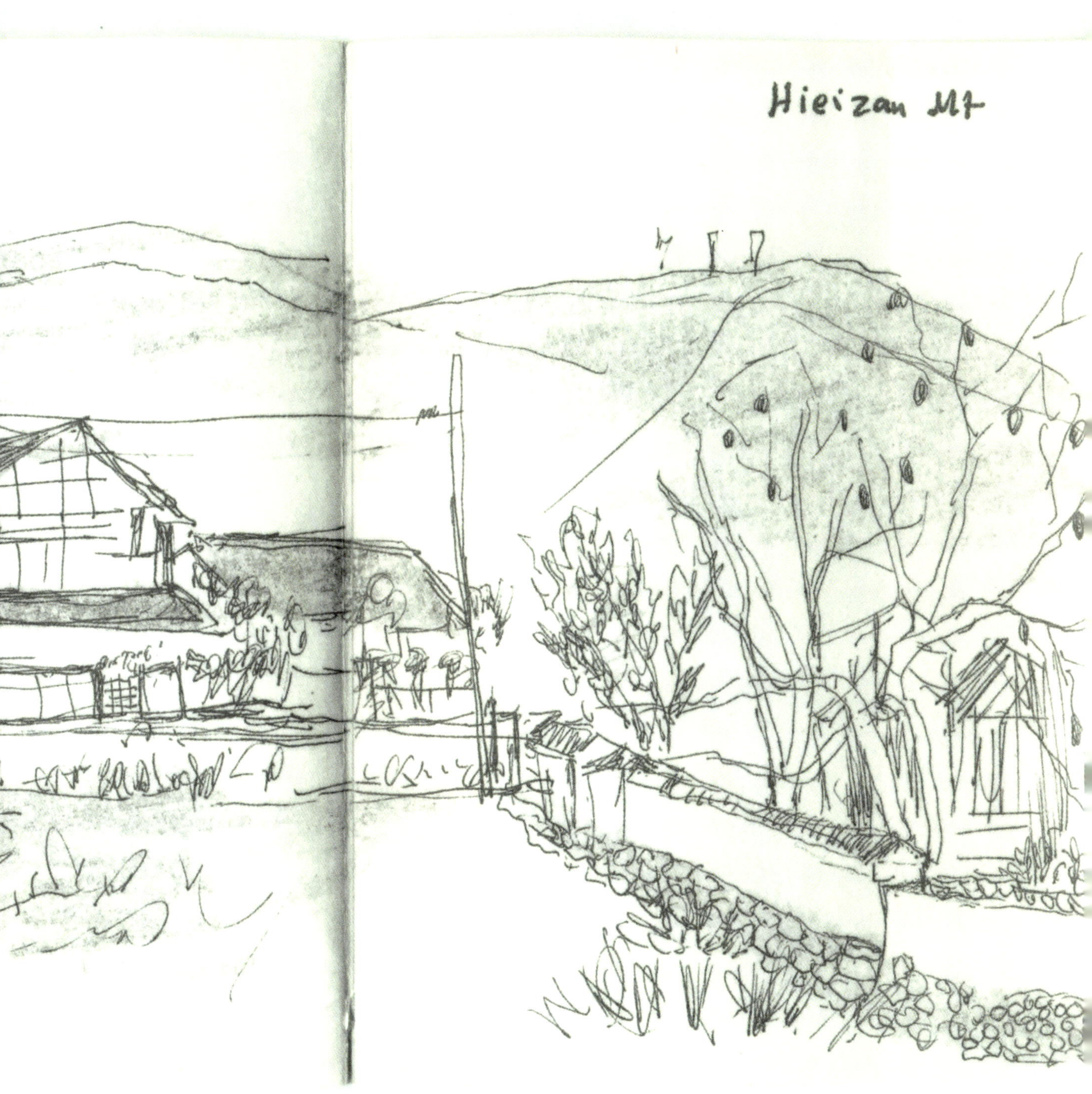

Hieizan Mt

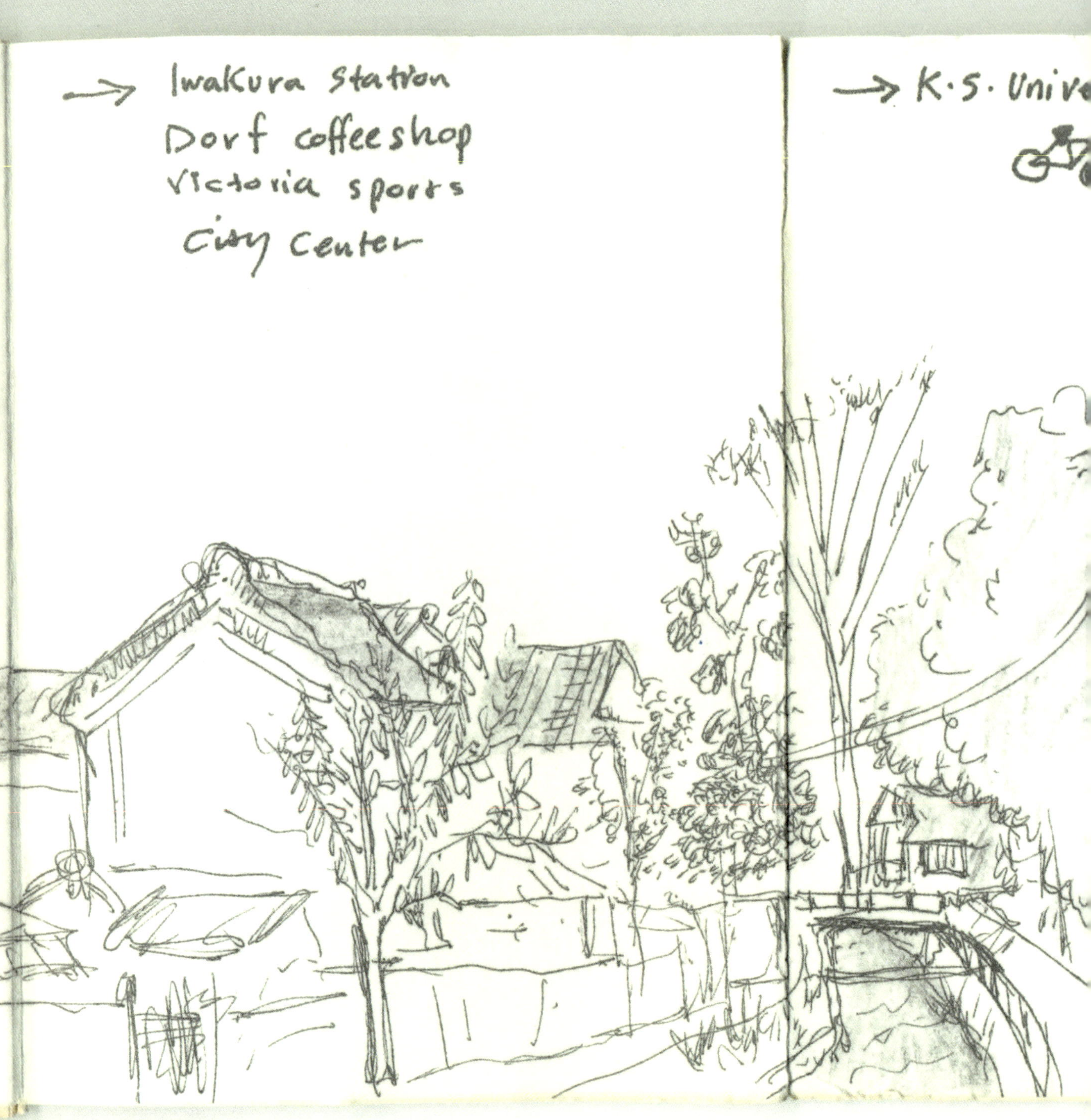
→ Iwakura Station
Dorf coffee shop
Victoria sports
City Center
→ K·S· Unive

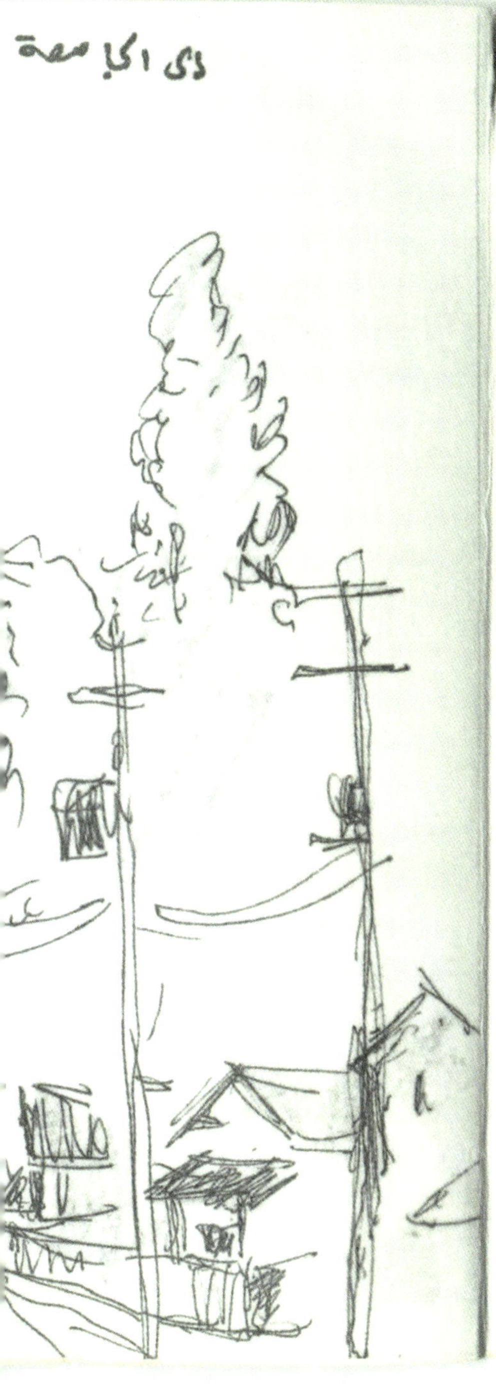

Iwakura Handscroll

Kyoto - Japan
30 Nov 95 - THU

Box 9761
Khorfakkan
Sharjah
U·A·E

٩٧٦١ ب ص
خورفكان
الشارقة

إ·ع·م

Iwakura Handscroll

Kyoto - Japan
30 Nov 95 - THU

Box 9761
Khorfakkan
Sharjah
U·A·E

ص ب ٩٧٦١
خورفكان
الشارقة
ا ع م

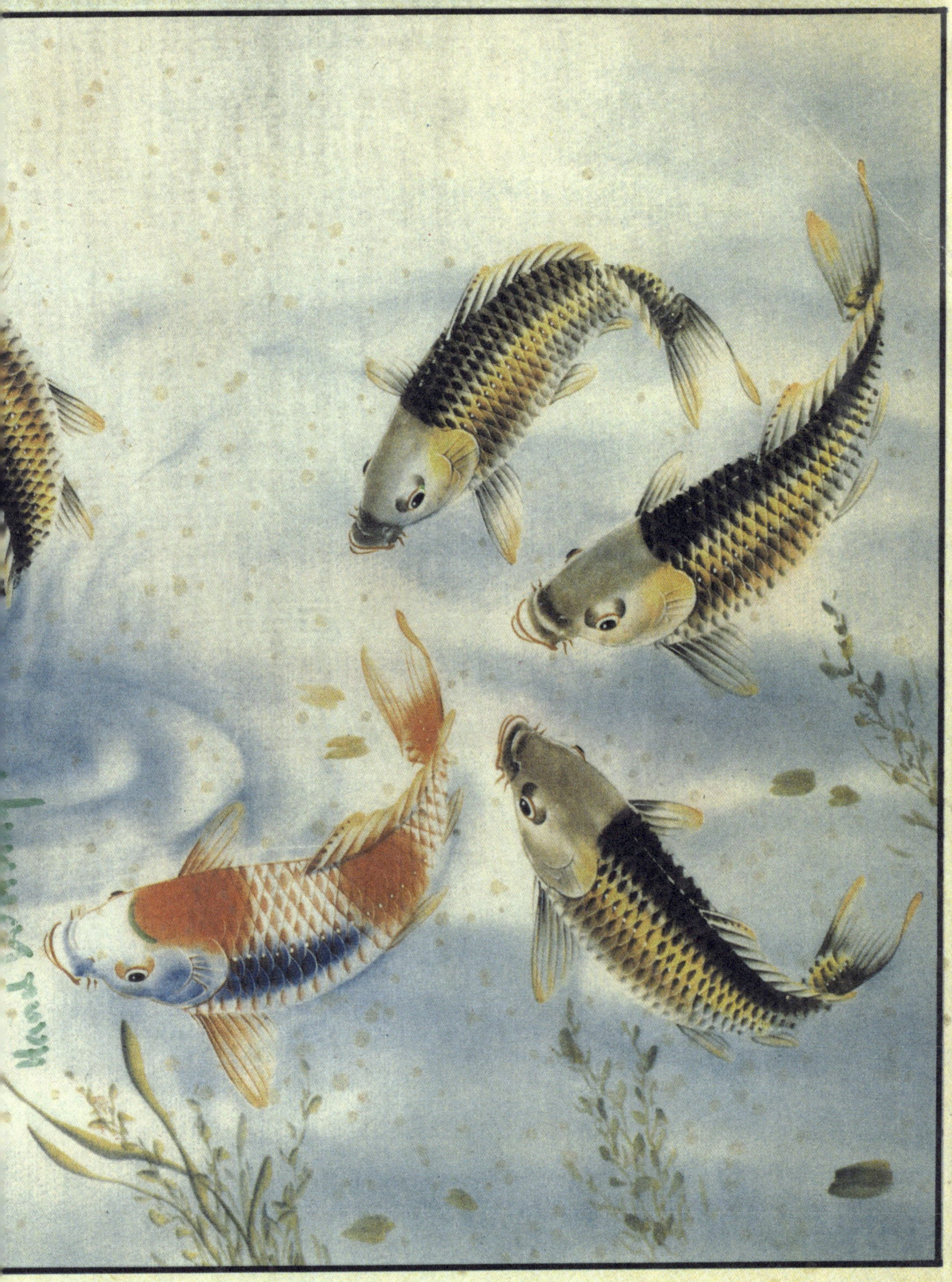

. NOTE CO.,LTD.

JAPAN

Alcoves And The
wilderness

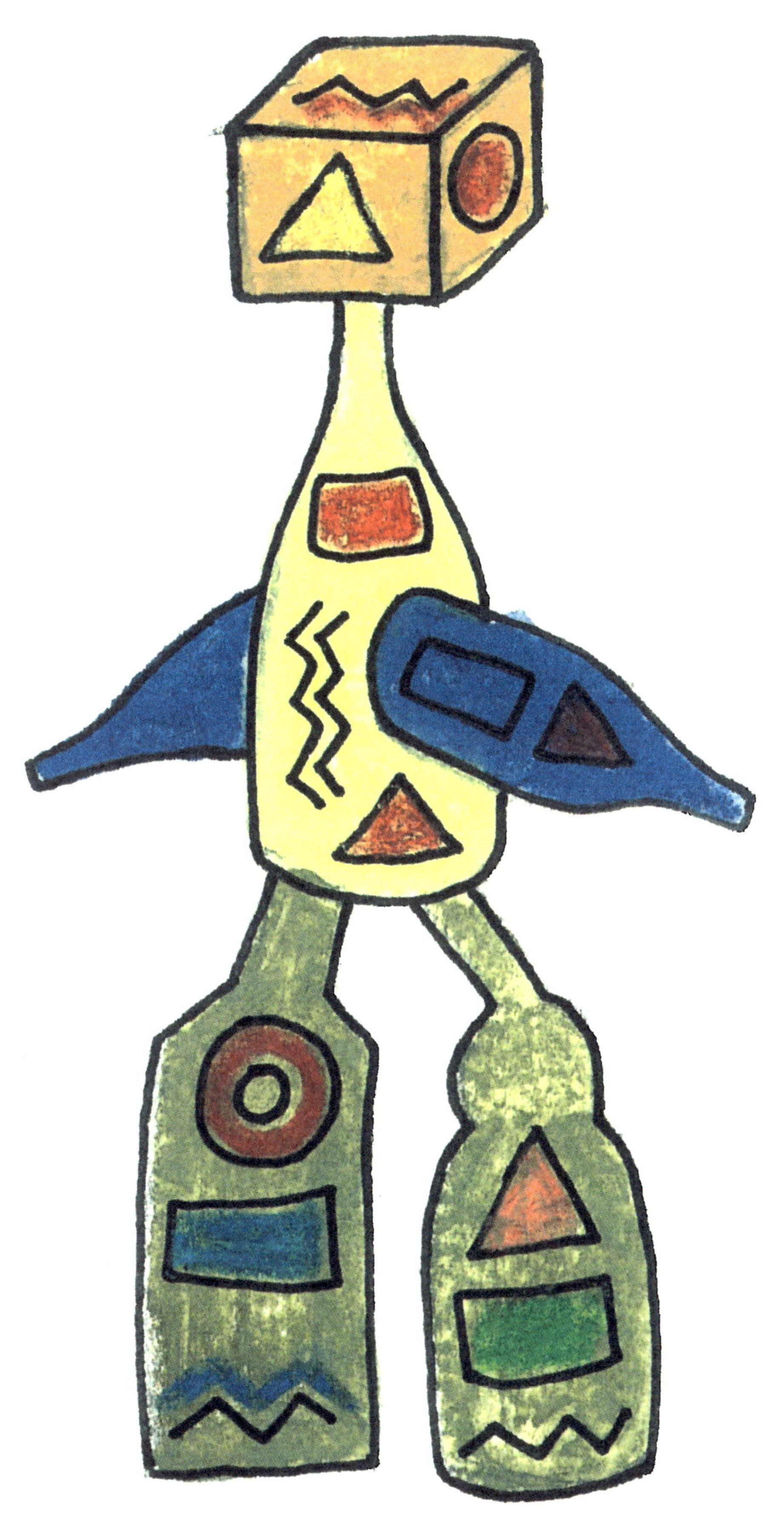

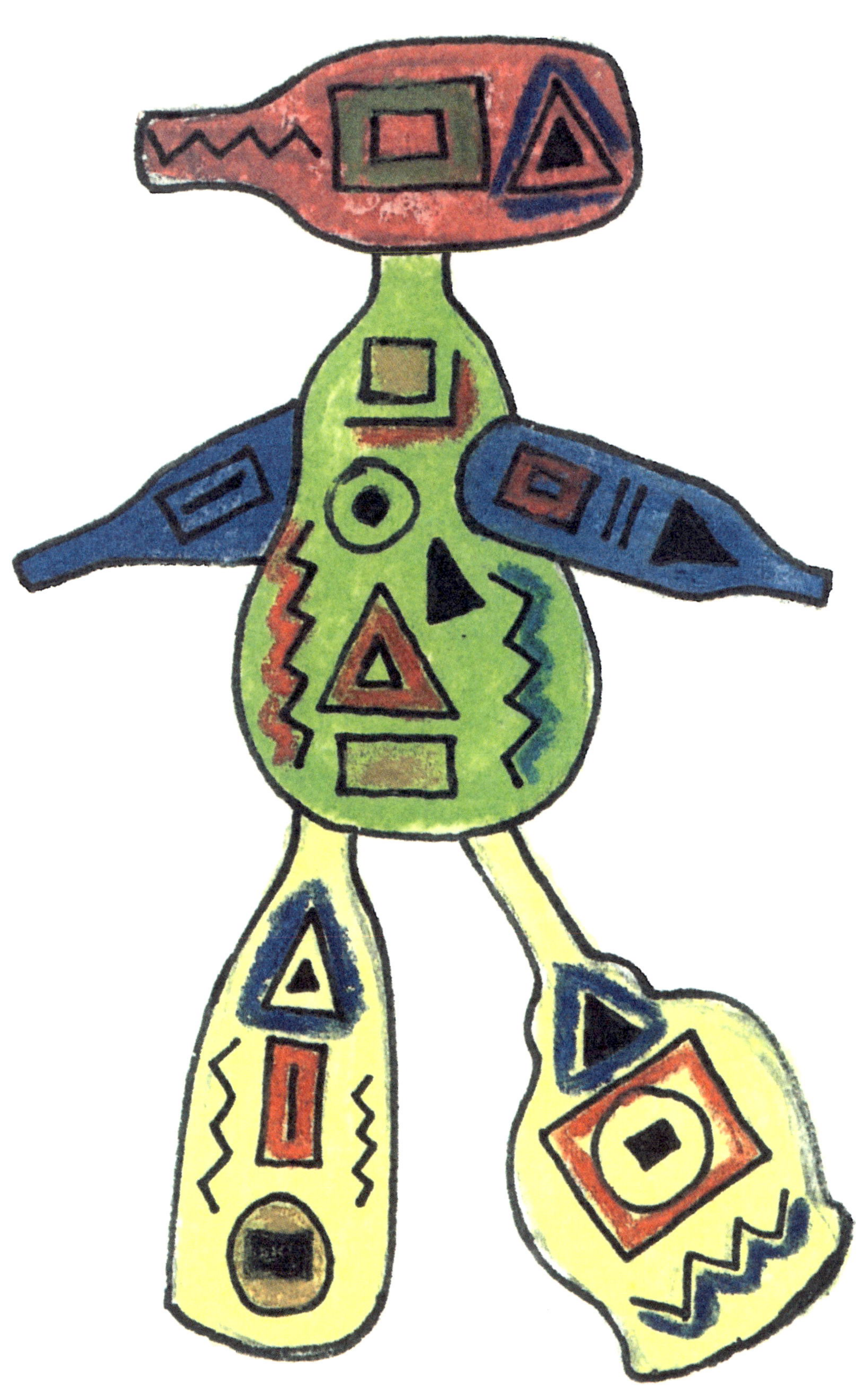

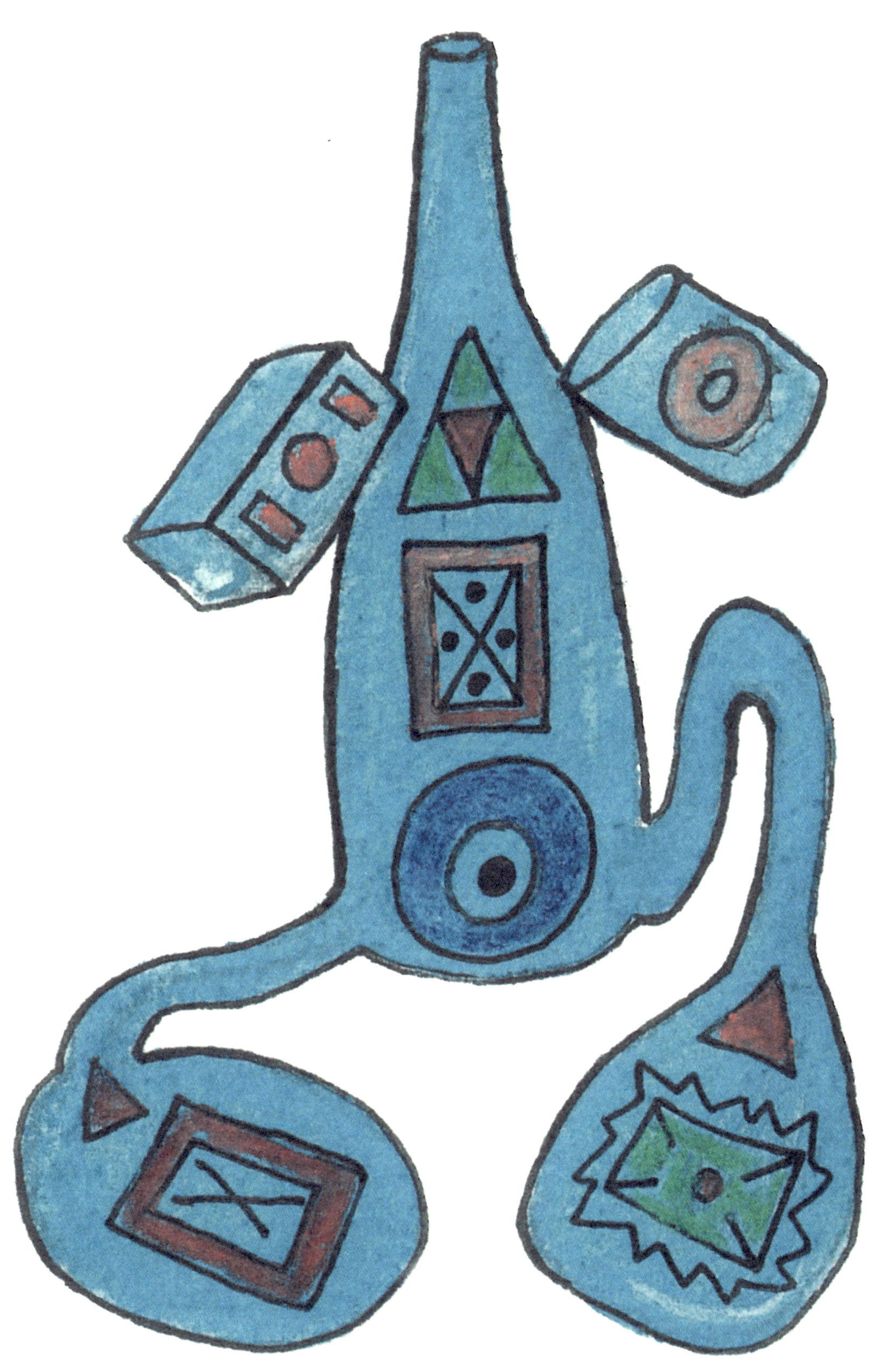

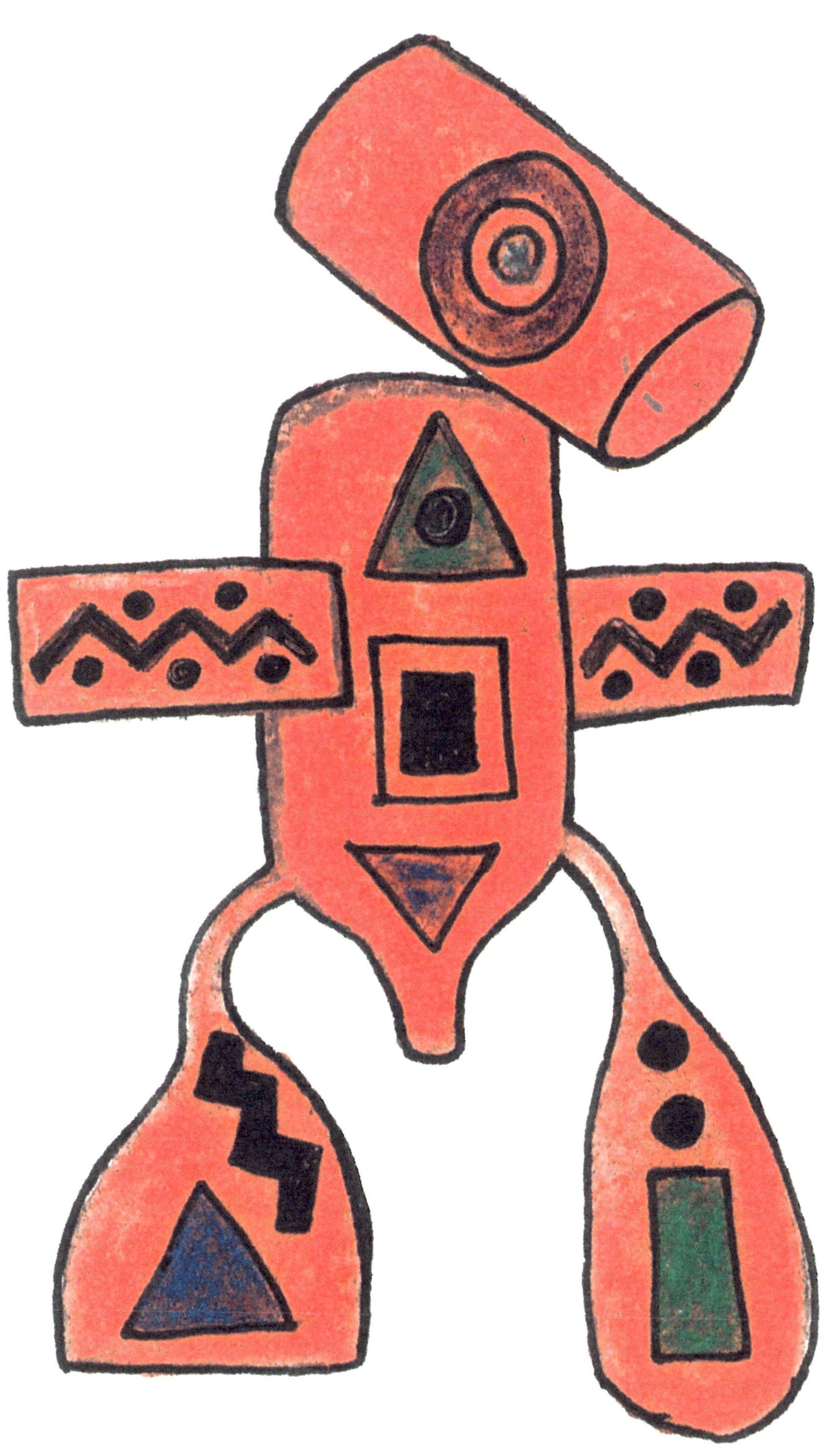

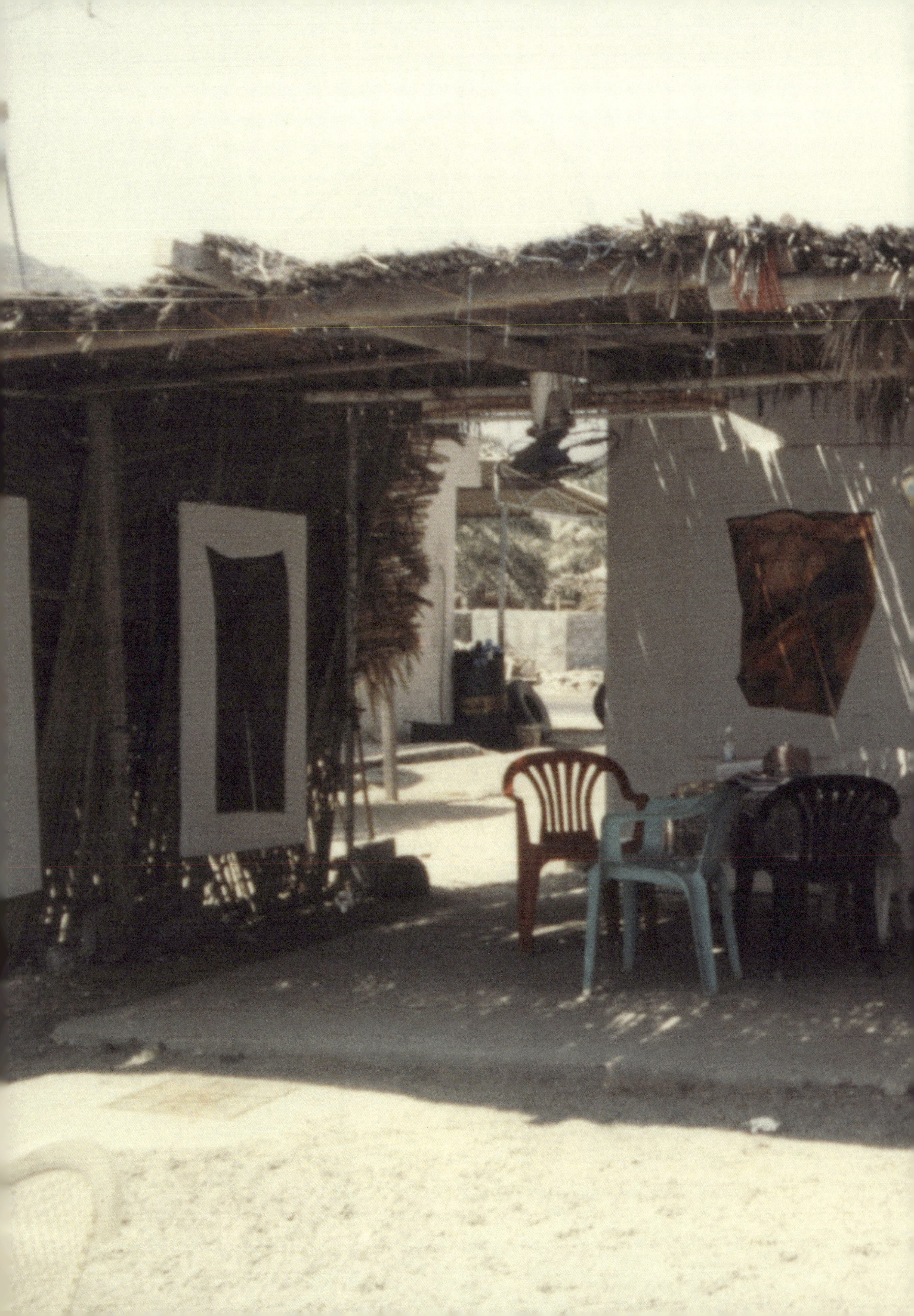

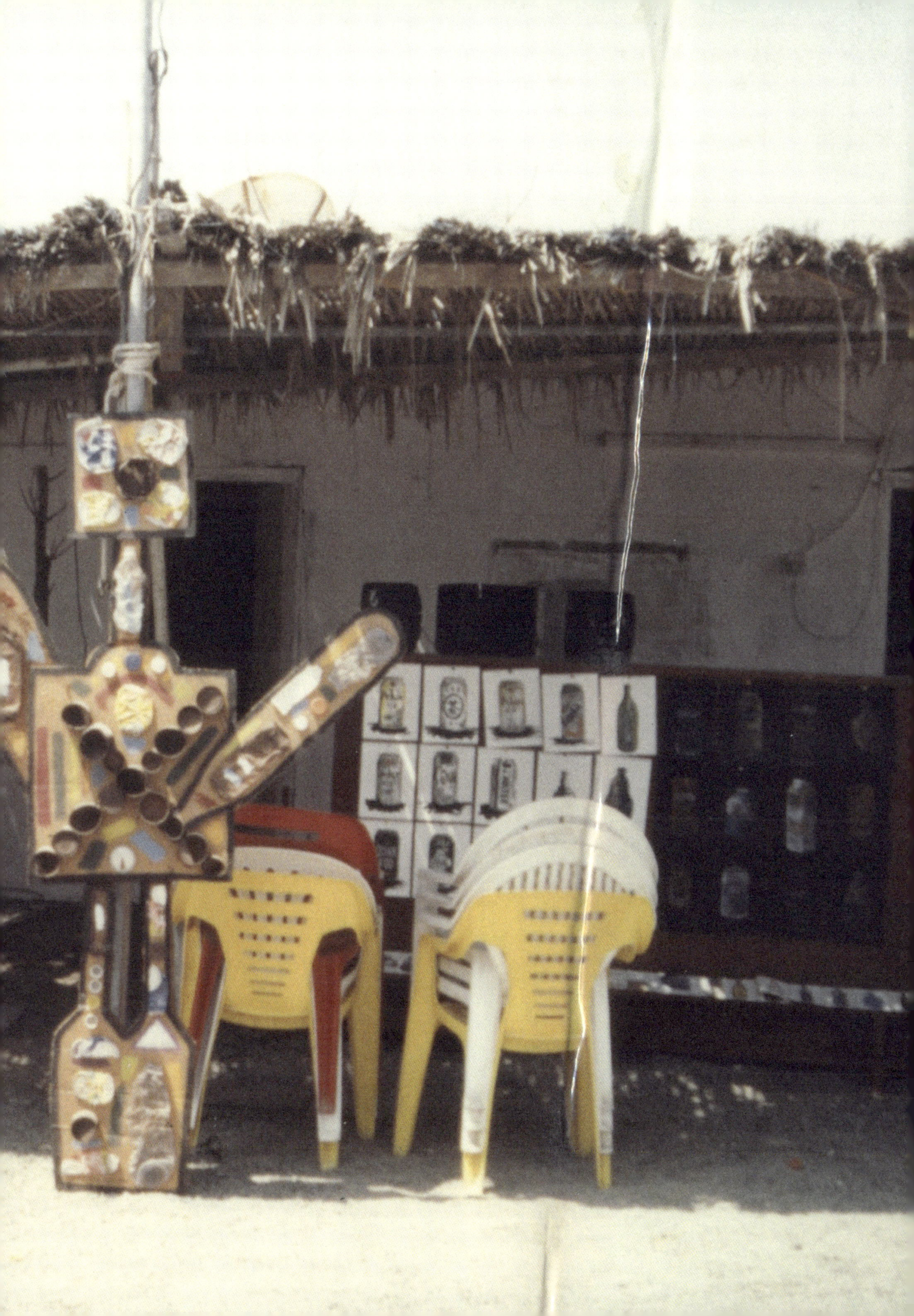

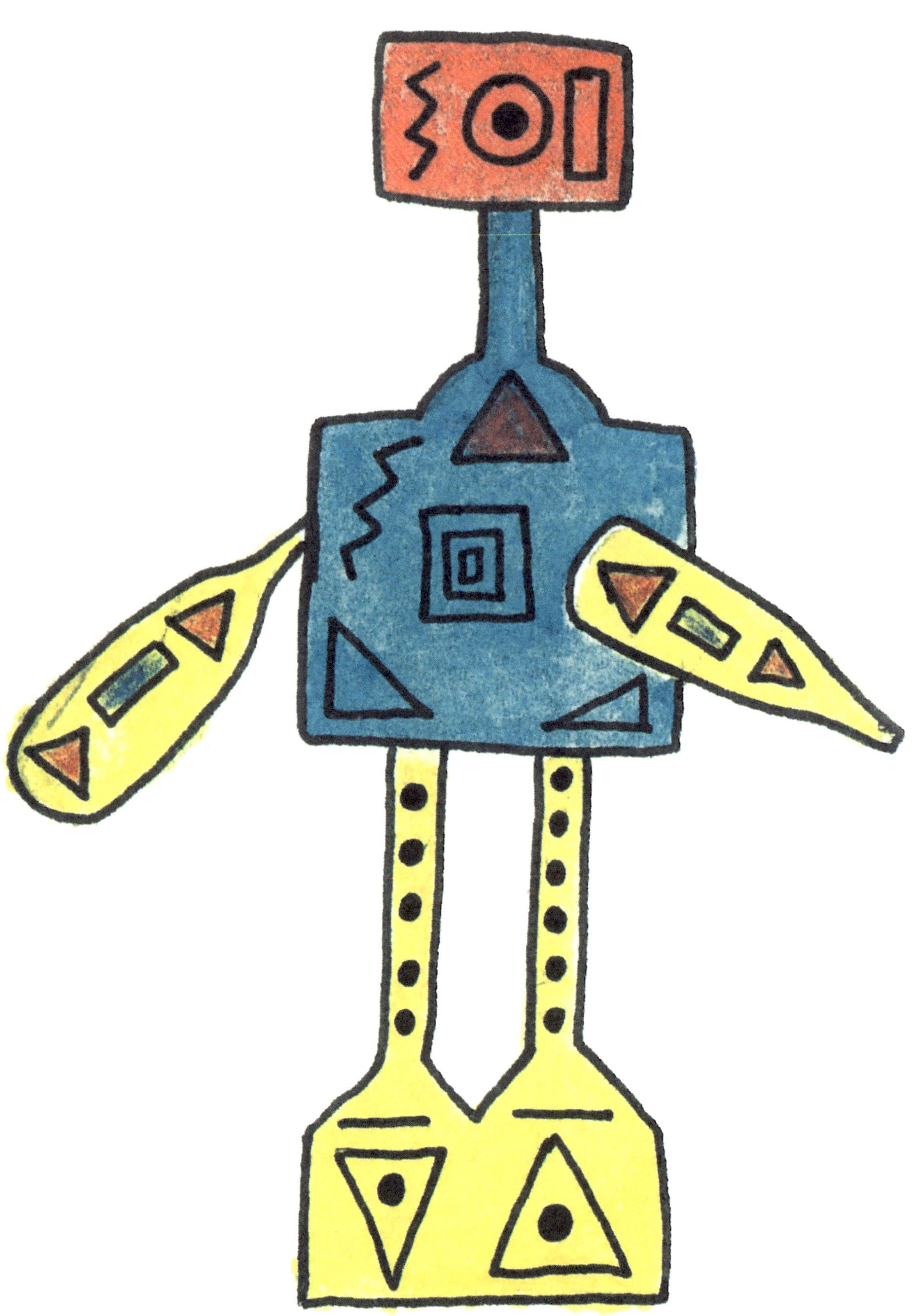

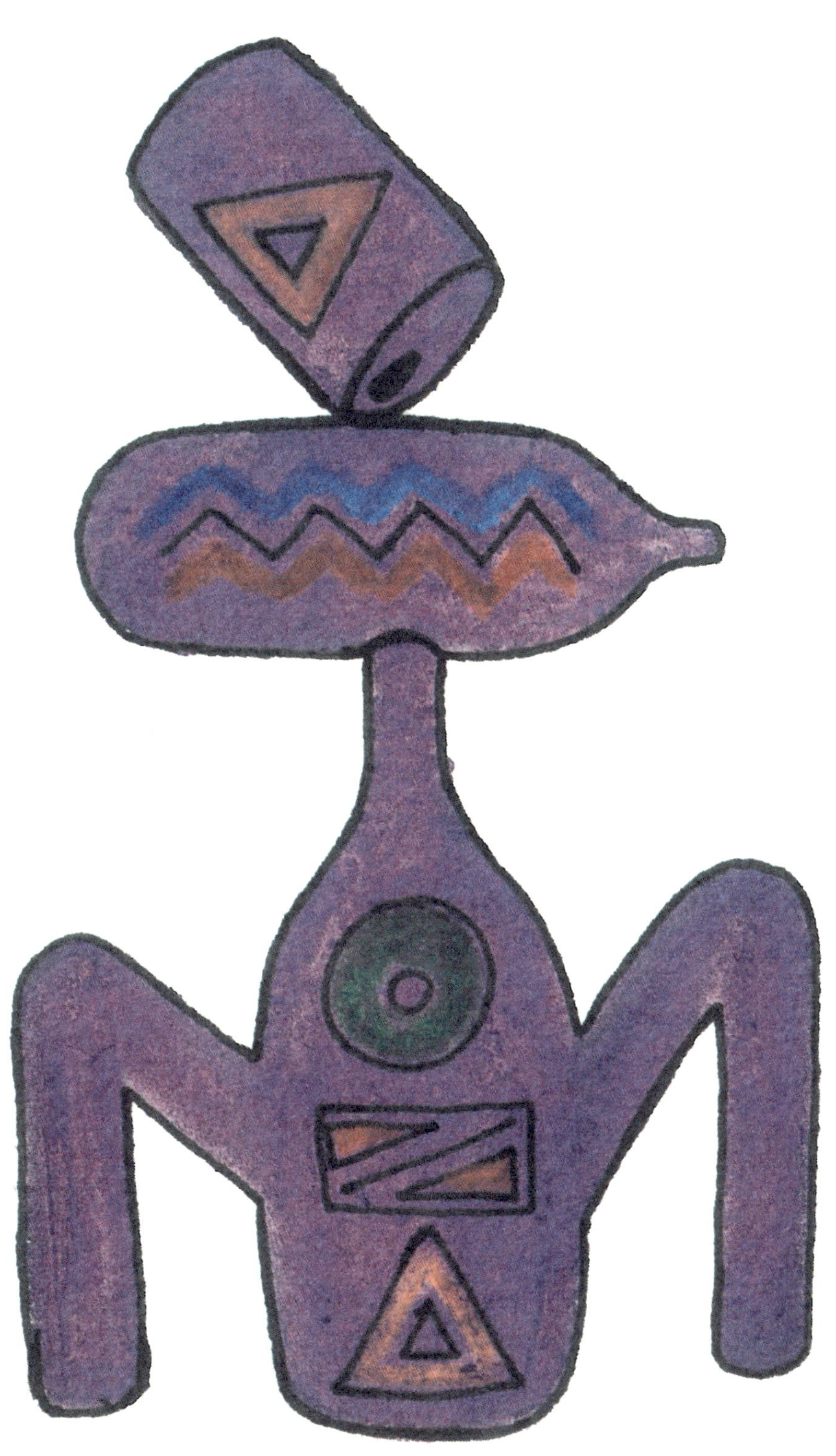

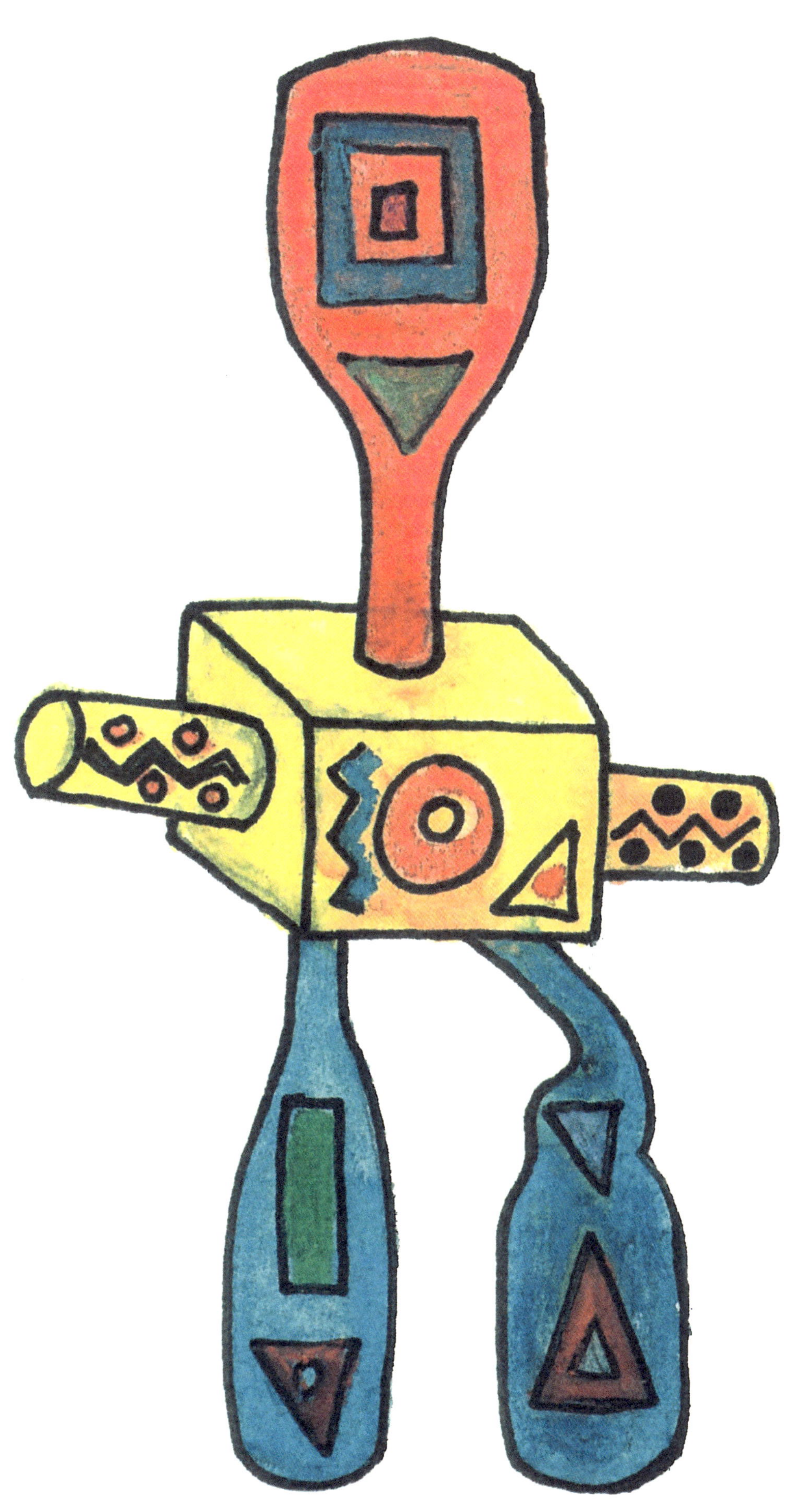

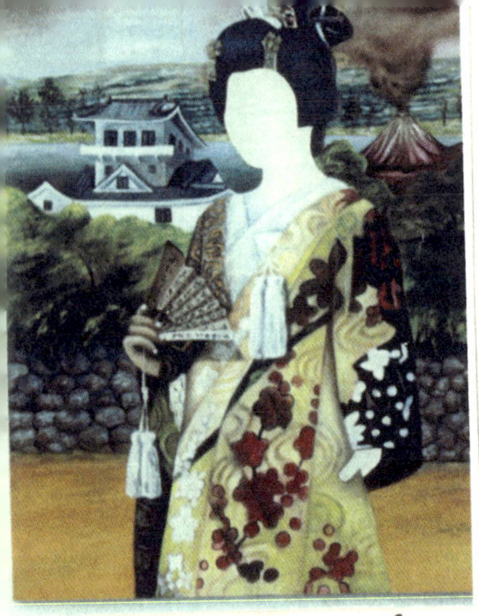
Oil on canvas · 1992 · 1 x 75 cm

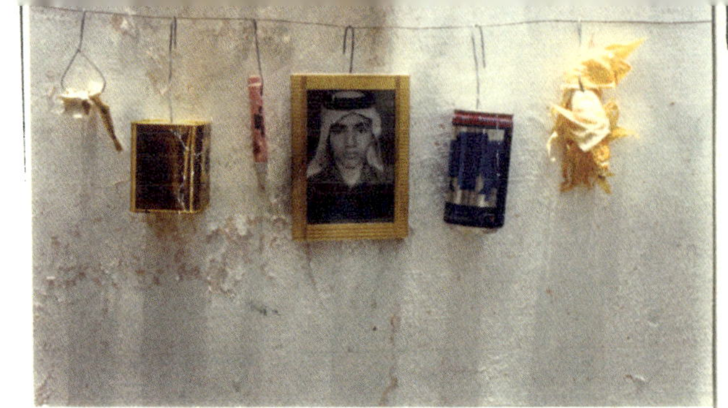
Detail : Line (circle & Line).

Abdullah Mohammed Al Saadi

P.O.Box: 9761
KhorFaka'an
United Arab Emirates

Mobile: (971)506292458
E-mail: alsaadi1800@yahoo.com

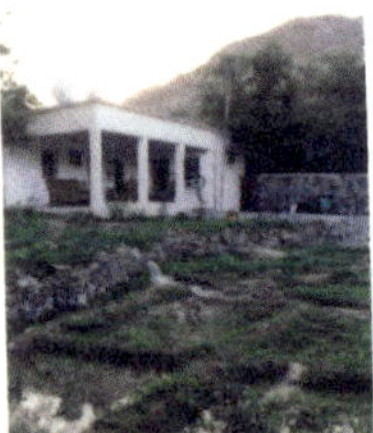

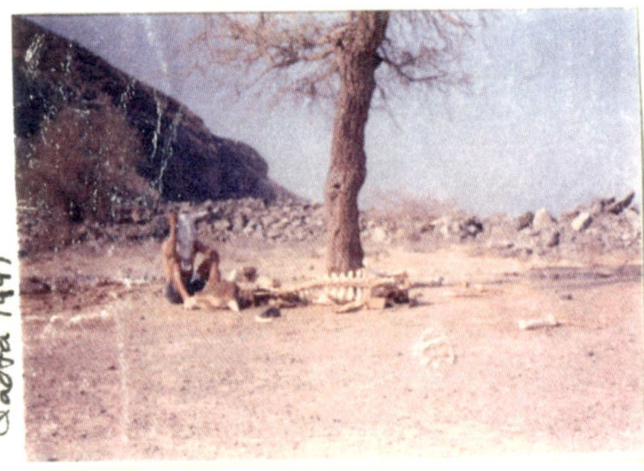
Qadfa 1991

Qadfa 1991

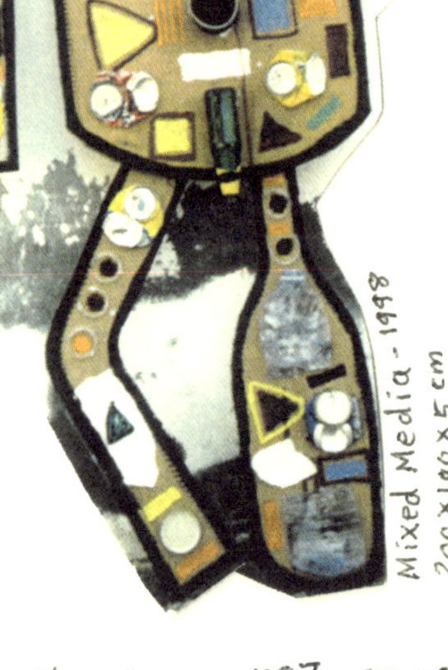
Mixed Media - 1998
200 x 100 x 5 cm

Oil on Canvas · 1987 · 67 x 87 cm

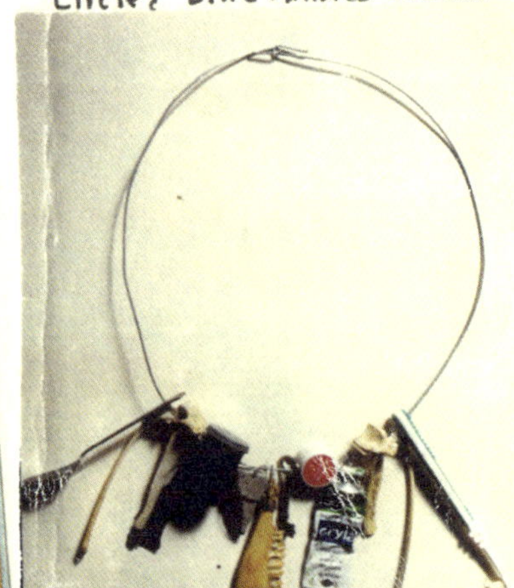
Circle & Line · Mixed media

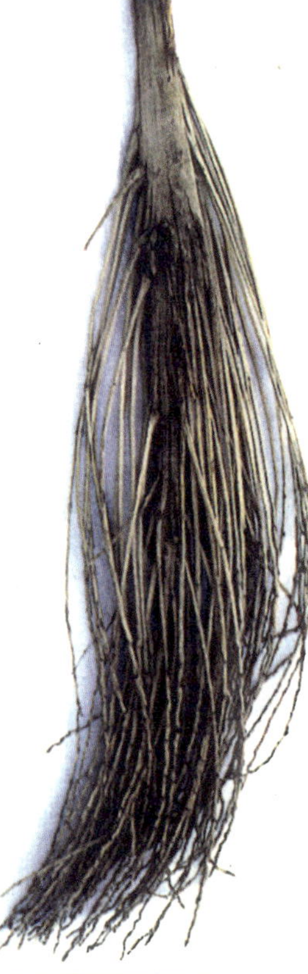
The 5th Solo Exhibition 2003 Lar

One morning, in Fujairah's coastal town of Sharm, Abdullah Al Saadi pulls off the Dibba-Khorfakkan Road, his vehicle coming to a halt at the entrance of Sharm Cafe. The smell of salt and the sound of lapping waves rouse his senses as he unloads the trunk. The day's first regulars arrive soon after, greeted by the sight of Al Saadi, nearly finished redecorating their neighbourhood haunt under the watchful, bemused eyes of its proprietors.

Al Saadi was himself a fixture at Sharm, and the idea of a cafe exhibition had been growing on him for some time. Since his return from his travels in Japan, he had spent hours there, either with his circle of friends or alone, drawing, writing poetry and meditating. Between rounds of coffee and lulls in conversation, Al Saadi would look across the cafe, note the layer of discarded cans spread across the floor and register the proximity of his location to both the Indian Ocean and the Hajar Mountains.

For three days, Al Saadi's works sat in the shade of Sharm's palm frond canopy or baked under the sun. Central to so many of these pieces was his enduring affinity for the beverage container in its many permutations, with over 50 such illustrations produced between the Emirates and Japan exhibited at the cafe. In a similar vein, lashed to two nearby support beams and facing the ocean, a pair of flat, totem-like assemblages – made of recycled water bottles and caps, soda cans crushed or cut into strips, and other geometric flourishes over irregular cardboard cutouts – stood frozen in fingerless greeting.

Alongside these illustrations and assemblages, he exhibited the *Circle and Line* (2003) series, consisting of objects gathered during his walks: slivers of animal jawbone, a toothbrush, shards of ceramic, a film canister, various stones and uprooted root sections, all strung on wire loops and displayed to garish effect. These works, in tandem with the landscapes and paintings he draped across the rocks and sands of the beach, also magnified the growing coastal pollution to which the cafe and its customers had inadvertently contributed.

For Al Saadi, cafes were controlled pockets of activity that allowed him to observe and absorb the local culture and language throughout his many journeys. They appeared in his mind as a series of interconnected way stations, grouped together not unlike the charms on his *Circle* works – seemingly unrelated but all drawn from the shores of his spatial memory.

This notion of way stations as stopping points for respite and reflection was also very much at play in Al Saadi's roving exhibitions collectively titled *Land* (2003). Loading up his new Nissan Defender with as many of his works as possible, the artist held solitary showcases in natural surroundings across Fujairah and Khorfakkan. Considering the implications of vehicle decoration as an often celebratory and propagandistic gesture, what is most interesting about these displays was Al Saadi's use of the Nissan's exterior as an exhibition space.

Land scrolls were spilling over the Nissan's hood in protective canvas sleeves. Its doors and windows are plastered with similar mountain and desert sketches, along with a self-portrait. Paintings, largely produced in the early 1990s, hover just above his campsite. The surrealist landscape, *Church of the Holy Family in Spain* (1992), pays tribute to his visit to Barcelona during his *Nippon Maru* voyage over a decade ago, and a second self-portrait hang from tree boughs. This was possibly the first time many of these works had been exhibited, displayed through Al Saadi's own authorship of exhibitions in 'nature,' departing from the classical and canonical white cube exhibition setting.

Today, Sharm has been crowded out by new seaside attractions, its ocean view obstructed by an artificial island and its winding strip of villas. The earliest indications of change manifested in Al Saadi's tongue-in-cheek prose poetry from his time at Sharm, in which fish flop onto shore in search of mineral water, empty plastic chairs race across the beach and capsize into the water and grazing sheep wonder to themselves whether the cafe serves cappuccinos or espressos. Similarly, the roads to his roving exhibition sites have long been forgotten, likely built or paved over, and his old Nissan has been retired, well beyond its mileage life expectancy.

Al Saadi does not, however, as Abbasid poet Abu Nuwas remarked, 'cry over stones.' To him, the living and the inanimate are all subject to the whims of modernity, a force as powerful as the ocean tides.

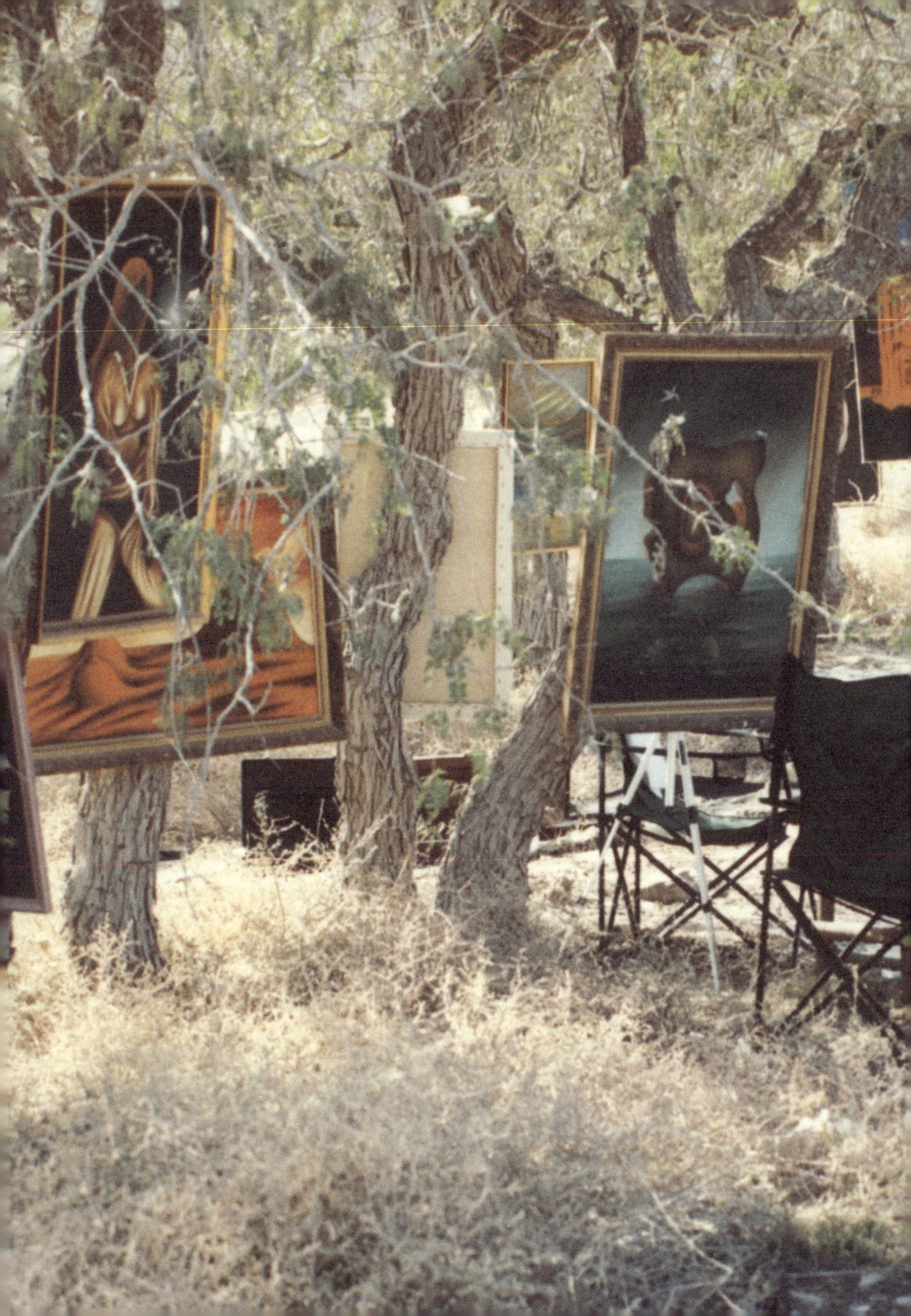

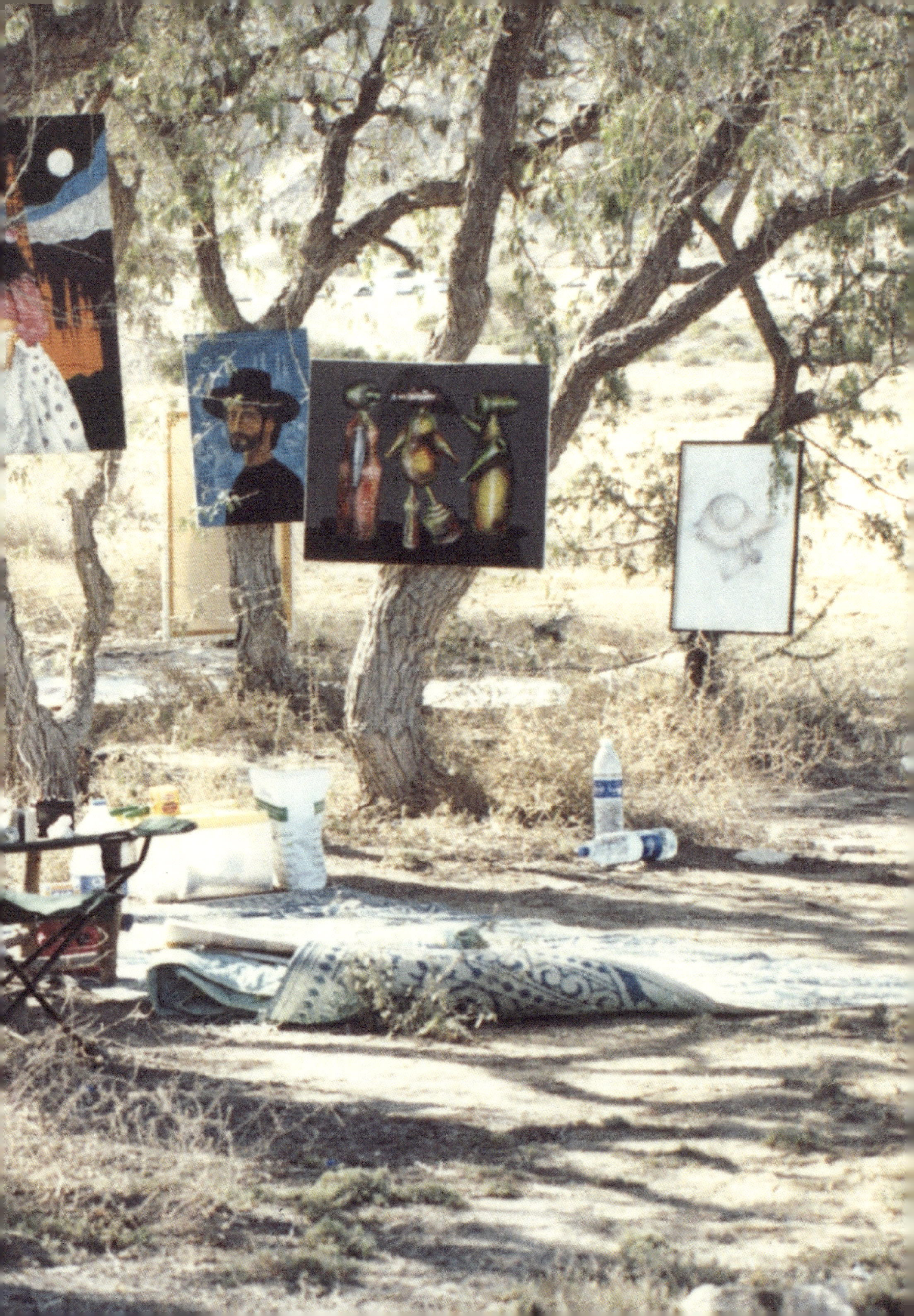

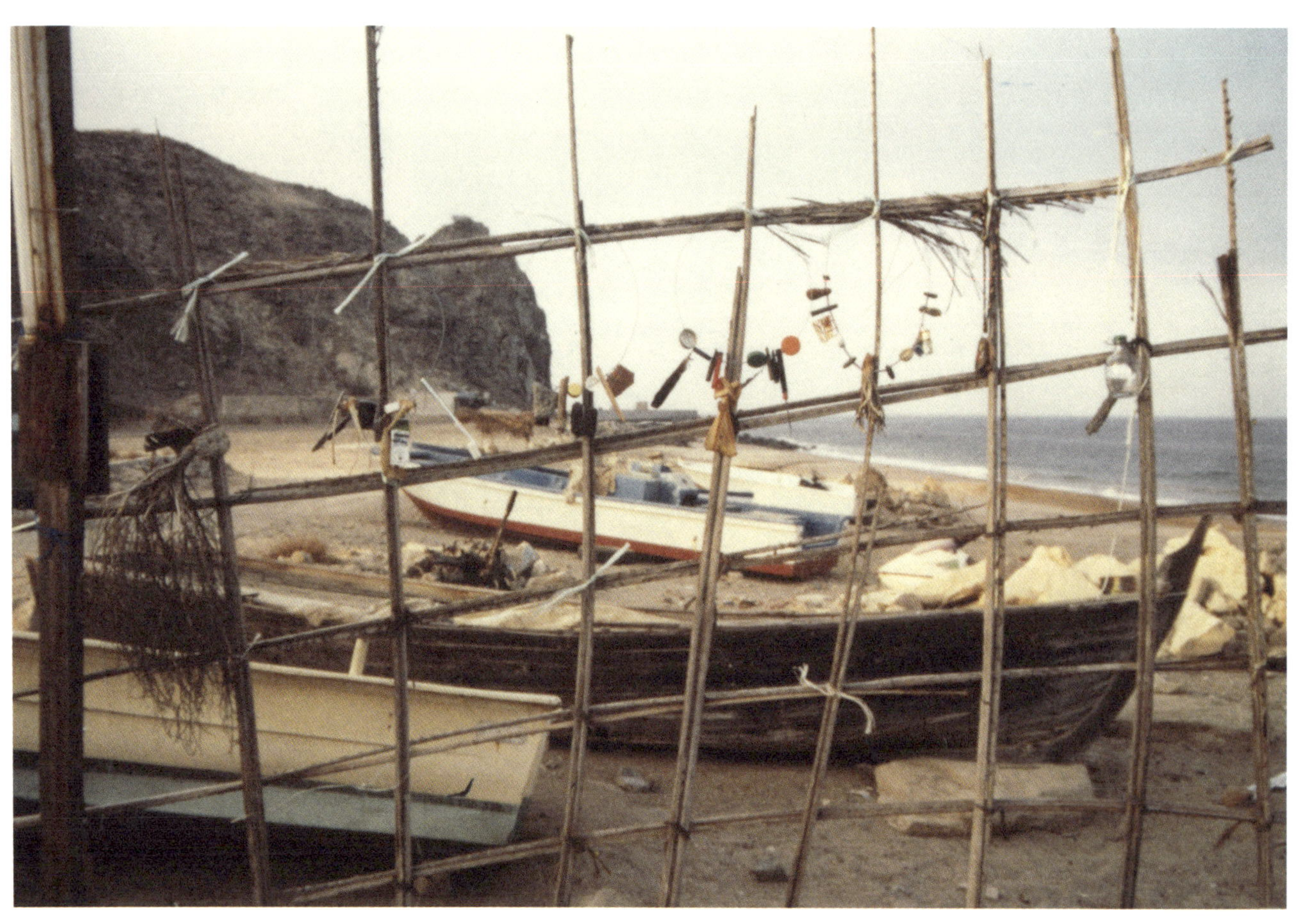

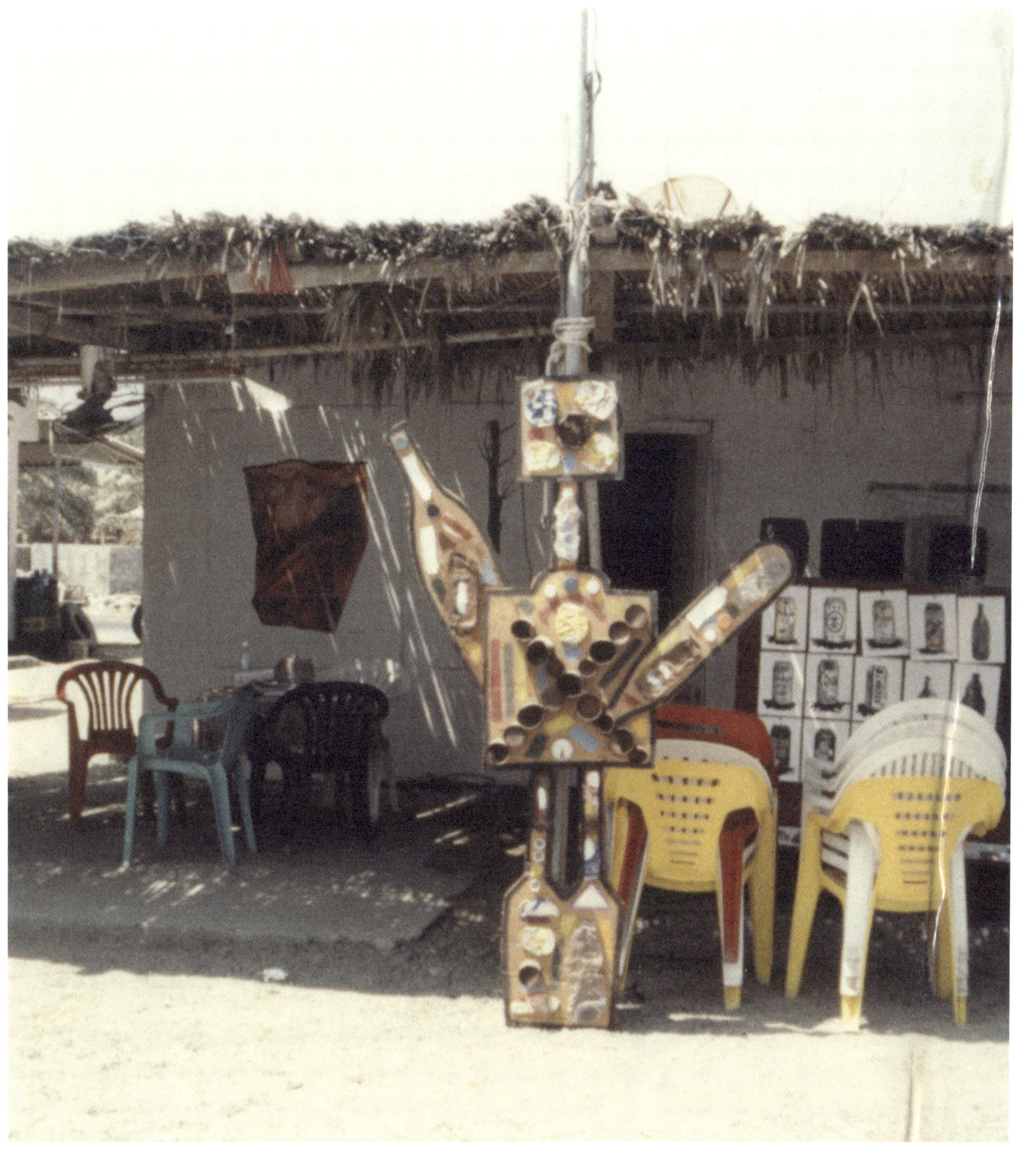

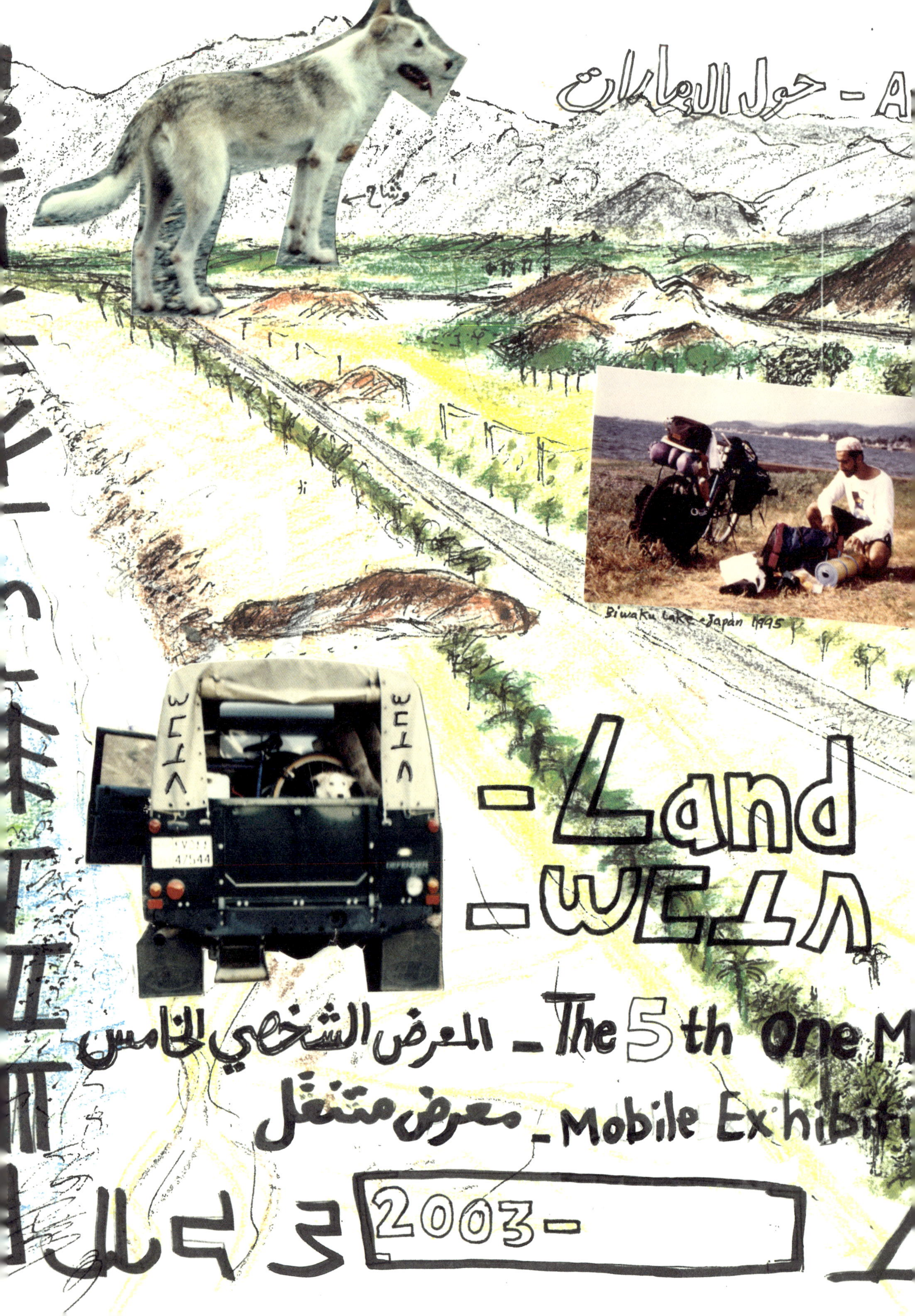
حول الإمارات - A
Biwaku Lake - Japan 1995
- Land -
- الأرض -
The 5th One M
المعرض الشخصي الخامس -
- Mobile Exhibiti
معرض متنقل -
- 2003

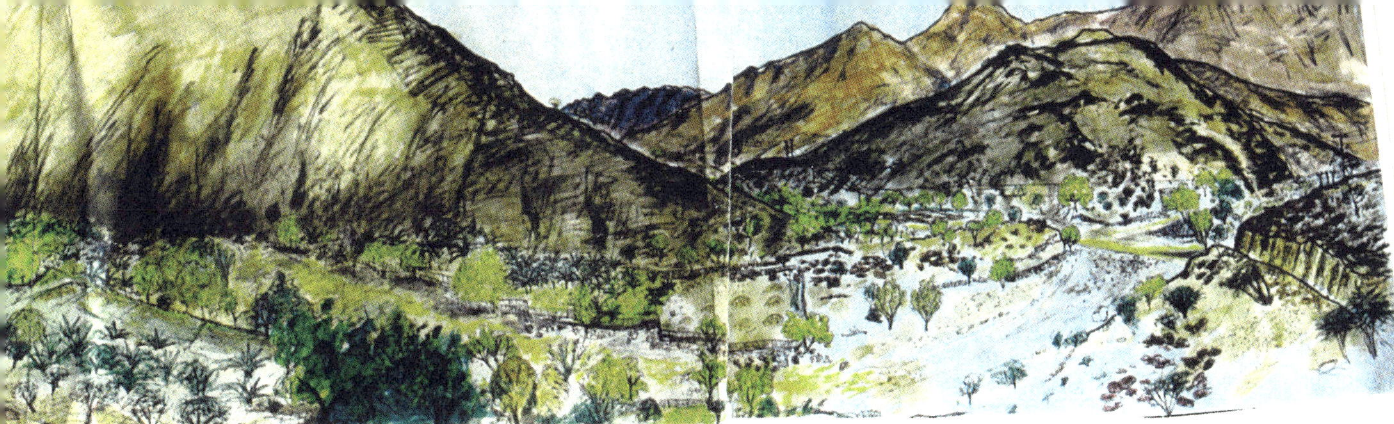

Detail : Wadi handscroll . Water color on paper . 2002 / 42 x 179 cm

My mother's letters (1998 - 2000)

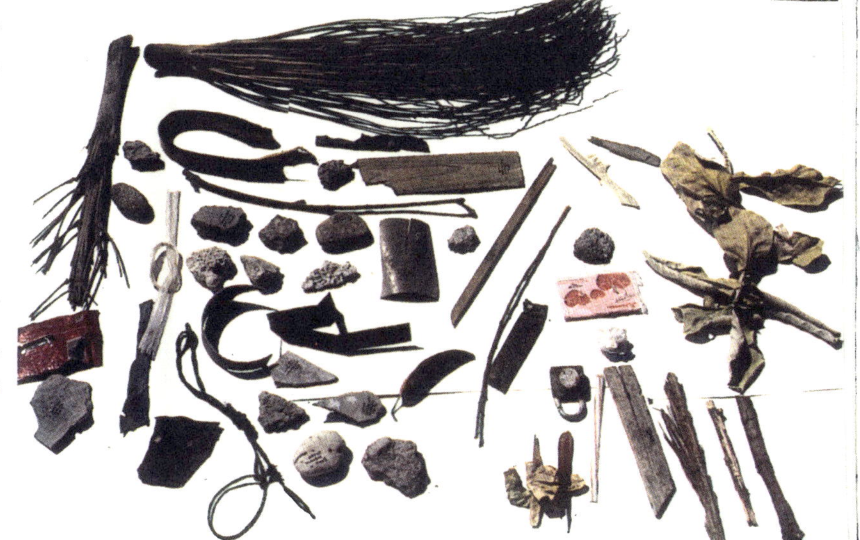

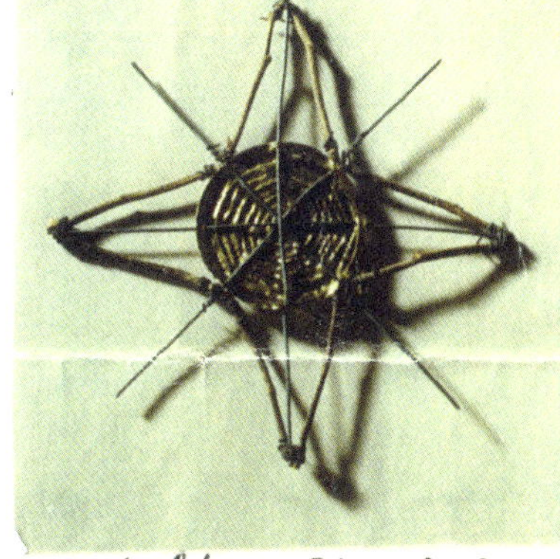

Circle & Line Star 20 x 20 cm

oil on canvas 1991 . 75 x 50 cm

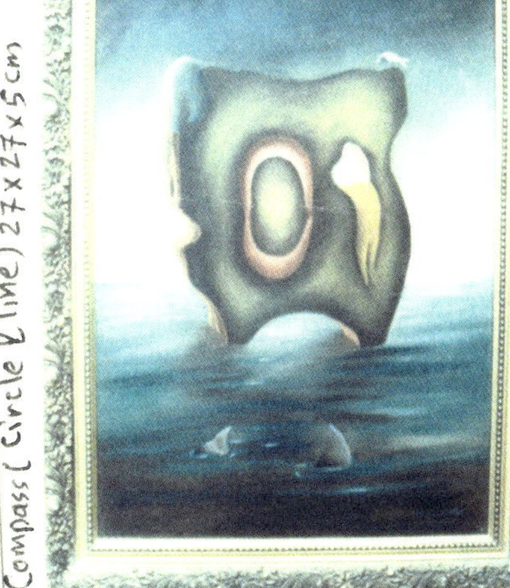

Compass (Circle & line) 27 x 27 x 5 cm

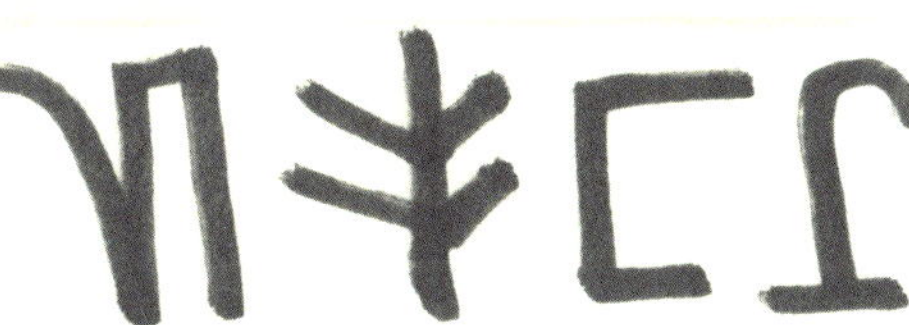

Mobile Exhibition . Fujairah .

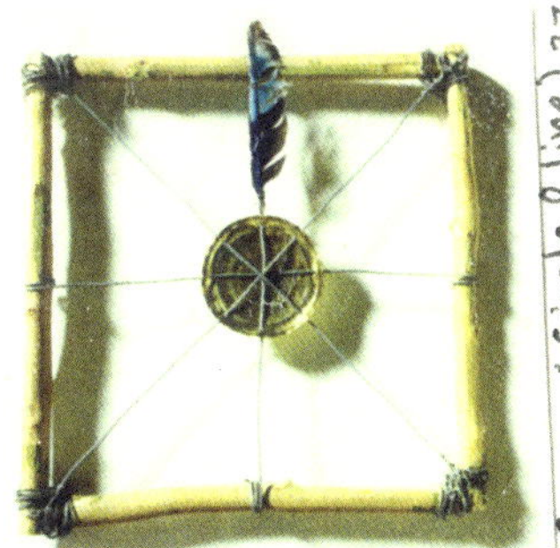

The 4th solo Exhibition . Sharm Café Fuj . 1999 .

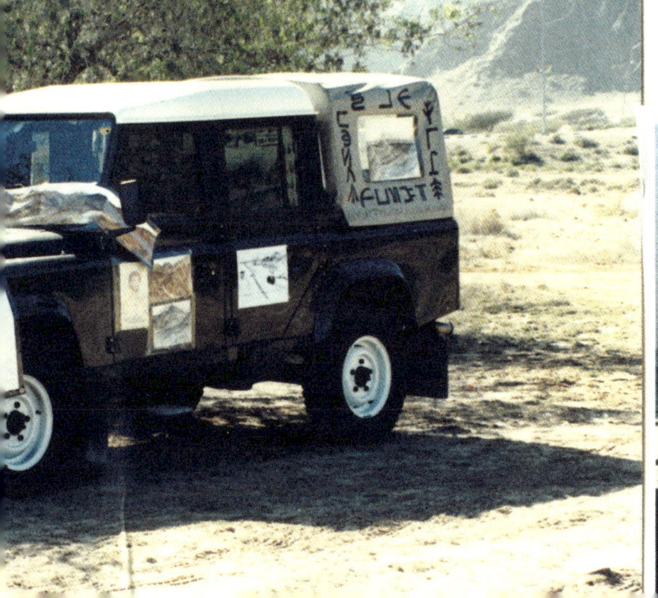

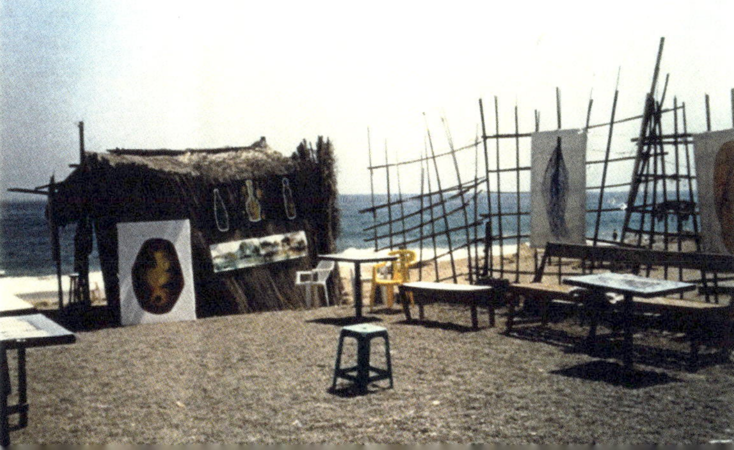

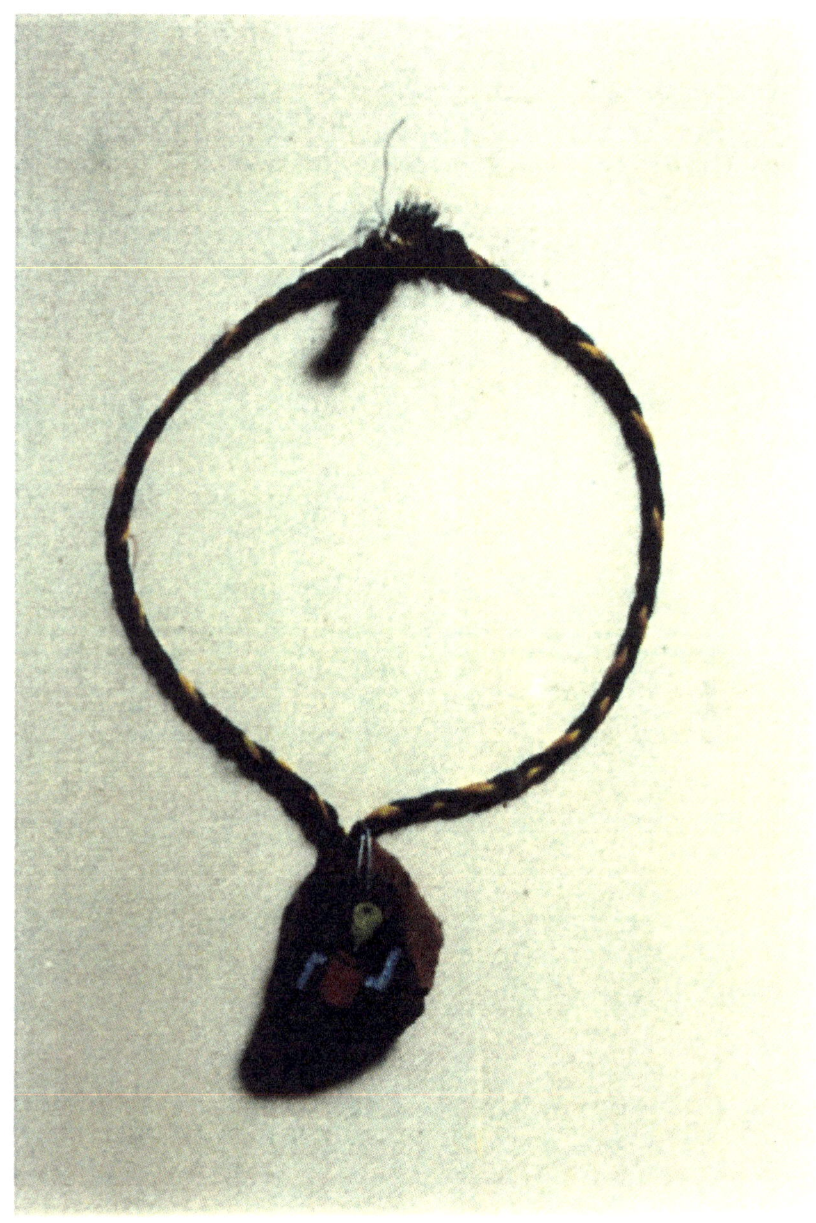

١٠الأحد ـ الشجرة

38

١. خيط من القطن بثلاثة ألوان صنعته أمي .

٢. قطعتان من الفخار ورسمة رطوطم . القطعتان عبارة عن صفارة قديمة توضع بينهما جزء من ورقة خضراء لشجرة الموز وتنفخ كآلة نفخ .

39

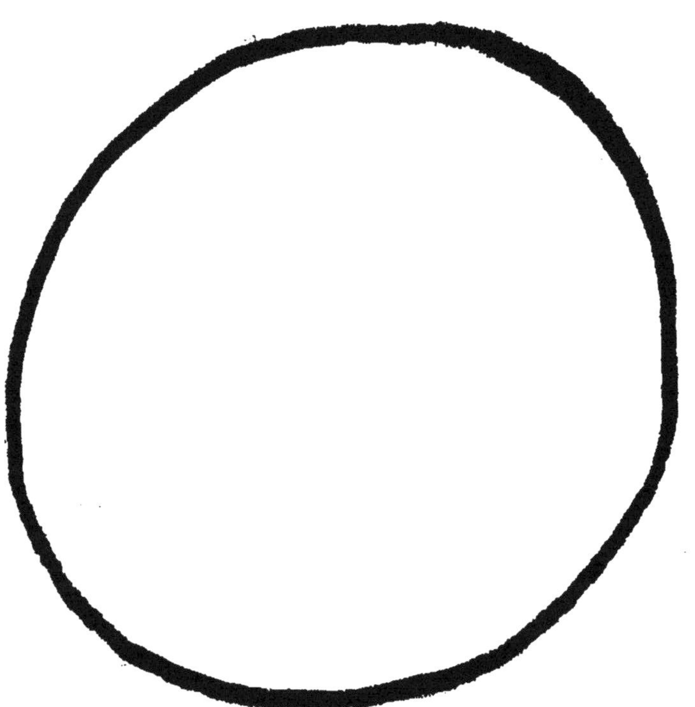

22

١. الدائرة

ـ تمثل الدائرة أطواق التأمل السبعة ، حدق بصرياً بالدائرة لترى الدائرة و ظلها (محيطها) ◎ ثم دائرتان متداخلتان و ظلهما ◉◉ ، ركز ذهنياً بالدائرة لتستحضر صوراً مادية تأخذ أشكال دائرية .

ـ لممارسة طقس التأمل الحركي أرسم دائرة كبيرة على الأرض و دور حولها من الخارج ثم أدخل وأخرج منها عدة مرات أو أحضر طوقاً واسعاً و

23

١٠ . قنينة دواء (رؤوس الجبال) .

١١ . لوحة (قط و قنينة)
اكريليك على ورق .
١٩٩٨ - ٢٩ × ٢٣ cm .

١٢ . قلم حبر من المعدن .

١٣ . علبة بلاستيكية (أرز) بداخلها
بقايا عش طائر .

١٤ . عازل ذكري بداخل كيس من
البلاستيك .

92

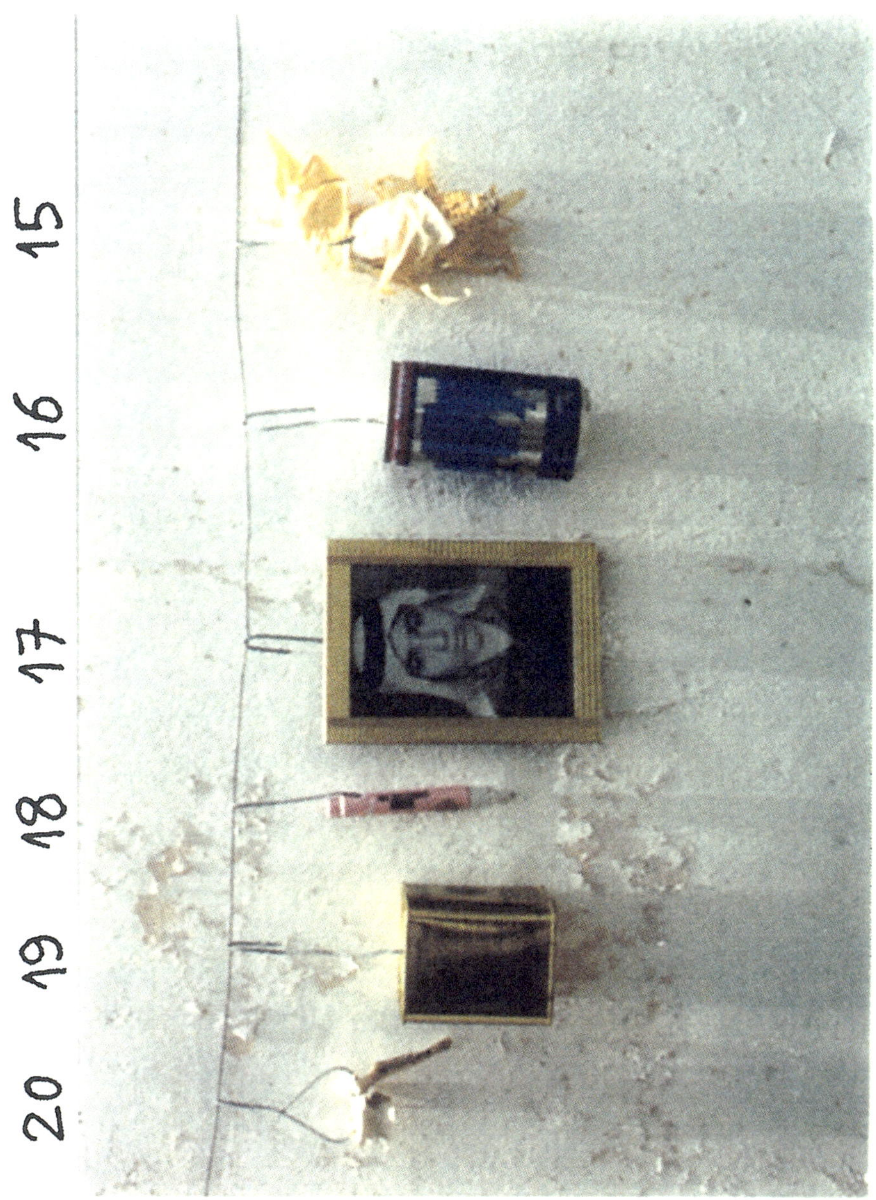

93

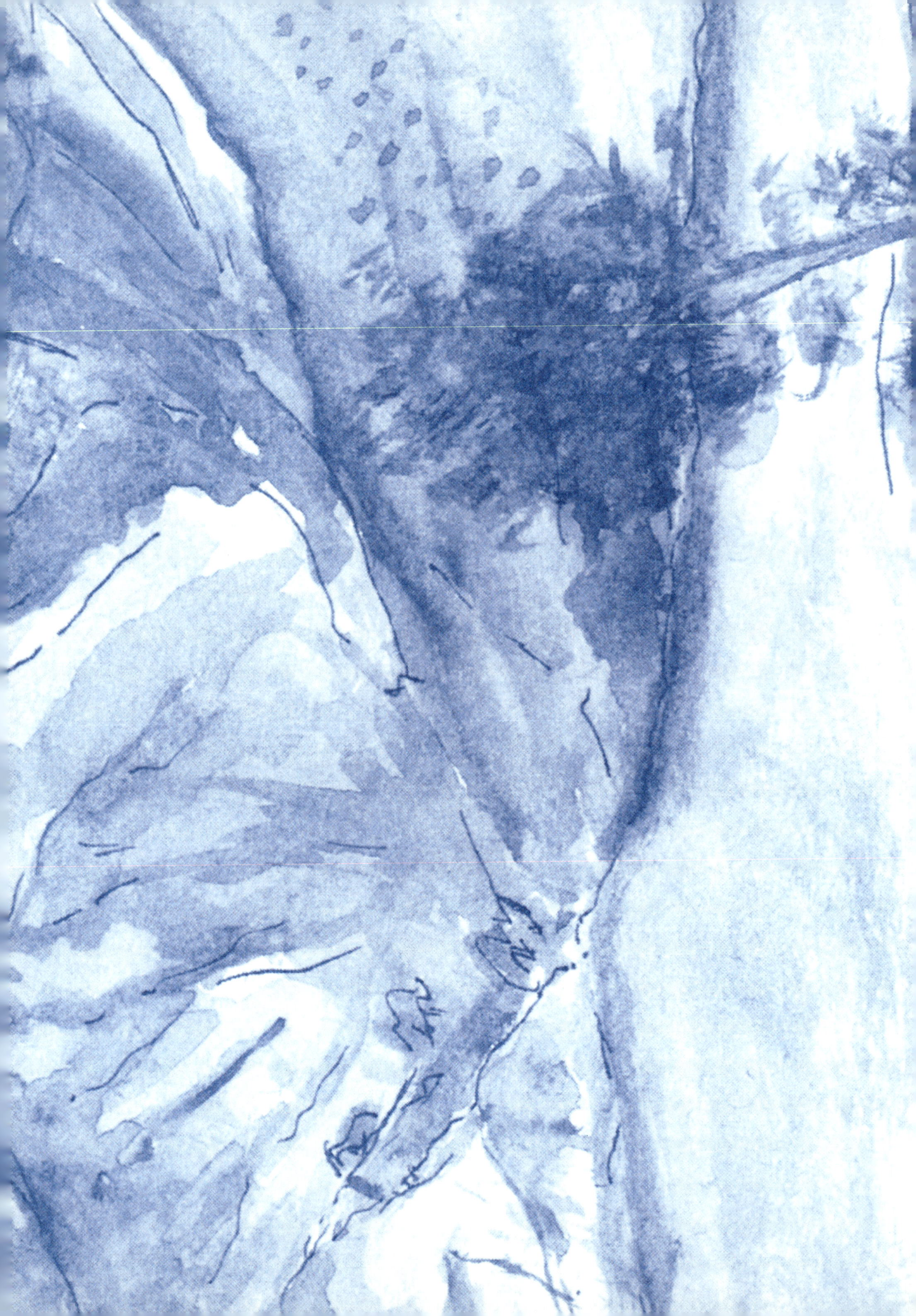

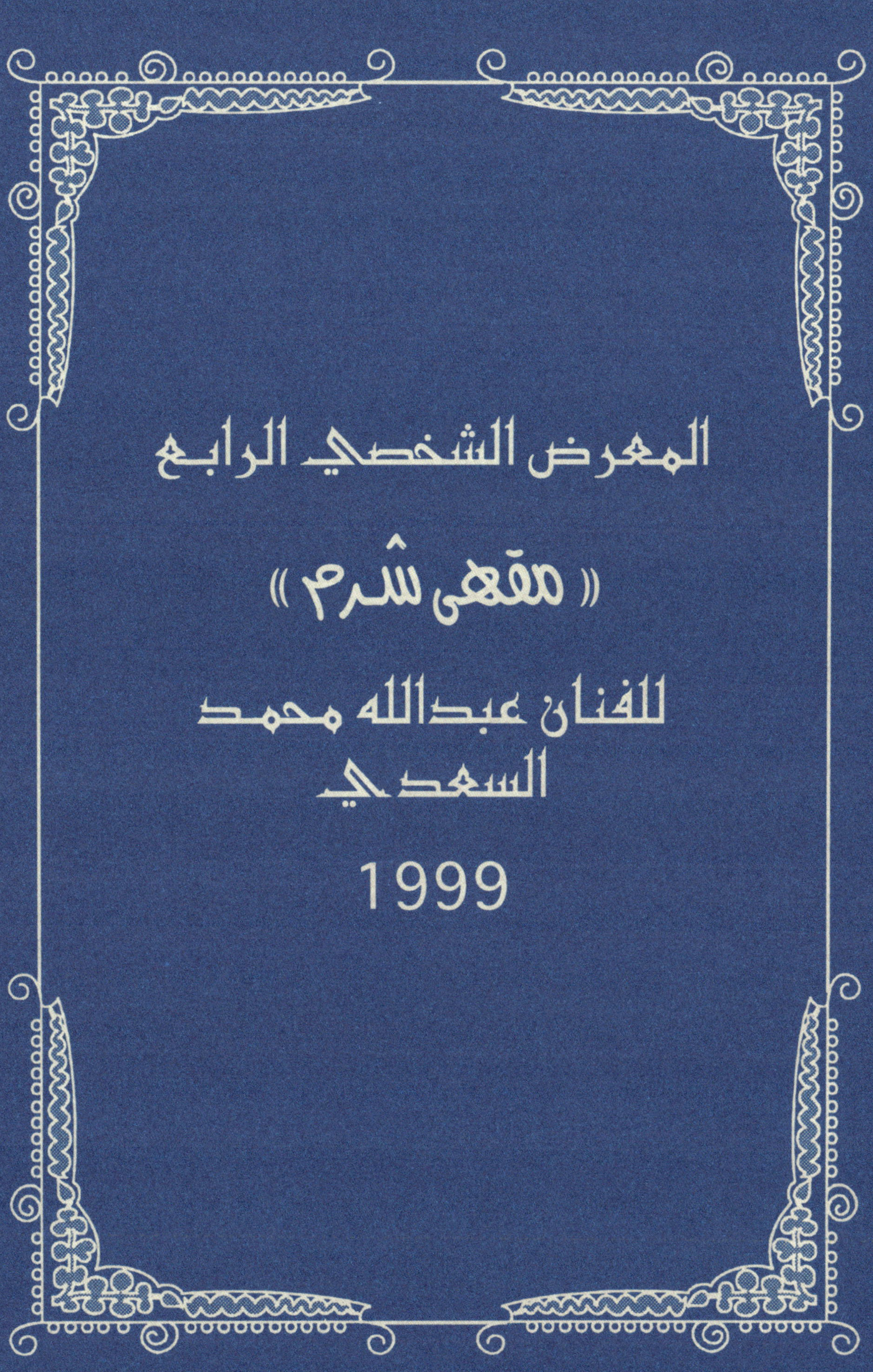

المعرض الشخصي الرابع

« مقهى شرم »

للفنان عبدالله محمد السعدي

1999

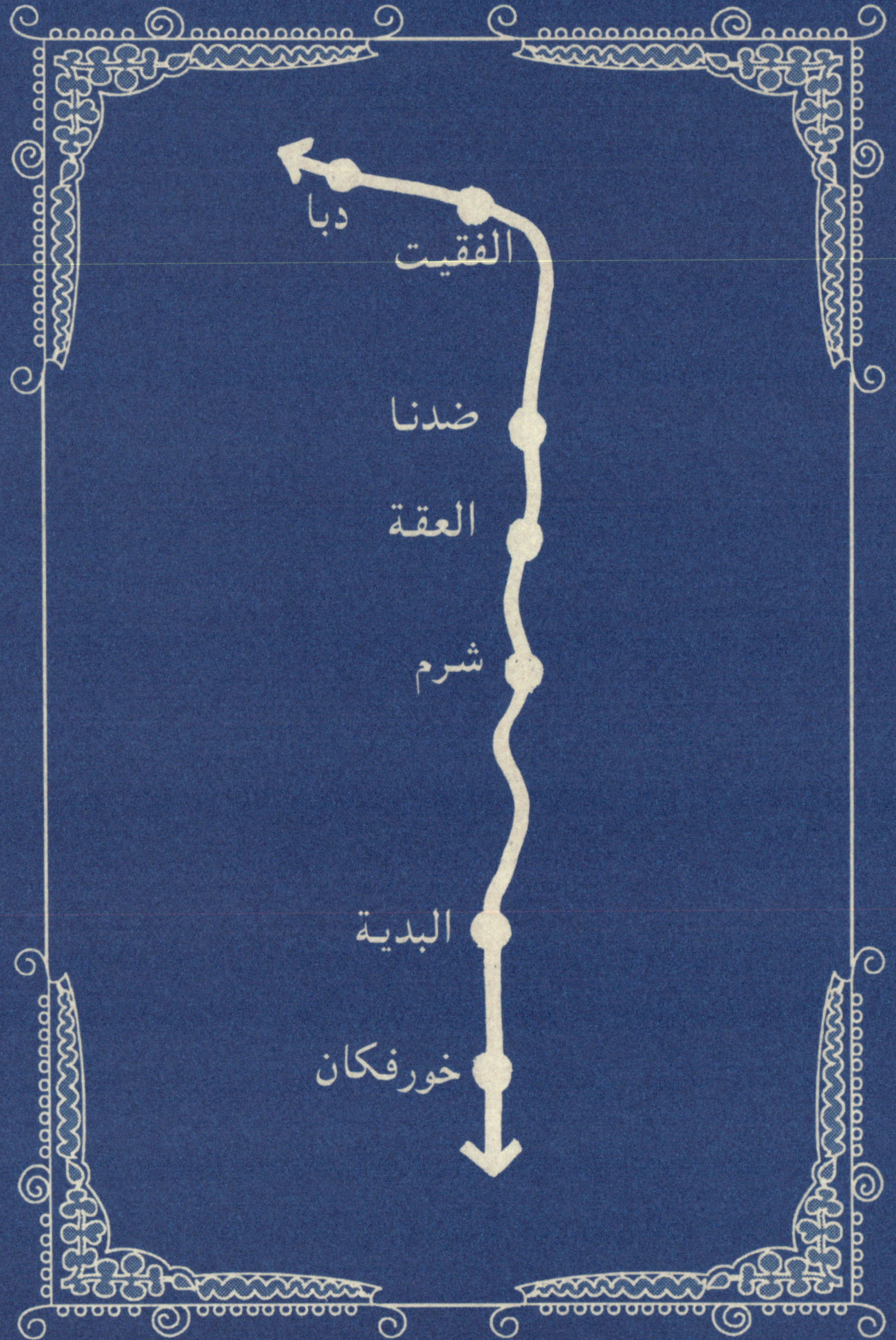

دبا
الفقيت
ضدنا
العقة
شرم
البدية
خورفكان

مقهى شرم

- يقع المقهى بقرية (شرم) التي تقع على طريق (خورفكان – دبا)

- يرتاد المقهى الناس، الحيوانات ، الطيور ، الحشرات، الهواء، الروائح، القمر والنجوم، الليل والنهار، الشمس، القوارب، والأشياء ويسكن بجواره البحر والرمل.

عبدالله محمد السعدي

1999

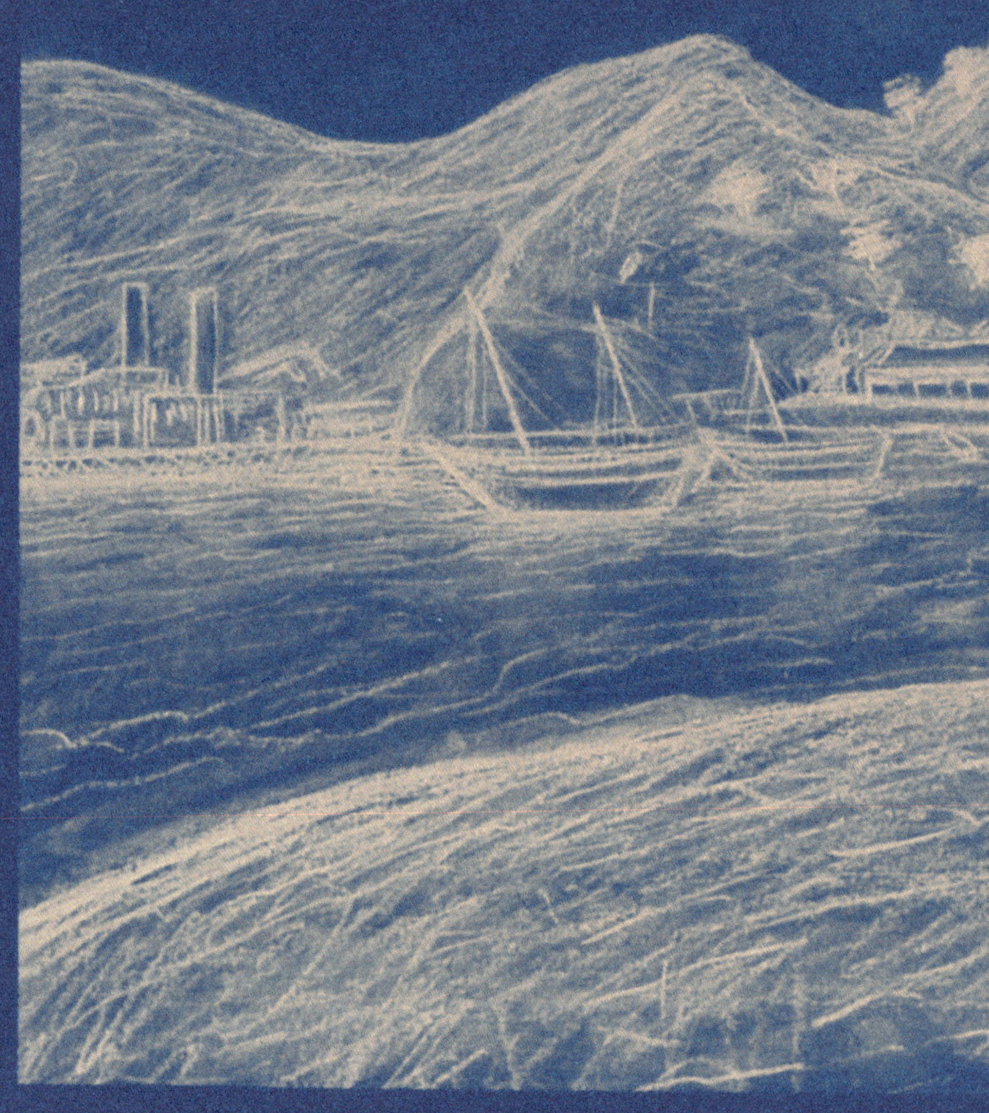

1993 (34x49 cm) ة

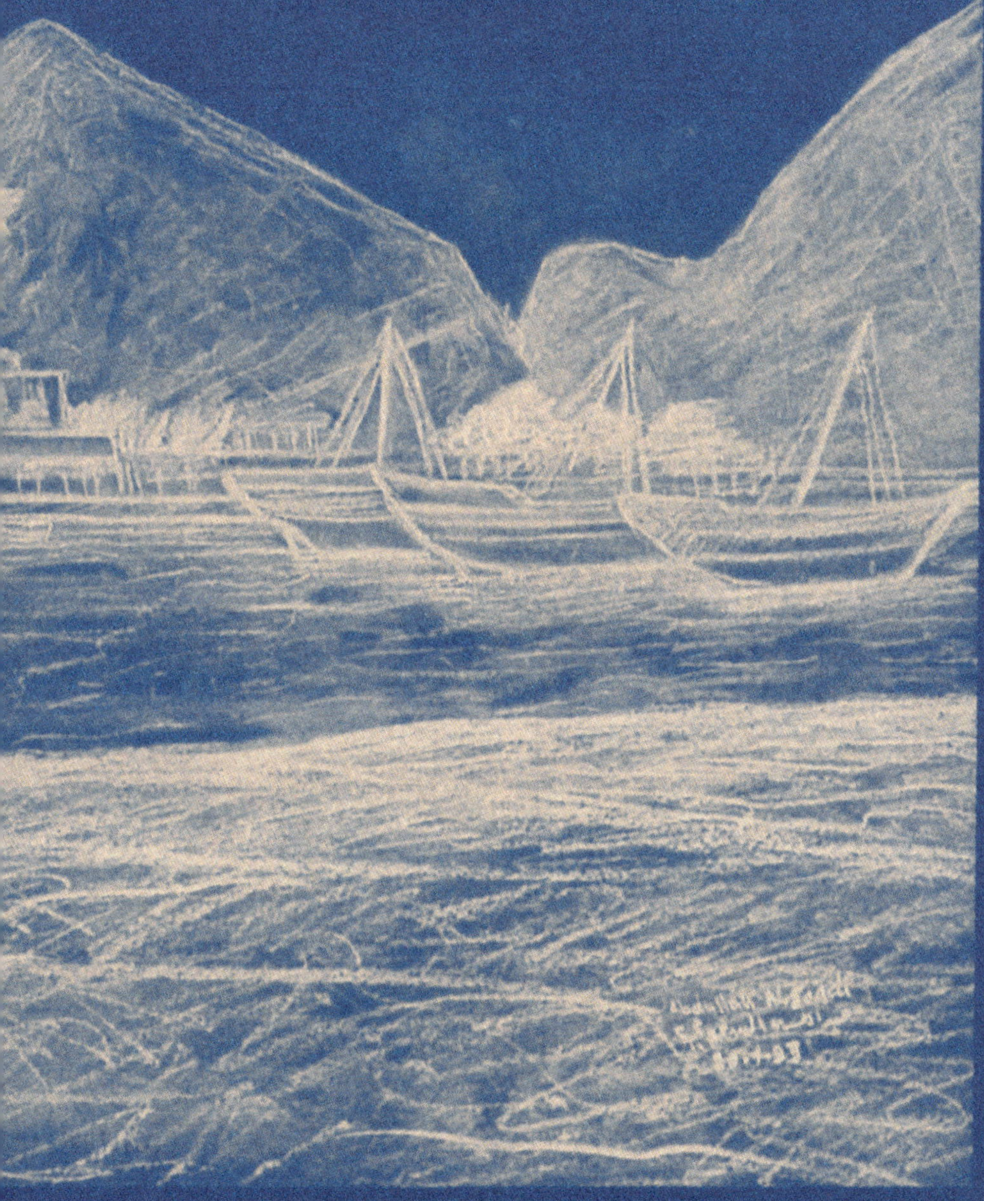

خورفكان - فحم على

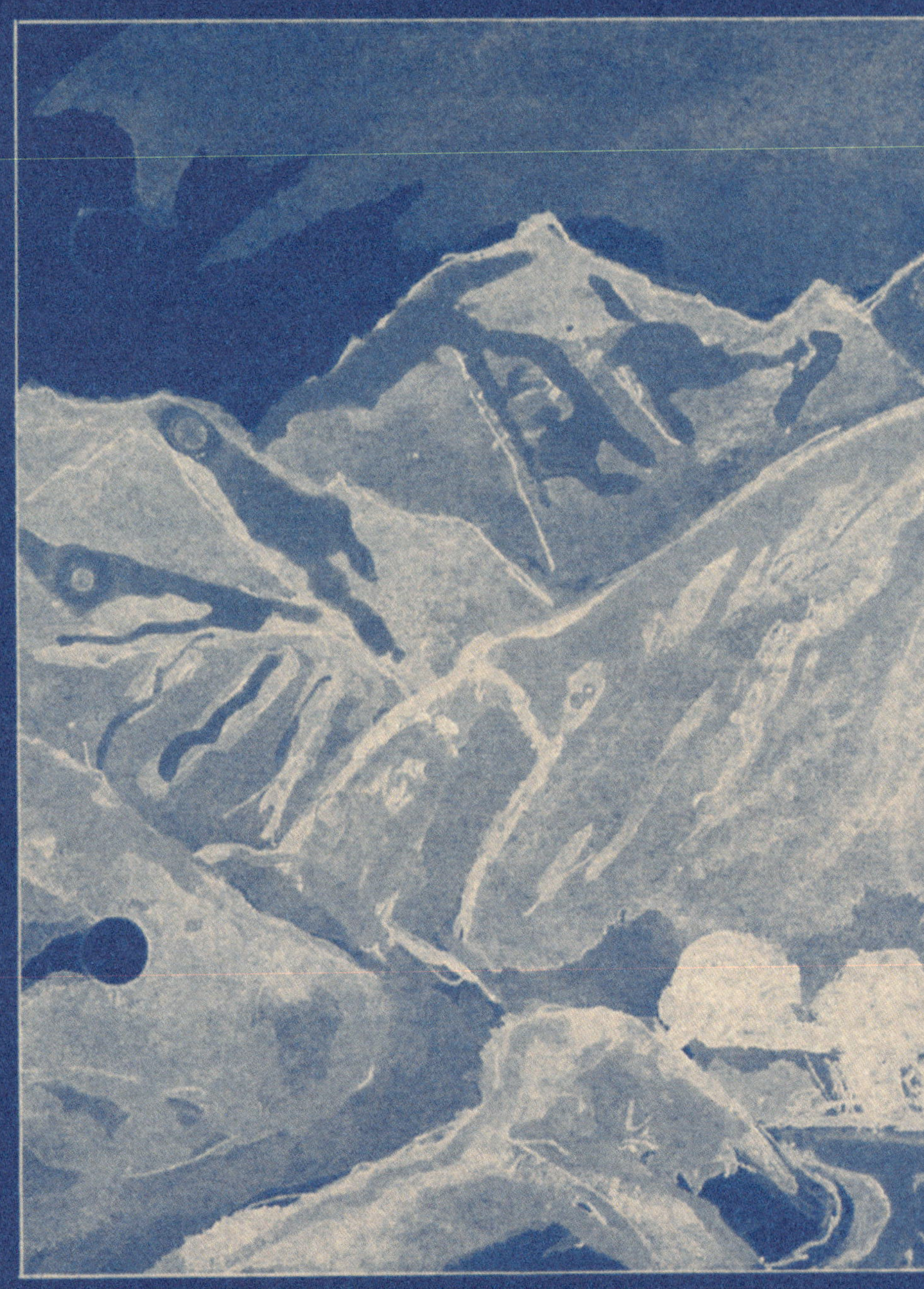

1997 (10x15 cm) ورق

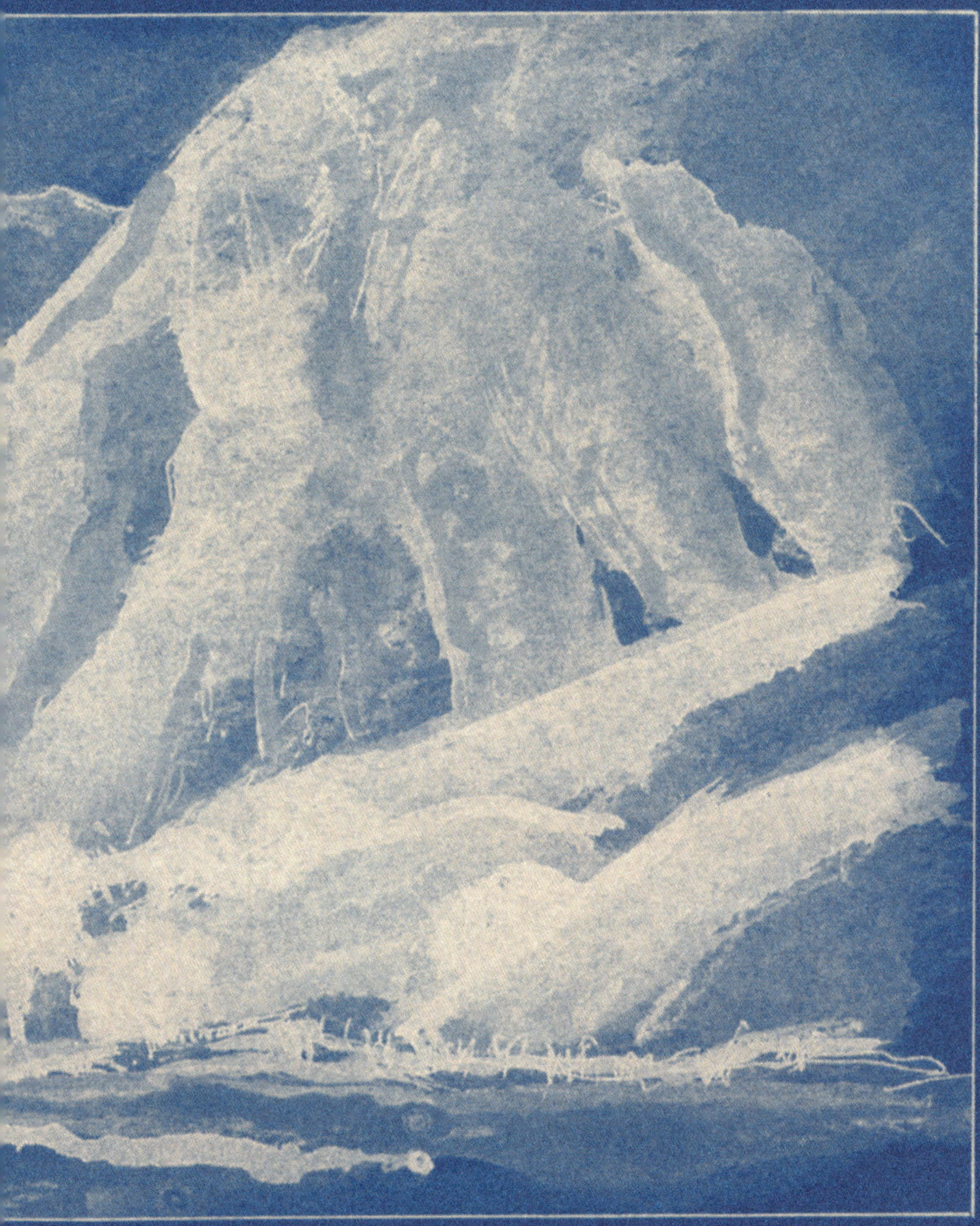

خورفكان (واديشي) حبر

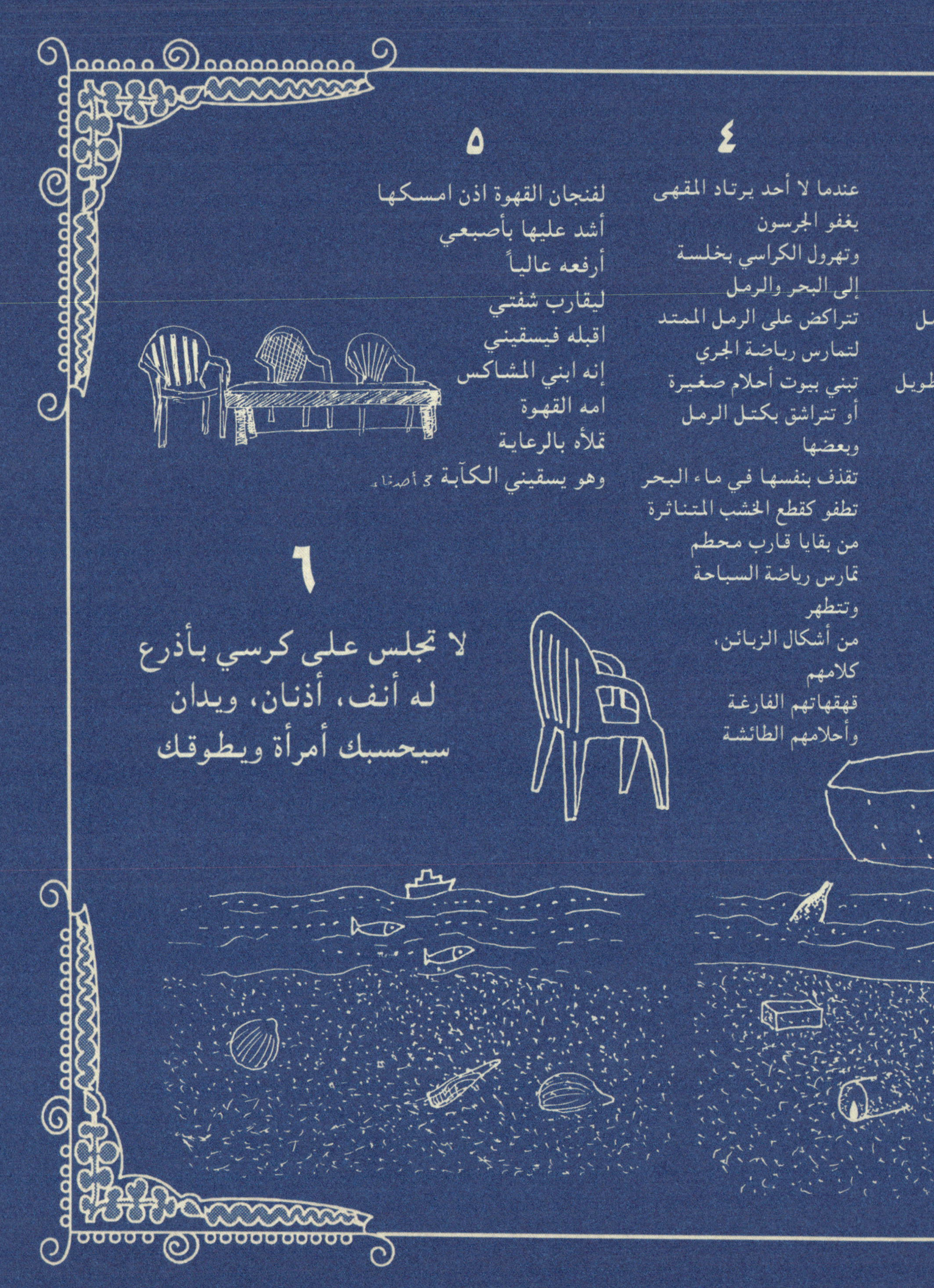

٤

عندما لا أحد يرتاد المقهى
يغفو الجرسون
وتهرول الكراسي بخلسة
إلى البحر والرمل
تتراكض على الرمل الممتد
لتمارس رياضة الجري
تبني بيوت أحلام صغيرة
أو تتراشق بكتل الرمل
وبعضها
تقذف بنفسها في ماء البحر
تطفو كقطع الخشب المتناثرة
من بقايا قارب محطم
تمارس رياضة السباحة
وتتطهر
من أشكال الزبائن،
كلامهم
قهقهاتهم الفارغة
وأحلامهم الطائشة

٥

لفنجان القهوة اذن امسكها
أشد عليها بأصبعي
أرفعه عالياً
ليقارب شفتي
اقبله فيسقيني
إنه ابني المشاكس
امه القهوة
تملأه بالرعاية
وهو يسقيني الكآبة

٦

لا تجلس على كرسي بأذرع
له أنف، أذنان، ويدان
سيحسبك أمرأة ويطوقك

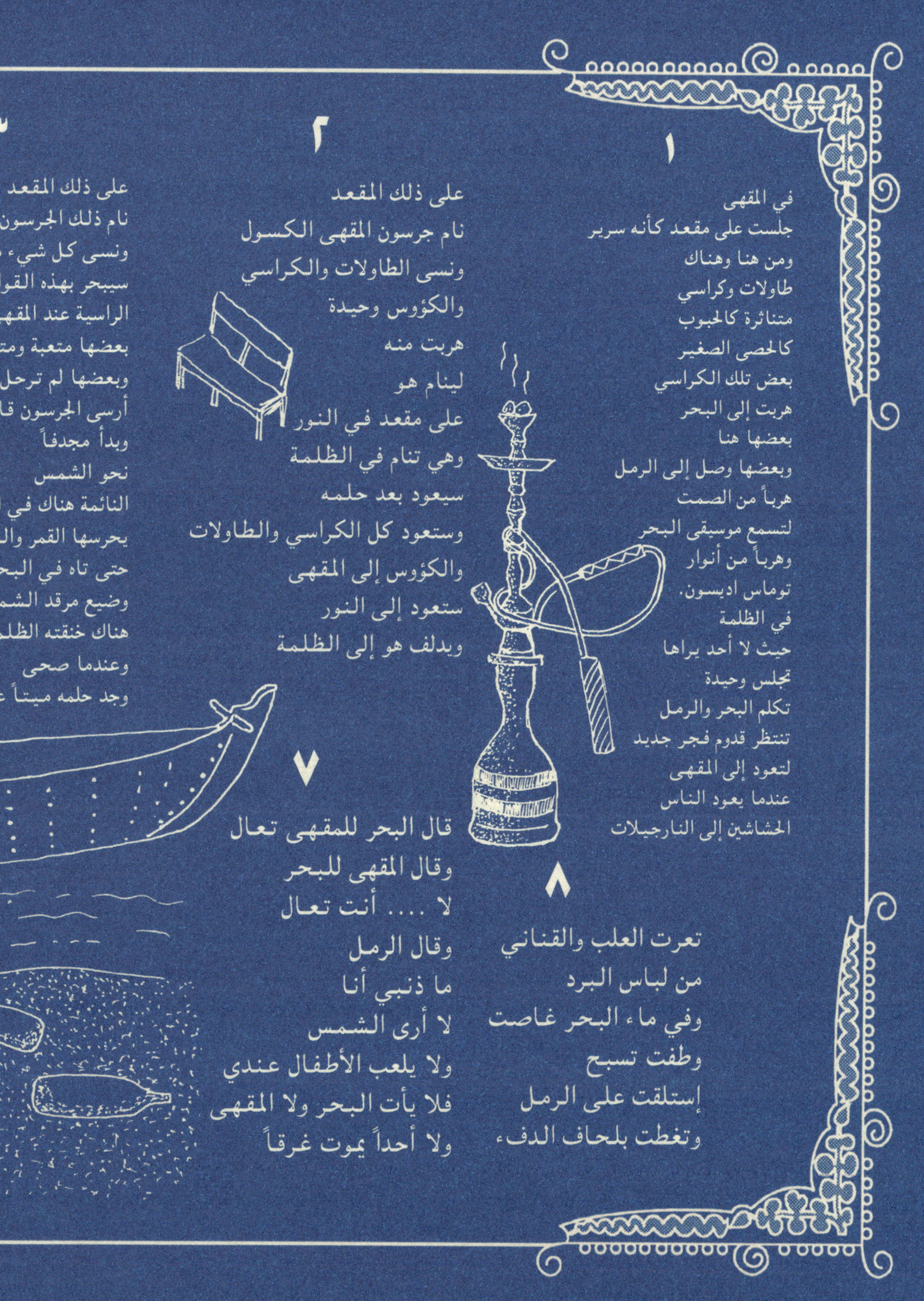

١

في المقهى
جلست على مقعد كأنه سرير
ومن هنا وهناك
طاولات وكراسي
متناثرة كالحبوب
كالحصى الصغير
بعض تلك الكراسي
هربت إلى البحر
بعضها هنا
وبعضها وصل إلى الرمل
هرباً من الصمت
لتسمع موسيقى البحر
وهرباً من أنوار
توماس اديسون.
في الظلمة
حيث لا أحد يراها
تجلس وحيدة
تكلم البحر والرمل
تنتظر قدوم فجر جديد
لتعود إلى المقهى
عندما يعود الناس
الحشاشين إلى النارجيلات

٢

على ذلك المقعد
نام جرسون المقهى الكسول
ونسى الطاولات والكراسي
والكؤوس وحيدة
هربت منه
لينام هو
على مقعد في النور
وهي تنام في الظلمة
سيعود بعد حلمه
وستعود كل الكراسي والطاولات
والكؤوس إلى المقهى
ستعود إلى النور
ويدلف هو إلى الظلمة

٣

على ذلك المقعد
نام ذلك الجرسون
ونسى كل شيء م
سيبحر بهذه القوا
الراسية عند المقه
بعضها متعبة ومت
وبعضها لم ترحل
أرسى الجرسون قا
وبدأ مجدفاً
نحو الشمس
النائمة هناك في ا
يحرسها القمر والن
حتى تاه في البحر
وضيع مرقد الشم
هناك خنقته الظلم
وعندما صحى
وجد حلمه ميتاً ع

٧

قال البحر للمقهى تعال
وقال المقهى للبحر
لا .... أنت تعال
وقال الرمل
ما ذنبي أنا
لا أرى الشمس
ولا يلعب الأطفال عندي
فلا يأت البحر ولا المقهى
ولا أحداً يموت غرقاً

٨

تعرت العلب والقناني
من لباس البرد
وفي ماء البحر غاصت
وطفت تسبح
إستلقت على الرمل
وتغطت بلحاف الدفء

١

على حبل الغسيل
...مات البحر الباردة.

١٢

هجر الناس ثيابهم وبيوتهم
ليغسلوا أجسادهم
في الغسالة عند البحر
لتجف تحت الشمس.

١٣

ترك خرطوم الماء
بيوت القرية عطشى
وجاء إلى البحر ليشرب

١٦

قفزت سمكة من ماء البحر إلى المقهى
لتشرب قنينة ماء معدني.

١٧

ألقت الشاة نظرة على المقهى من بعيد
وتسألت : ياترى أتوجد بالمقهى
قهوة كابتشينو أو اكسبرس !!

١

...م، ترتعش ، تتعرق
...الغسيل في مرج وهرج
...ون، تتطهر من
...من قبل المتبقية،
...أفواه الكريهة.

١٨

لأنه لا توجد بالمقهى
غسالة صحون أو غسالة ثياب
لذا يغتسل الجرسون في البحر.

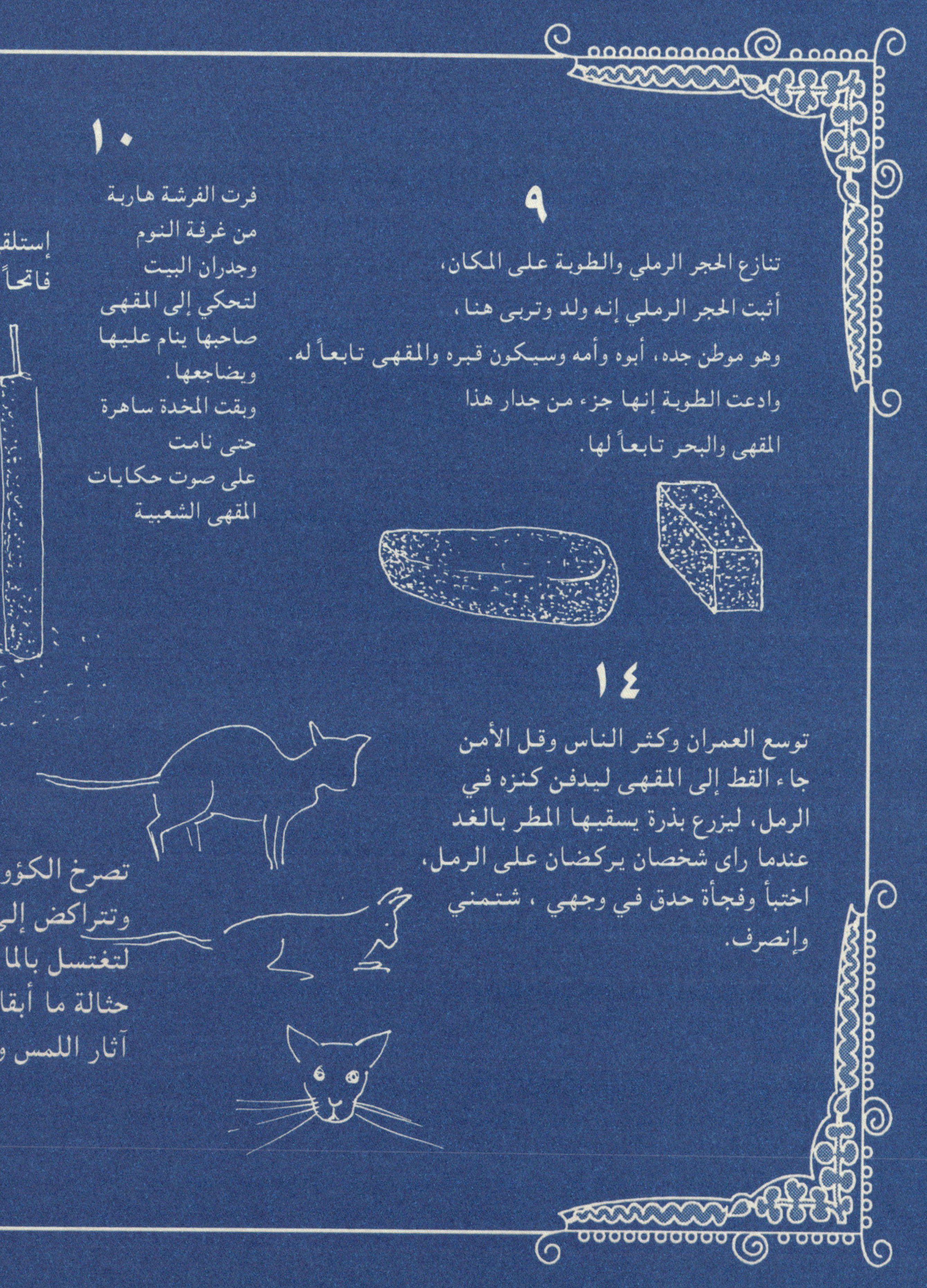

٩

تنازع الحجر الرملي والطوبة على المكان،

أثبت الحجر الرملي إنه ولد وتربى هنا،

وهو موطن جده، أبوه وأمه وسيكون قبره والمقهى تابعاً له.

وادعت الطوبة إنها جزء من جدار هذا المقهى والبحر تابعاً لها.

١٠

فرت الفرشة هاربة
من غرفة النوم
وجدران البيت
لتحكي إلى المقهى
صاحبها ينام عليها
ويضاجعها.
وبقت المخدة ساهرة
حتى نامت
على صوت حكايات
المقهى الشعبية

إستلقى
فاتحاً

١٤

توسع العمران وكثر الناس وقل الأمن

جاء القط إلى المقهى ليدفن كنزه في الرمل، ليزرع بذرة يسقيها المطر بالغد

عندما راى شخصان يركضان على الرمل،

اختبأ وفجأة حدق في وجهي ، شتمني وإنصرف.

تصرخ الكؤوس
وتتراكض إلى
لتغتسل بالماء
حثالة ما أبقاه
آثار اللمس و

ورق ی (10x15 cm) 1997

خورفكان (واديشي) حبـ

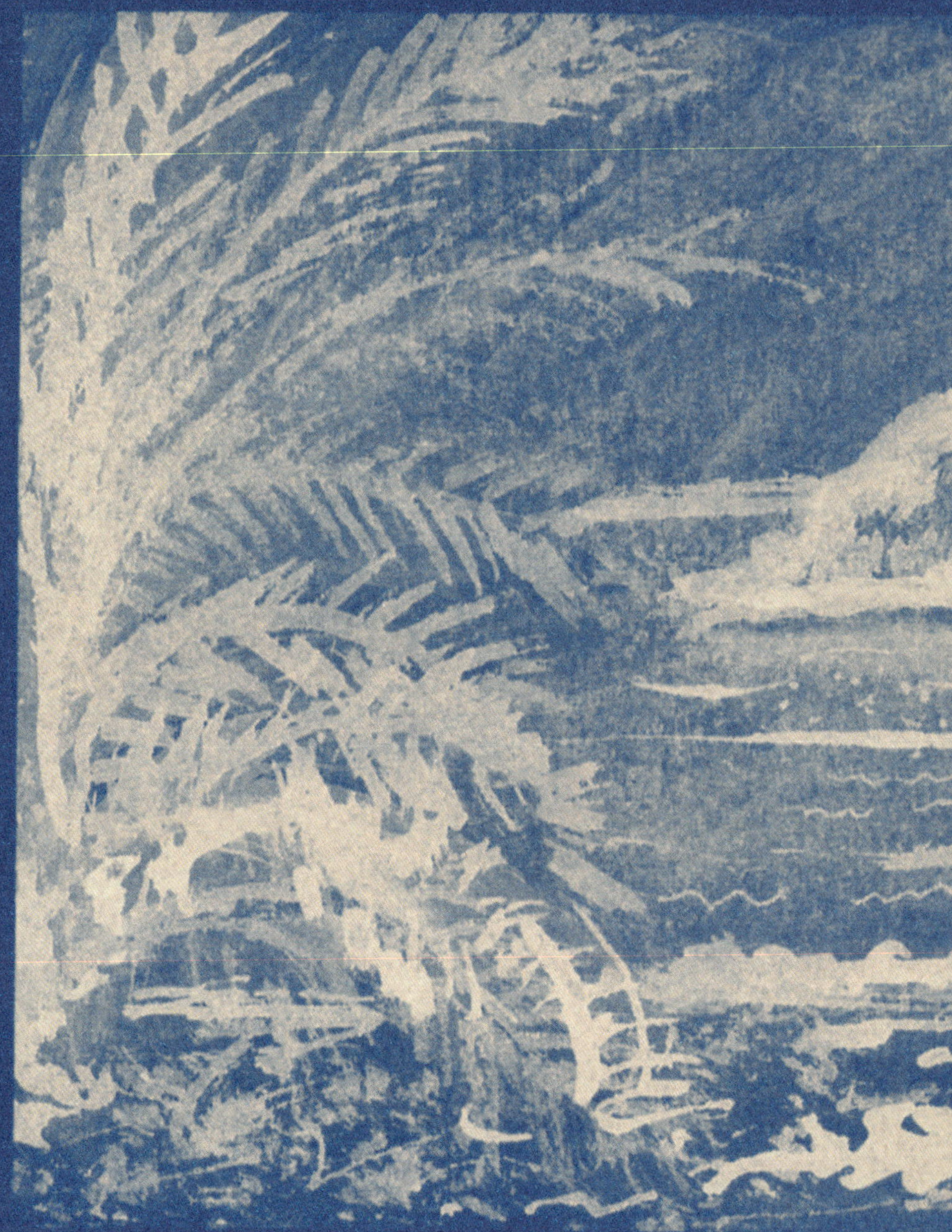

1999 (10x19 cm)

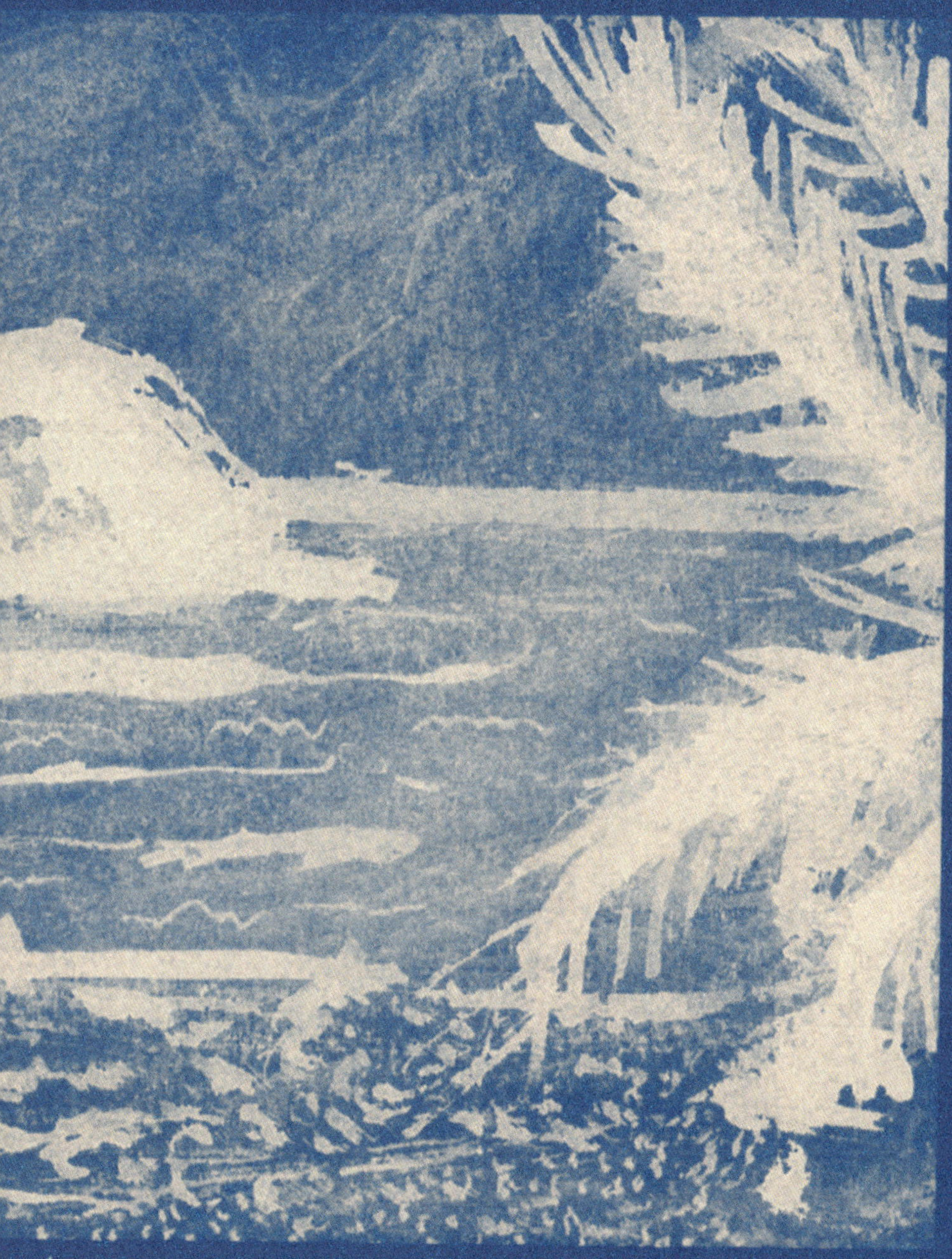
الفقيت - حبر على

- عبدالله محمد السعدي ١٩٦٧.

- مدرس – خورفكان

- ليسانس لغة انجليزية – جامعة الإمارات

- عضو جمعية الإمارات للفنون التشكيلية

- سافر مع سفينة شباب العالم ١٩٩٢

- درس في اليابان ٩٤ – ١٩٩٦م

- يشارك في معارض داخلية وخارجية

- دورة في جامعة ادنبره – اسكوتلندا ١٩٩٨

- أقام ثلاثة معارض شخصية

P.O. Box : 9761
Khorfakkan - Sharjah, U.A.E.
Mobile : 050-629 2458
Tel. : 09-2383209
E-mail : alsaadi9@emirates.net.ae

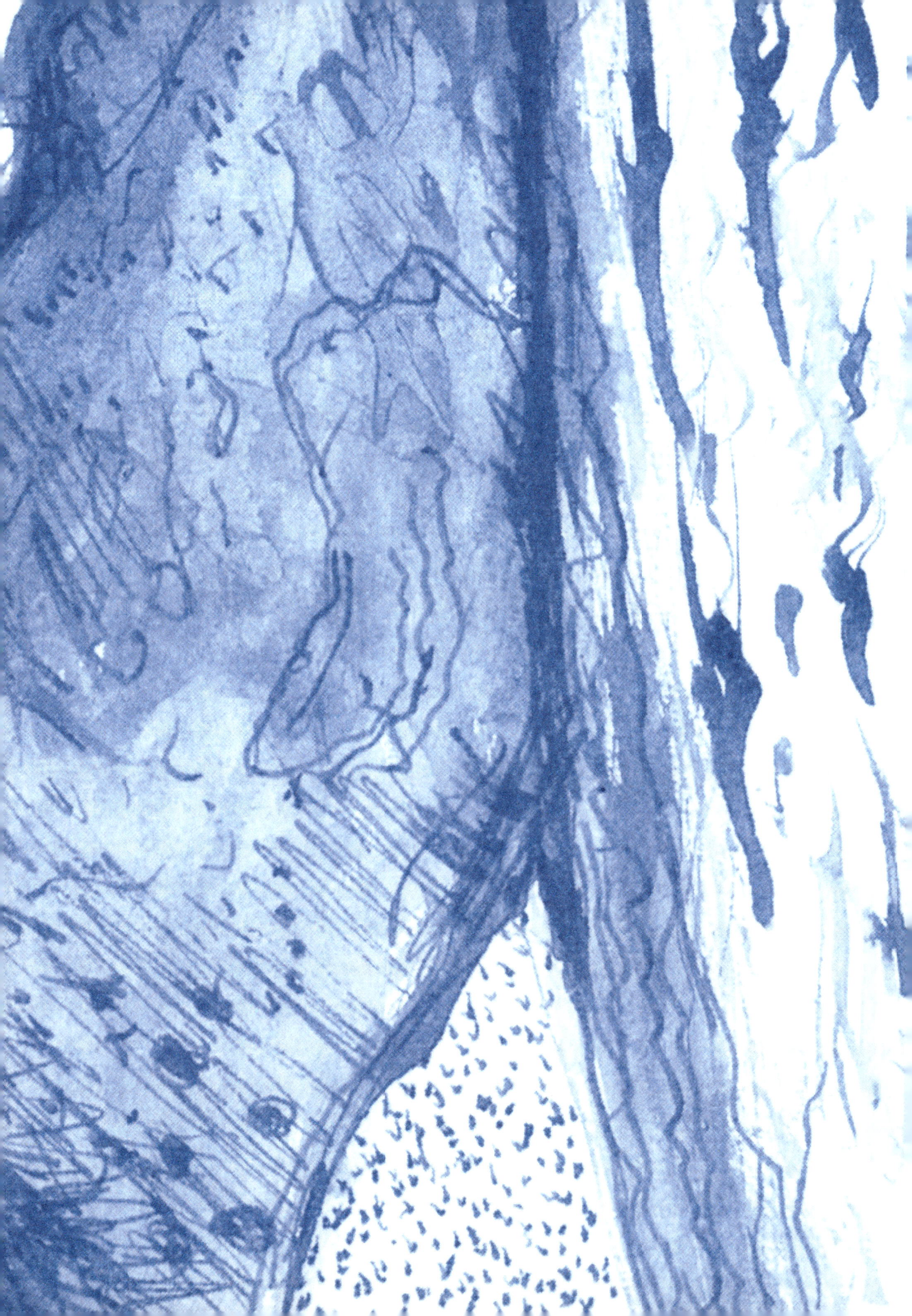

Abya Yala

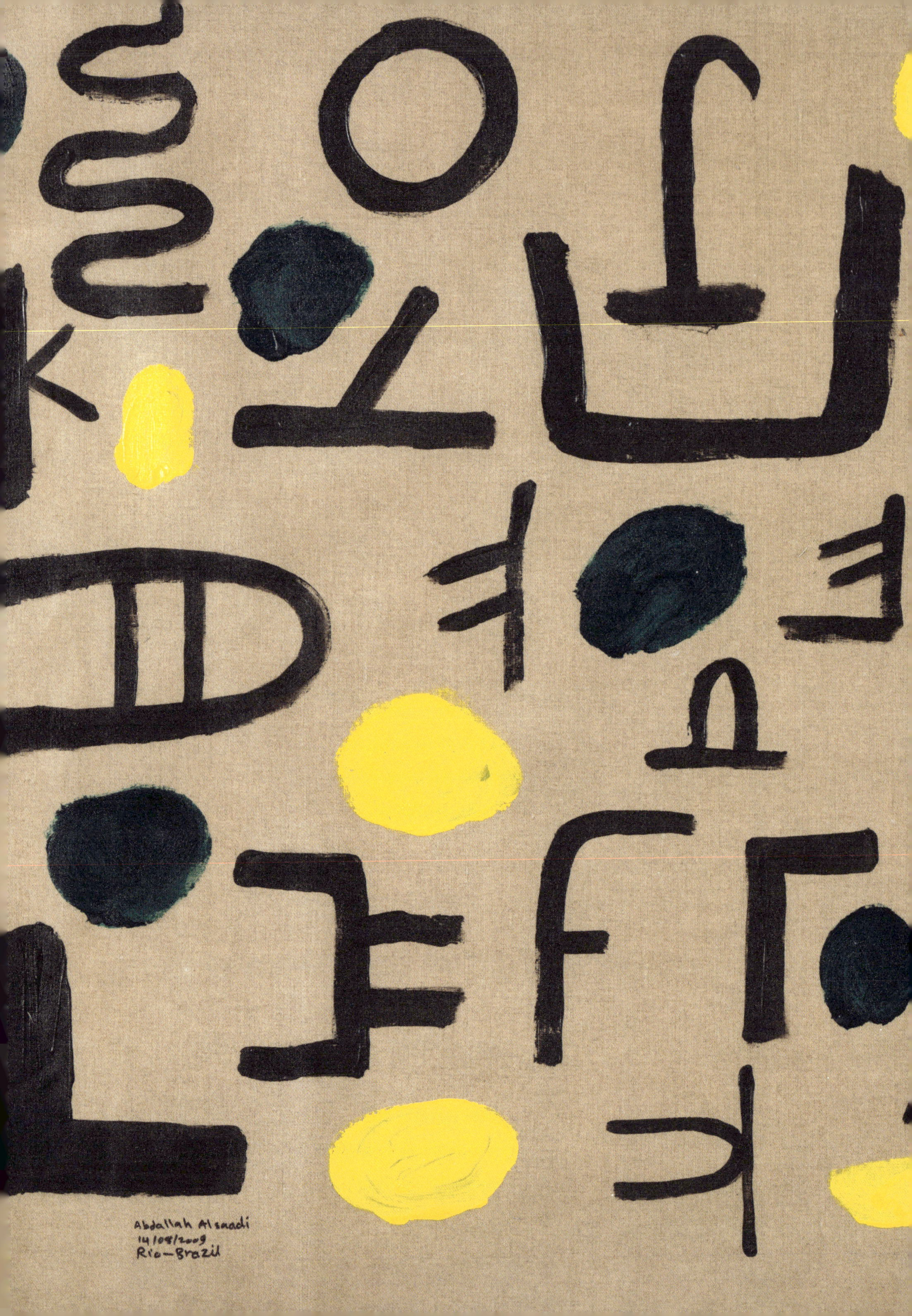

Abdallah Alsaadi
14/08/2009
Rio-Brazil

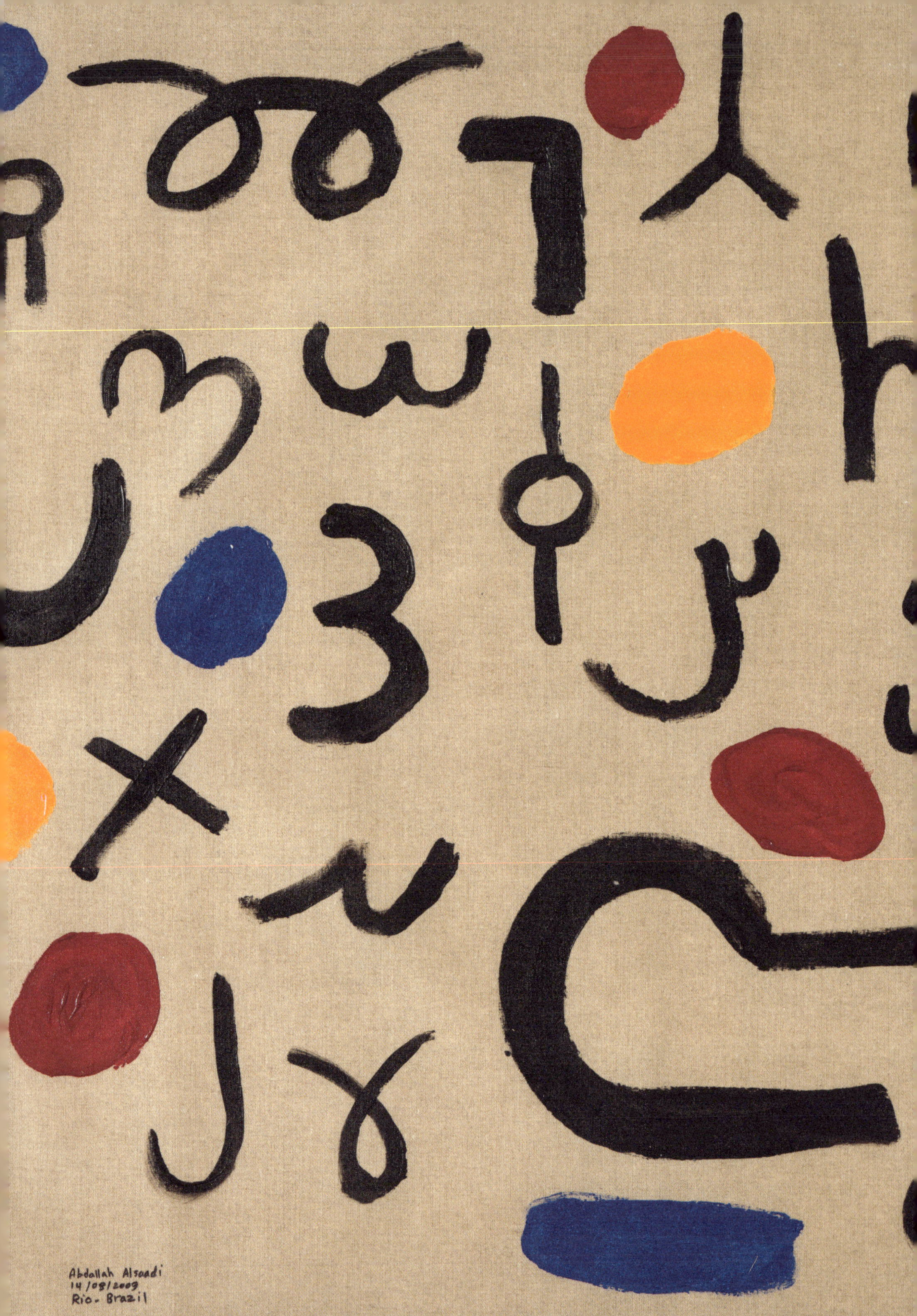

Abdallah Alsaadi
14/08/2009
Rio. Brazil

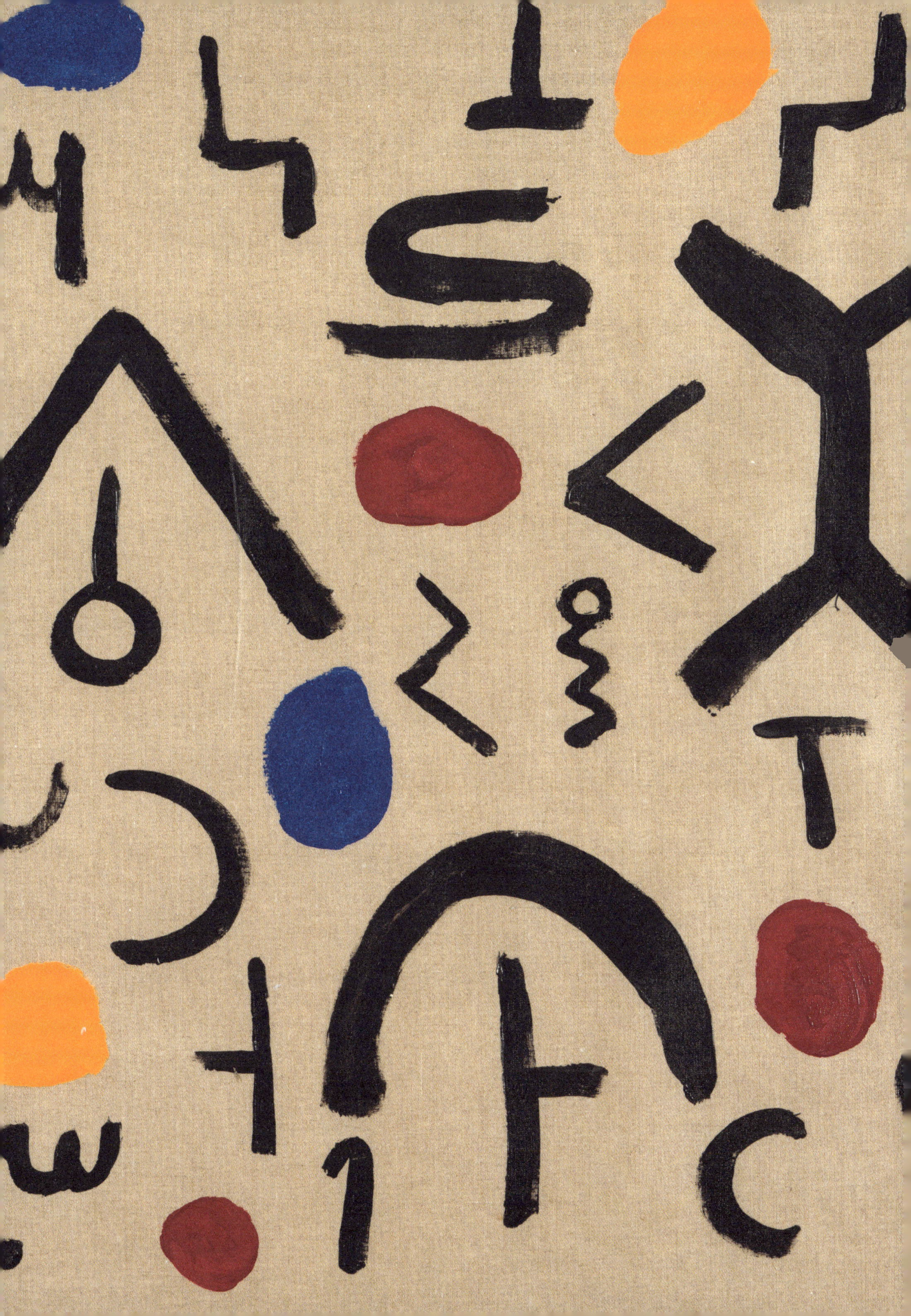

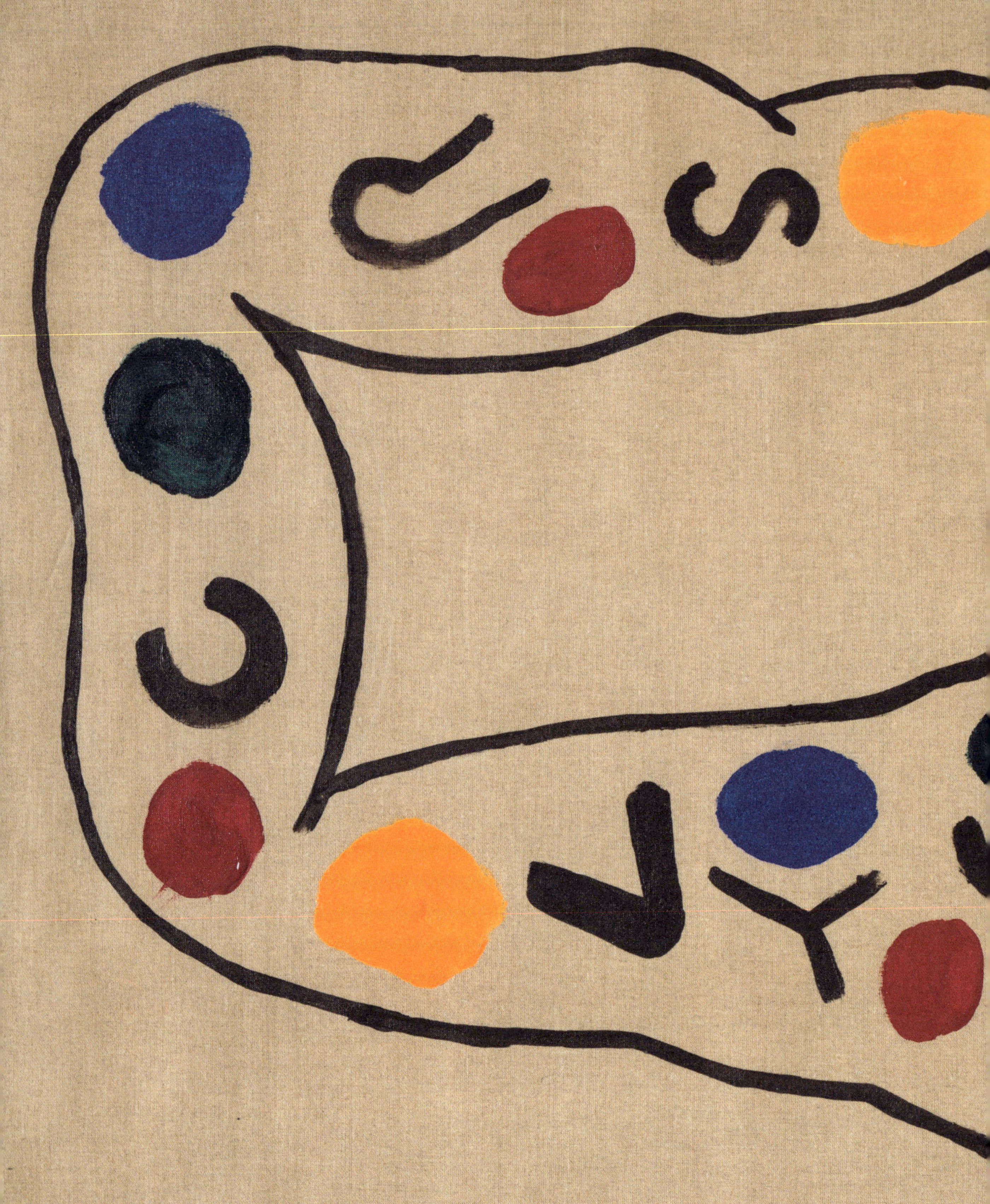
Abdallah Alsaadi
15/08/2009
Rio - Brazil

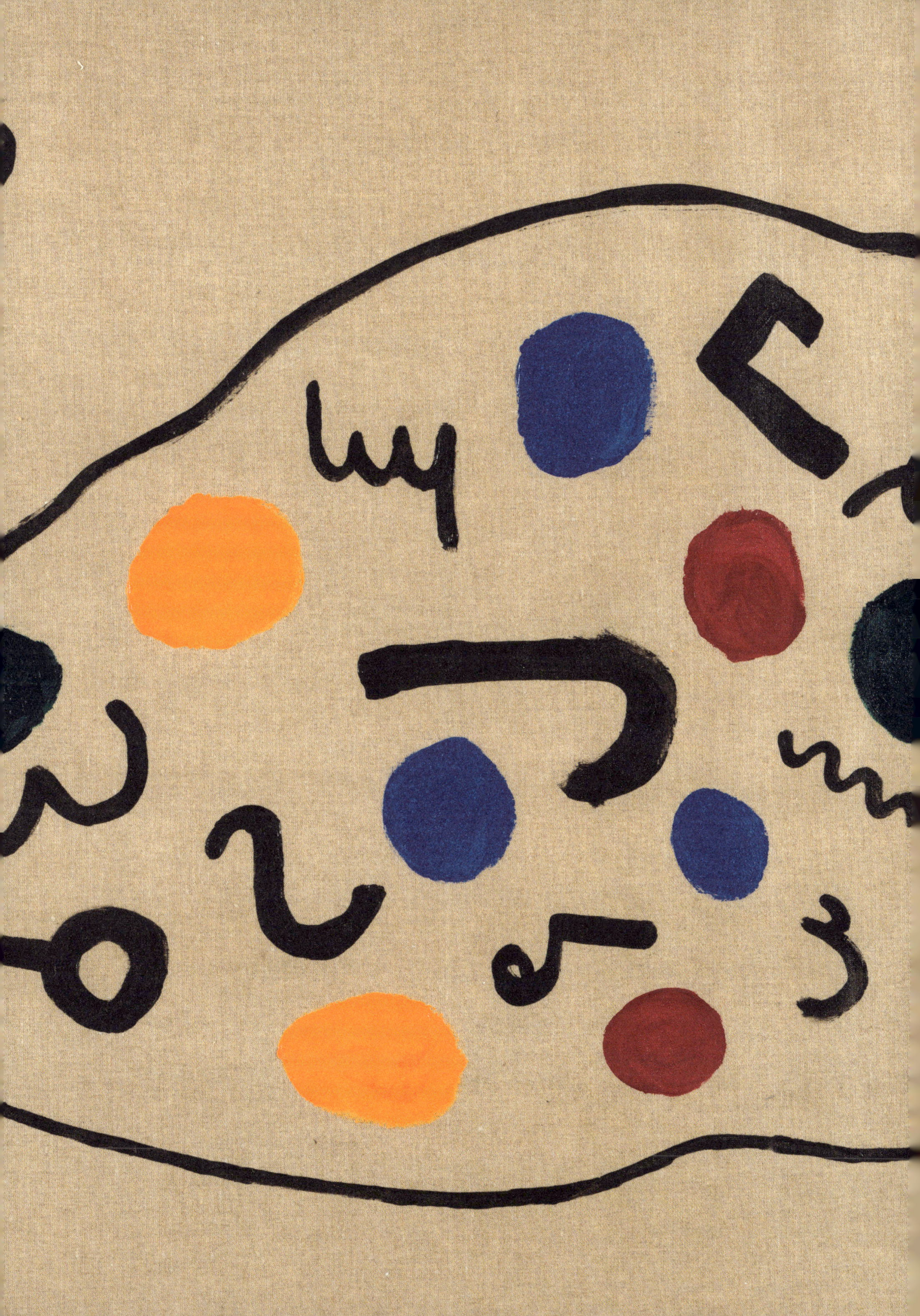

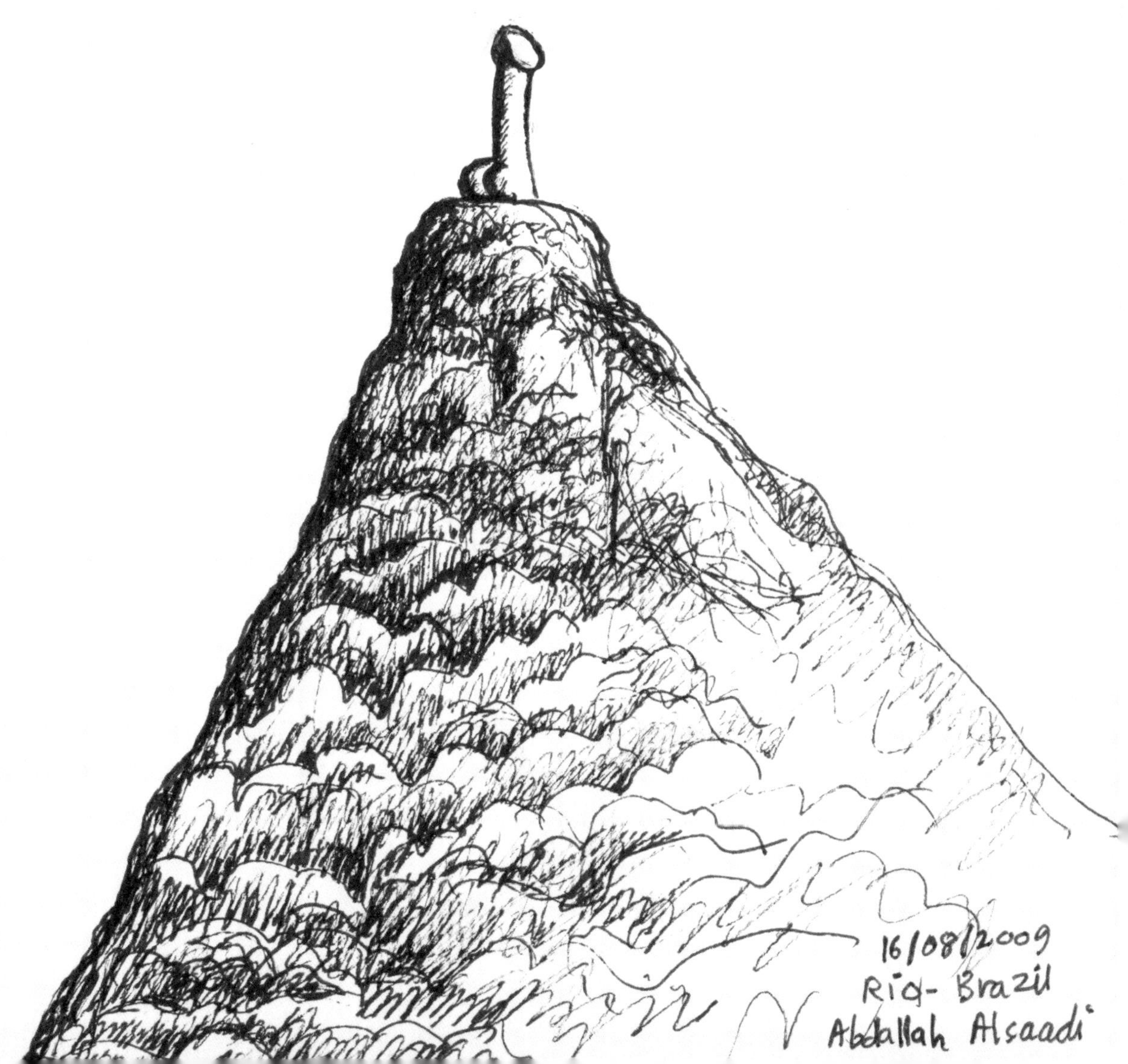
16/08/2009
Rio- Brazil
Abdallah Alsaadi

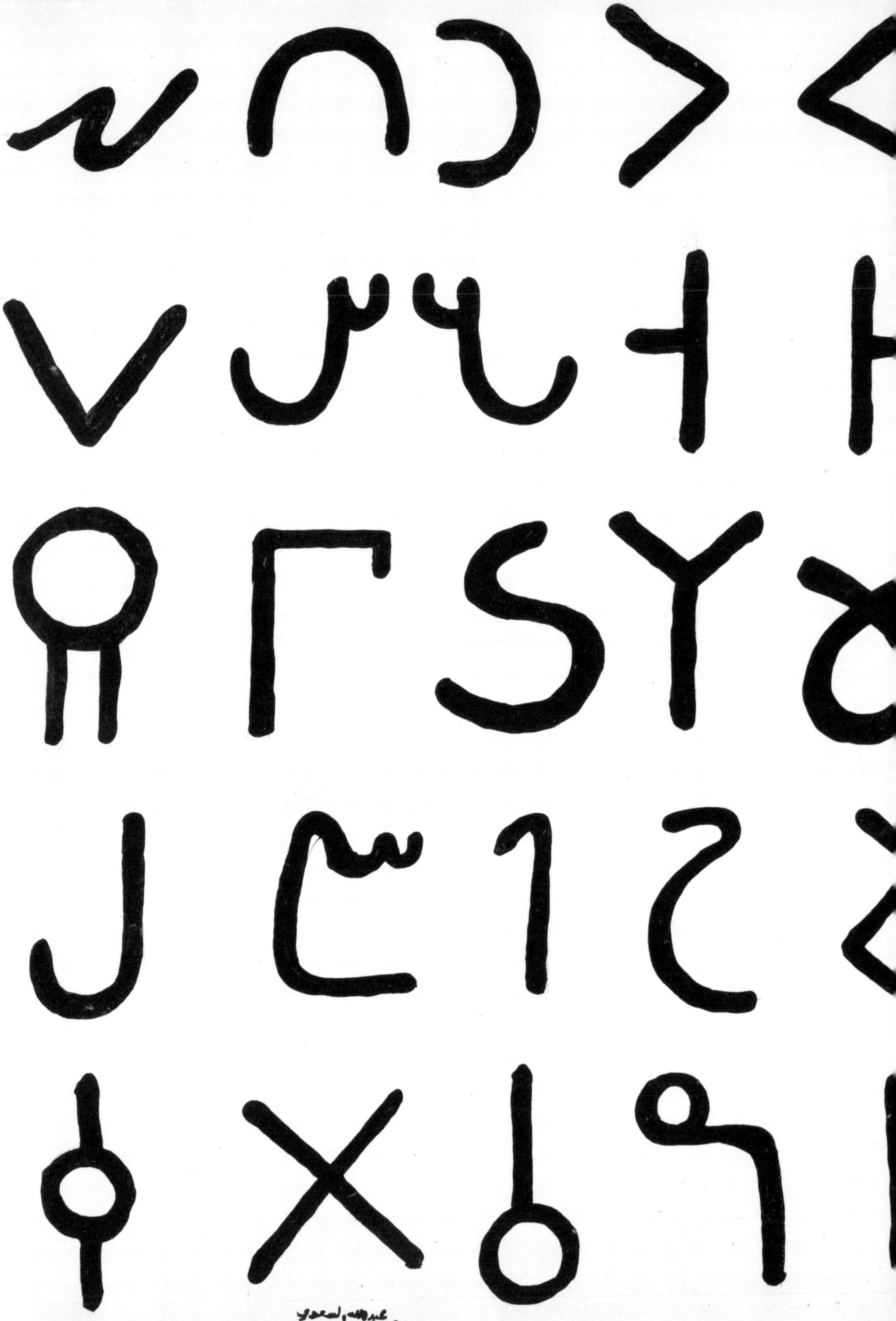

08.2009 : Rio

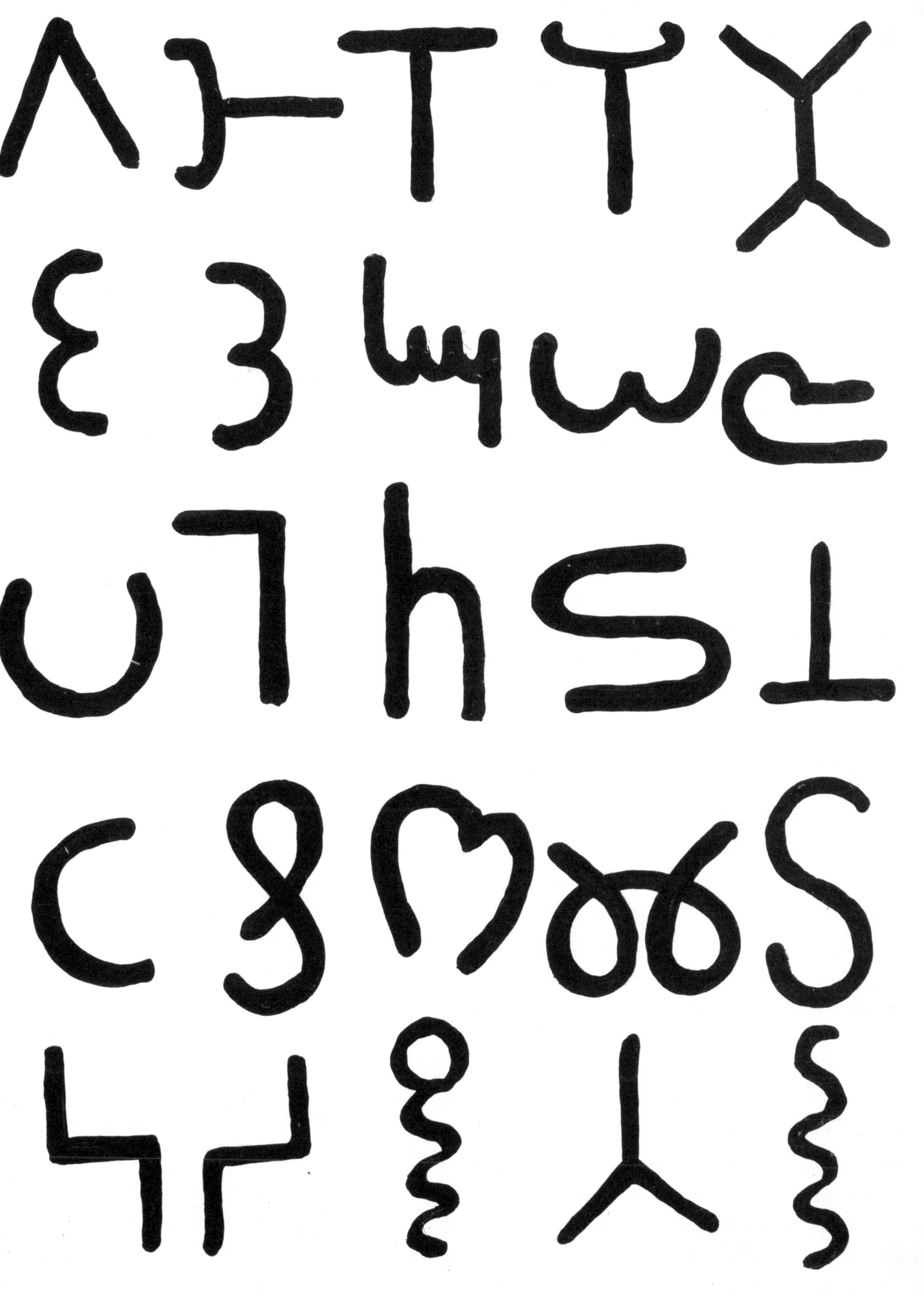

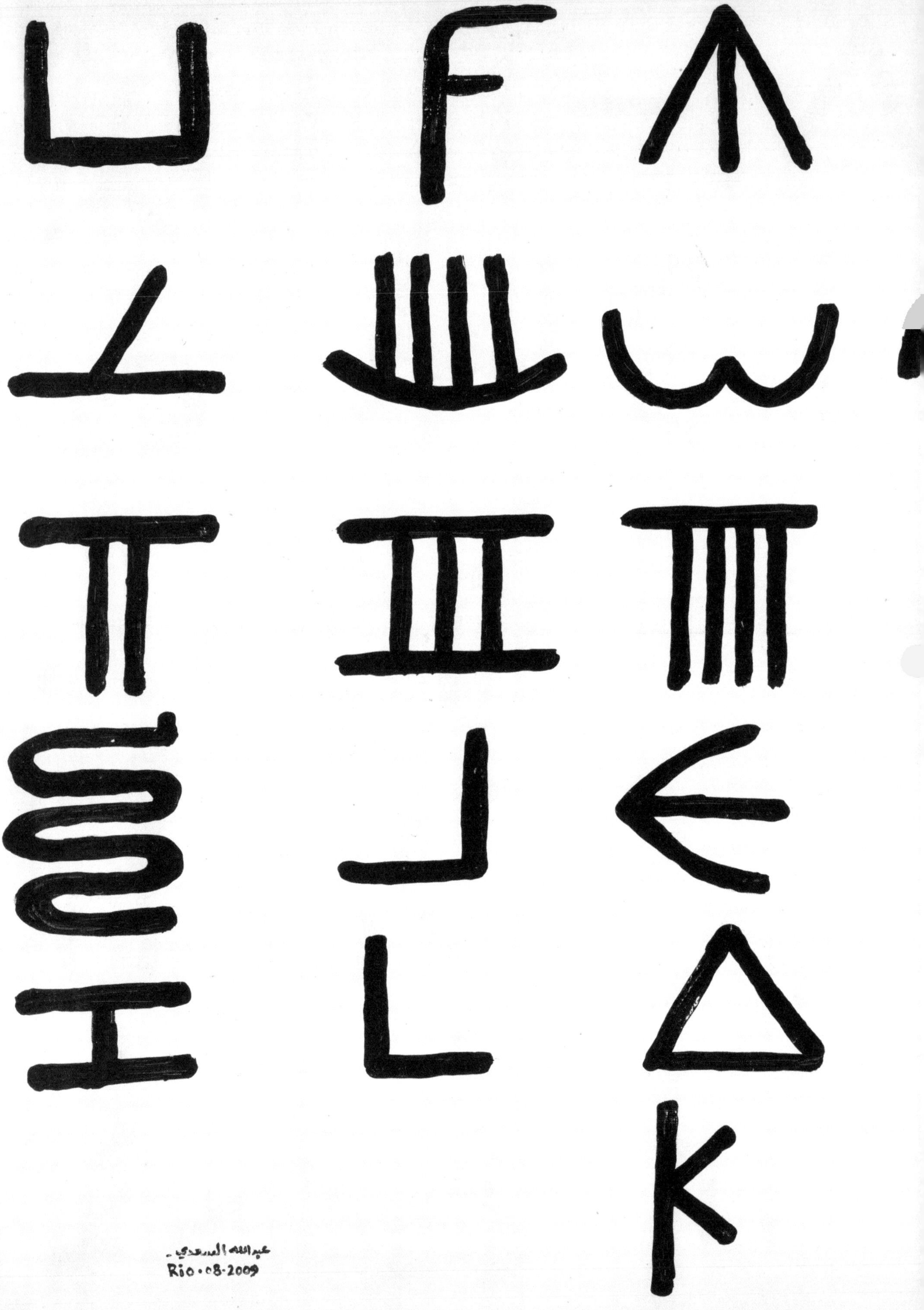
عبدالله السعدي
Rio·08·2009

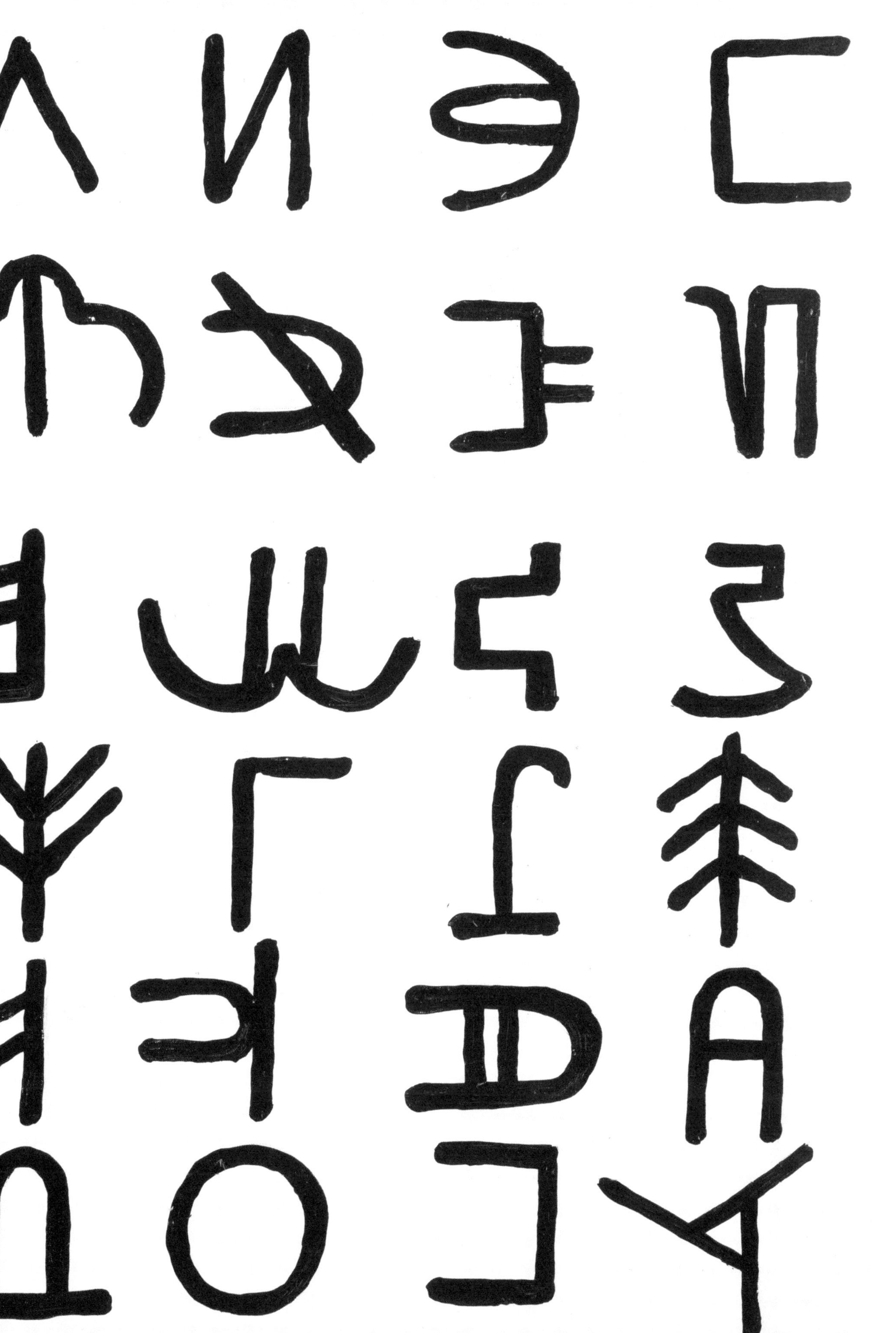

Hotel São José
Avenida Sete de
Setembro , 847-Centre
Salvador - Bahia

هذا هو الأفطار البسيط من
الساعة 06:00 ← 09:00 .
بعد الأفطار عدت إلى الغرفة وخرجت بعد ذلك
أمشي حتى وصلت إلى جهة البحر من هناك وعند
النصب التذكاري ، ترى لقلعة في البحر ومن هناك
البواخر والمراكب والقوارب في المرسى ومن هناك
قلعة ساو مرسيلو

[Bahia.
Marina]

[Forte de São Marcel

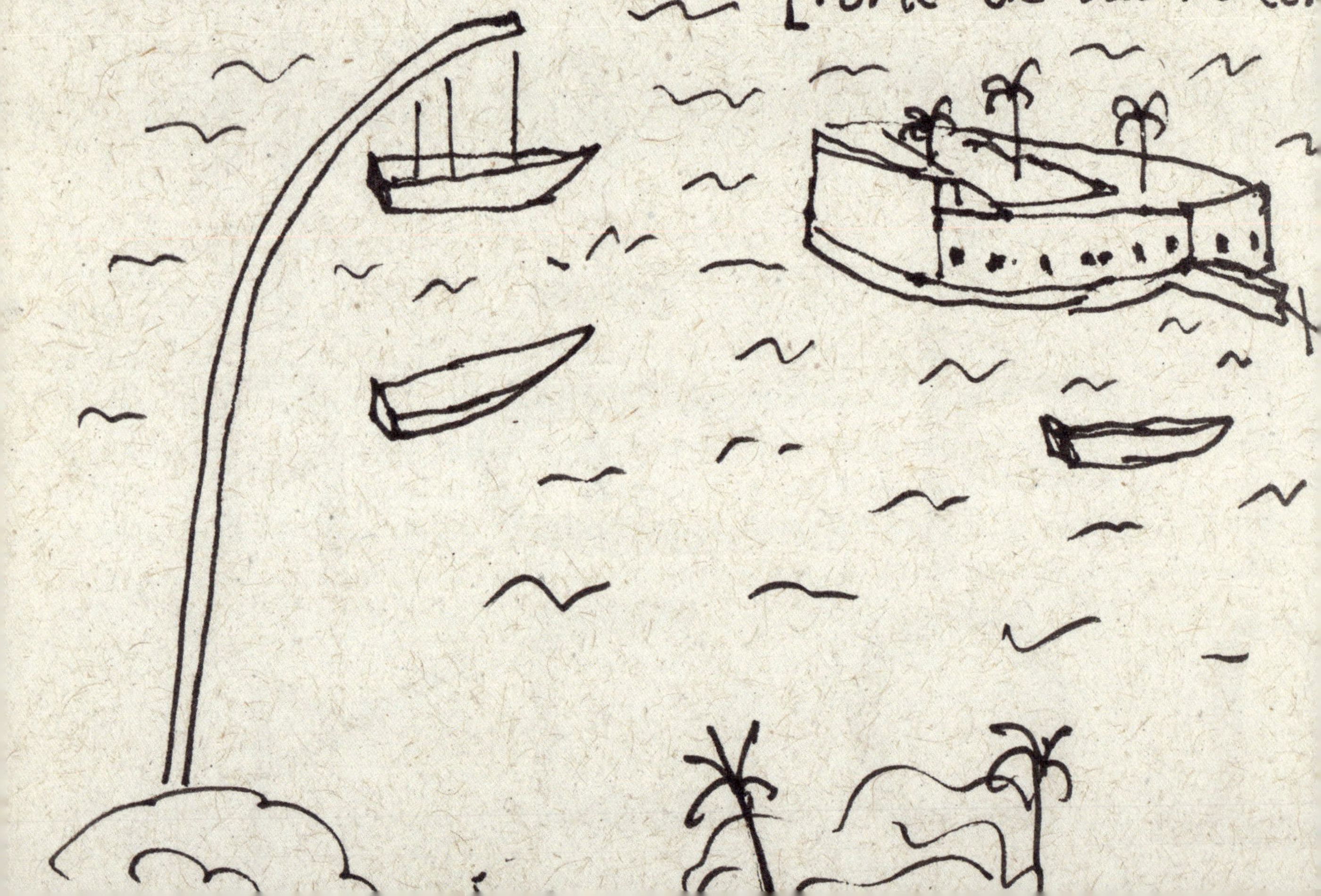

Arriving at the 26th edition of the world's second-oldest art biennial, gatherers milled about the Ciccillo Matarazzo in São Paulo. This imposing three-storey modernist structure of 30,000 square feet, designed by the celebrated Brazilian architects Oscar Niemeyer and Hélio Uchôa and named after the biennial's founder, was inaugurated in 1954 for the city's fourth centennial. Curated by German critic and art historian Alfons Hug, the 26th Bienal de São Paulo convened 135 artists for *Free Territory*, which envisioned the artist as architect of a boundless world of aesthetics that transcended day-to-day conflict. The result was a largely medium-specific curatorial method. In one of his first international debuts as an artist, Abdullah Al Saadi represented the United Arab Emirates.

The ground floor, with a ceiling over seven metres high, was occupied by large-scale sculptural works, the naturally-lit second floor by painting and video. Photography, a connecting factor, spanned the entire pavilion. At the biennial, Al Saadi presented his then ongoing work, *My Mother's Letters* (1998-2013), which refracted the non-verbal communication between the artist and his mother. For this project, he collected and categorised miscellaneous objects left at his doorstep, indicating visits she had paid him while he was away or preoccupied. Through years of systematisation and rendering of these keepsakes into a series of increasingly fluid, numbered diagrams, he derived an alphabet using elements of Japanese hiragana, katakana and Arabic diacritics. Accompanied by a selection of landscapes, *My Mother's Letters* illustrated the relationship between mother and son through a language unique to Al Saadi's locale.

His debut in Brazil was prompted, in part, by new developments in the exhibition model of the Sharjah Biennial. Its sixth edition, the first led by Hoor Al Qasimi, had adopted a decentralised approach, abandoning the national representation model which had characterised the Sharjah Biennial editions from 1993 to 2001. Enabling a more fluid, less state-centric approach than the 'Qawmiya' that had previously governed the event, the 2003 edition looked to bridge wider cross-cultural relationships, with trade and migration as sources of affinity and new media and mediums such as video, performance and public interventions as points of emphasis. In this new constellation, Al Saadi and other local artists, such as Hassan Sharif and Karima Al Shomaly, were represented as local artists whose practices had continuity within the permutation of the local arts scene.

A year later, these same works exhibited in São Paulo were shown in Buenos Aires, Argentina, at a Museo Nacional de Bellas Artes group exhibition, granting Al Saadi even wider exposure in the South American art scene. Al Saadi returned to South America in 2009 through Abu Dhabi's now defunct Emirates Foundation for an artist residency with the Largo Das Artes centre. His barren apartment in lush, hilly Rio de Janeiro presented a clear view of the famous Christ the Redeemer statue, as well as sightings of monkeys that often strayed from the nearby forests into the city streets. The majority of Al Saadi's journaling and art-making took place in the living room. His meals were either delivered or taken at the nearest restaurant, which was about a 40-minute walk away. With no other boarders and little companionship beyond visits from his host and the centre's curator, Al Saadi's stay was a productive, though largely solitary, one.

When Al Saadi wasn't preparing for his exhibition *(100) One Hundred,* at Largo Das Artes, named after the 100 journals milestone he reached while in Brazil, he was visiting as many museums and galleries as possible and making day-long bus trips to neighbouring Salvador, Paraty, São Paulo and Iguazú Falls, near the Argentinian border. By capturing these locations in his paintings and works on paper and fabric, he primed himself for future interpretations of the Emirates' own geography.

His study of the sweet potato (known locally in the Emirates as *findale*), then in its early stages, also gained another dimension during his stay at Largo Das Artes. Cultivated by both Al Saadi himself and his father, the root vegetable is thought to have originated in some form within South America. Having already exhibited selections from the project at his solo show *Findale* (2008) at EFAS as well as in Rio de Janeiro, he would go on to explore the sweet potato's migration and proliferation across West Asia in what remains one of his longest-running series.

Al Saadi, who saw some of Madha in Rio de Janeiro and its surrounding forests and peaks, felt more at home in Brazil than he ever had on his other travels. A month of Portuguese language study at the Catholic University of Rio, as well as conversations with his host, complicated this kinship slightly. The name Abdullah, he learnt, was often a catch-all term for Arab immigrants, particularly labourers who travelled to make their living. A popular folk poem paints a picture of Abdullah the travelling salesman, going up and down the hill with his suitcase. Its opening three-word refrain, *rala, rala, rala,* and the infinitive form, *ralar,* refer to someone thin and hard-working, respectively. Al Saadi noted, more positively, that its local pronunciation brings it especially close to *hala,* i.e. Arabic for welcome.

The cultural, geographic and linguistic parallels Al Saadi gleaned during this five-year period spent in and out of South America would inform some of his most ambitious mid-career works, later realised across the mountainous and coastal regions of his youth. He also began to encounter and work with a new transnational and cross-disciplinary arts scene through the biennial format, first with Sharjah and then in São Paulo. The biennial as a space for experimentation and new artistic ideas paved the way for the 'outsider' and non-formally trained art that Al Saadi made, and continues to make, to become part of a multi-nodal and deterritorialised art world.

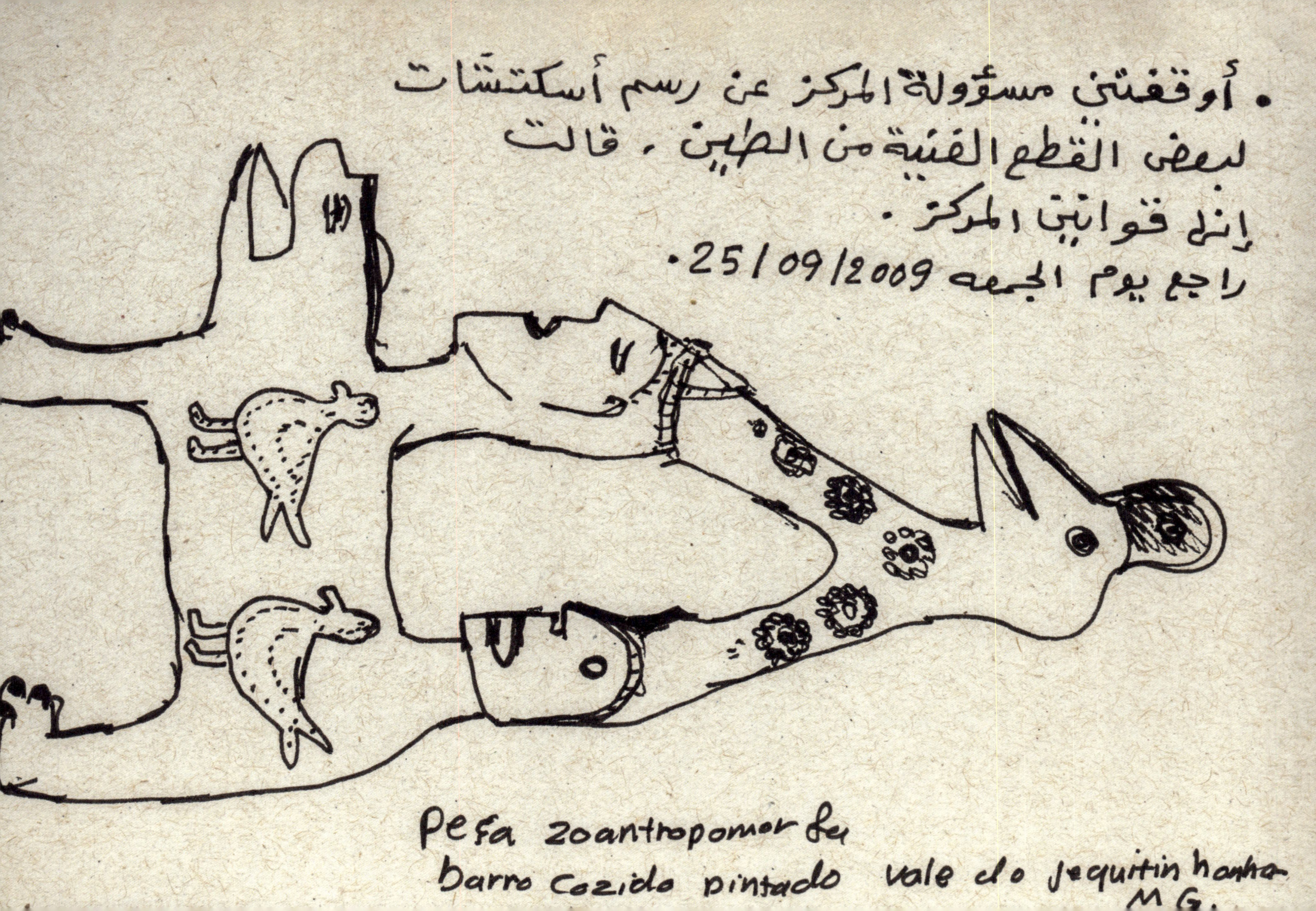
• أوقفتني مسؤولة المركز عن رسم أسكتشات
لبعض القطع الفنية من الطين . قالت
إنني قوانين المركز .
راجع يوم الجمعة 25/09/2009•
Peça zoantropomor fa
barro cozido pintado   vale do Jequitin hanha
M.G.

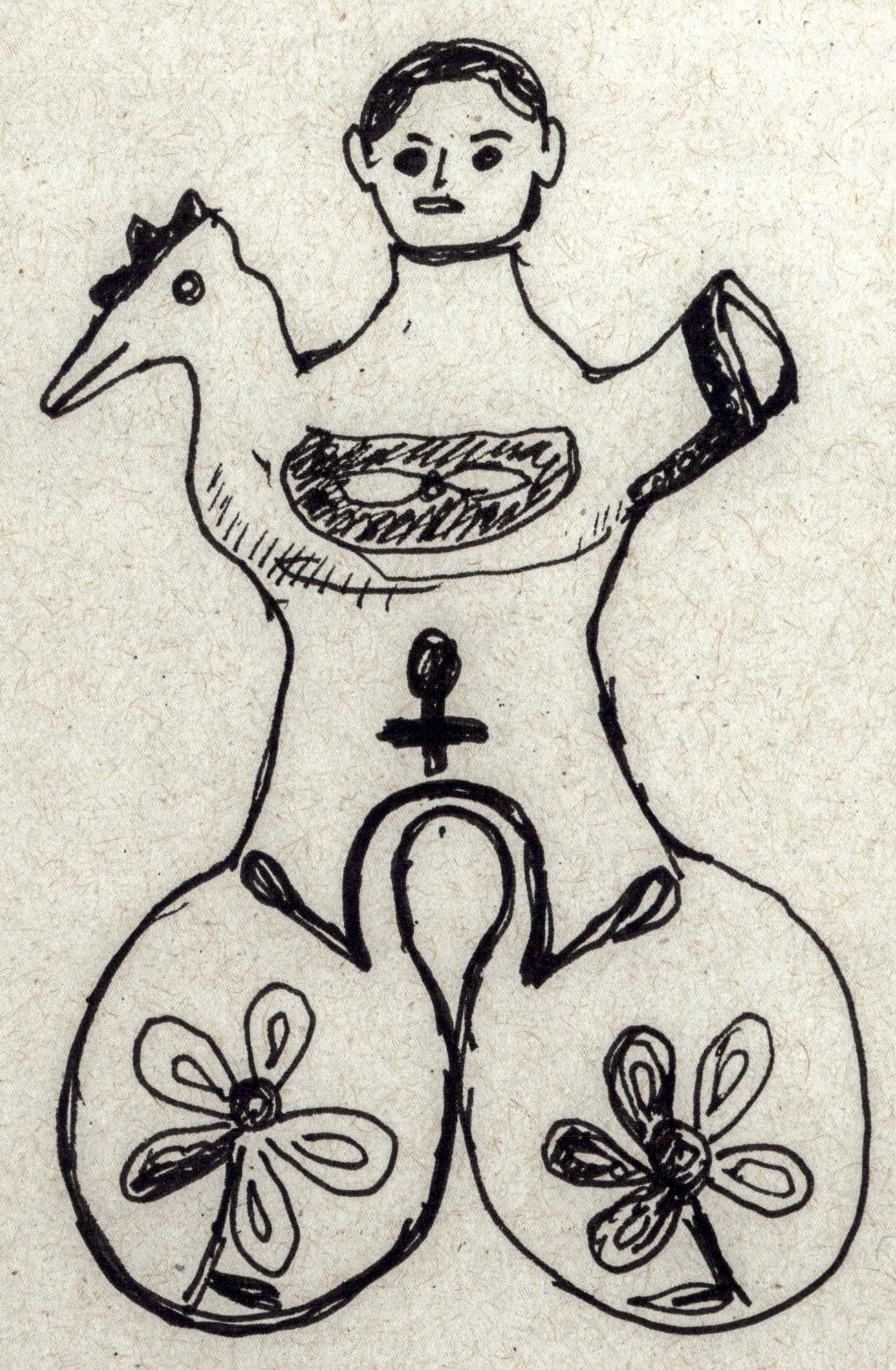

Centro de Referência
do Artesanato Brasileiro

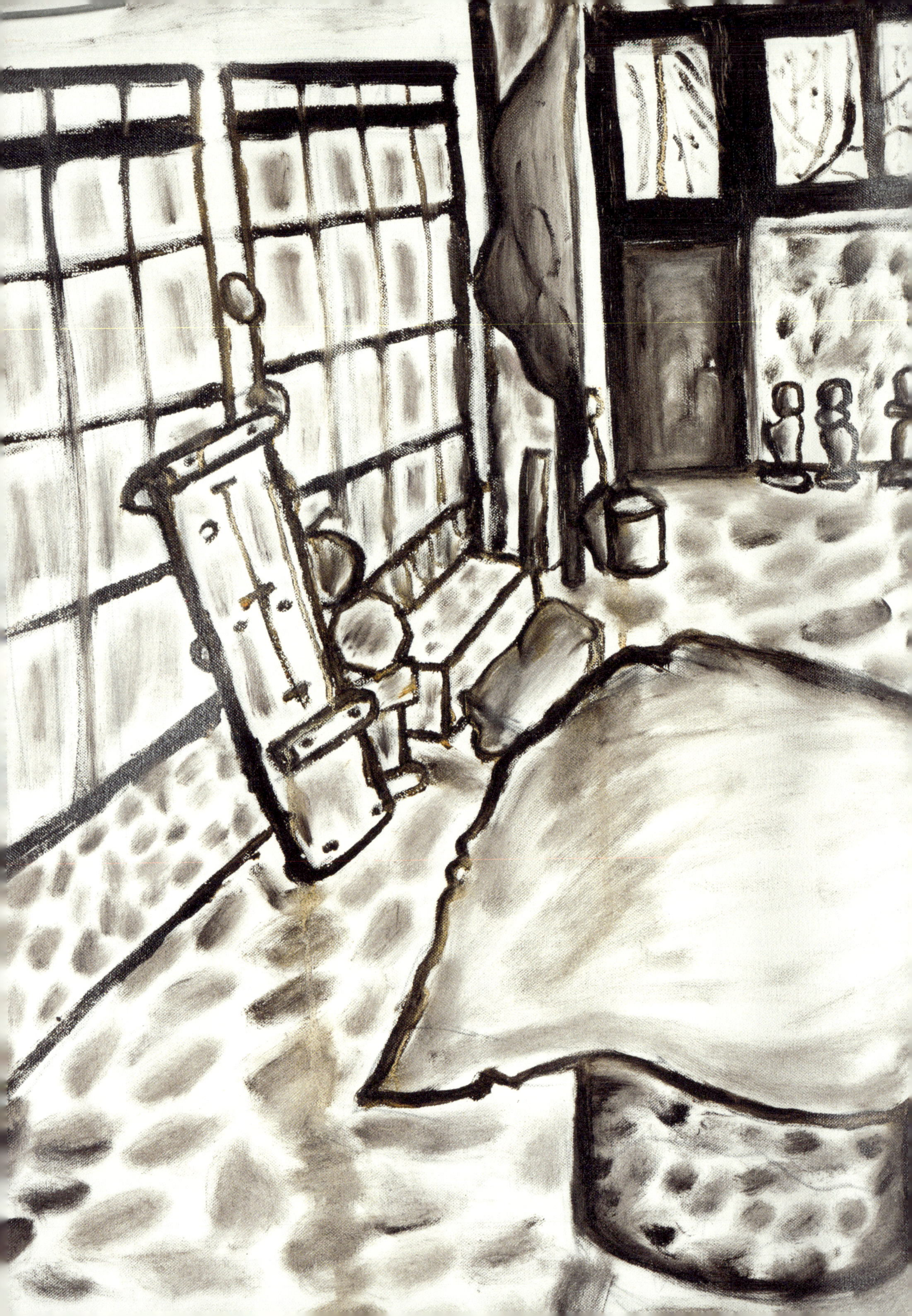

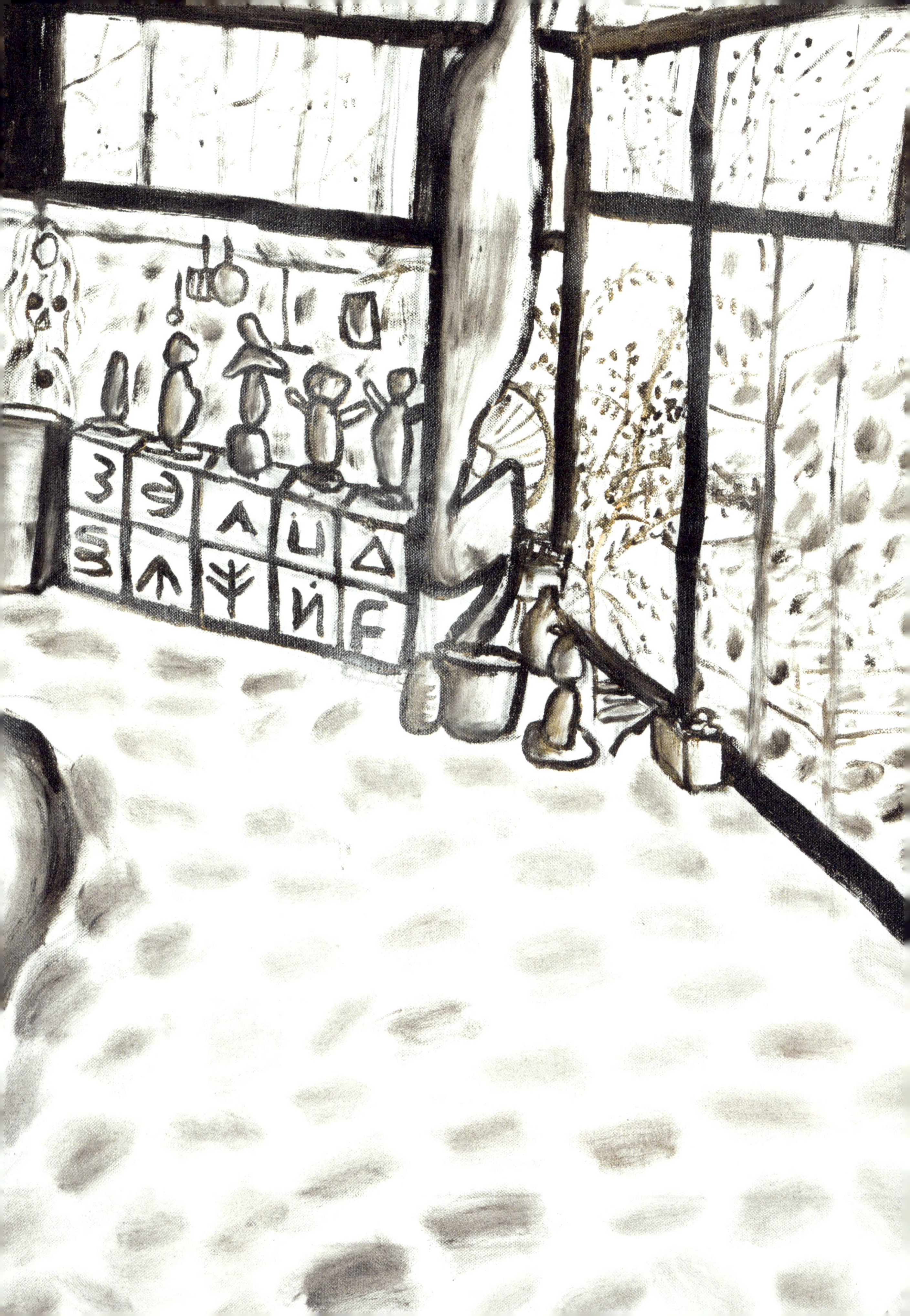

o Brazil
Os Estados unidos
a Coréia

o americano   a americana
o coreano   a coreana
                     a cubana
                     a austriaca
                     a egípcia
o cubano,   a Ale
o australo   Egito
egípcio

o Japão
a polonês
o chinês

somos
sou
são

Nós somos
Vocês/eles são
eu sou
ele é
Você/você
ela é Brazil

17/10/2009

X

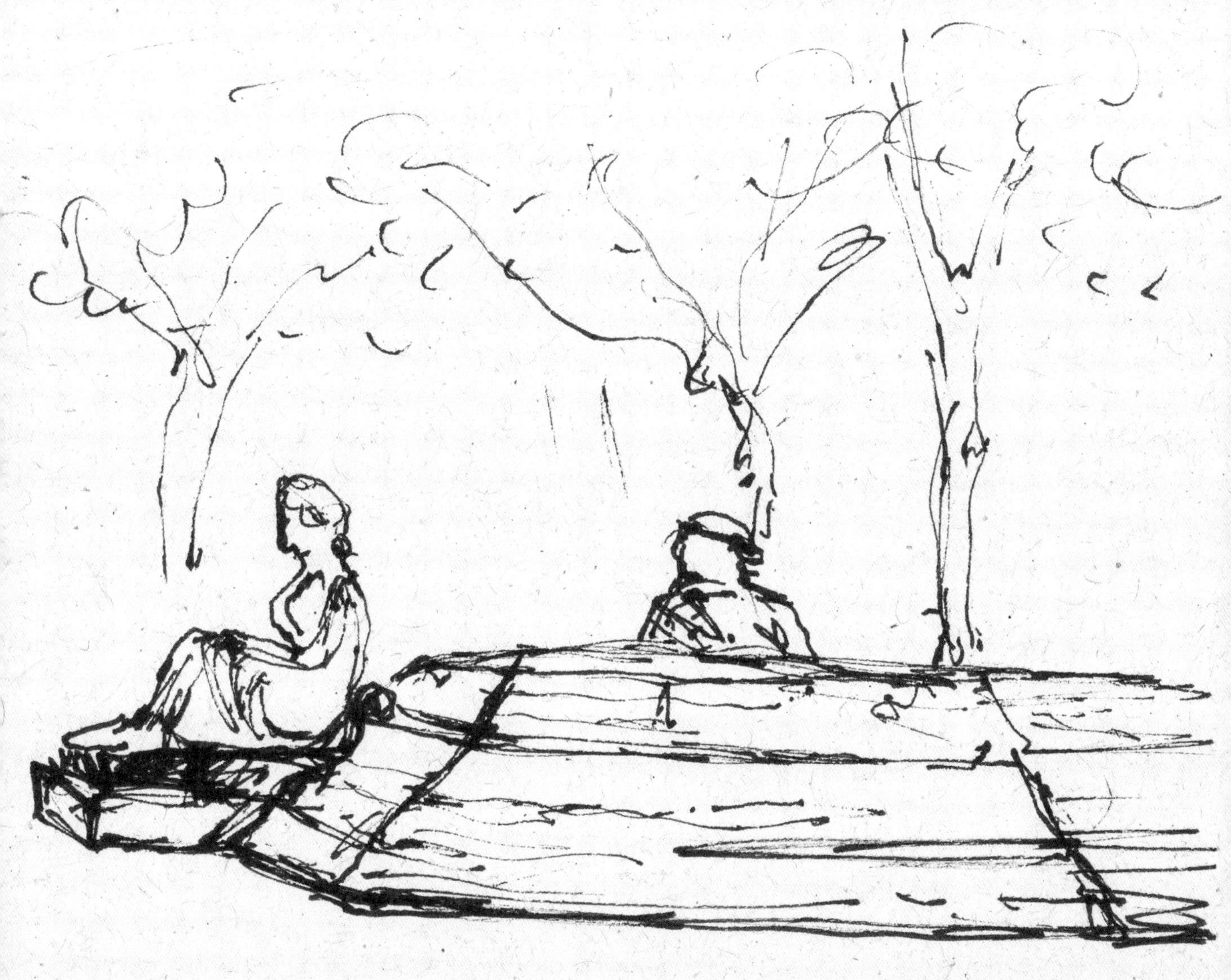

06:00 صحوت من النوم في مدينة سلفا دور، في
غرفتي رقم 104 بفندق : Hotel São José
أخذت حماماً . لبست ملابسي وذهبت لتناول
الأفطار في غرفة الإستقبال . قطع بسكويت،
عصير فاكهة ، قطعة جبن مع زبدة وقهوة و
قطعتا فاكهة من الأناناس،

رسائل أمي

My mother letters

98 – 2000

By

Abdallah Alsaadi

عبدالله محمد السعدي

2003

9

الرسائل	النوع	العدد
1•15•33•47	معدن	4
2•9	إسمنت (اسبستوس)	2
3•4	حجر بحر مرجاني	2
5	حجر بحر رملي	1
6•7•10•12•16• 19•21•43	رمل، إسمنت وحصى	8
8	ورق محارم	1
11•14•22•25• 30•39•40	خشب شجر طبيعي	7
27•32•36•37	ورق شجر طبيعي	4
17•23•38	خشب مصنع	3
13•24•31• 42•44•45•46	بلاستيك	7
18•29•41	نايلون	3
20•26•34•35	حجر جبلي	4
28	جلد صناعي	1

** جدول رسائل (1998•1999•2000)

10

أيام الأسبوع	الرسائل	الزيارات	اليوم	الشهر
—	1	1	—	1
—	—	—	—	2
—	1	1	—	3
—	—	—	—	4
—	1	1	—	5
Sat • Tue • Mon	3	3	6•2•1	6
Mon	2	1	27	7
—	—	—	—	8
Wed	1	1	16	9
Thurs • Fri	3	2	22•9	10
Fri • Fri • Fri	3	3	27•6•4	11
Mon • Fri	2	2	14•12	12

■ جدول رسائل (1998) •

107

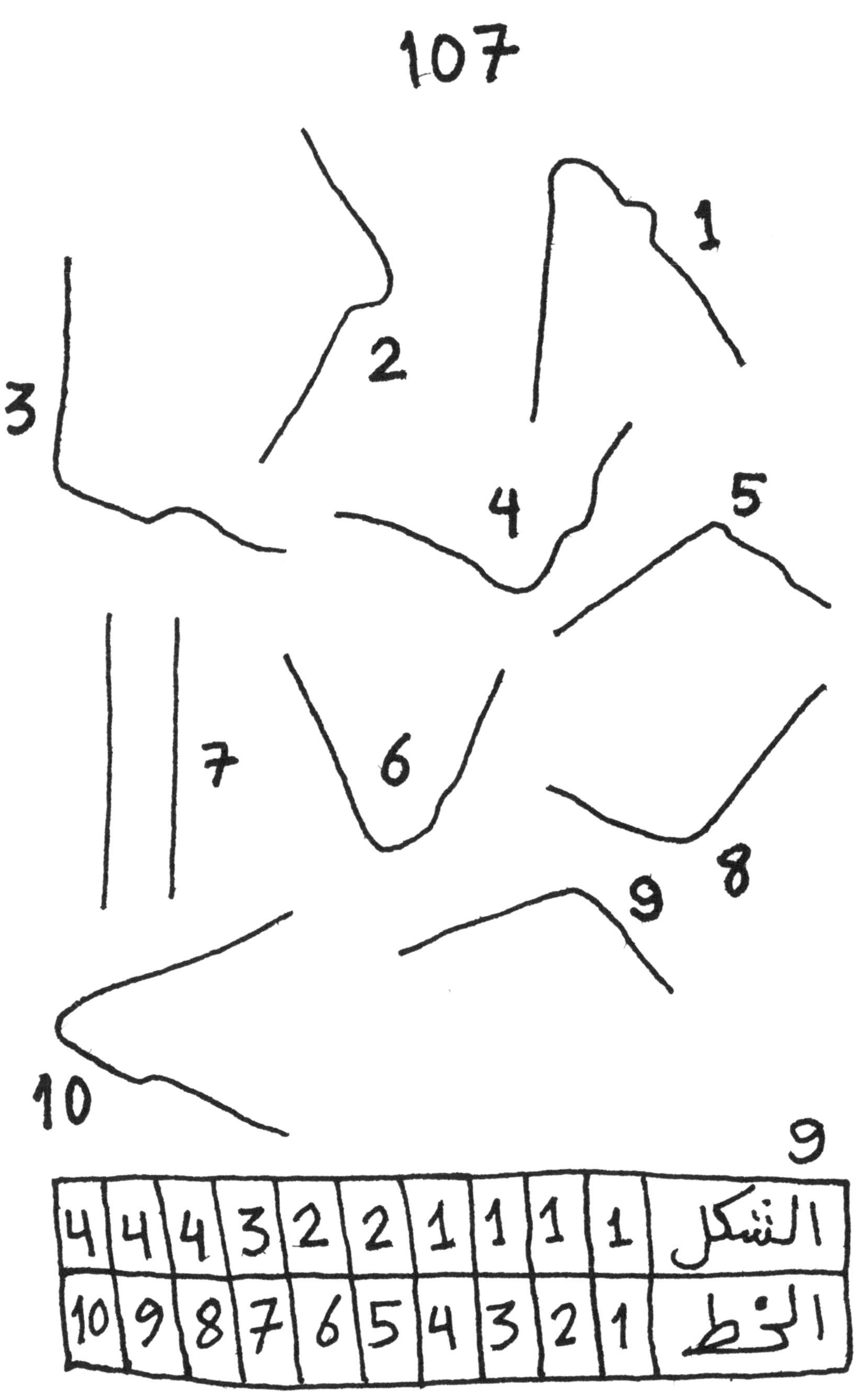

الشكل	1	1	1	2	2	3	4	4	4
الخط	1	2	3	4	5	6	7	8	9	10

110

رسالة

(11)

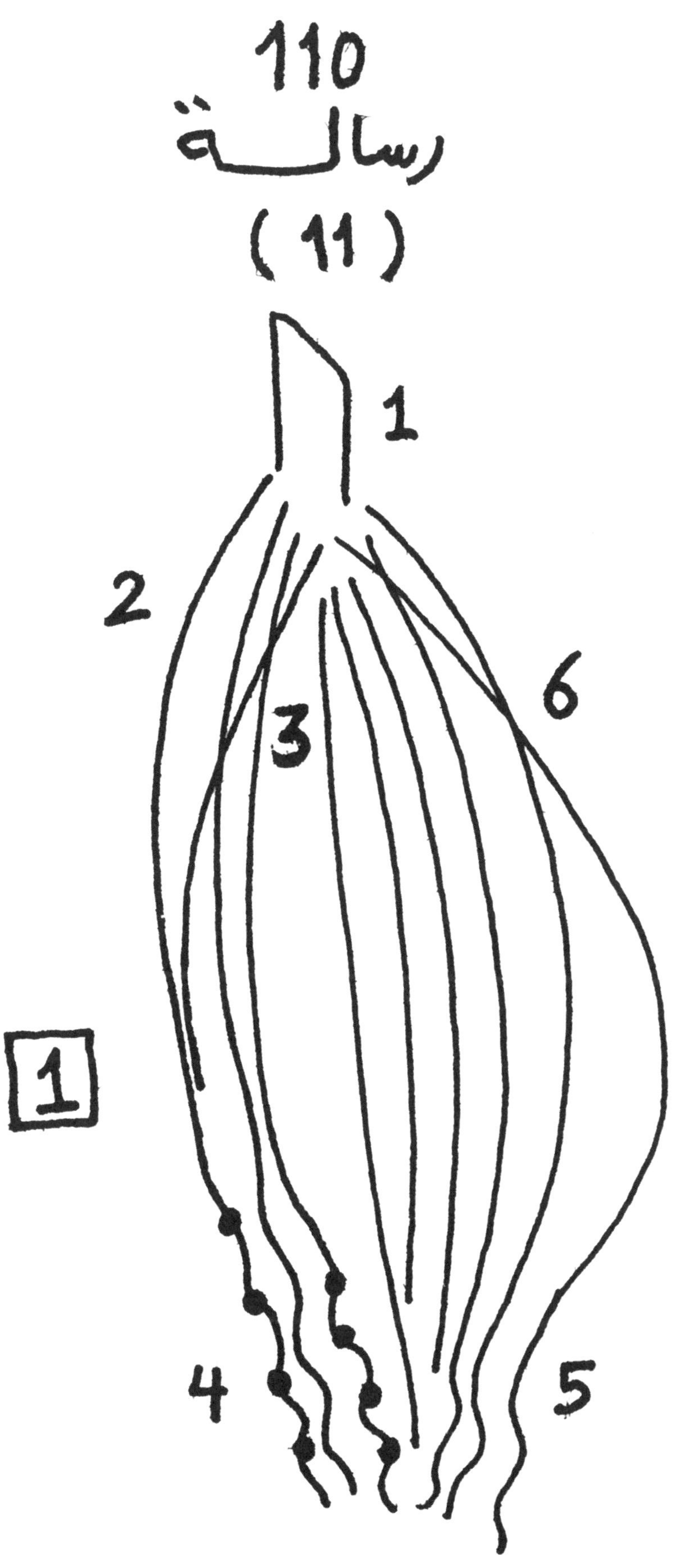

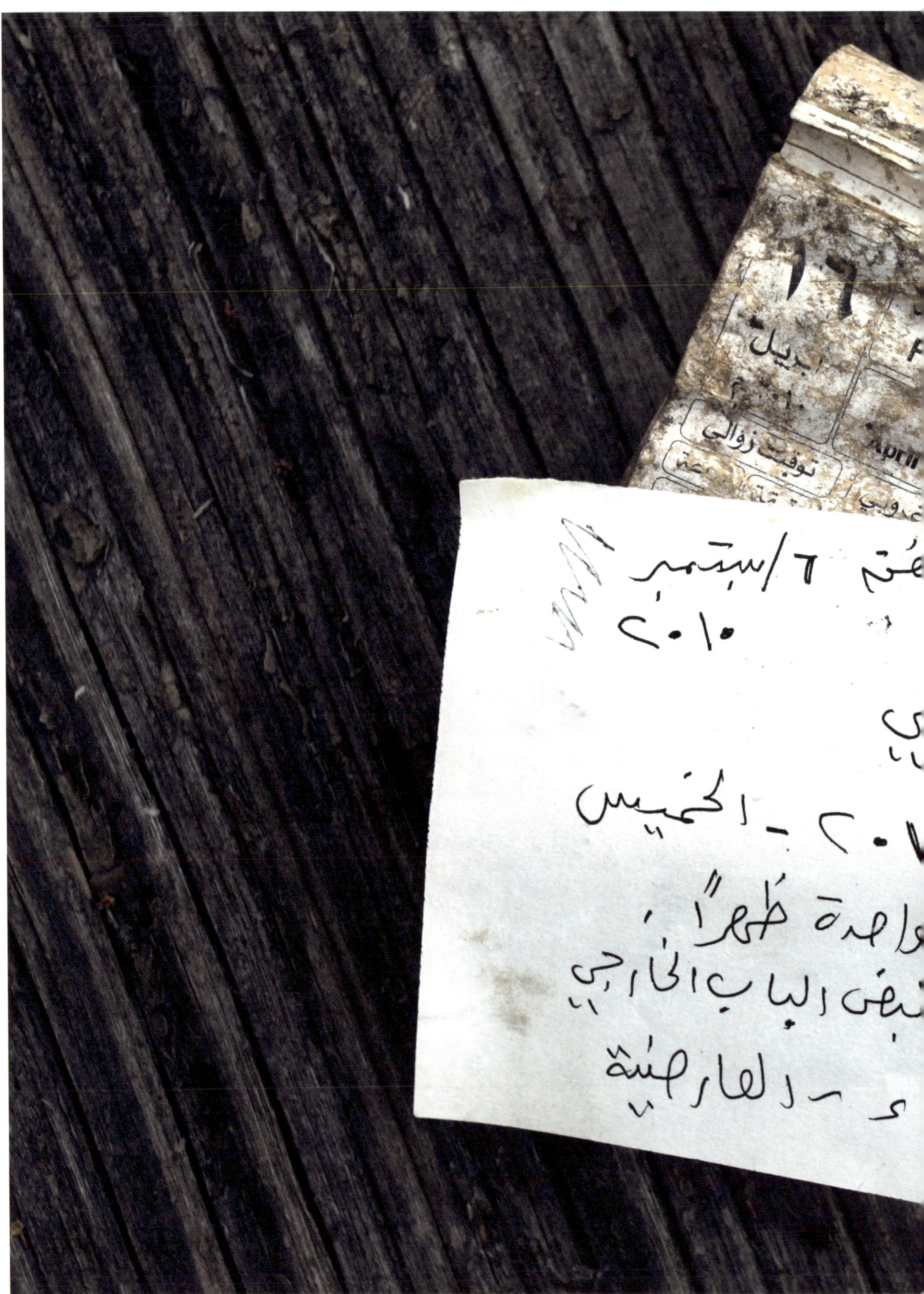

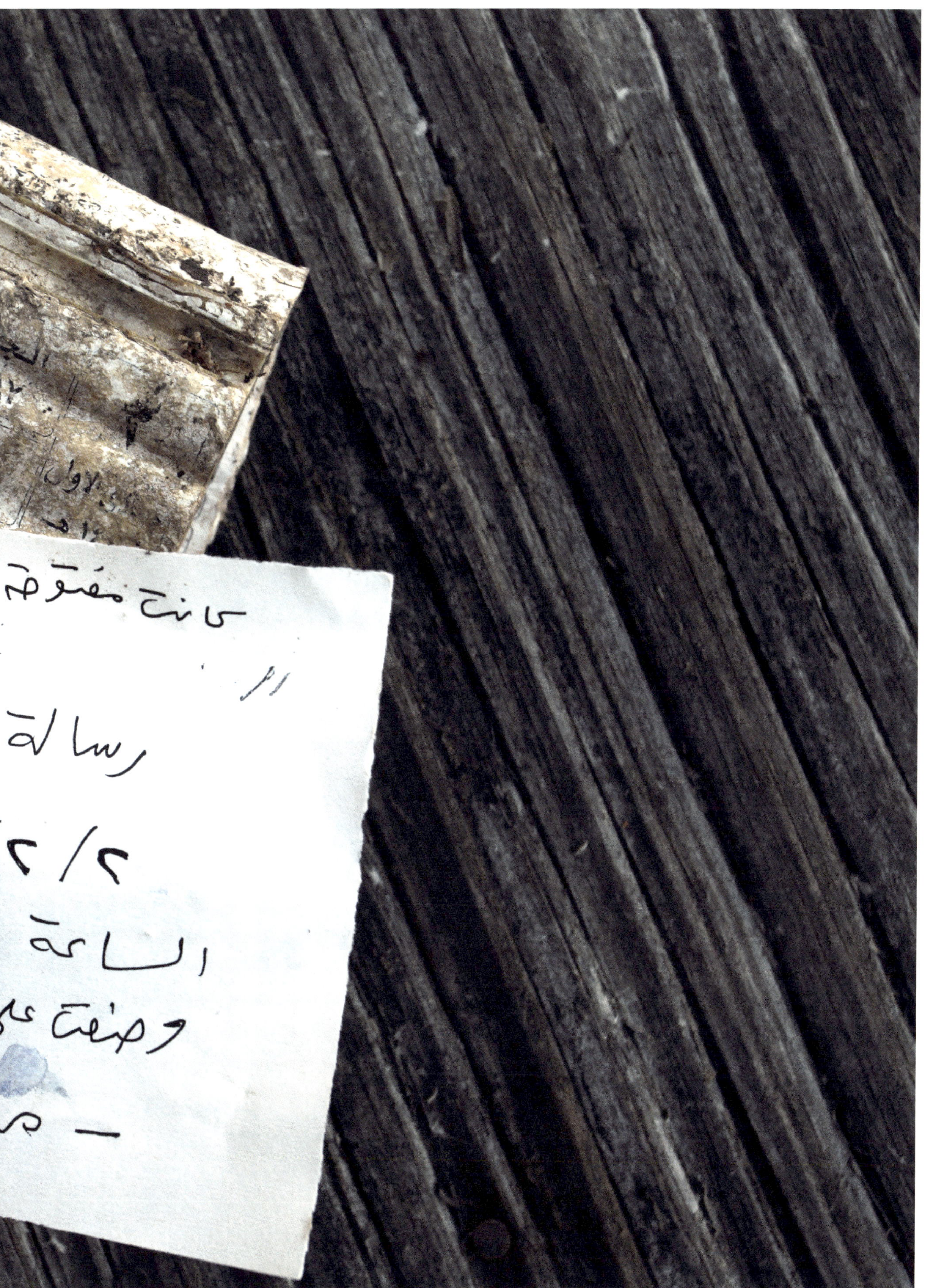

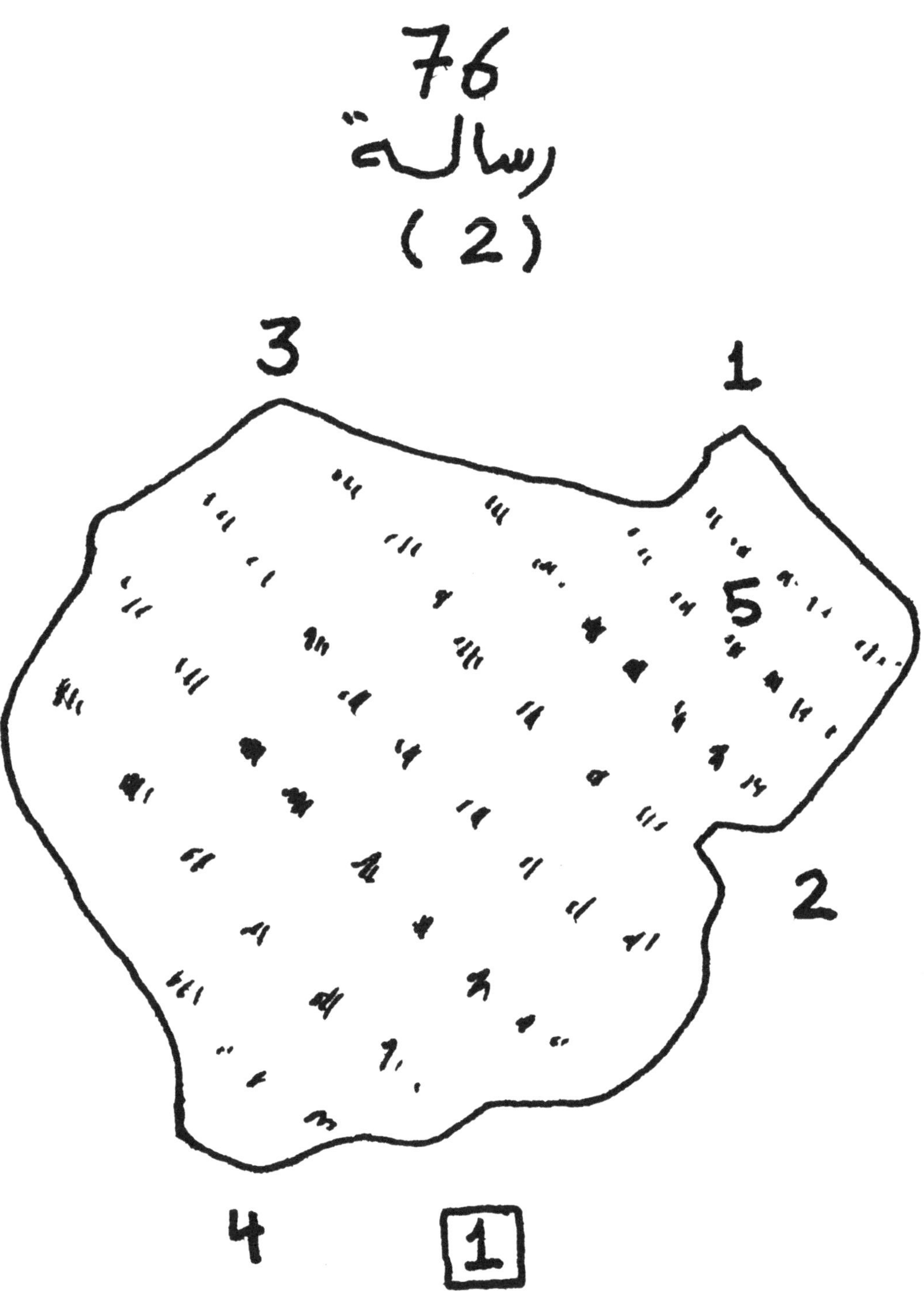

76
رسالة
(2)
3
1
5
2
4
1

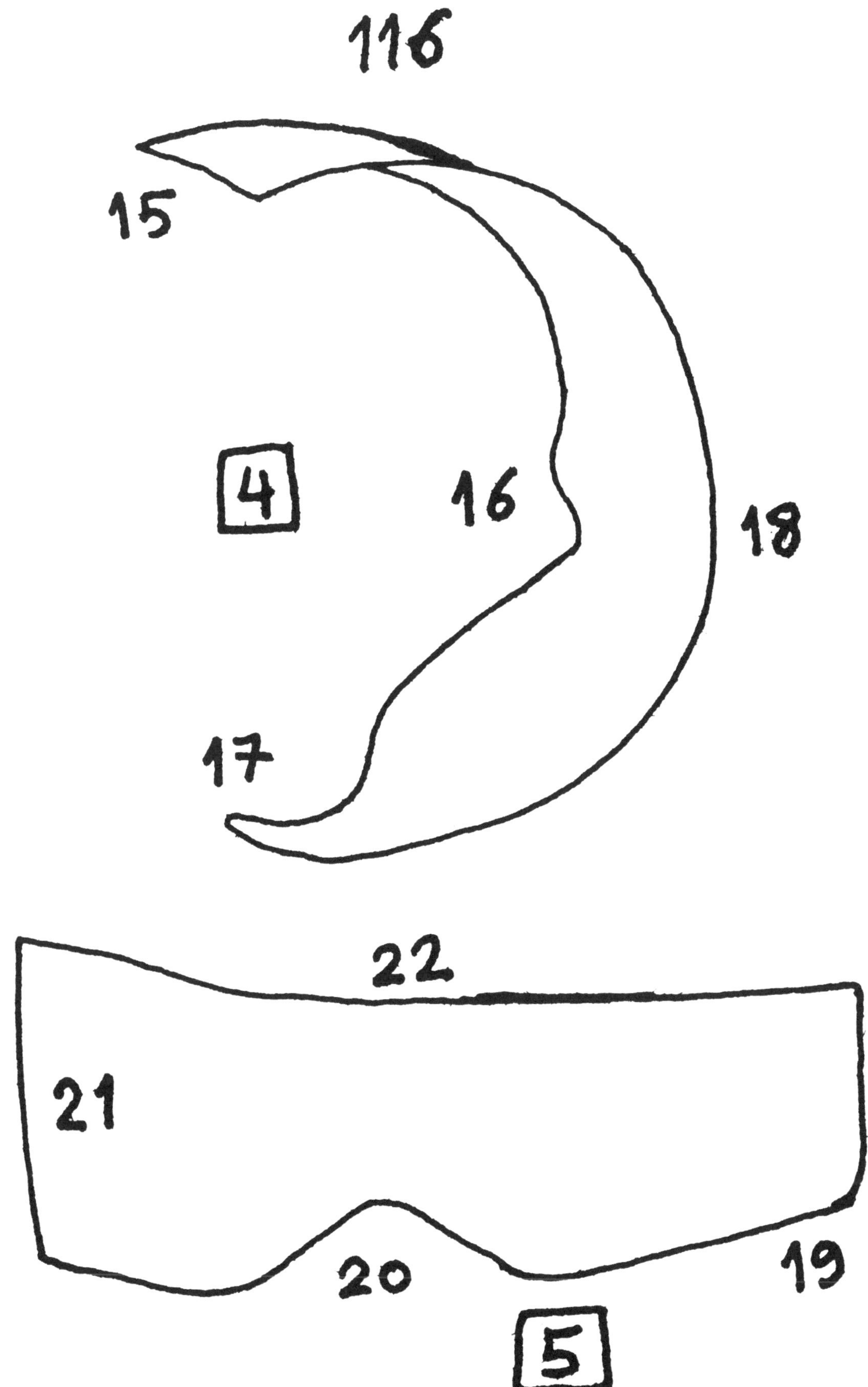
116
15
4
16
18
17
22
21
20
19
5

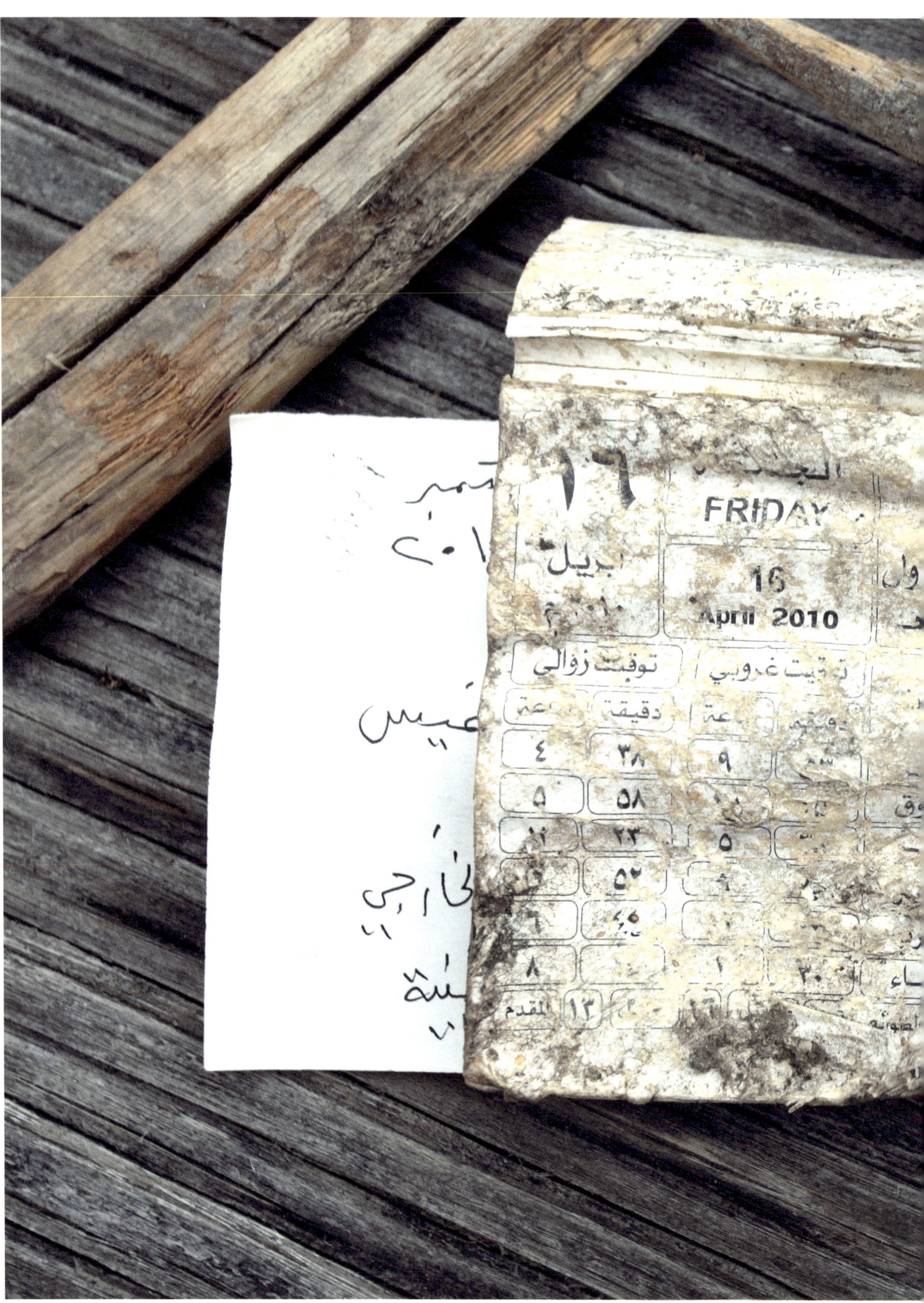

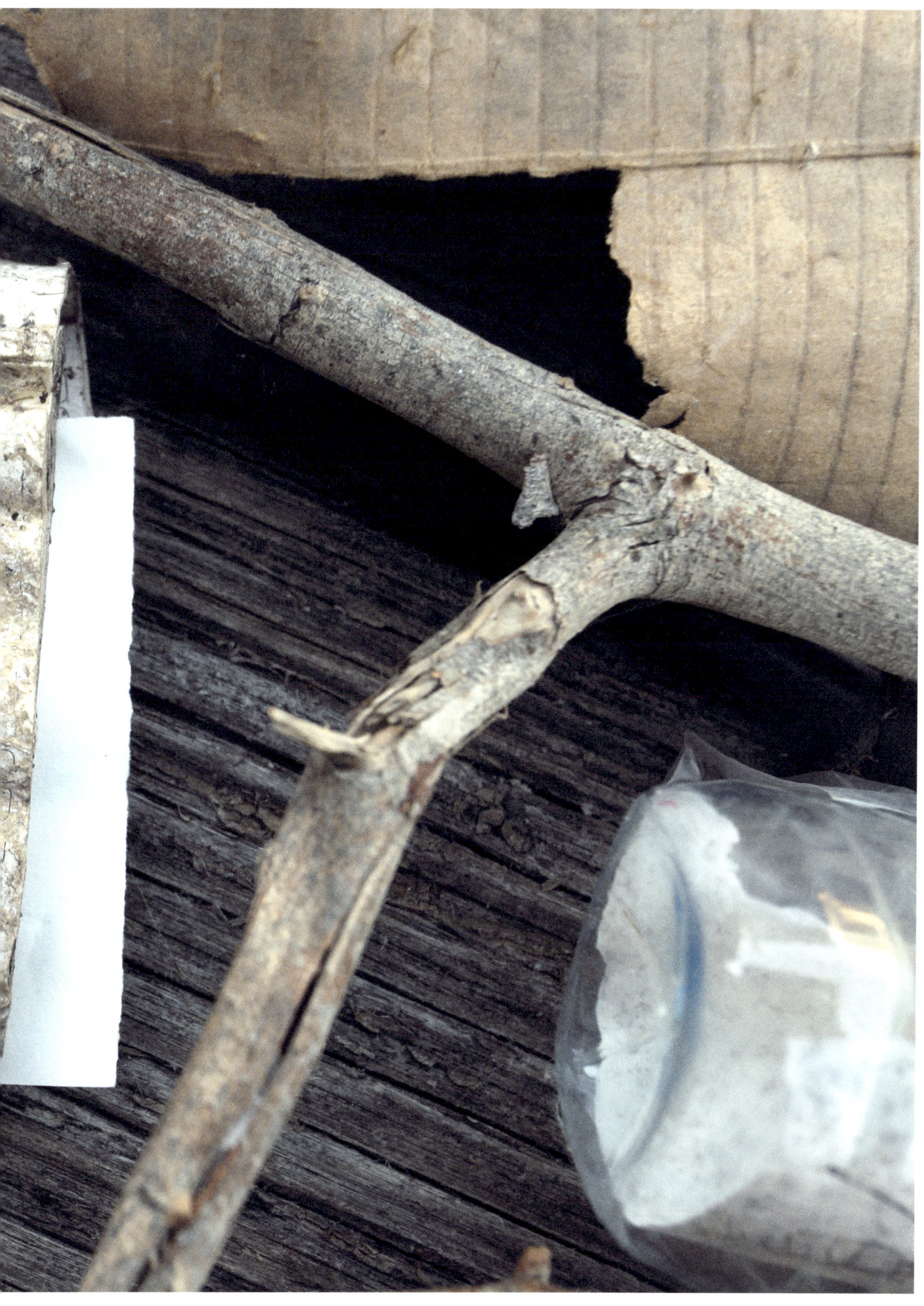

Marende✳✳✳

Marende✳✳✳

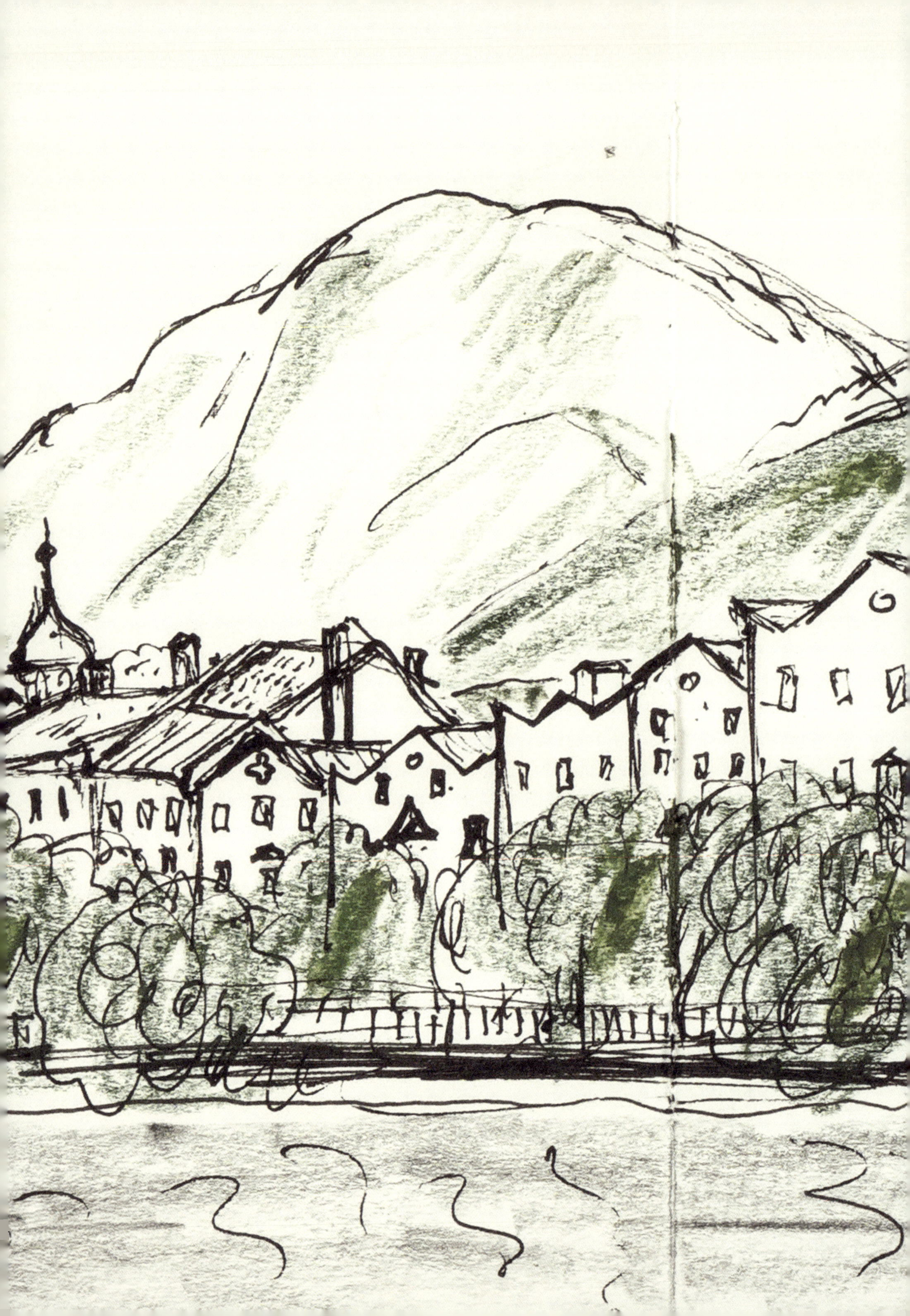

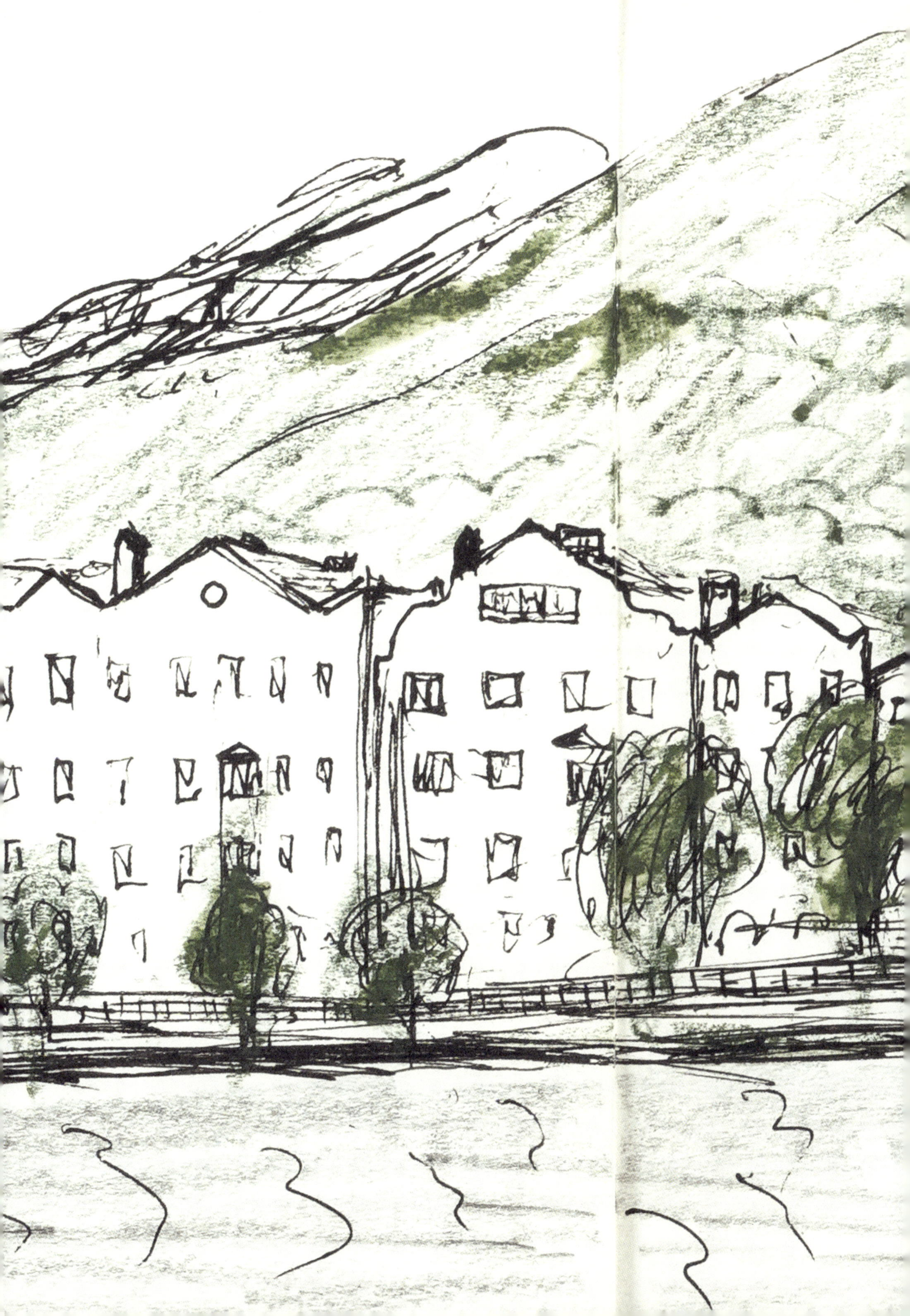

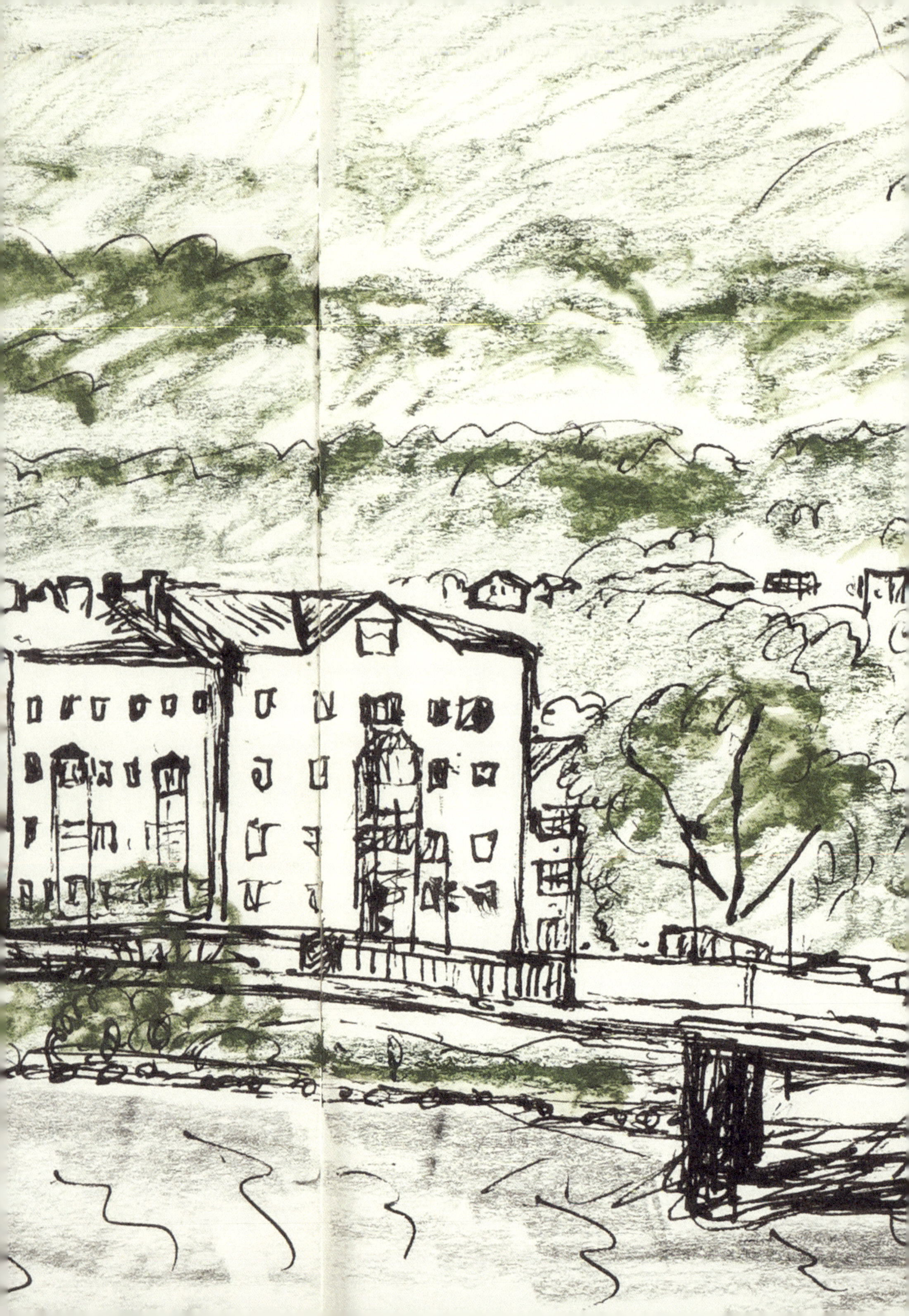

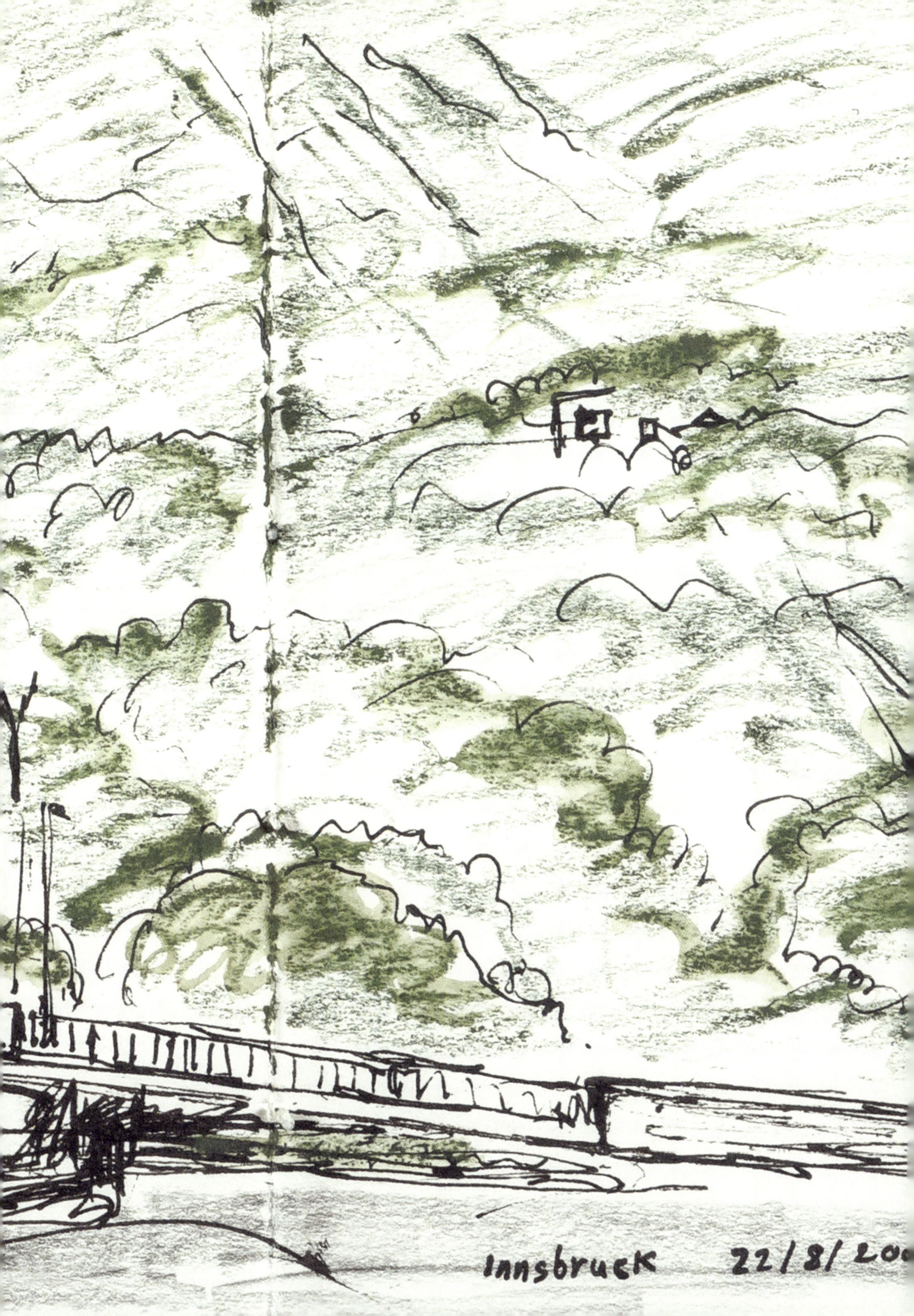

Innsbruck 22/8/20

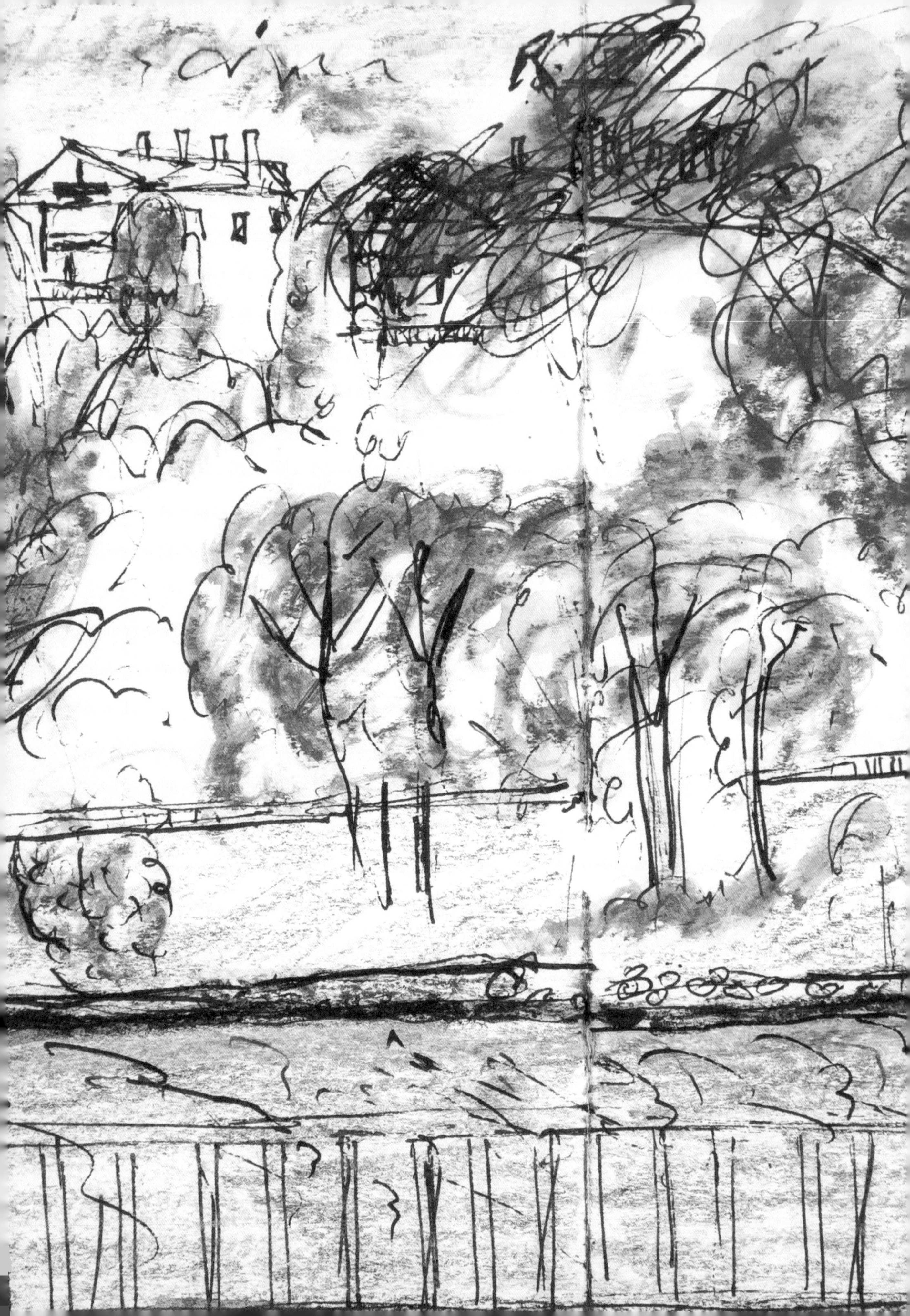

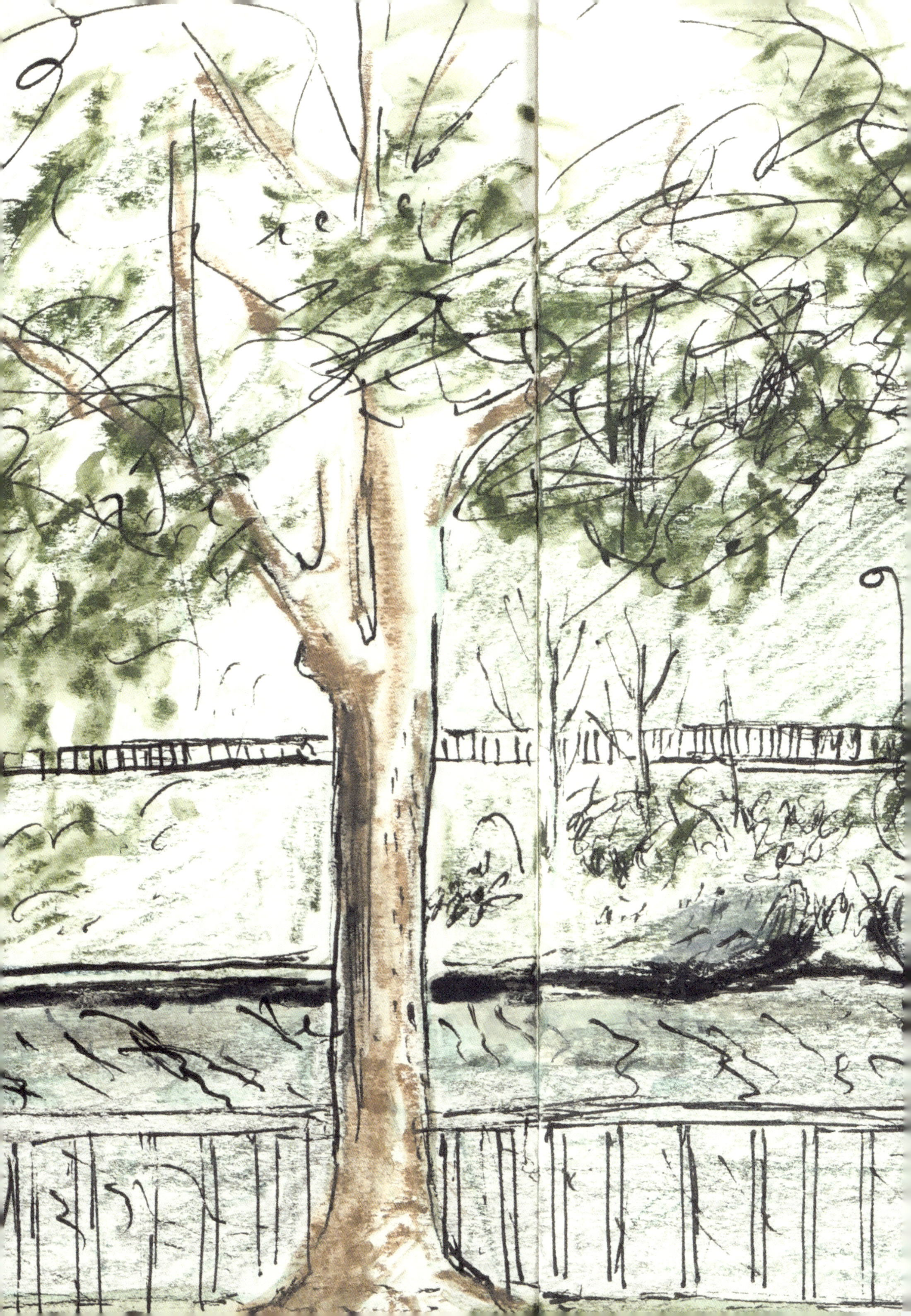

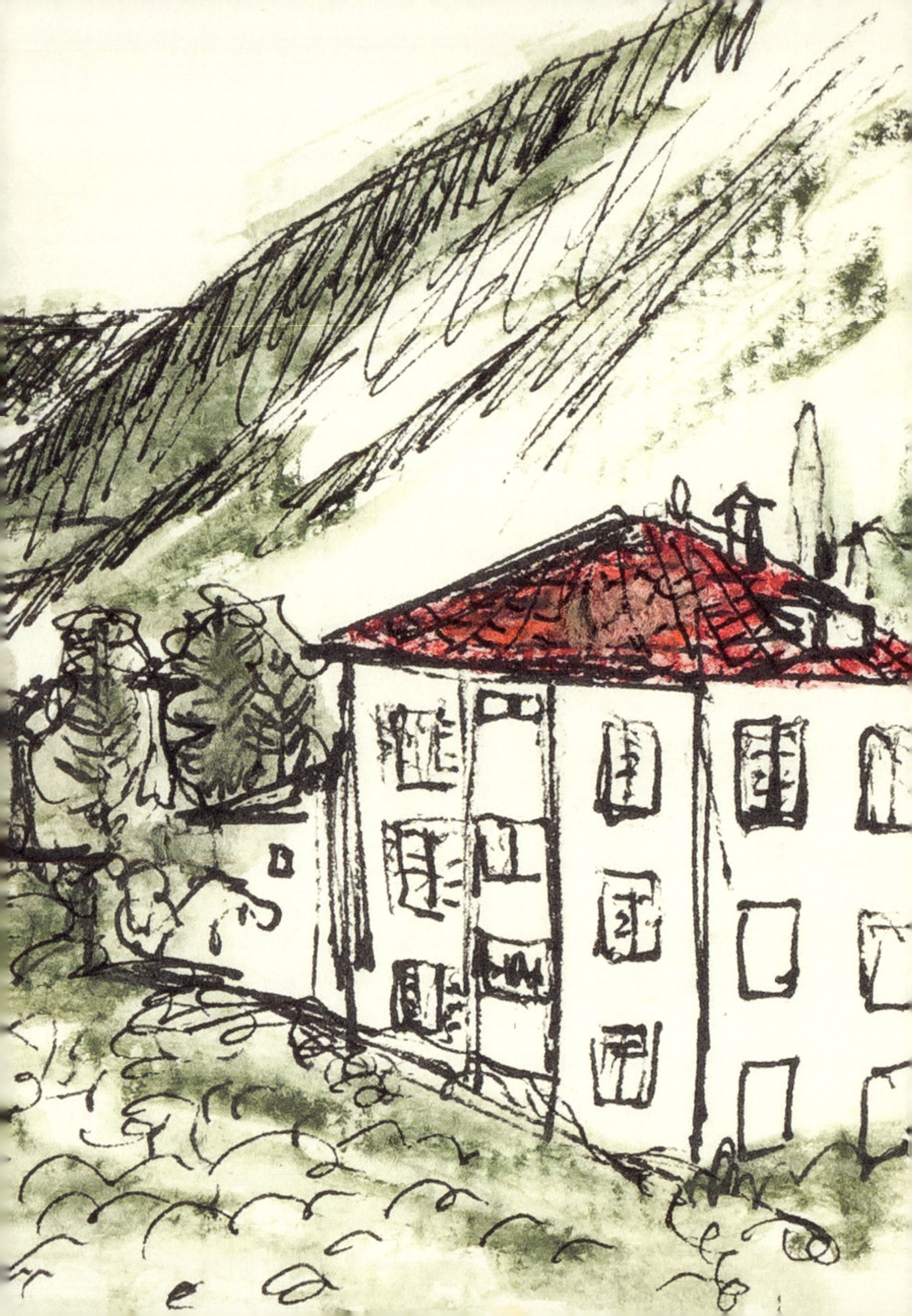

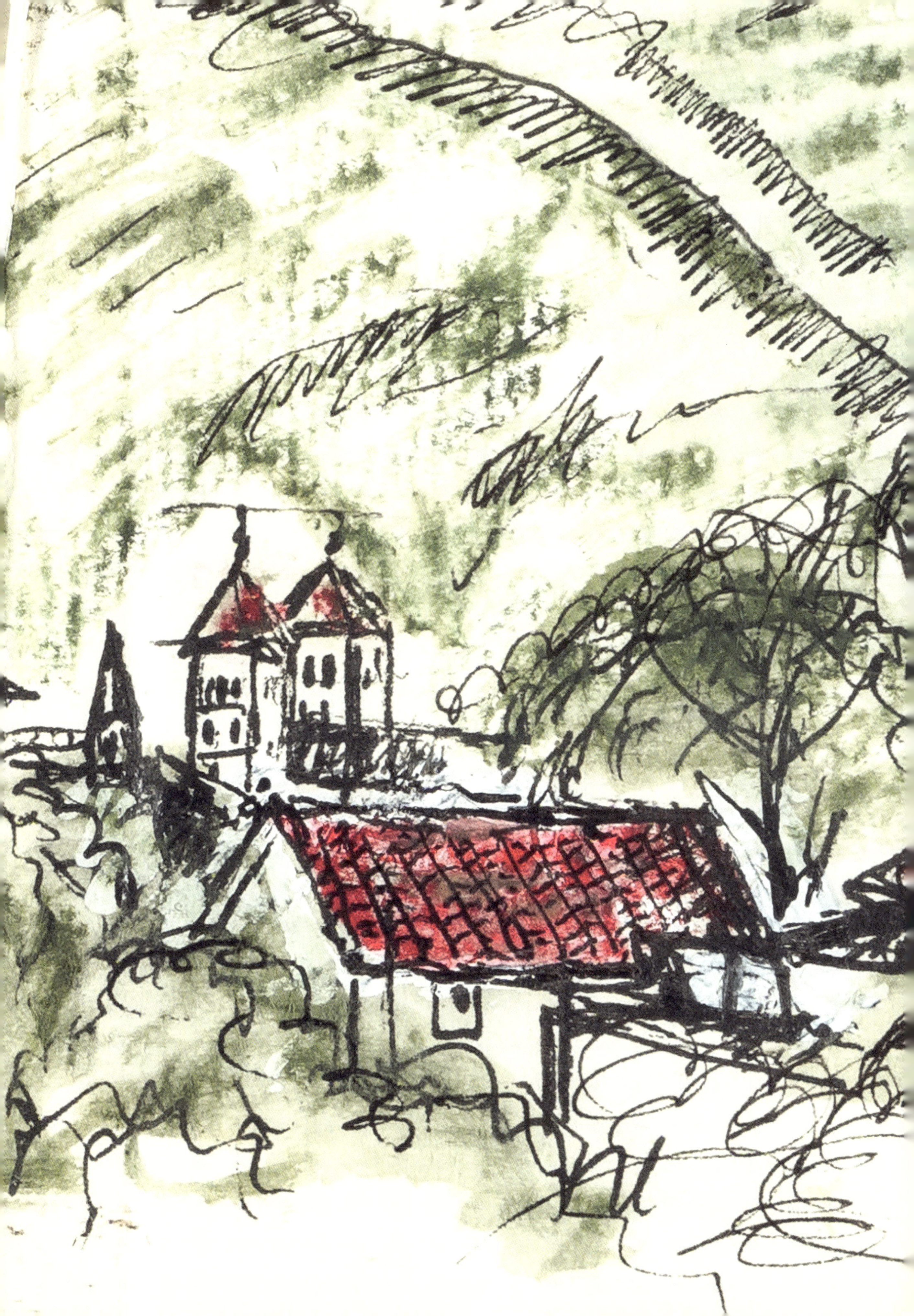

بقدر ما هي أسكتشات ويوميات
كتبتها عن تجربة فنية عشتها
في النمسا في المدن التالية :
Innsbruck ، Salzburg ، Wienna
وجزء من إيطاليا في مدينة Bolzen
(Bolzano) ومدينة Verona .

من 1 July إلى 10 September 2008
ضمن برنامج تبادل ثقافي بين حكومة
إمارة الشارقة و وزارة الثقافة بالنمسا.

المصدر : يوميات رقم
[88، 87، 86، 85، 84، 83]

Six hours from Dubai to Vienna, and Abdullah Al Saadi barely slept. He woke to sunlight streaming through his cabin window, catching his first glimpses of the city through bleary eyes. Breakfast was served an hour before they landed at the Vienna International Airport on 1 July 2008. A three-hour train ride finally brought him to Salzburg, the first stop of a three-month artist exchange programme arranged by the Government of Sharjah and the Austrian Ministry of Culture.

From his spacious quarters in the Land Salzburg artist space, he had a clear view of the Salzach, the river that had powered the city's salt trade economy until the early 20th century. For the month he spent there, Al Saadi would walk with and against its currents, through its medieval old town, past renaissance and baroque architecture, its tree-lined banks busy with tourists, families and dog-walkers out to enjoy the beginning of summer.

The first book Al Saadi read there was *Water and Dreams*, French philosopher Gaston Bachelard's treatise on the poetics of water across different cultures. It set the tone for a month in which rain was ever-present: whether sketching at a waterfront cafe, reading or journalling at the Volksgarten Park or exiting one of the city's many museums.

With the weather left unchecked in the absence of air conditioning and ceiling fans, natural phase change dictated the mood of Al Saadi's day. When it rained, he rushed to find shelter for himself and his notebooks. When he left his window open at the artist space, water would pool on the floor. It was two weeks into his stay before he even thought of carrying an umbrella.

One of Salzburg's recent claims to fame is the fact that much of *The Sound of Music* (1965) was filmed at Nonnberg Abbey, Mirabell Gardens and the hills bordering the city. Salzburg in July embraces the spirit of that film, with its citywide music festival, impromptu live bands and abundance of riverside buskers.

Al Saadi's growing musical interest was piqued by visits to a museum dedicated to the Salzburg-born composer Wolfgang Mozart and to the Sound of Art exhibition at the Mönchsberg branch of the Museum der Moderne Salzburg, with its display of early futurist and fluxus sound art. At the Salzburg Museum, an item from its historical instrument collection caught his eye: an ocarina, the oblong wind instrument commonly used in Central America, the shape of which Al Saadi likened immediately to that of a sweet potato, the central focus of his long-term project, *Findale*.

In the first days of the festival, amid singing, dancing and drinking, he walked the streets with a newly purchased ocarina hanging around his neck. To Al Saadi, the body records everything it sees, hears and touches. While not a musician, having the instrument close to his chest was a meditative ritual that allowed him to be guided not by a map or itinerary but by an internal compass pointing him to new experiences and chance meetings.

On 1 August 2008, Al Saadi arrived in Vienna and took up residence on Blattgasse Street, near the Hundertwasserhaus, an expressionist architectural landmark designed by Austrian artist Friedensreich Hundertwasser.

The birthplace of Gustav Klimt and Egon Schiele as well as the resting place of Mozart and Beethoven, Vienna is also renowned for its centuries-old coffeehouse culture. As legend has it, after the second Turkish siege of Vienna was broken in 1683, Franz George Kolschitzky, a Viennese military officer who had lived in the former Ottoman Empire, found a few bags of coffee beans in an abandoned camp. He recognised their value, altered the traditional recipe by adding milk and sugar and opened the city's first coffeehouse. Similar to their role in the Arab world, these establishments soon became preferred gathering places for artists, writers and intellectuals.

Al Saadi, however, needed no history lesson to appreciate this connection. Picking up where he'd left off in Salzburg, he flitted between the city's cafes and as many of its 100 museums as possible. These were storehouses not only of European heritage, but also of the Arab and Islamic worlds. Vast imperial collections from the Habsburg Empire, as well as discoveries from Austrian-led archaeological digs in the 19th and 20th centuries, had long since trickled down to many of the city's public collections that Al Saadi visited.

From there Al Saadi left for Innsbruck, the capital of the Austrian federal state of Tyrol, to attend a month-long symposium held by the International Academy of Ceramics. Alongside local artists as well as participants from Mexico, China, Estonia and other parts of the world, Al Saadi learnt the ins and outs of the medium: from the coarseness of red clay and the high firing temperatures of white clay to the difference between a rib tool and a loop tool to the anatomy of a kiln. Aside from a handful of irregular mugs and bowls, Al Saadi naturally put most of his energy into a set of clay sweet potatoes and ocarinas.

The real value of the symposium for Al Saadi, however, lay in the glimpses of Tyrolean life during the group's day trips – its architecture, cuisine and mountainscapes, which reminded him so much of home and the promise of consistent company.

About an hour and a half from Innsbruck, up roads lined with fresh vegetation and over narrow suspension bridges, is the village of Vent. Situated within the Ötztal Valley and the Schnalskamm Mountain range, it flows with glacial streams in the summer, its milk cows and alpine horses grazing on green fields after the winter thaw.

Over a lunch garnished with wildflowers, one of the artists asked their waitress if she knew where to purchase cured cowhides. The farmer who could oblige her, the waitress said, would be back in time for *marende*. Used in parts of Austria and South Tyrol in Italy, *marende* refers to a simple, hearty meal in the late afternoon or early evening, a traditional platter of bread, cheese and cured meats paired with wine or beer and served as a welcome respite after a day of physically demanding activity.

Marende, marende, Al Saadi would turn the word around in his head, applying his own form of linguistic analysis to it. Given its resemblance to the phrase *ma'a al-ghadaa,* or 'with lunch' in Arabic, he concluded that it pointed to some undocumented exchange between Europe and the Arabic-speaking world.

Two days after his trip to Vent, Al Saadi went to Bolzano in South Tyrol. Dotted with vineyards and fruit orchids and surrounded by Alpine mountain ranges, this city was one of his first stops in Italy. Alluding to its history as a key trade point for centuries, Bolzano's language, architecture and culture are equal parts Mediterranean and Austrian. Piazza Walther, the city's bustling main square, was named after celebrated medieval lyric poet Walther von der Vogelweide, who first made a name for himself as a travelling singer before being granted a fiefdom by the Holy Roman Empire.

Coming face to face with Ötzi, the famous natural mummy exhibited in Bolzano, Al Saadi was first drawn to the dozens of faded tattoos running across his body. Researchers have found that these markings also correspond to sites of injury, degeneration and sickness. The fact that Ötzi was found so close to where Al Saadi had discovered the word *marende*, that he bore similar branding marks induced by folk medicine and that he had died in the middle of his own journey made Al Saadi feel oddly close to him – as close as one could feel to a man from the Copper Age.

Verona, the next stop on Al Saadi's brief Italy tour, brought him deeper into wine country, to the Arena di Verona, one of the world's best preserved Roman amphitheatres, and Castelvecchio, a 14th-century fortress that now serves as an art museum spanning the Medieval and Renaissance periods. Contemporaneous with Castelvecchio's heyday, Dante Alighieri took refuge in the city after his exile from Florence. In 1865, Verona erected a statue of the poet to commemorate the seven years he spent there, pouring over manuscripts in the Capitolare Library and writing a significant portion of his *Divine Comedy*.

Back in Vienna via Innsbruck, Al Saadi spent his final days in Europe completing his last panoramic city scroll, ticking a few more museum visits off his list and whiling away the hours reading and people watching at Stadtpark. With his funds dwindling and a run-in with two plain clothes policemen spoiling his taste for the city, he took one final day trip to Melk, a town in Lower Austria along the Danube River. From there he sketched his way through a four-hour round trip boat ride to nearby Krems, passing the 12th-century Schloss Schönbühel, Dürnstein and Aggstein castles as well as the riverbed where archaeologists unearthed the Venus of Willendorf in 1908. Al Saadi had seen the figurine, dating back to Paleolithic times, days prior at the Natural History Museum.

Three days later, Al Saadi decided that his European summer was well and truly over. He was going home with six notebooks of sketches and diaries as well as works on paper, stone and ceramic knocking around in his luggage. More than anything, what finally drove him home instead of hopping on a train to Belgium was boredom and loneliness. The loneliness he had managed to keep at bay his entire trip was finally catching up to him.

In the introduction to *Marende* (2008), a book chronicling Al Saadi's time in Europe, he states outright that he did not set out to write a travel guide. Containing nearly every journal entry and illustration he produced in those three months, the book is a testament to this belief and a rejection of the label of 'tourist' itself.

To Al Saadi, a tourist plans their trip around destinations that are deemed touristic, armed with cameras, in his own words, to defend against the fallibility of memory. His movement was much more spontaneous, his primary experiences scrupulously documented over more than 600 pages, always searching for new connections between art, land, literature, music and everyday life.

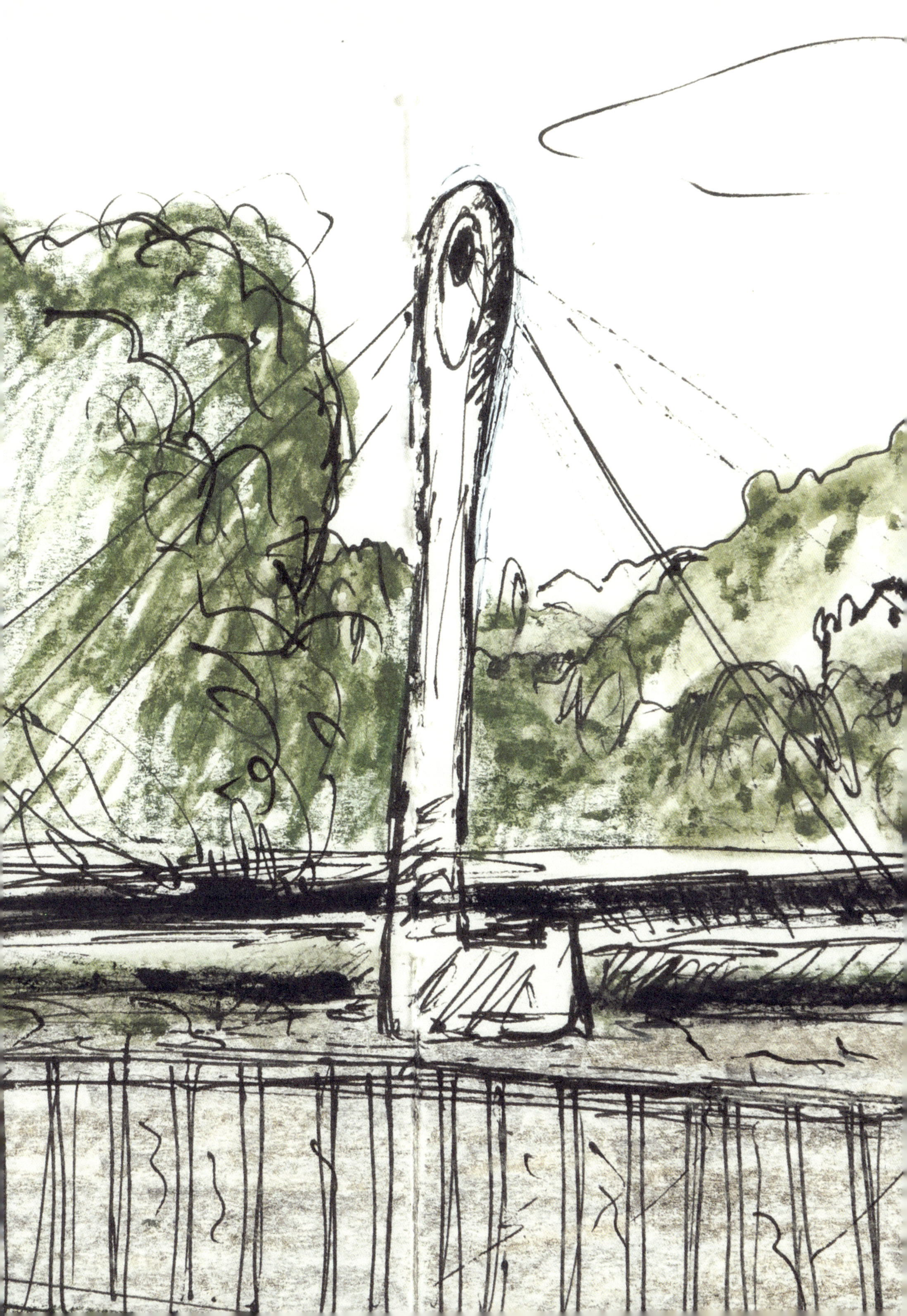

مغينِدا

Marende

Rofenhöfe 2.011 m

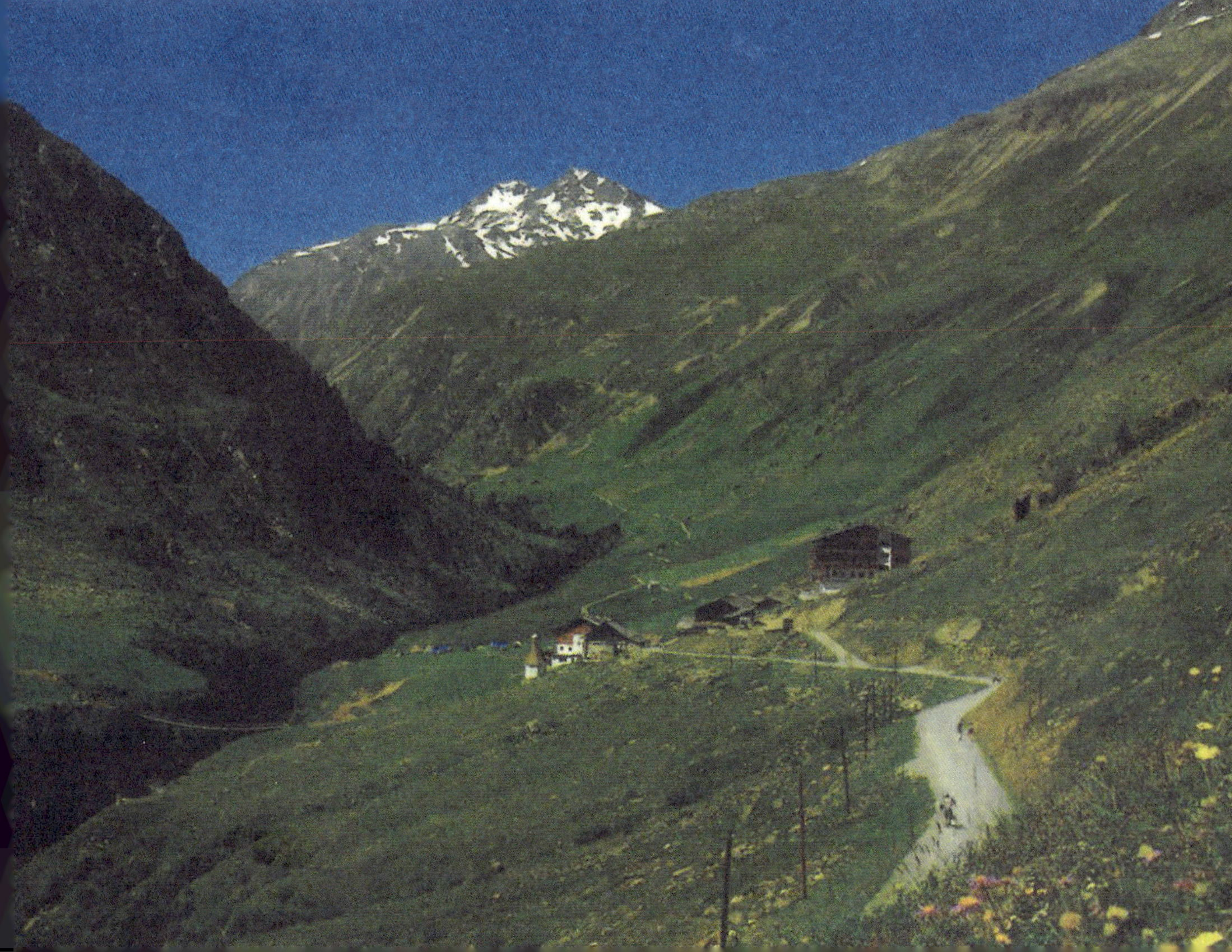

مغيّنداً = مع الغداء

Marende = With lunch

By

Abdallah Moh'd Alsaadi
عبد الله محمد السعدي
2008

All rights reserved for
the artist.

Flöckner
DER BÄCKER DER SALZBURGER
SEIT 1837

- Bill Viola (A portrait on light and
  heat 1979 (·video film),
-
  memory surface and
  metal prayers 1977

____

مشيت قليلا من دون هدف محدود حتى وصلت في
متحف

Museum der Moderne
Salzburg

حينما هذا معرض لثلاثة فنانين ؛

- Hiroshi Sugimoto,
- Nan Hoover   .
- Bill Viola .

März - Juli 2008

المعهود بالاعمال الكبيرة ... في الاروقة ، لكن ...
متحف المشي في الغابة ... والمدينة والآمنة القديمة .

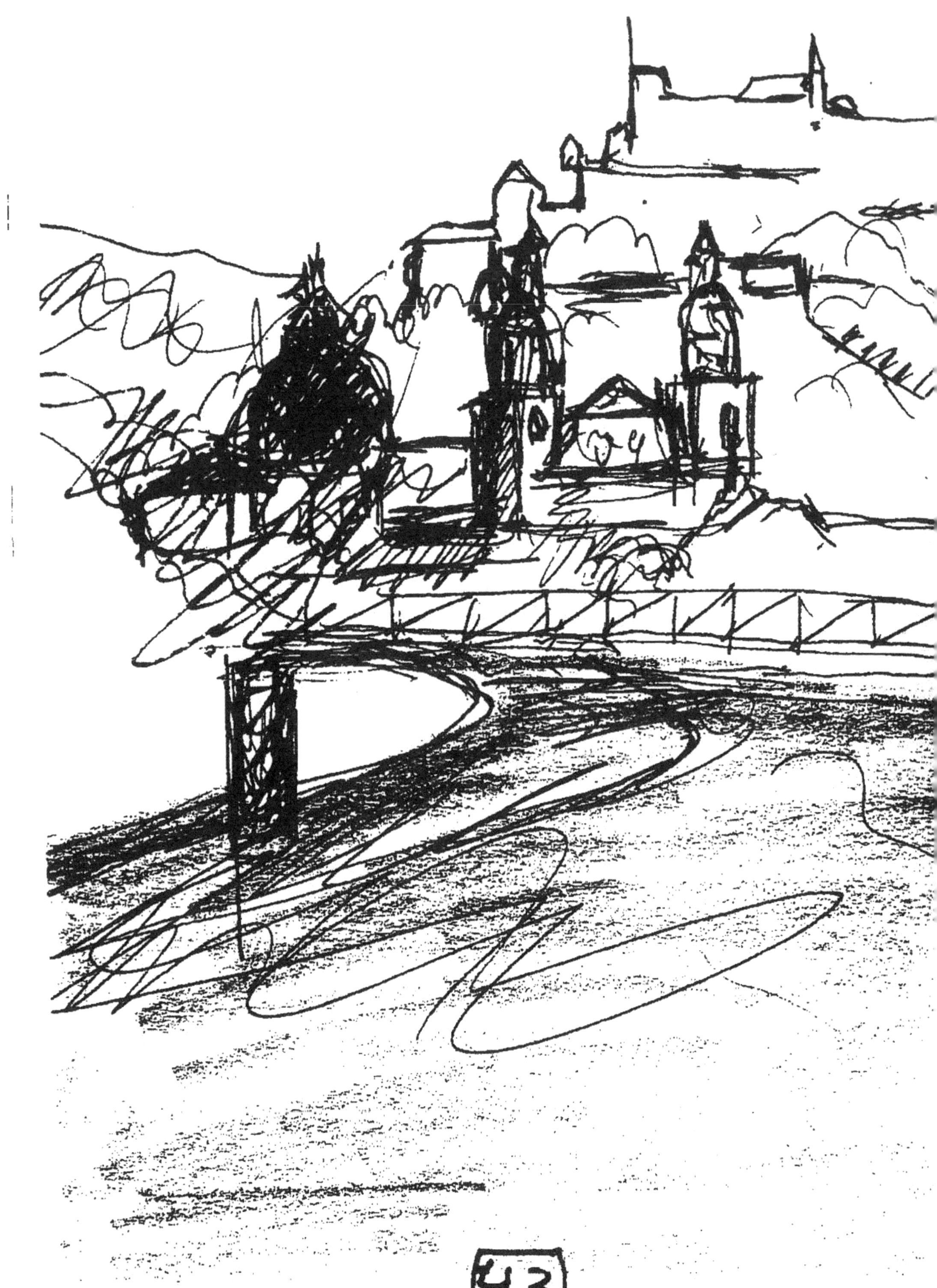

43

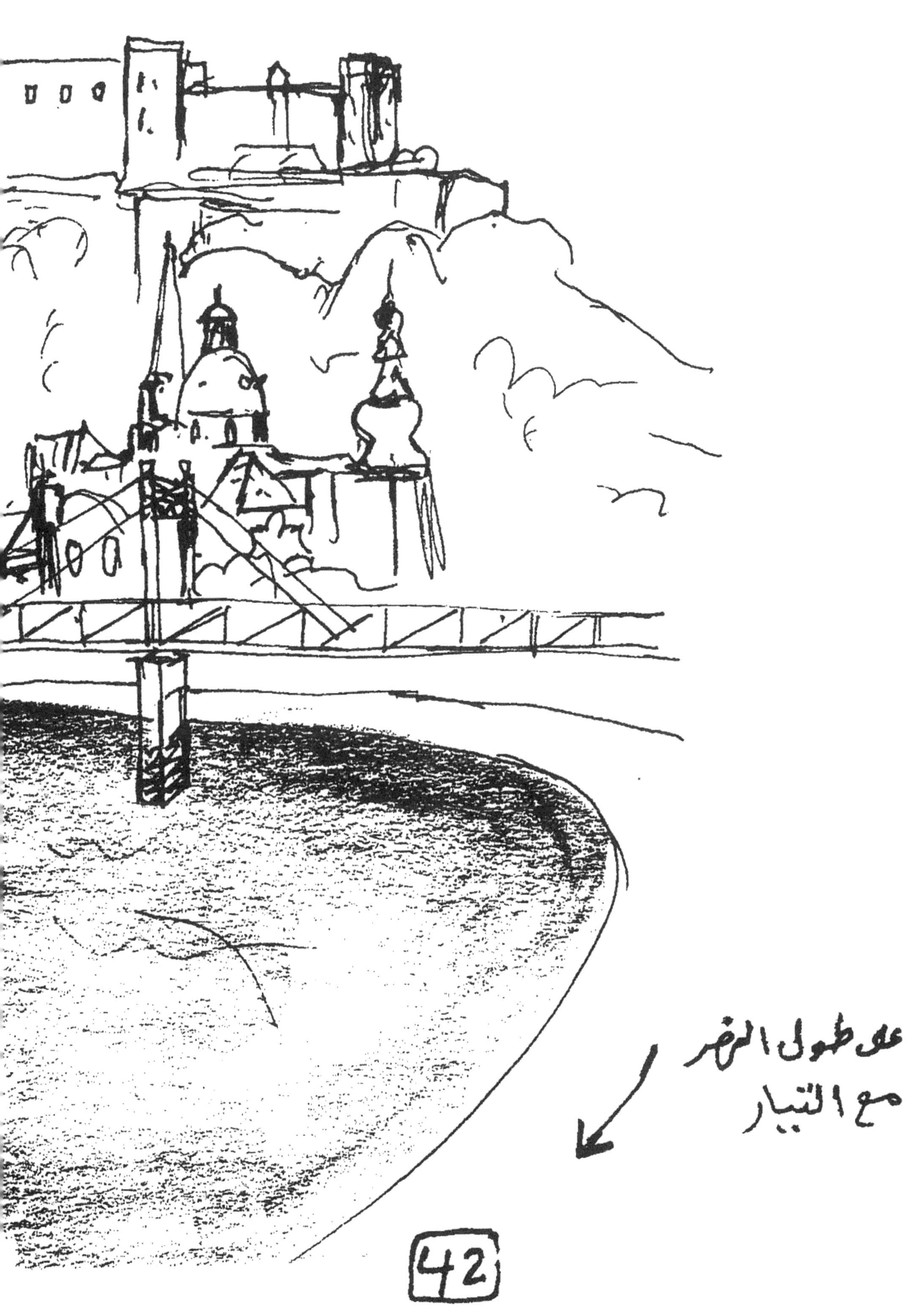

على طول النهر
مع التيار
42

دخلت الحديقة . Franz Josef . كنت أريد
جلوسي على مقعد للقراءة لكن لم أجد مقعداً .. منزاهت
مشي على ضفة النهر ... جلست على مقعد .. قرأت
قليلاً في كتاب الماء و الأحلام؟ ... تركت الملكات
تعبت المشي ... وبعد ساعة بوابات لسيارة تتبلد
تعب .. فأحسست أن السماء قد تمطر .. فقررت
سودة .. لكن كنت قد مشيت لمسافة بعيدة
بت رياح قوية ... وتحركت السحب .. ونبأة بسقط
مطر بغزارة ... فأسرعت للاجتماع تحت شجيرما
وفي نصف ساعة هذا المطر قليلاً فأسرعت مايغرا
كانت ملابس قد تبللت لكن خفت أن تتبلل
لي .. الكتاب ودفتر يوميات كنت أقرأ
يس القرطاس ...

بعد عودتي وبعد ساعتين سقط المطر مرة أخرى .
ت كالعادة أترك النافذة العلوية مفتوحة
هذا اليوم وجدت مسلم المطر قد دخل الغرفة
.. عندما كنت في الخارج قد دخل الغرفة

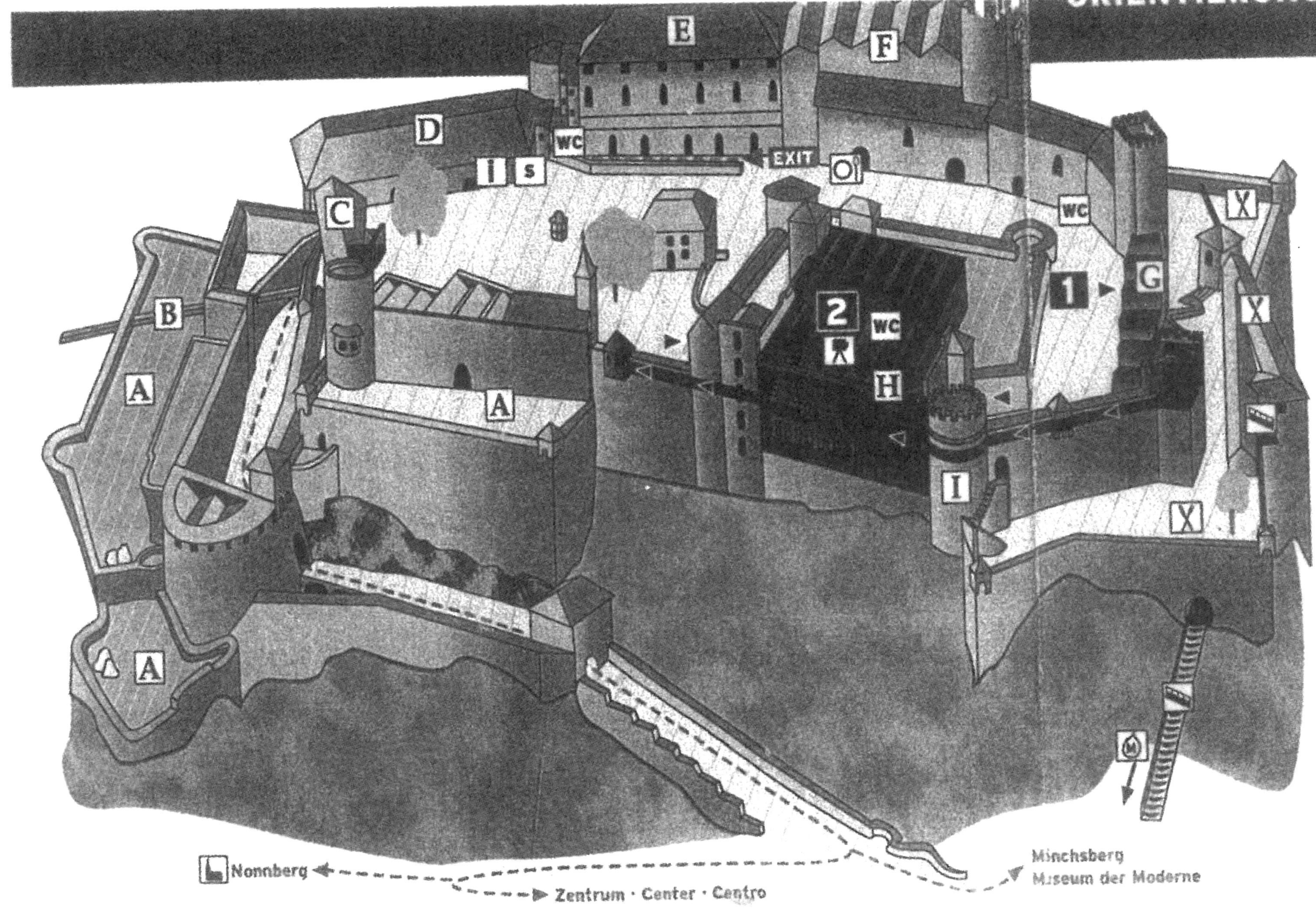

E
F
D
WC
EXIT
I s
C
WC
B
1
G
A
2
WC
H
A
I
X
X
X
A
Nonnberg
Zentrum · Center · Centro
Minchsberg
Museum der Moderne

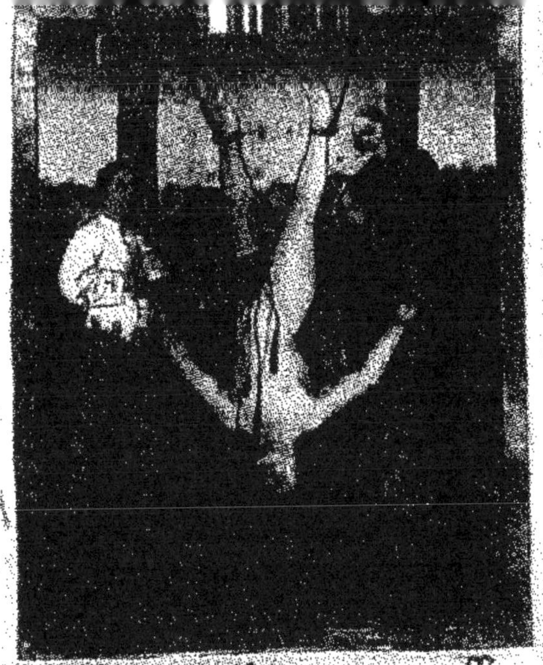

جدت المتلفة و أخرجت
...ب و قريب من متحف
[Papyrus] جلست في الظل
ليلا وعدت أمس . بقايا جدران
حجرات متبقية منذ العهد
الروماني تبدو وأسفل الشارع
حائط بجدار وسياج و من
هنا وهناك عربات الخيل تحمل
سياح من ولى .
كنت متعباً لذا توقفت في
[Palffy] رشفت قهوة cake au lait وبعد نصف
ساعة تابعت طريقي عائداً ماشياً الأوبرا لكن
درت في طريقي متحف
[ALBERTINA]

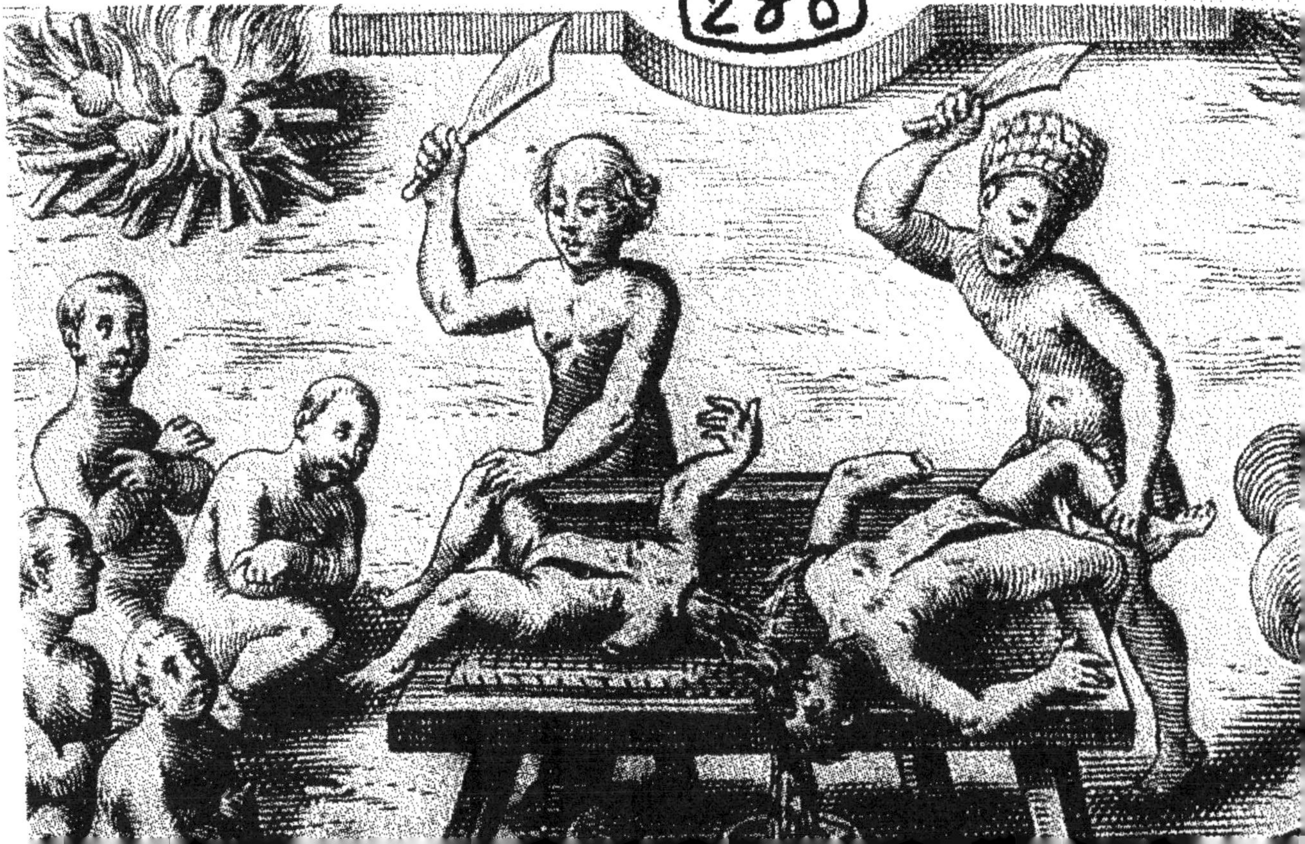

286

بعد خروجي من المتحف زرت المكتبة الوطنية (National Bibliothek) لزيارة معرض:

Blutige Geschichten

هناك صور كثيرة وكتب معروضة تحكي من طرق التعذيب والقتل والاضطهاد منذ القديم إلى الآن. حتى صورة الرئيس العراقي صدام حسين موجودة والرئيس غاندي و غيرهم. المكتبة مليئة بالكتب القديمة.

wiener staatsoper
ticket
für Erwachsene
€ 3,—
inkl. 10% USt

STAATSOPERNMUSEUM
007244
STAATSOPERNMUSEUM

In Kooperation mit
Info-terminals developed
SIEMENS
Global network of innovation

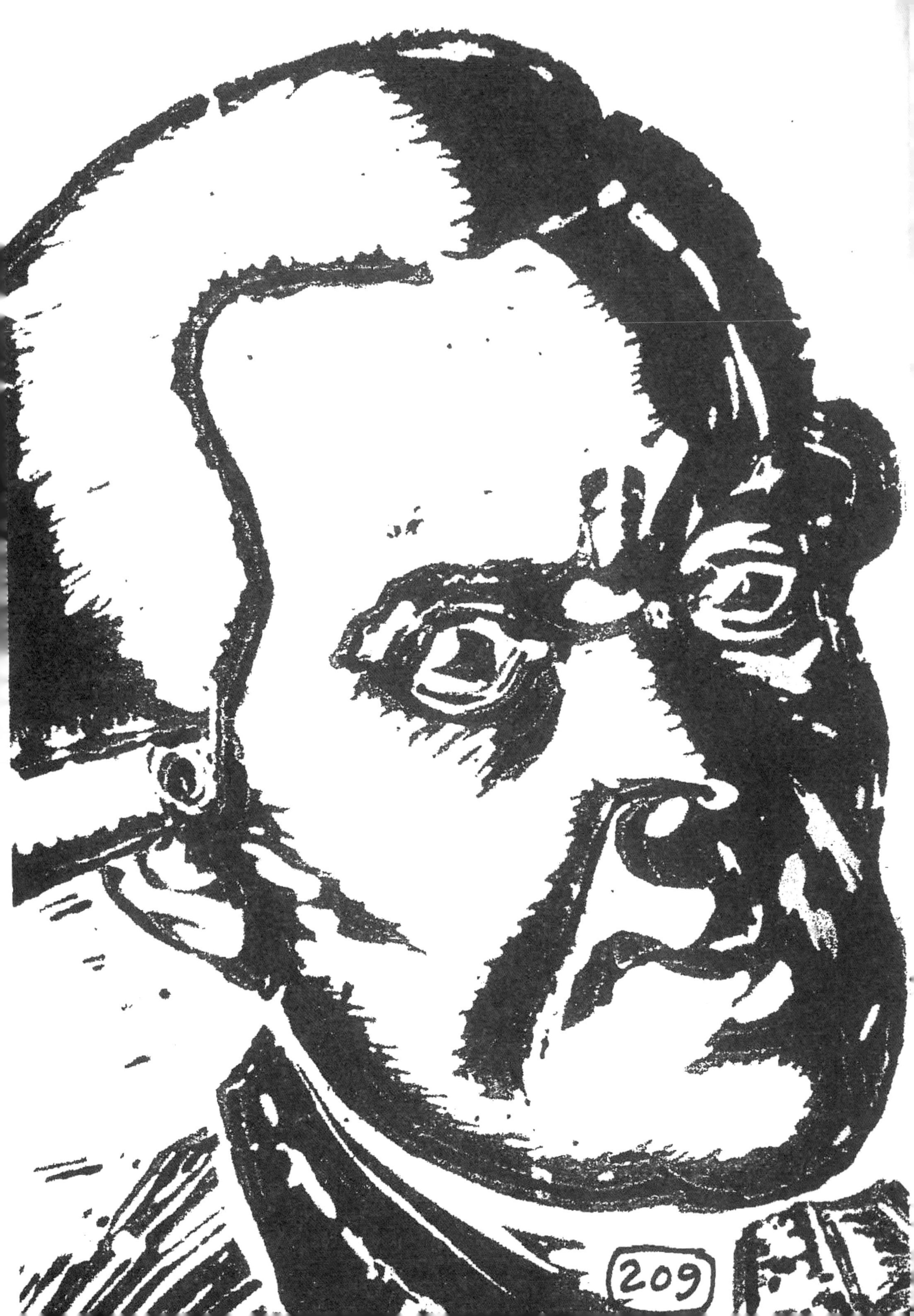

209

Lawrence Sterne
Tristram Shandy

بعد عمودي وجدت انه رقم [220] هو أيضاً رقم
عند الصفحات من ١- 220 من كتاب رسائل أمي القا
صورتها كمشروع فني ... وكما قلت لـ
Irina إنه عندي كتاب : مختارات من الشعر الروسي ، و بما
إنك روسية فأصبحت هناك علاقة أو رابط بين
أحداث وأسماء وأشياء من حياتنا .. و بمعرفتي
كأنك تفتحين لي الكتاب لقراءته . و بمعرفتي
20:00 من قاعة [Kunstlerhaus] ما هرة للفنان
الصيني Li Singsong أنا ومترجمته من الصينية الى الأبلغ
بعد المي فترة عدت الى الغرفة ... التقيت بـ اميليو
وتحدثنا عن مشروعي الفني الحالي لكن المشكلة في الجمهور
شاشره2 هذا عند أنا ا دفتر اليوميات في الجمهور
رقم [86] . دفتر رقم [85] دفتر اليوميات الجديد
لدفتر [89] لدفتر اليوميات [85] دفتر مكمل (اكتشف
نفت عند الثامنة مساء ليلاً ... هنا النهار أطول لذا يبس
المرء ان الأيام أكثر طولاً وزمنا .. لا يهم هذه آخر
صفحة من دفتر اليوميات وعلى الصفحة المقابلة صورة
الموسيقار هايدن Haydn وشكراً
[308]

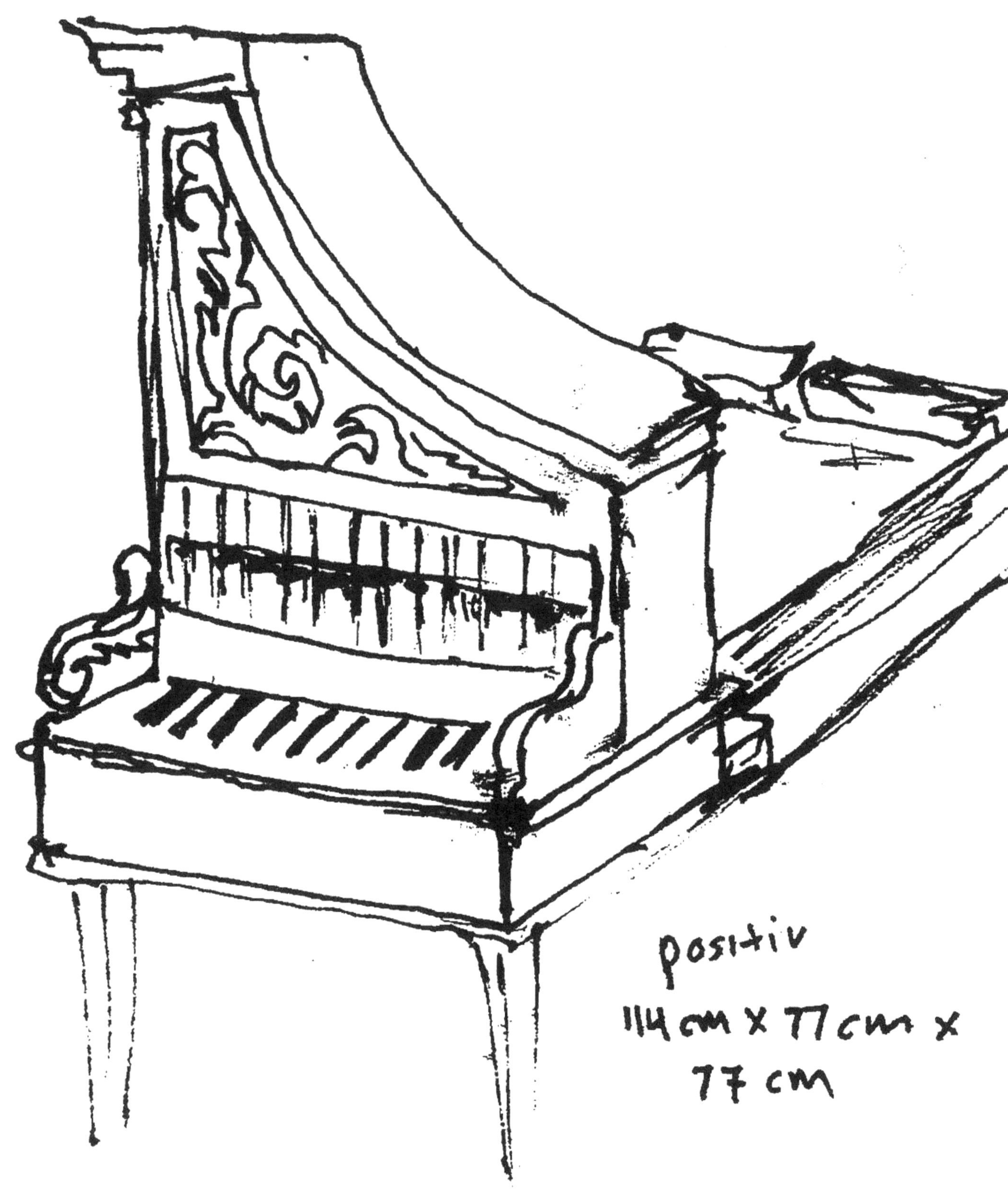

positiv
114 cm X 77 cm X
77 cm

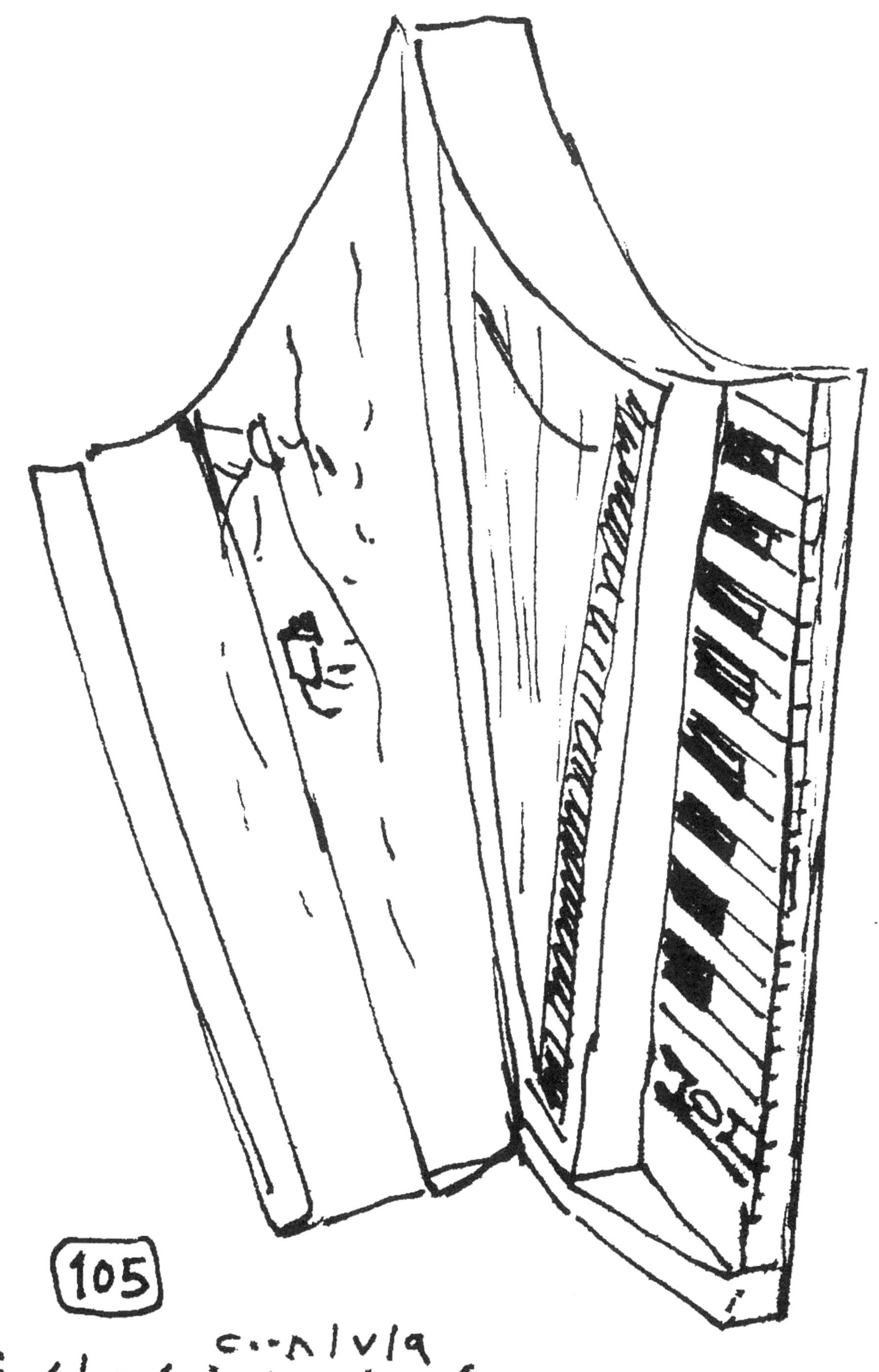

[105]

٦٠٠٨/٧/٩

مجموعة أمكنشتات لبعض الآلات الموسيقية
من
[Spielzeugmuseum]

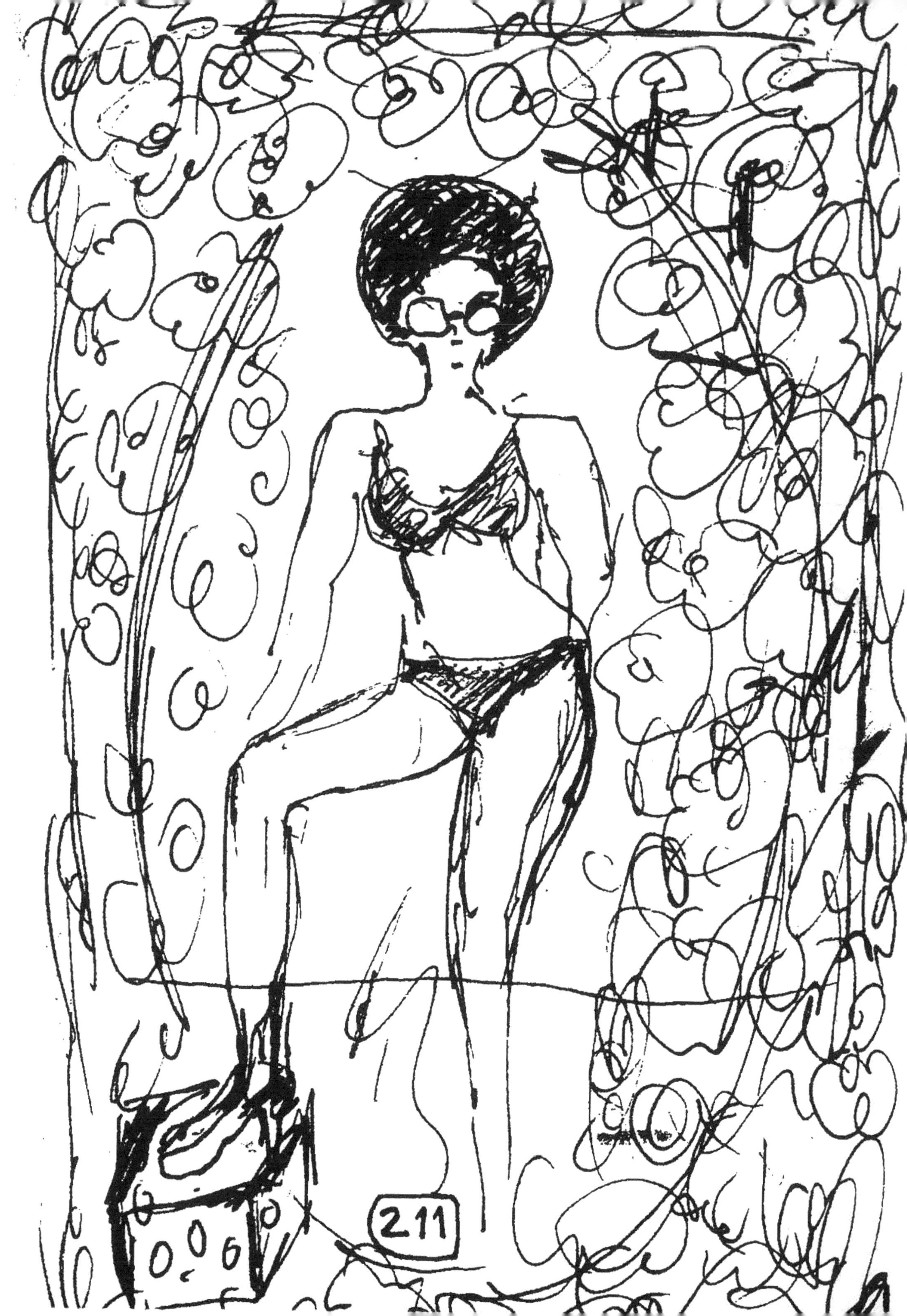
2.11

هنا يمكن مشاهدة الصخور من بعد ...
من الجبل وأحياناً تنهار
بسبب الأمطار وغيره لذلك تتشكل
عقبة لدى السكان القاطنين
عند سفح الجبل .

لم يتبقَّ كثيراً ...
كانت Irina تشم وتلمح
الزهور المتاخمة للبحيرة .
هو وربما ، كانتا تمشيان
ببطء ...
استقلينا سيارة أجرة
عائدين لأننا حجزنا لنا طاولة
من المطعم
لتناول العشاء

كانت الساعة السادسة مساءً ؟ عدنا الى المطعم .. تناولنا العشاء .. صحن سلطة لذيذة ، وصحن
سمك مع البطاطس وبعده حلوى بفواكه berry البنفسجي كما أتفقد ... بعد ساعة
أو أكثر ركبنا السيارة عائدين . بنى بحيرة القرية ... من يسميني سمعت وعلى ...
قالوا لي أنه بنت أحمر ...

نستمع إلى الأغاني اليمنية. كان اميليو قد استأذن للخروج قبل وصولك [برباره] وقد تناولنا الأمطار معاً و قررنا الذهاب لزيارة بحيرة Mond وتعني Moon اي القمر وهي تعني بحيرة [Mondsee] اي بحيرة القمر لأن شكلاً يشبه القمر .

كانت برباره
تقود وانسياره
وتتعالى الموسيقى
اليمنية من المسجل
والتراث اليمني
حاضراً دائماً
لدى برباره
فرأينا طريق اشترينا
عليه الفواكه
الطازجة من الاكشاك
وتابعنا الطريق حتى
وصلنا الى بحيرة القمر [Mondsee]
هناك وسط العشب والخضرة والأشجار
وجدنا راحتنا ... تقدمت على الحشيش
وهناك عائلات كثيرة ... تركت المكان وجلسنا
مقاهي المقهى أوالمطعم ... رفضنا القوة

وقررنا بعد ذلك المشي
رغبتنا فيها عبر المسار
الغابة .. وتابعنا المشي
منها عند واستمر
لنباتات قديم من أيام
الديناصورات، وأكل
berry الذي ينمو طبيعياً
تحدثنا معا
نهايات بسبب
الأمطار وتقتلع
وتوشحار كما حدث
اربع سنوات
أمضيتي به زوجة

اميليو
تابعنا المشي حتى وصلنا
إلى بحيرة [Attersee]
وهي أكبر البحيرات
يمارس الناس التخييم
السباحة وركوب

Mondsee

Brezen

Salzburger

متى كى اسفوا يقربوه من التأثر بالصبغ
و بجزء من تجربته .

خرجنا من هناك عائدين نيا جريلق
نتسرامى على أطرافه البيوت
الجميلة على شرفاتها ترى الورود و الأزهار
و من بعيد ربما نشم رائحة روث
الأبقار و لون أخضر يكسو كل شي
أما قطعة الجبن هذه فقد جربتها
و أكلت البارحة ، لقد اشتريتها بعد
عودتى و خروجى إلى المدينة .. ما أطيع
أنا فى المدينة لكن تقاس المسافة
كوالى عشرة دقائق مشياً على الأقدام
أما ركوب العربة التى يجرها حصانان
فلم أجرب ركوبى . والبارحة رأيت
المقف "chariot"
كما تسمى . تناولت سندويش
شوربا

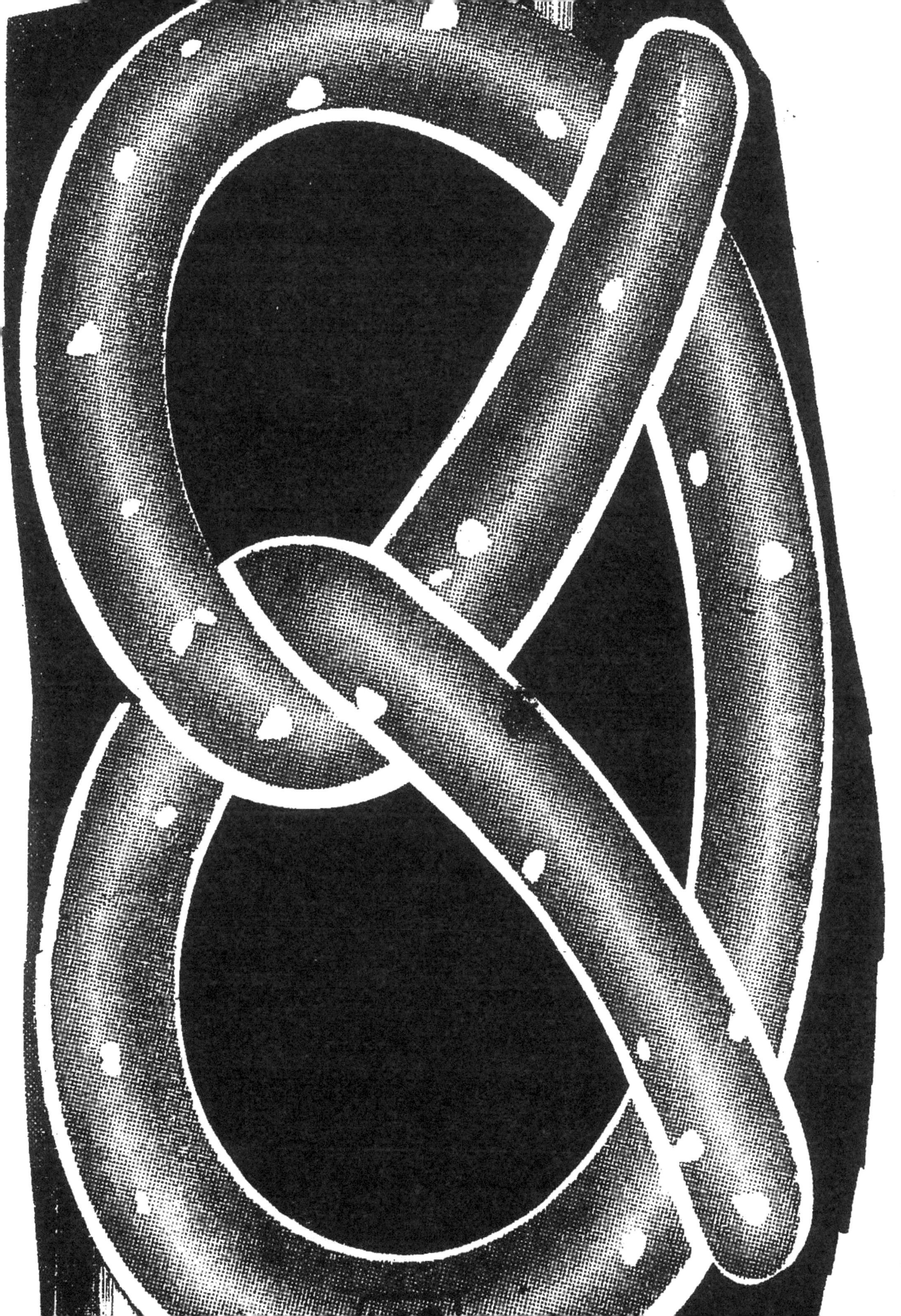

Hoor AlQasimi
In Conversation With
Abdullah Alsaadi

Hoor Al Qasimi (HAQ): To start, I would like to ask you about the works that you included in the exhibition at the Sharjah Art Foundation and about the title of the exhibition, *Al Toubay*, which, as you mentioned to me, has a connection to your mother?

Abdullah Al Saadi (AAS): I undertook a comparative journey to South America where I documented similarities between my homeland and South America. 'Al Toubay' is the Arabic name for a piece of equipment used to make bread, which I consider to be a staple of universal nourishment. Bread generates and links us to one another. Bread also reminds me of my mother, and this is why I titled the exhibition *Al Toubay*.

HAQ: What is the back story of the comparative journey featured in this exhibition?

AAS: I was inspired to make this trip as a result of three prior journeys which covered the areas surrounding my home and the northern emirates near the Omani border. I called the first one the *Camar Cande's Journey* (2010–2011), named for my travelling companion and donkey. *The Watermelon Journey* (2013) covered a mountainous area, and the paintings I made during that period were inspired by the red colour of watermelons. On the third journey, which also took place in Roos Al Jibal, I reflected on the unsettling nature of communities who endure moving from one place to another, such as the Roma. Most of my production during this trip was in the form of entries in my diary. On this trip, I had two books about the Roma with me, and while reading them, I compared my life with theirs. I felt an affinity as I was camping, cooking and moving from one country to another. Although the areas I was moving through were near each other, I felt anxious when I moved from one village to another, as if I had departed for another country.

HAQ: Could you elaborate more on this sensation of anxiety associated with your journeys? How does it also relate to your context and upbringing?

AAS: I believe it has something to do with an inherited obsession with moving and travelling across a landscape that similarly the Roma suffer from. These are problems that have troubled me since childhood. My family moved in the winter from the palm farms in Madha, which is in Omani territory, to Khorfakkan on the east coast of the Emirates, and we would return to Madha the in summer. I found such upheavals stressful. They continue to haunt me in my current life. Now I move between Nahwa and a village in Masafi. While doing this journey, I started to feel like a roamer and practised rituals of what feels like uprootedness. To move from place to place, the Roma, as an example, use animals. Yet when I was a child, my family used a car to move around and transport items. In my practice, I use other forms of mobility, such as animals, to show affinity with the Roma.

HAQ: Yes, animals and other non-human entities take a central and critical role in your practice and the journeys you make, such as in Camar Cande, where the donkey and the dog come in almost as your co-authors….

AAS: When I was young, I bred donkeys. I decided to go on this particular trip to draw some natural landscapes. I visited this area in the northern emirates and Oman before on a bicycle, but this time I wanted to write in my diary about my feelings, emotions and relation with animals. I planned this project five years before I started the trip.

Another co-author of the trip was my friend Abdulrahman Al Muaini, who drove the car that was loaded with everything we needed for the journey. I made the journey on foot, the donkey in front of me and the dog behind me. The donkey and the dog were tied with one rope. We walked for hours and then camped. During the trip I worked on my drawing and drew a road map, and while camping I worked on my paintings. I produced 150 paintings in addition to a video and some photos. This trip was tiring, but it brought me closer to animals, especially to the dog and the donkey, despite the fights they had with each other.

HAQ: Animals also accompanied you on the 'Al Toubay' journey, the eponymous title of the exhibition?

AAS: I was accompanied by animals during the 'Al Toubay' trip. I also used the red colour of the watermelon in drawing the mountains. This idea came when I was eating watermelon with my son. He told me that watermelon is like a mountain. And so I was inspired by him. After the Camar Cande journey, I thought of going on another similar trip, with more animals this time. But that would require more people and more cars. As a result, I came up with the idea of engraving animal figures on stones to represent the real animals that would have accompanied me on the journey. I took 10 stones with me, each one representing a different animal.

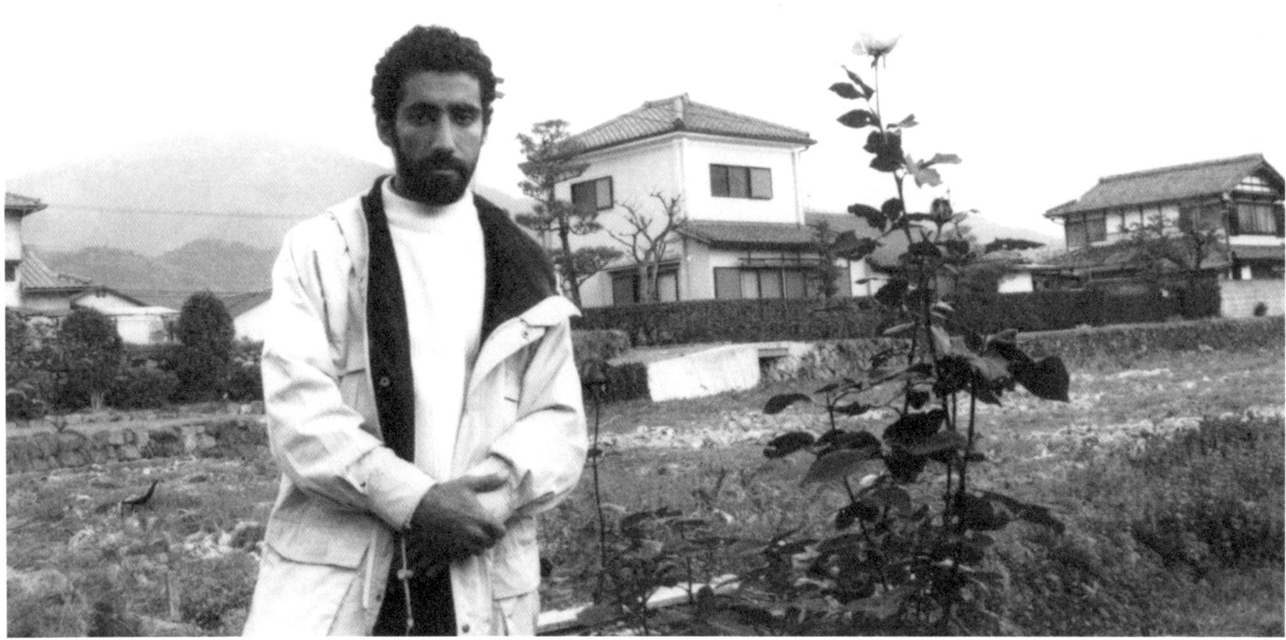

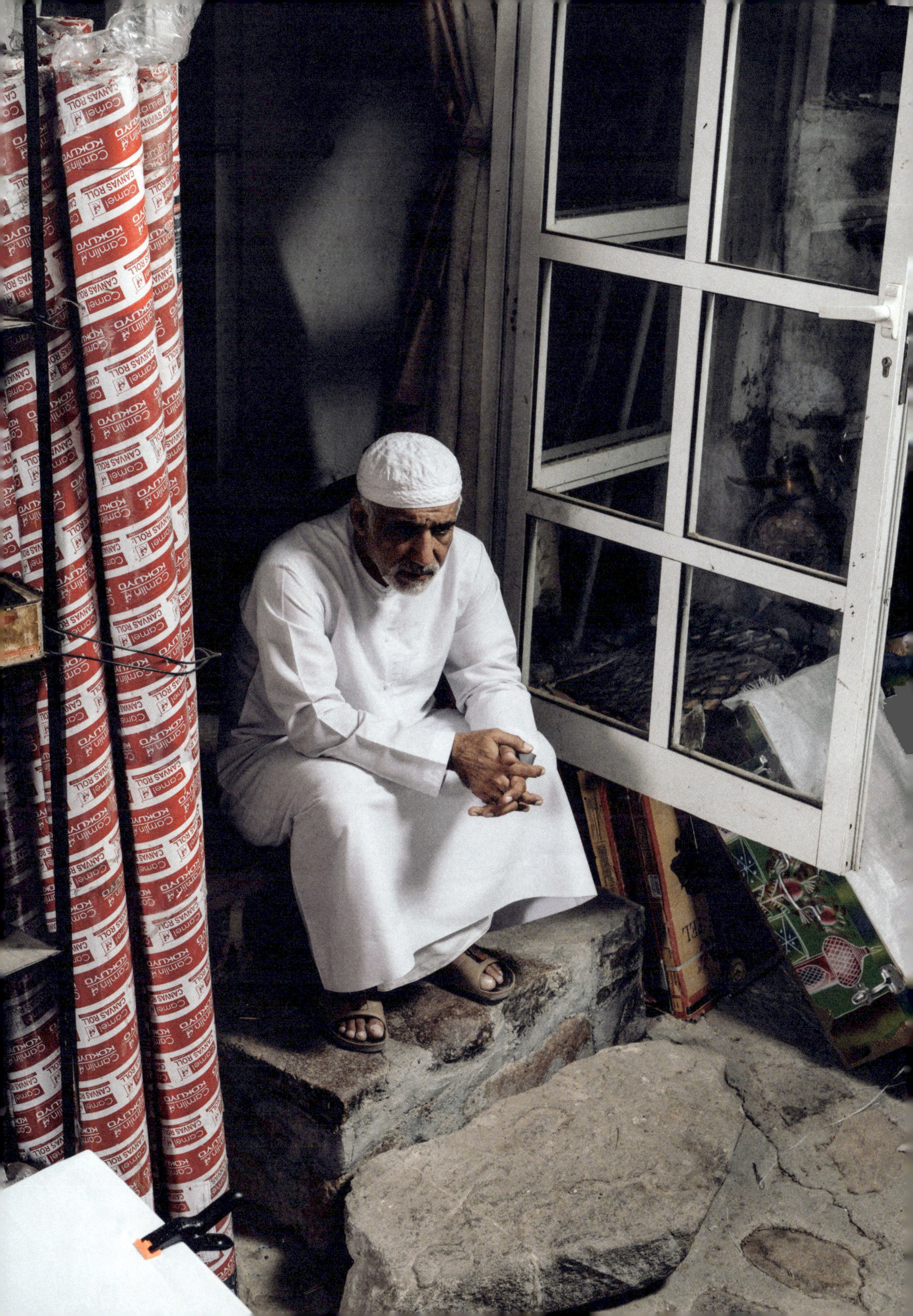

Through my writing and by maintaining rituals that I would do back home – like placing food out for my cat after taking my dinner, which I did for the cat engraved on stone – I felt this performance helped me reflect on my creative writing.

HAQ: It also echoes another work of yours, *Scarecrows* (2013), where the function of the scarecrow used in agriculture is somehow criticised and unveiled and the bird or other avian entities are positioned as co-authors.

AAS: The inspiration for the scarecrow idea was the Christ the Redeemer statue in Rio de Janeiro. I observed the similarity between the statue and the palm scarecrows that we use in gardens here. The idea materialised, and I started to produce scarecrows for this project. In the past, people from my community used whatever materials were available in their homes. I added a base for the scarecrows so as to facilitate moving them from one place to another. I also added photos of a donkey or a woman to adorn the scarecrows. In the past, the farmer used scarecrows to scare birds, but in the end I tried to reveal that the farmer is in essence scaring themselves. It is about flight and fight, where humans project their wishes to fly, but at the same time, they fights birds when thye use the scarecrows. From my perspective, I believe that birds have the right to eat.

HAQ: In addition to animals, your acts of journeying and walking simultaneously position other objects and non-sentient entities, such as the slipper, or flip-flop, as expressed in the work *Stone Slippers* (2013).

AAS: The flip-flop can be considered part of an identity. In the past, people from all different social classes wore flip-flops on their visits, travels and everywhere. They represented freedom and comfort. Pieces of rubber tyres were even added to them in some communities so they would not crack. The situation is different now. Flip-flops are only used at the sea or in bathrooms, and they are not appropriate to wear for social visits and salons. The word slipper even suggests a slippery thing. If we were to wear stone slippers, the entire concept changes. The slippers become heavy and burdensome and thus can be reflective of life in general. In the past, life was simple, but nowadays it is much heavier, more complicated. There is also a relationship with the earth – when we wear the stone slippers, we feel the heat of the stone. The stone slippers are also part of this journey, because walking is an essential component of making a trip, and walking reminds me of my mother.

HAQ: You touch on an important aspect here of the extension of your life and its rituals into an artistic practice. Where and when do you consider the formations of your practice as an artist?

AAS: I think in my diaries. I have been writing in my diaries for 25 years, since I was in secondary school. Also drawing. The oldest drawing that I still have I made when I was 12 years old. It was about a folk dance, and I used wax crayons to colour it. I had a collection of works I did from second grade to secondary school. This collection remained in my school in Masafi, but when I returned to take it, I was told that it had been destroyed.

I still have a notebook from intermediate school. My brother and I went to boarding school in Masafi, and while at school we used to draw in the afternoons. My brother was a good painter during this time, but he stopped drawing as he got older. Boarding school had a considerable influence on me. It was like home. I lived with other students on weekdays, and we only visited our homes on Thursdays and Fridays. This also contributed to a sense of ongoing movement and perhaps anxiety, apart from my family's seasonal lifestyle. School became a life in itself, and students had their own independence. In the 1970s and 1980s, life was difficult even with family, especially for those who lived in a village where there were not any schools. It was better to stay in the school dorm where everything was available, including food and money. Students were given pocket money of 300 AED, which was quite a lot at the time. Life was good! Later on, I moved to Sharjah to complete the second and third secondary classes. Then I joined the Emirates Fine Arts Society (EFAS).

HAQ: What was it like being in Sharjah at the time, and who from EFAS influenced your work?

AAS: Travelling and experiencing Sharjah at the time was special. I made friends and met poets, writers and artists. I remember that I first met with Hassan Sharif and was mostly influenced by him and his ideas. I was still a student, and I visited EFAS only once a week. Nevertheless, I participated in the its activities. Even after I enrolled in the university, I maintained my connection with EFAS. Over time, I began to chart my own path in terms of the direction my work was taking. I realised that the migration and journeys which characterised my life set me apart from other local practitioners.

HAQ: So when do you think you began to incorporate this into your practice?

AAS: When I first went abroad. When I finished my university study, I applied for a study programme in Japan, and I was accepted. My experience in Japan was good, especially since it was the first time that I had studied abroad.

Before this, I first visited Japan in 1992 through my participation in a youth programme called Ship for World Youth. Every year, 12 to 20 young people from different countries travel to Japan and sail on the Ship for World Youth for two months, visiting different countries and destinations. I visited Sri Lanka, Singapore, the Red Sea, Alexandria and Cairo, Spain, and Muscat. There was a special programme and scheduled activities in each location we visited. After the study programme, which provided us with a monthly stipend and accommodation, I studied at Kyoto Seika University. I was a research student, and I was not obliged to attend classes, but I did some work with one professor. During this period, I began to produce works in my own artistic style. I stayed in Kyoto for about a year and a half.

HAQ: I believe it was also the same time period when you started making and experimenting with scrolls. Was it in Japan where you learnt about them?

AAS: Yes, it was during this period that I became acquainted with this Japanese art form. The first scroll I did was for a place in the vicinity of my home. At that time, I started drawing scrolls in my own style, which was different from the Japanese method. A scroll is like an open, endless road with large surface areas and more room for freedom of expression than a painting, which can be restricted and limited by a frame.

HAQ: It seems that your work began with the page and works-on-paper, but when you encountered the scroll, it helped you expand and express the transience and openness that your life's journeys symbolised for you. When did you start actually using found materials and objects, such as stones, from your journeys in your works?

AAS: A few years after I came back from Japan, I started incorporating these elements, as in *My Mother's Letters* (1998–2013). My mother was illiterate. When she visited me and she didn't find me at home, she used to put small stones or whatever objects were available at the entrance of the studio to let me know that she had been there. When I came back, I realised that she had come. Sometimes she came while I was sleeping, and I wouldn't hear her knocking, and again she put her small stones at the door. Putting her stones on my doorstep was like a language, a form of communication between us. Illiteracy does not impede communication among people. By 2013, after my mother passed away, these objects became an artwork and a much bigger project. It has taken many years to document this project, shuttling between Khorfakkan and Madha.

At some point, after my mother bought a phone, things changed and the stones and letters became less frequent. I found it a difficult transition, but I recognise convenience often forces things to change.

HAQ: What was your thinking process for using letters composed from stone and other materials you collected as a project?

AAS: I drew, numbered and wrote comments about them. When I didn't have enough information about a particular letter, I relied on what I had written in my diaries about the letters. I started to construct a type of alphabet derived from the lines and contours of each letter as a way to document and organise the letters. For example, I collected a line or two from each letter, collecting 28 to 30 lines in total, similar to an alphabet system.

I studied every line and chose from the group of 28 to 30 the easiest or most straightforward line. The line I chose is similar to the hiragana and the katakana, which are components of the Japanese written communication system. While I was in Japan, I studied how to write Japanese alphabets, which had a great influence on me. The Japanese alphabet is comparable to the Arabic alphabet. I had a problem in terms of the vowel points in the Arabic language, which don't exist in the Japanese language. For that purpose, I used the hamzah(ء), tanween (ً) and shaddah (ّ)and others used in Arabic.

This work was an endeavour to create a means of communication and a private language. Through this work, I made my mother try to read and write.

After *My Mother's Letters*, I produced several alphabet systems that were specific to unique works, such as the 'Birds' and 'Sweet Potatoes' alphabet systems. Over time, I began to think that every work creates its own unique alphabet.

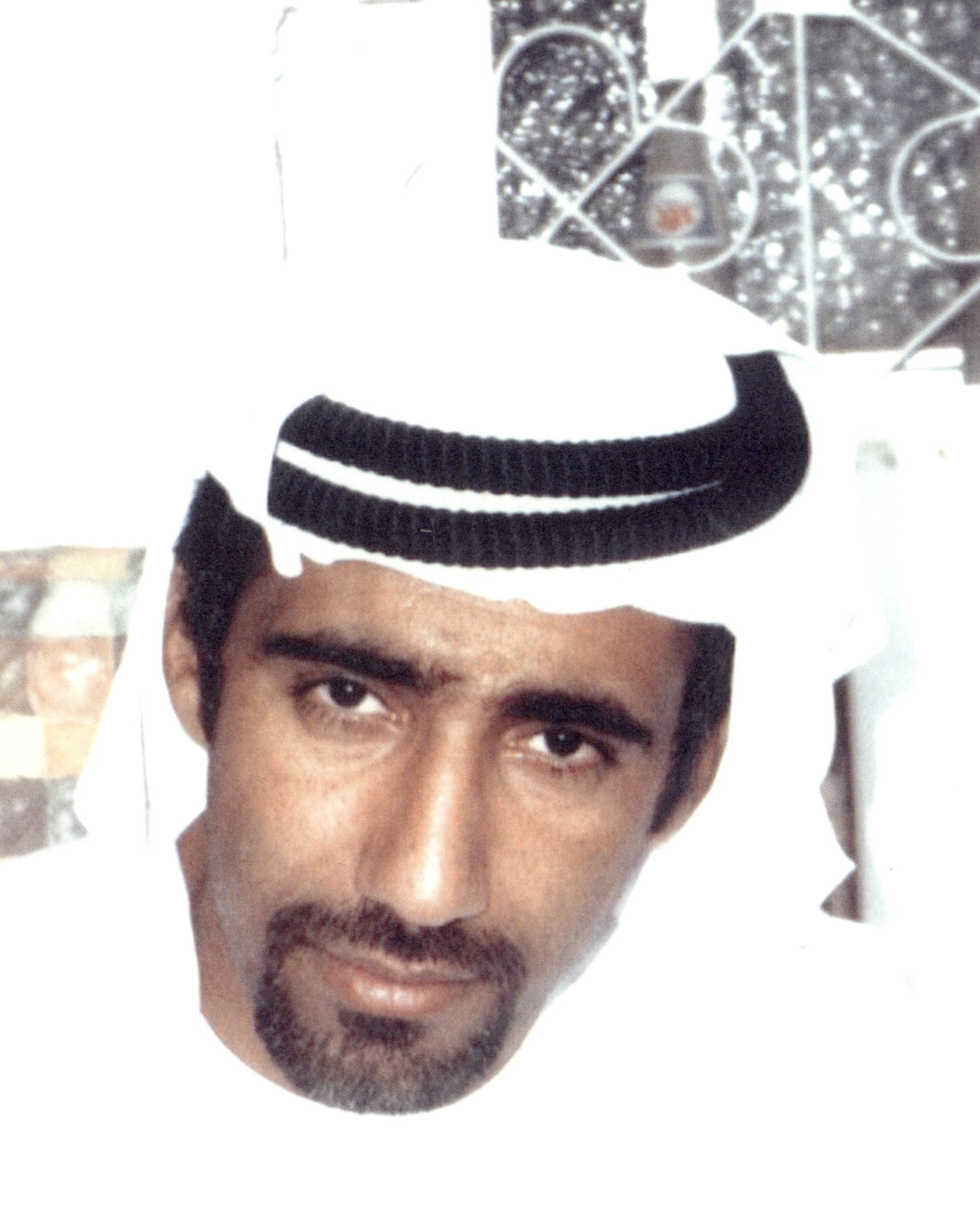

HAQ: The 'Sweet Potatoes' project also has a relation to your family as well as relations between the Emirates, to South America…

AAS: Yes, it relates to the farming activities of my father. Before my father died, he used to plant sweet potatoes and sometimes bought them from the market when water was not available due to a lack of rain. In the same manner that I created an alphabet system for *My Mother's Letters*, I collected the sweet potatoes and drew them. Then I derived lines from them, and from these lines, I extracted the Sweet Potatoes Alphabet. From these alphabets, I made works from clay, drawings, and sculptures on stone, in addition to works related to music and others related to jewels and gold.

Sweet potatoes are said to have originated in South America, specifically from the Lake Titicaca area around the border between Peru and Bolivia. The 'Sweet Potatoes' project is not limited to the Emirates but also extends to South America as a result of my comparative journey there.

In this project, I tried to explore similarities and differences between my culture and South American culture. For example, the *falaj*, which in our country is a channel dug in the ground or on the surface, is similar to the river in South America, but they are different because the falaj is dry while the river contains running water.

HAQ: Apart from domestic spaces, family relationships and heirlooms used in your works, you also have used the 'natural' landscape and public spaces as artworks or venues. Can you tell me more about this?

AAS: I organised an art exhibition in a coffee shop in Sharm that I used to go to with my friends. I sat in the same place, meditated, wrote poems and made drawings. One day, I noticed some discarded cans strewn about the shop. I also noticed some houses nearby with a washing machine that had been thrown away. This coffee shop was a simple one. It had a certain connection with the area and was located very near the sea. I spontaneously began working on the exhibition, which lasted for three days. I hung my works in the morning and removed them in the evening.

In the beginning, the regulars didn't pay much attention, but after a while, they noticed how the paintings hanging on a wall near the sea or the mountains had a connection with the environment. This art exhibition is a documentation of my works.

HAQ: Then how do you feel when you exhibit your works in museums and other places without this relation to the environment?

AAS: When I hang a painting in a coffee shop, the visitor may not notice it, or it may not be within his or her interests. The painting in a cafe is a part of the environs of the cafe. But when you hang a painting in a museum, it will be the visitor's centre of attention, not the wall on which it is hung. In this situation, it will not have any relation with the museum. The relation will be with the spectator's eye.

HAQ: In the last two decades or so, your works have gone around the world. How do you feel about that, especially after you have exhibited in contexts with little relation to your own landscapes of affinity? External viewers may not be able to contextualise or understand your work or space.

AAS: The place of the work changes, and the work goes to another place, but the work remains as it is. It is like a journey…it departs.

HAQ: That seems very apt for you and your work. How about other artists' views and perceptions of your work?

AAS: I have only met a small number of artists, so I have not been influenced by artists' works. But sometimes I have found similarities between my works and other artists' works. Our works meet but the concept differs.

HAQ: Then, what do you think about the way in which your works were presented for the exhibition *Al Toubay* at Sharjah Art Foundation? What do you think about presenting the works in traditional coastal heritage homes?

AAS: The intimacy of the old houses was perfectly suited for my artworks, particularly *My Mother's Letters*. The way in which the exhibited works were curated highlights the connections between each collection. 'Al Toubay' is connected with the trip, and the trip is connected with *Camar Cande's Journey* and *The Watermelon Series*. It shows continuity and connection, a sort of unending journey, harking back to my childhood up to my maturity as an artist.

– Conversation recorded in Sharjah, 2014

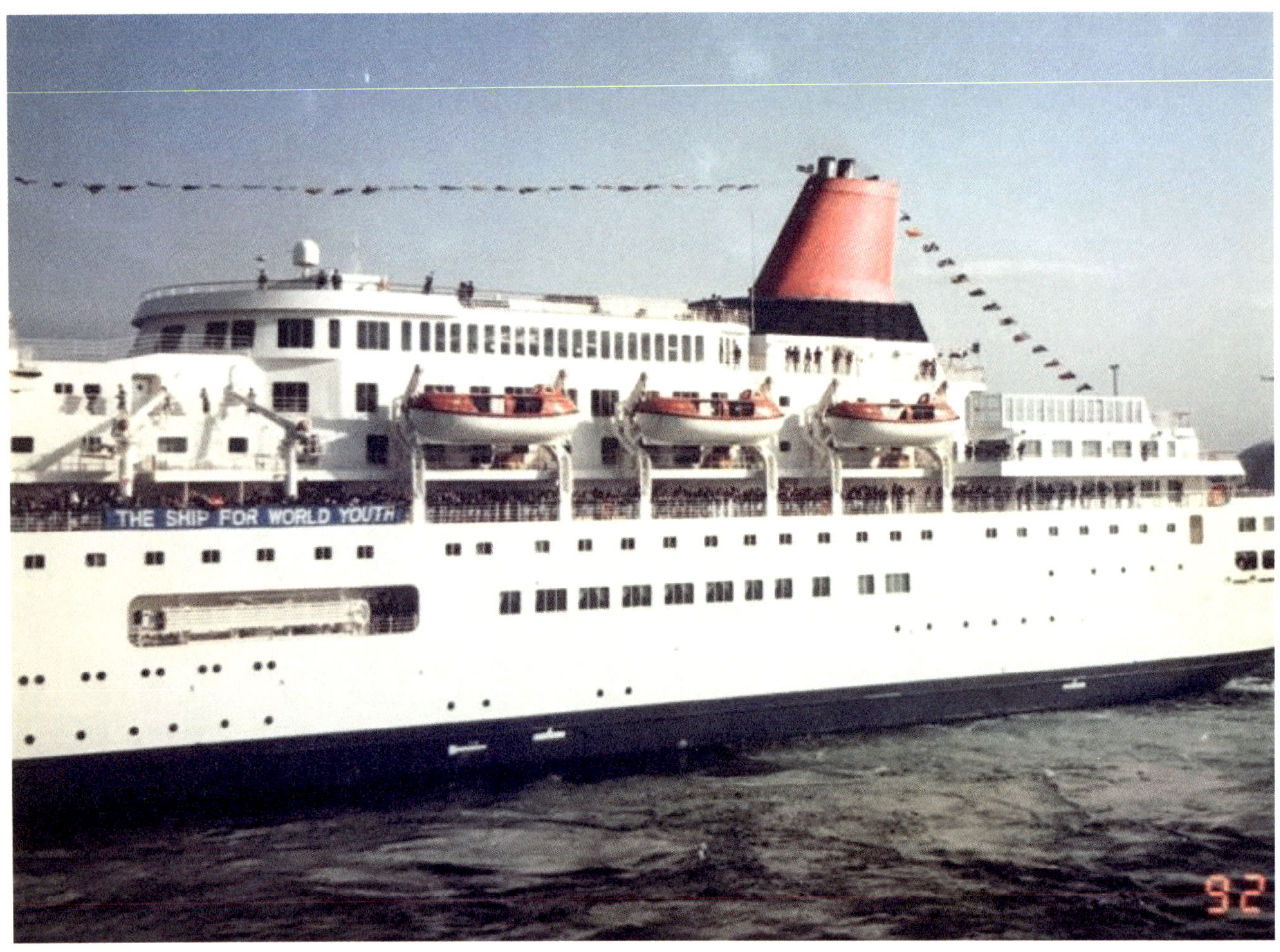
THE SHIP FOR WORLD YOUTH

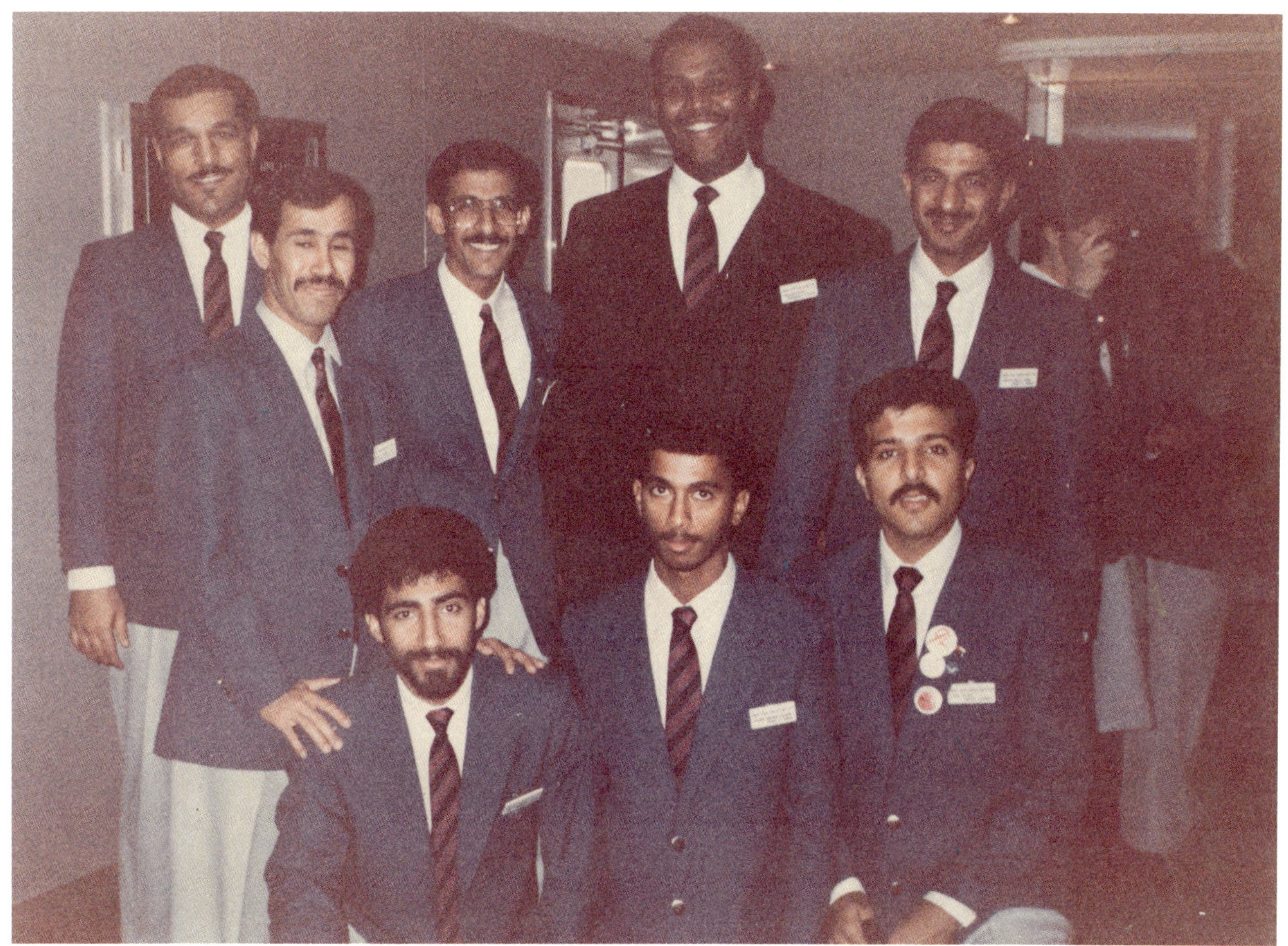

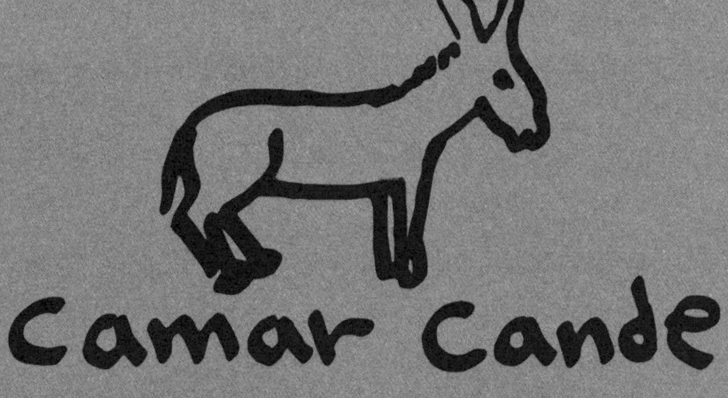
Camar Cande

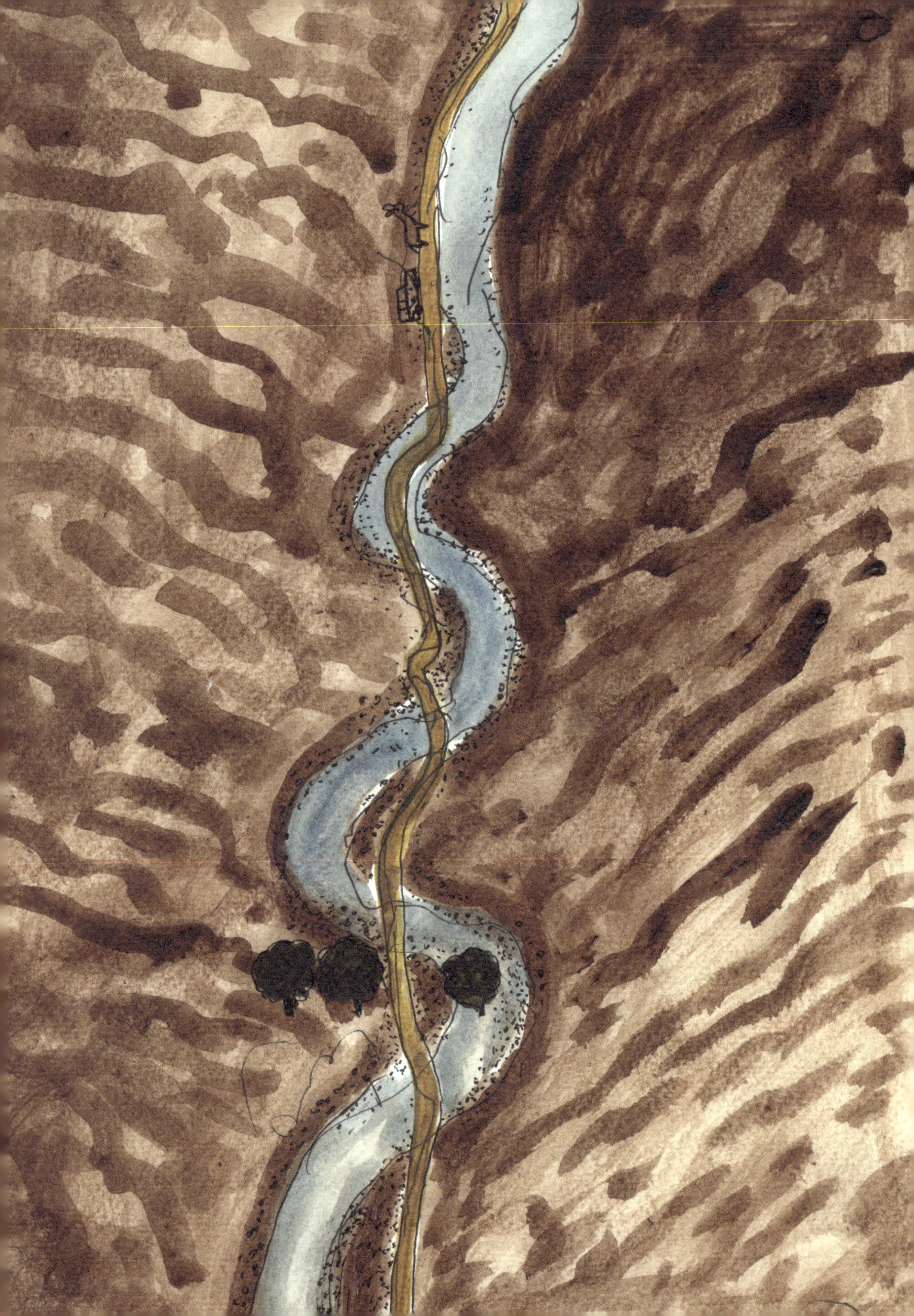

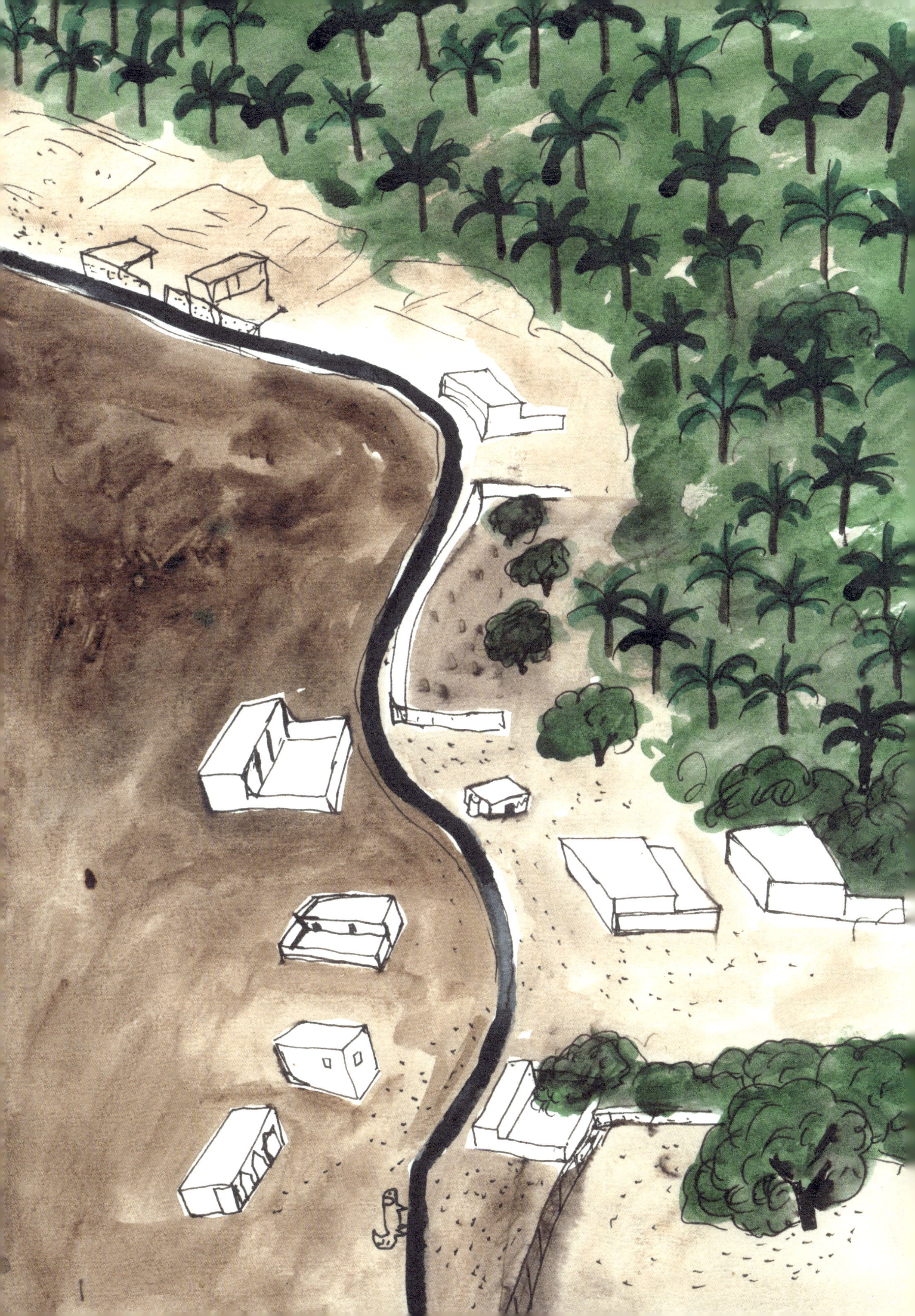

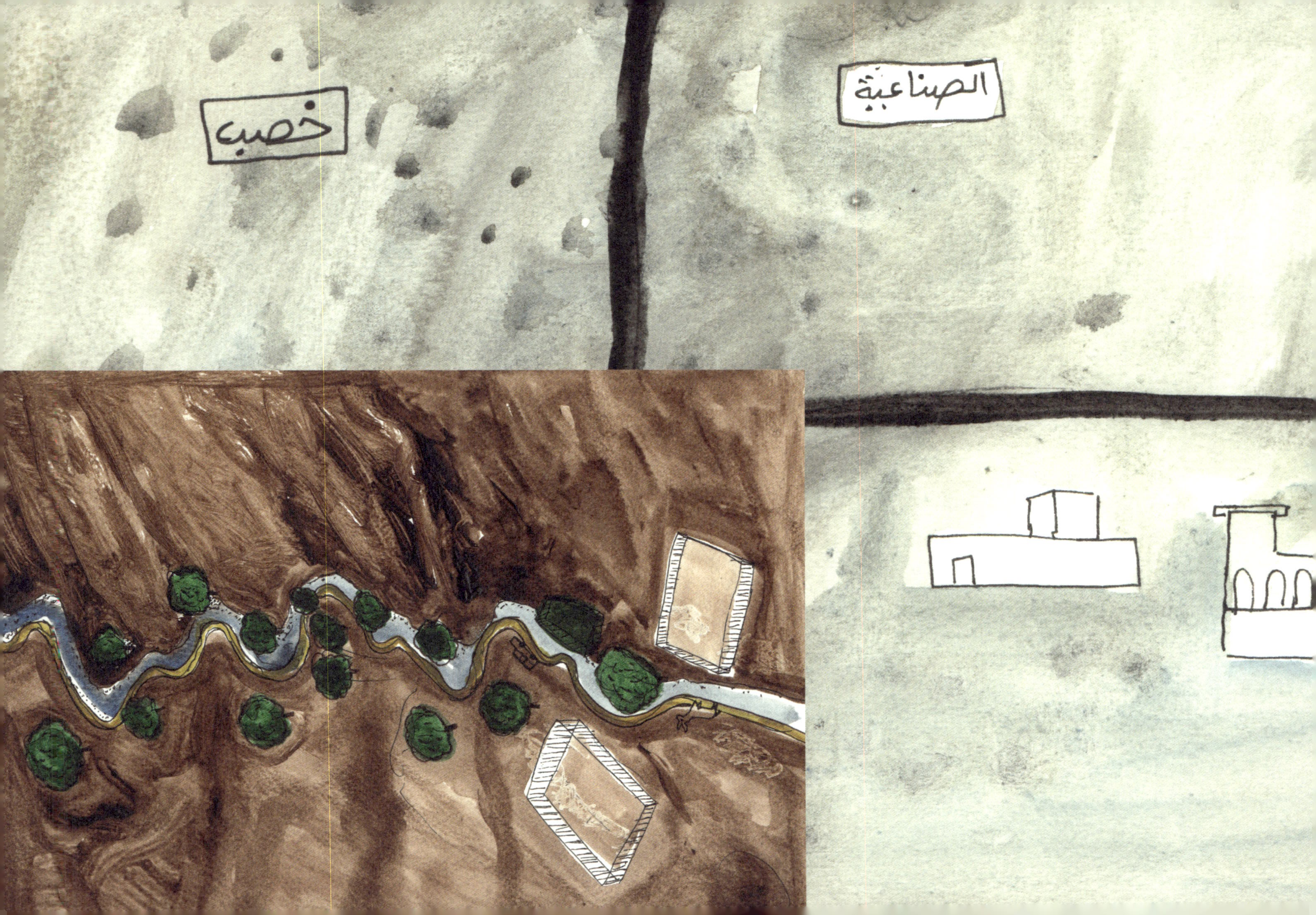
خصب
الصناعية

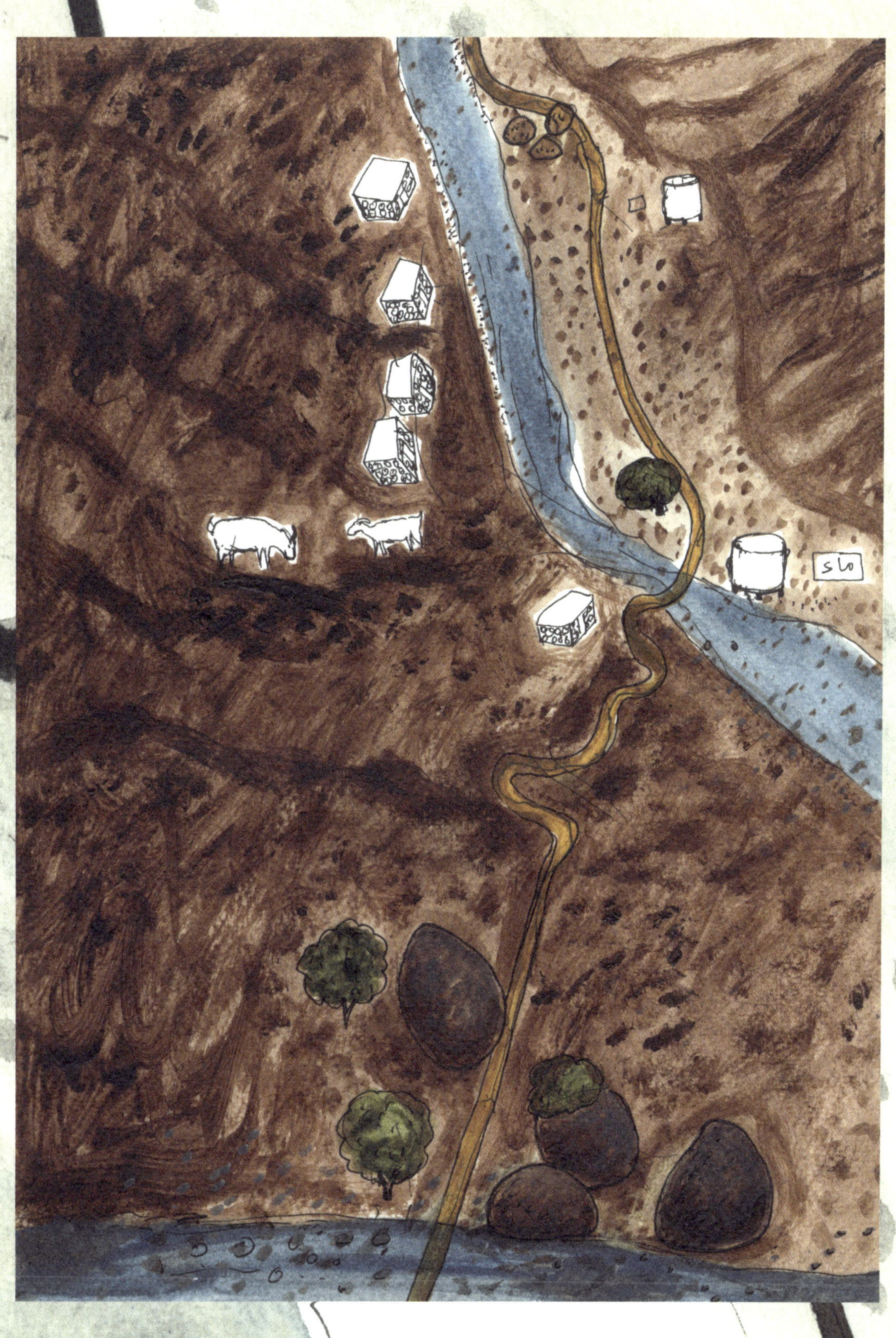

slo

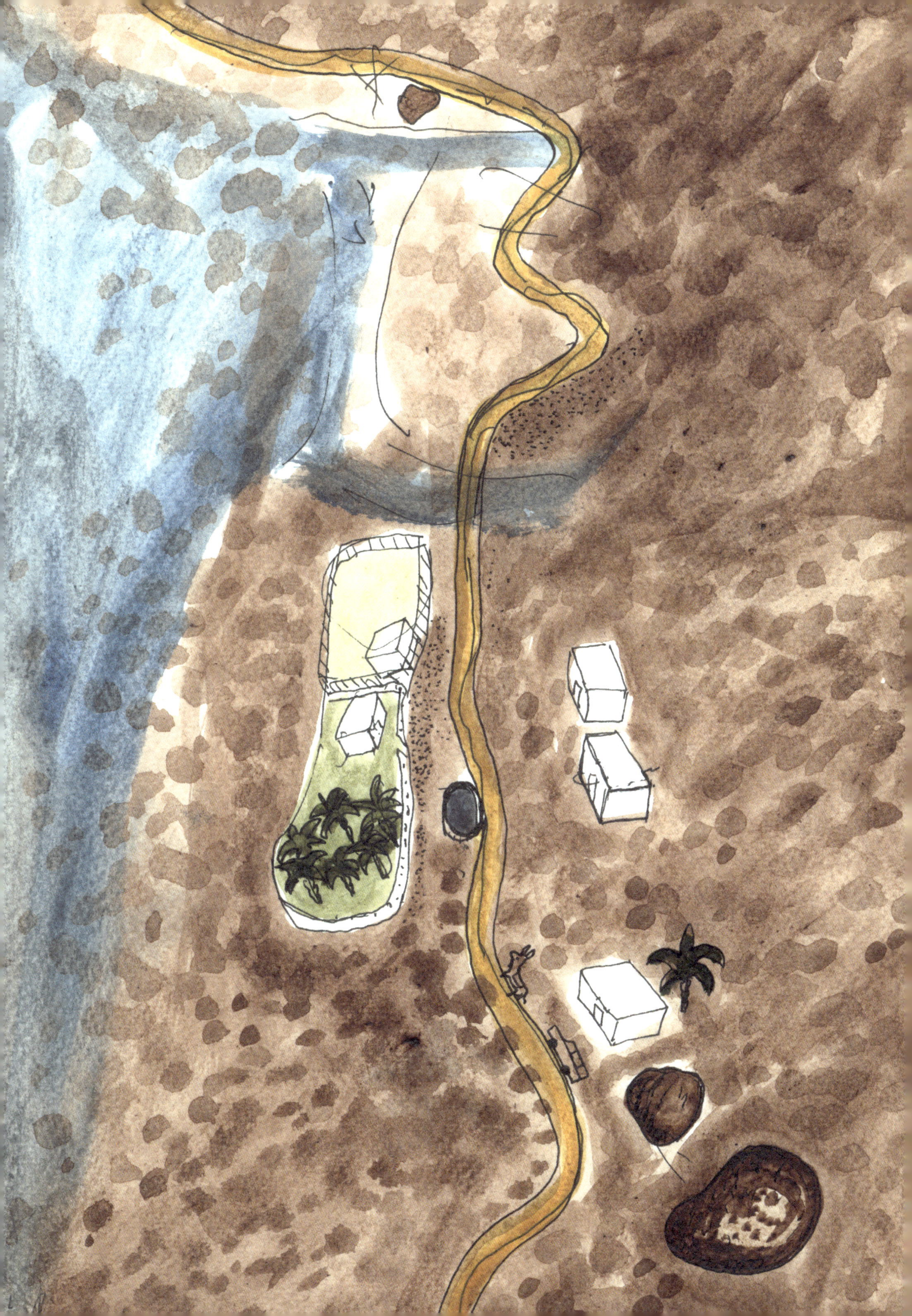

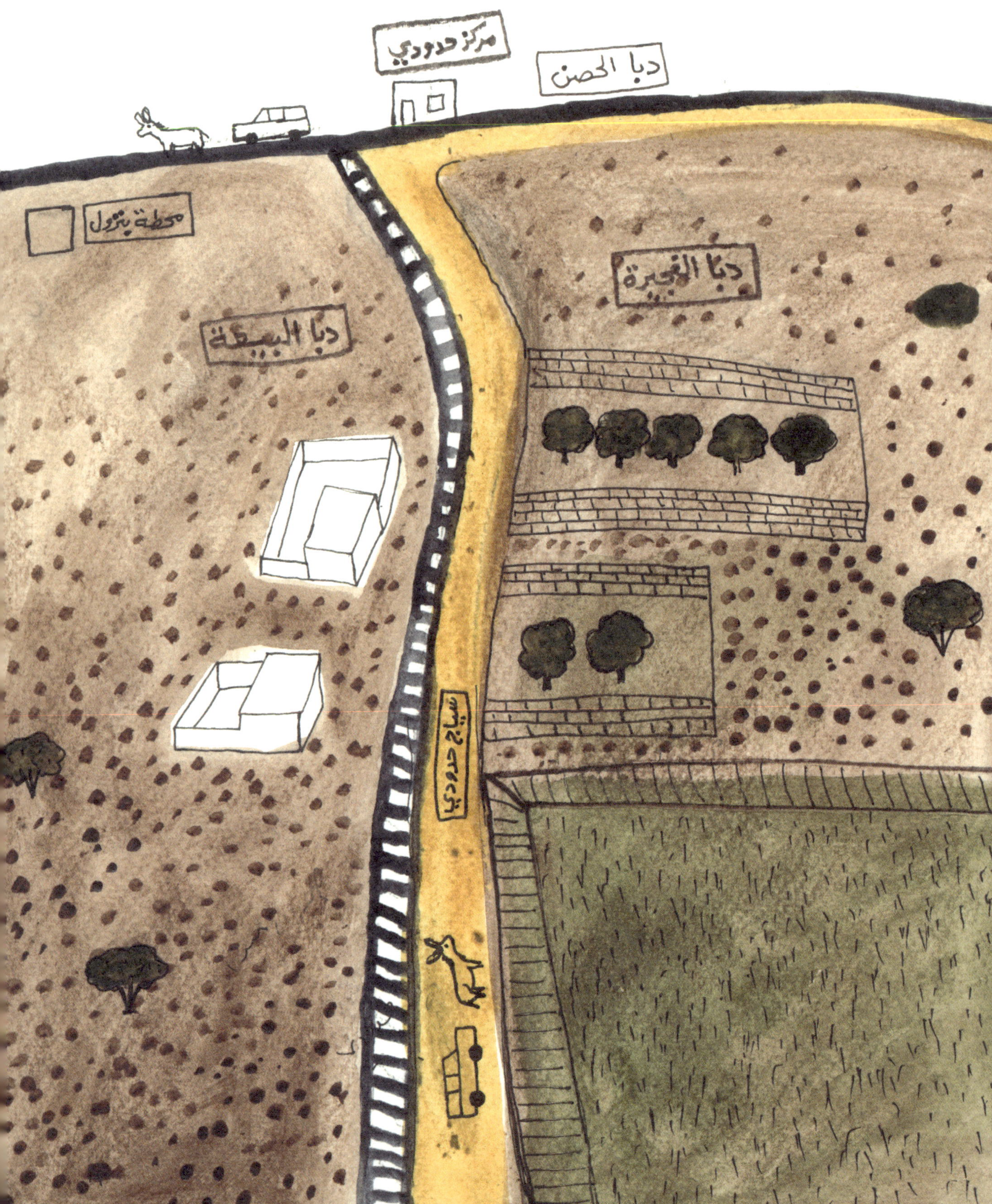

مركز حدودي
دبا الحصن
محطة بترول
دبا البسيطة
دبا الفجيرة
سياج حدودي

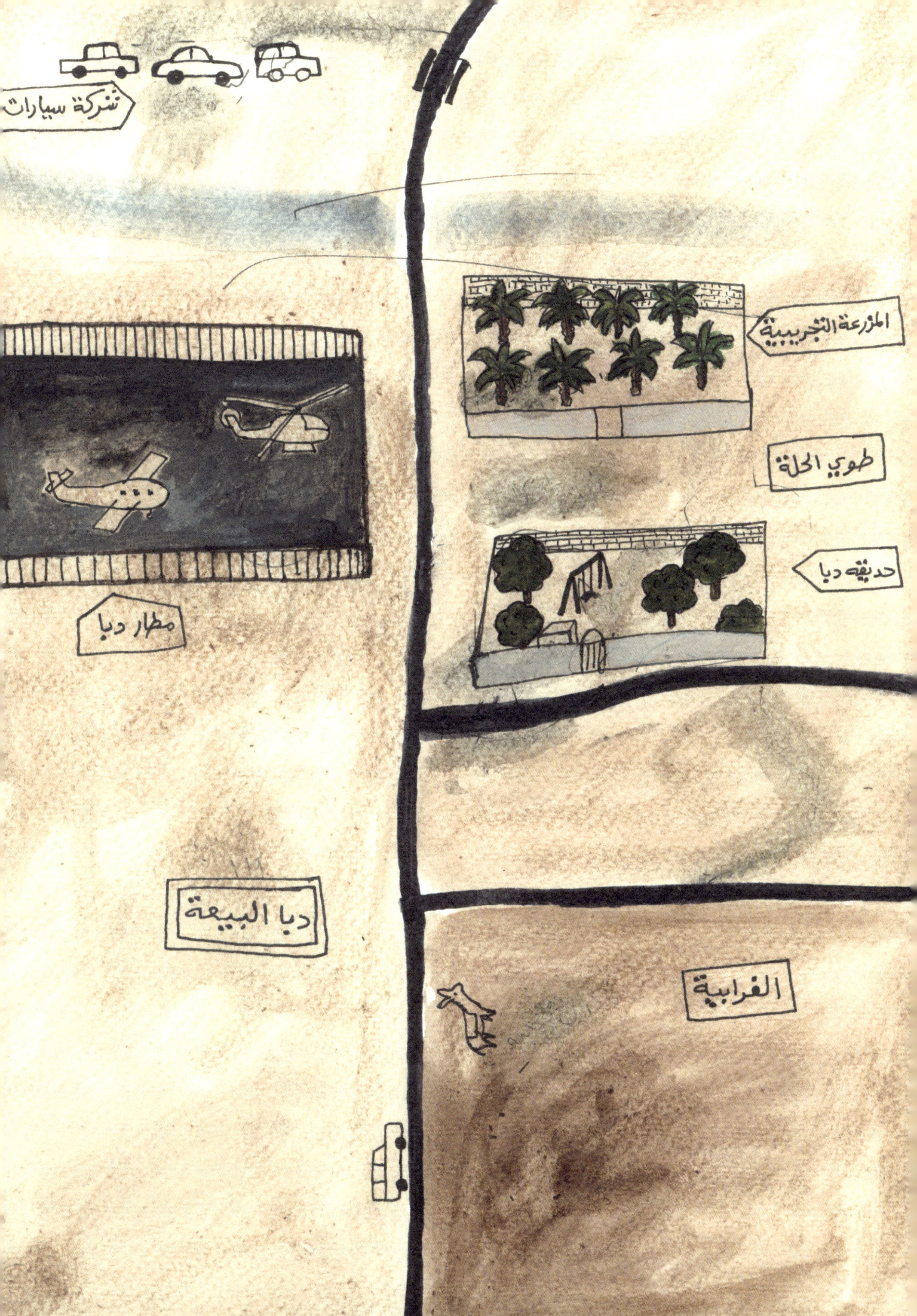

شركة سيارات
المزرعة التجريبية
طوي الحلة
حديقة ديا
مطار ديا
ديا البيعة
الغرابية

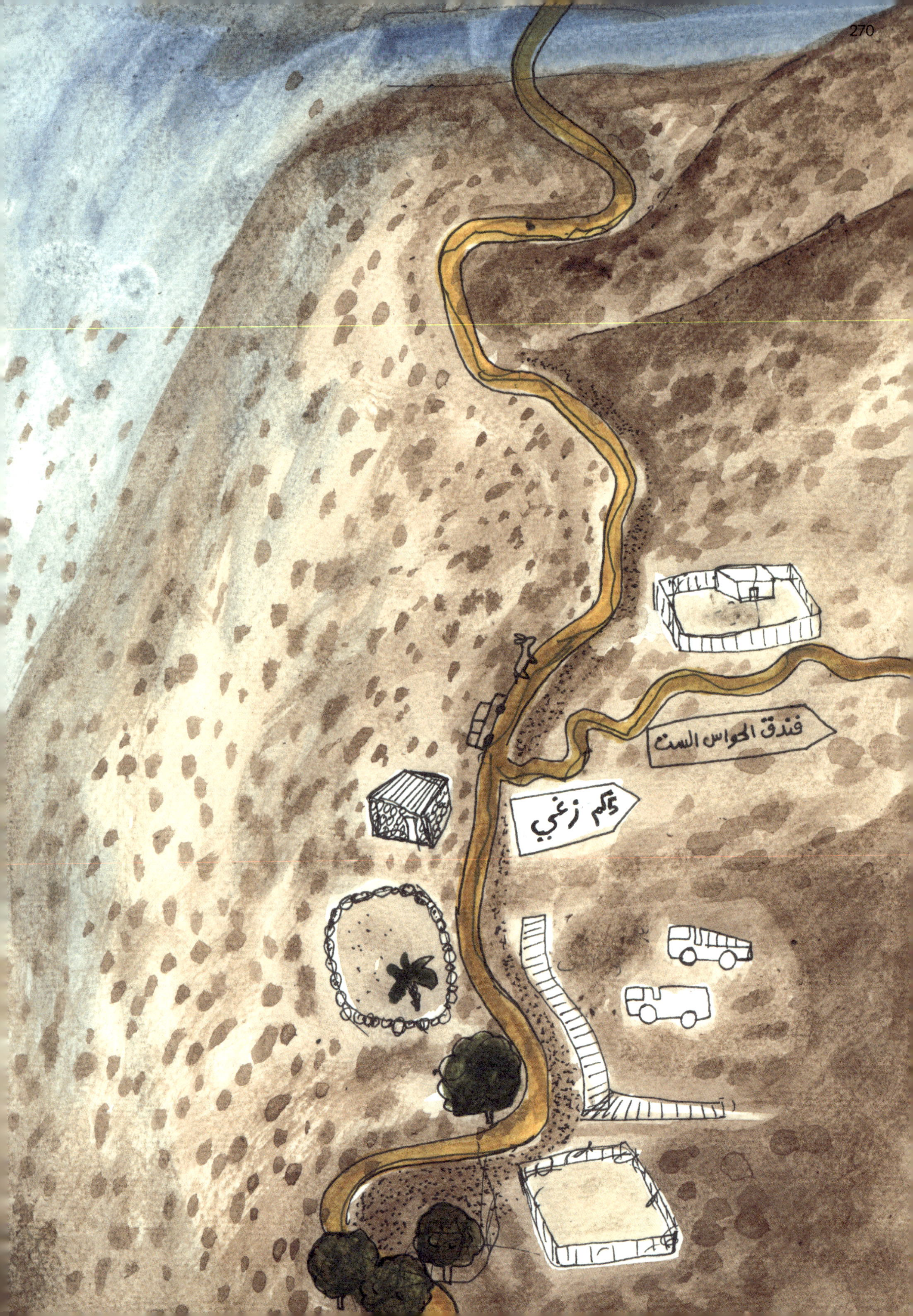

فندق الحواس الست
٥ كم زغبي

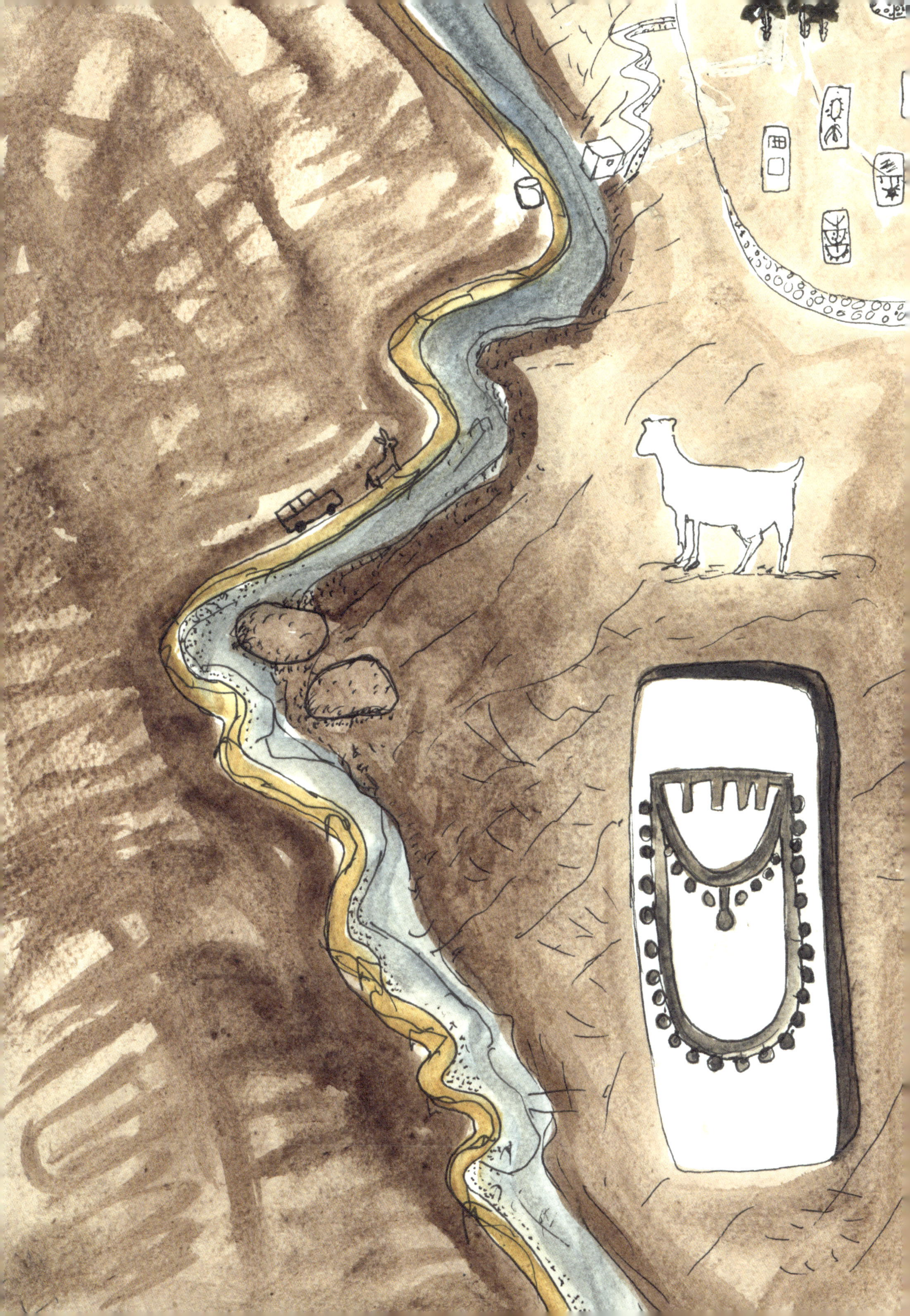

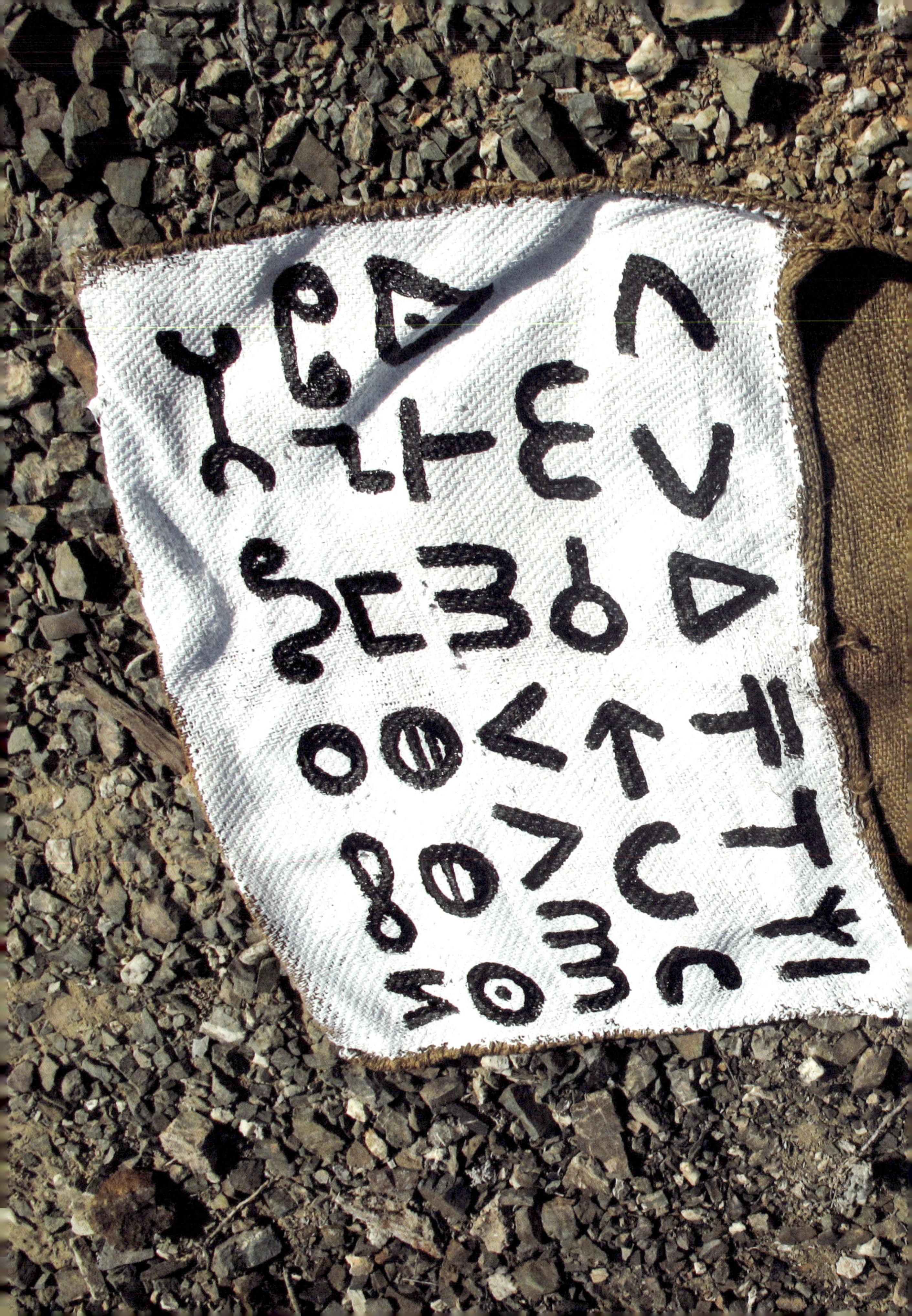

The 700-kilometre Hajar Mountain range spans the northeastern edge of the Arabian Peninsula, running through the contemporary lands of the Emirates and Sultanate of Oman, and culminates in the Musandam Peninsula, or Roos Al Jibal as its dwellers, Abdullah Al Saadi among them, call it. Its highest point, Jebel Shams, as well as Wadi Ghul, are colloquially referred to as Oman's Grand Canyon, attracting hikers and mountaineers historically and presently.

Several decades of archaeological research have also designated Hajar and its surrounding territories as repositories of prehistoric Arabian history and culture. Boulder and rock art throughout its mountains and wadis depict marine life, such as anemones, fishes and turtles; ibex-like figures and leopards; humans standing, seated or riding; geometric patterns; and ancient Southern Arabic script. In recent decades, engravings of automobiles and other signs of modern passersby have surfaced in parallel to these inscriptions. At the ancient oasis settlement of Bat, a UNESCO World Heritage Site, a vast necropolis has been discovered that includes both a cluster beehive and over 100 cairn tombs.

Hajar was also the site of one of the Gulf's most unique modern land disputes. The Omani exclave of Madha, home to Al Saadi's family's date palm farm, is situated near the eastern foothills of the Hajar Mountain range. Surrounded by the Emirate of Sharjah, Madha was a hotly contested object of dominion, due in part to its considerable water resources. This tension persisted until as recently as 1971, when an agreement brokered by the British protectorate granted it to the Sultanate of Oman. Functioning today as an exclave of Oman yet enclaved by the Emirates, it expresses the unique political-territorial demarcations found all over the Gulf, such as the Musandam Peninsula and Nahwa, in which divergent territorial settlements belong to different emirates or countries. As Hajar's history continues to be unearthed, Al Saadi writes his own. The foundations of his practice – walking, cycling, map-making, found object collecting and landscape painting – first took shape within the range's wadis, pathways and neighbouring settlements. These approaches were developed independently of a clear canonical understanding of urban-based art methodologies. Instead, he sought to reconcile his innate desire for travel, a deep connection with nature and the imperative to amplify ancestral knowledge.

More than two decades of travel and art making, much of them spent against the backdrop of the mountains, had prepared him for what would come to be known as the definitive era of his career. The works Al Saadi produced between 2009 and 2017 during journeys across this region were not only some of his most ambitious, but also marked the beginning of curating his travels, walks and trails as artistic practice and output. Staged in 2014 by Hoor Al Qasimi at Sharjah Art Foundation, the solo show *Al Toubay* – Al Saadi's first instance of long-term institutional involvement in the Emirates outside of the Emirates Fine Arts Society – would prove particularly fruitful.

The multimedia installation *Camar Cande's Journey* (2010–2011) documented a 20-day trek through the Hajar Mountain range, its northernmost Roos Al Jibal, and several of its surrounding towns and villages, including Madha, Masafi and the Omani port city of Khasab. In many of the resulting watercolour landscapes, Al Saadi's dog, a donkey named Camar Cande and a pickup truck driven by his friend, artist Abdulrahman Al Muaini, appear as barely perceptible blips guiding viewers through winding mountain roads, dry riverbeds and sparsely populated settlements. These compositions differ greatly from previous detailed scrollworks of urban and natural landscapes, instead providing aerial views with rough, muddled brushstrokes, varying scales, minimal labelling and almost childlike depictions of infrastructure, seemingly produced in quick succession from photographs or memory.

An accompanying video work also reveals a central conceptual facet of the project: neither Al Saadi's dog nor Camar Cande specifically served as mere beasts of burden, guardians or modes of transportation; rather, they stood as equal companions throughout the trip. Exhibited first at Sharjah Biennial 10 and then in the *Al Toubay* show, its reception gave Al Saadi the confidence and support to hone the geographical and thematic elements of this first project and to attempt more layered interpretations of his walking and journeying practice.

Camar Cande and Al Saadi's dog would later join him on separate solo journeys that tested the limits of these interspecies companionships. This dynamic took a more symbolic turn in his work *Ten Engraved Stones with Animals* (2013). Here he substituted for live animals with a collection of talismans, which served as mnemonic devices evoking each would-be animal's corresponding virtues.

The Watermelon Series (2013) furthered Al Saadi's fantastical approach to landscape painting. Another unlikely collaborator, his son, compared the colour of the Hajar Mountains to the fruit's bright red flesh, prompting Al Saadi to reimagine familiar hiking trails through a new chromatic lens. These works make up *The Comparative Journey* (2013), informed by parallels between Al Saadi's trips to South America and the Emirates' geography, biodiversity and culture.

After *Camar Cande's Journey*, journeying and walking as part of Al Saadi's practice evolved into readings of Latin prose, Spanish poetry and Sufi writings as well as echoed histories of the Silk Road and itinerant communities that accompanied Al Saadi on these outings. This new direction facilitated more embodied experiences, situating his own exploits and diaristic practice within a wider global literary lineage.

For Al Saadi, who had made his debut in Sharjah so many years before as a student, *Al Toubay* at the Sharjah Art Foundation was not a retrospective but a homecoming.

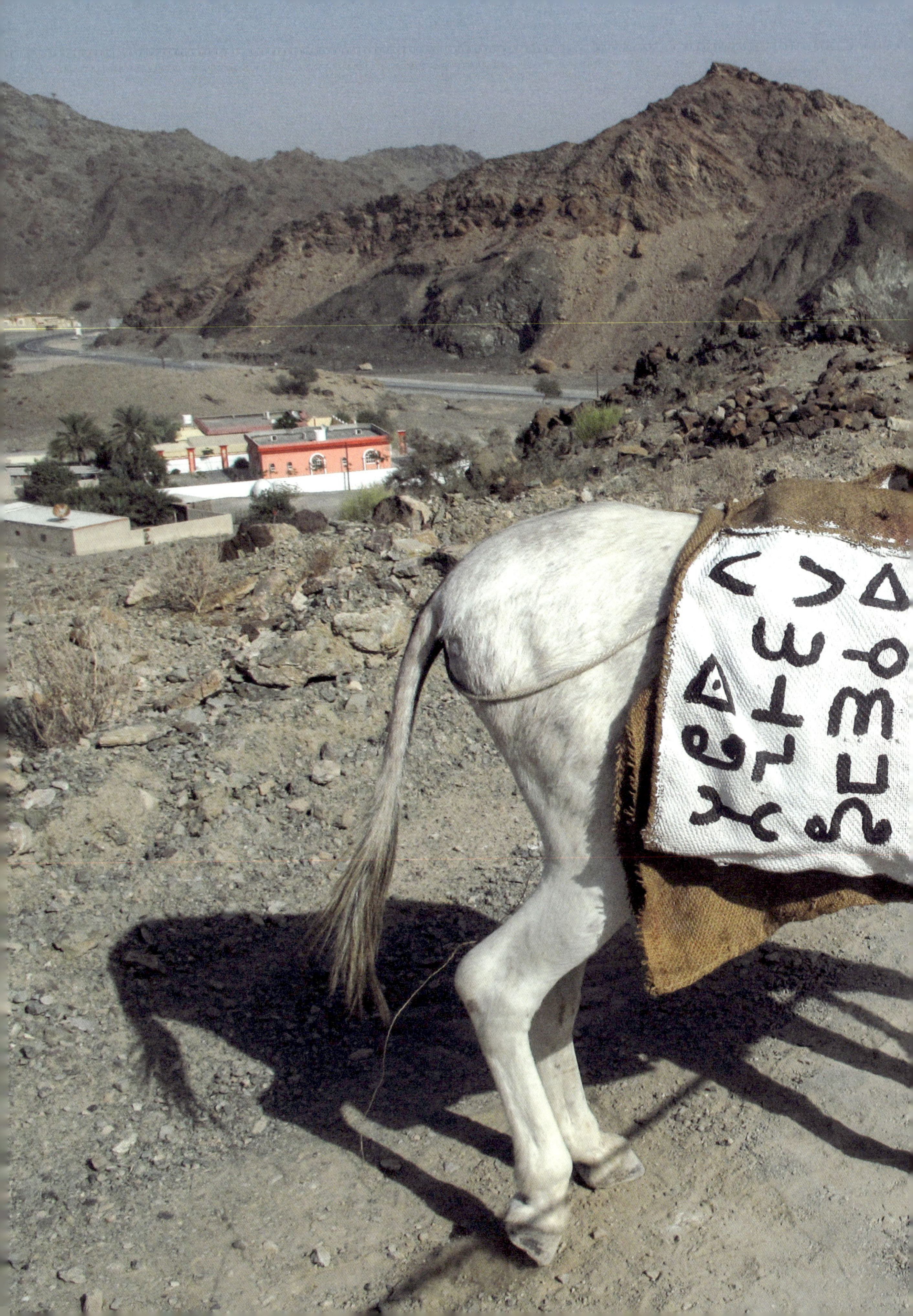

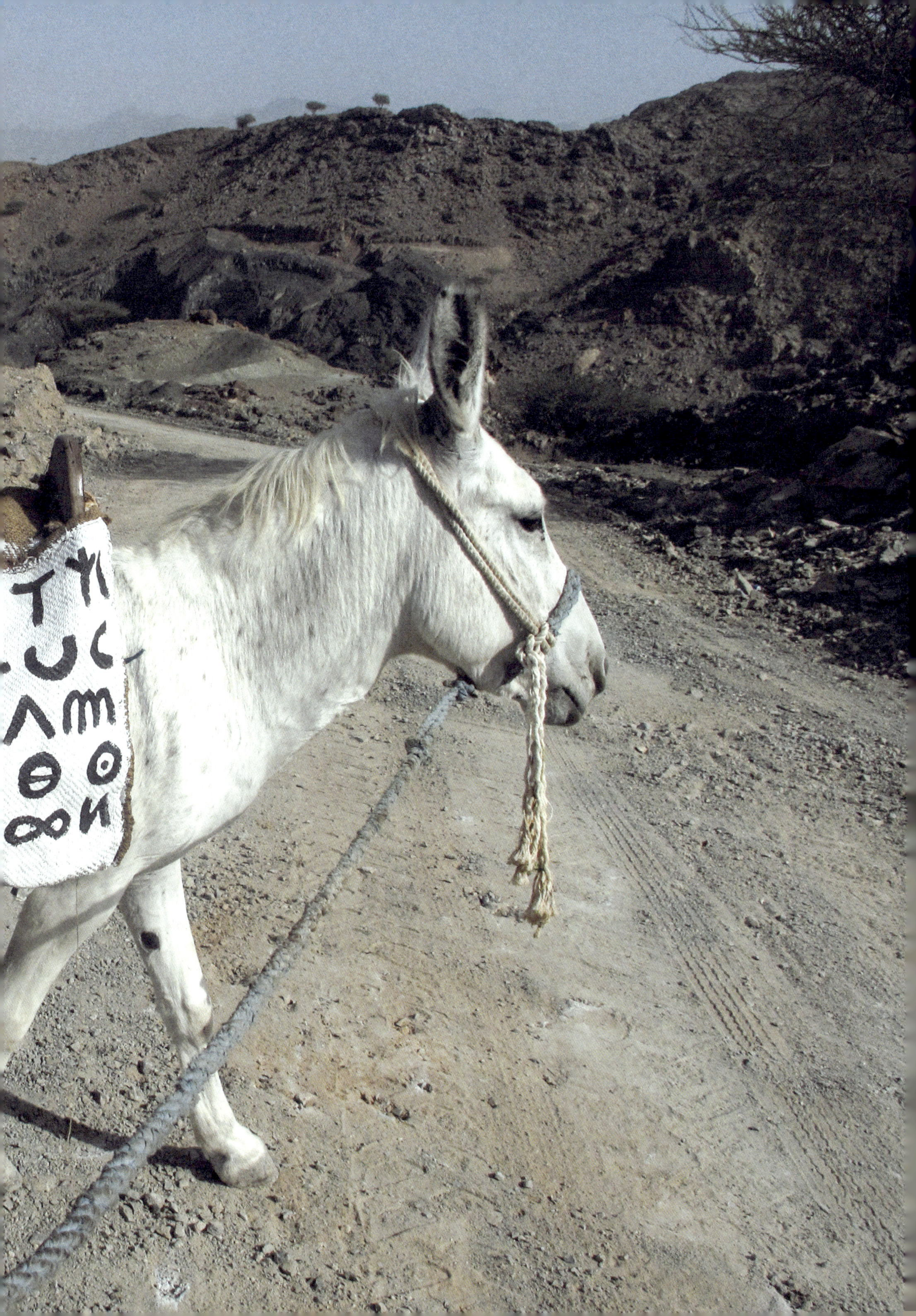

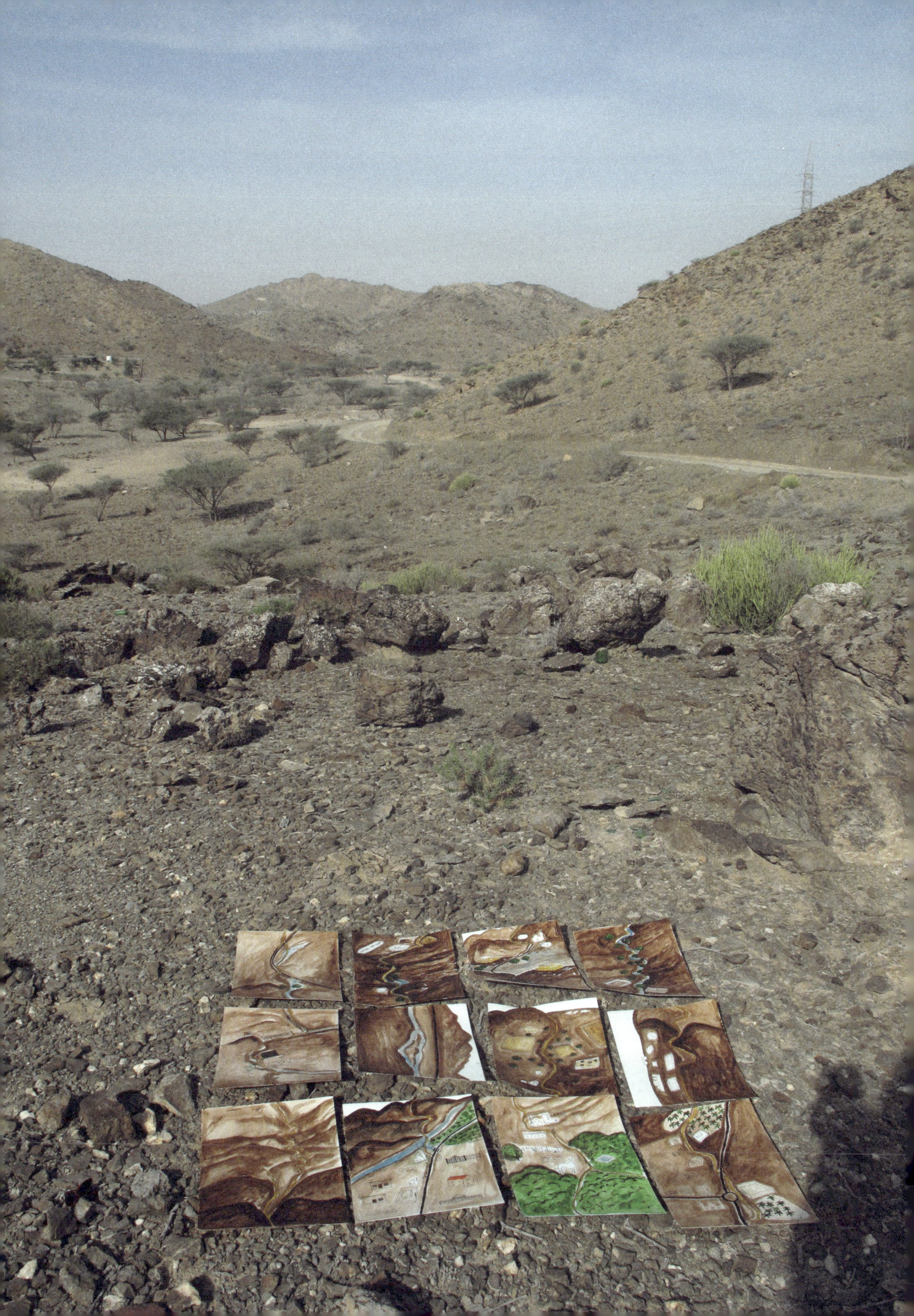

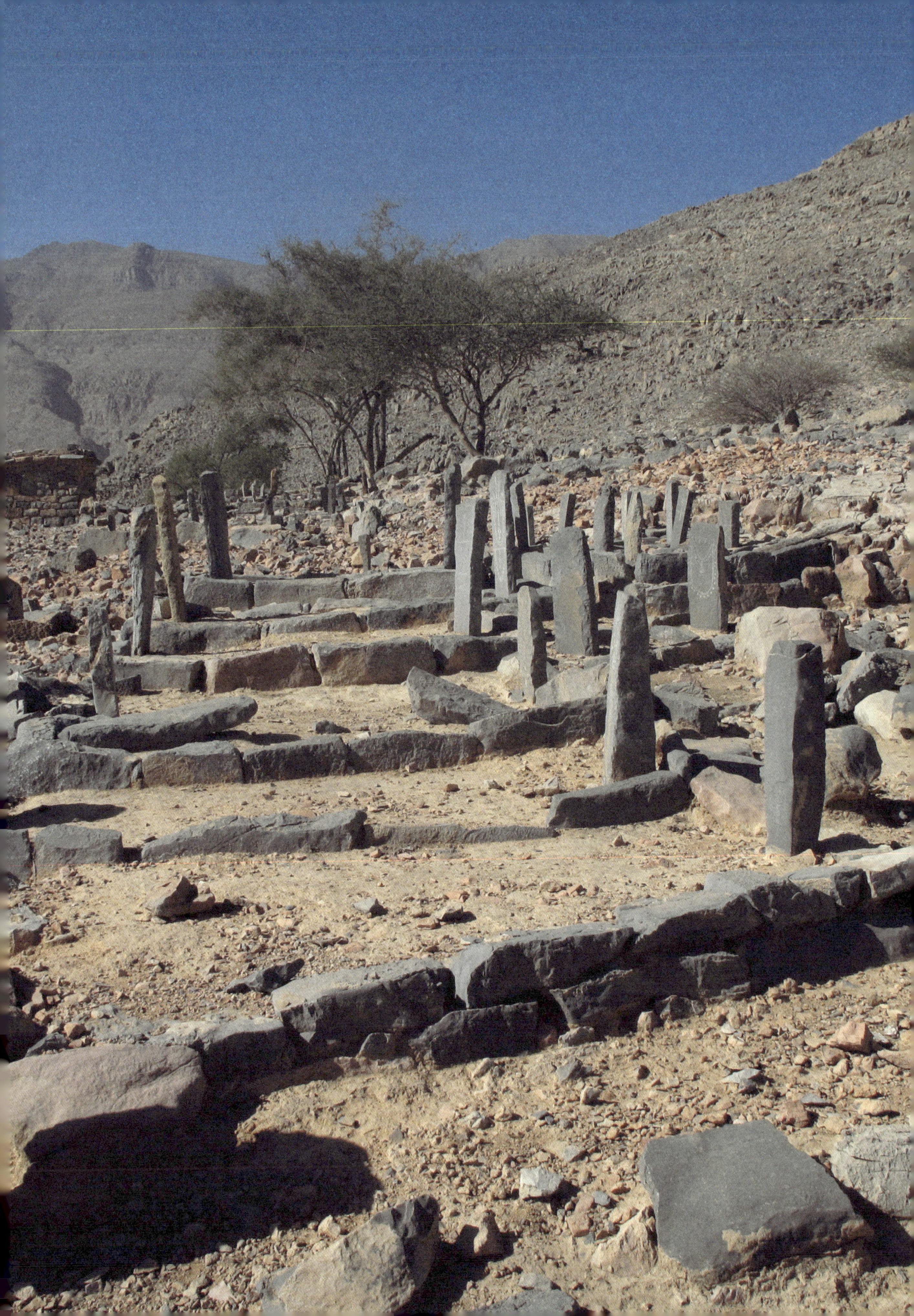

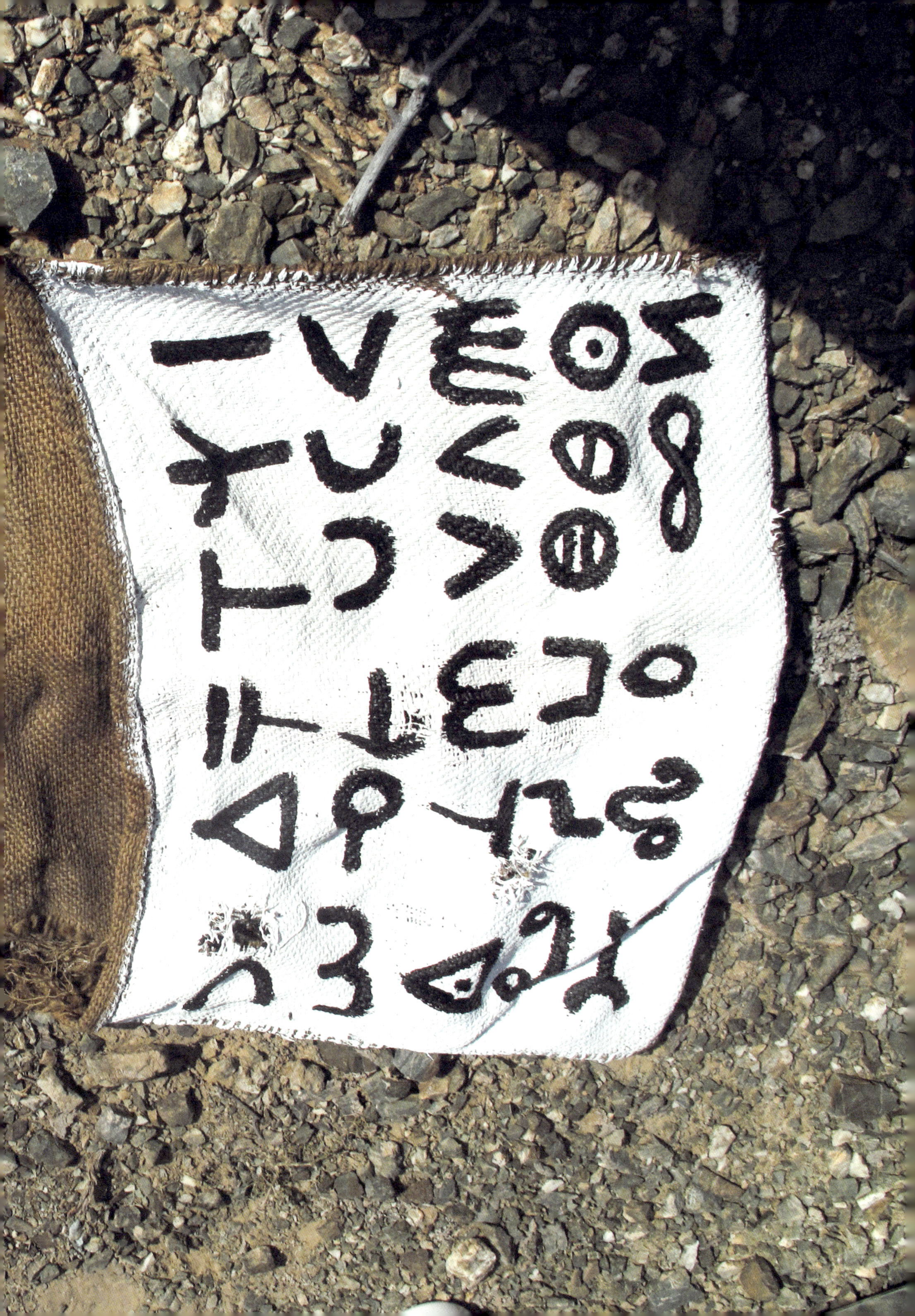

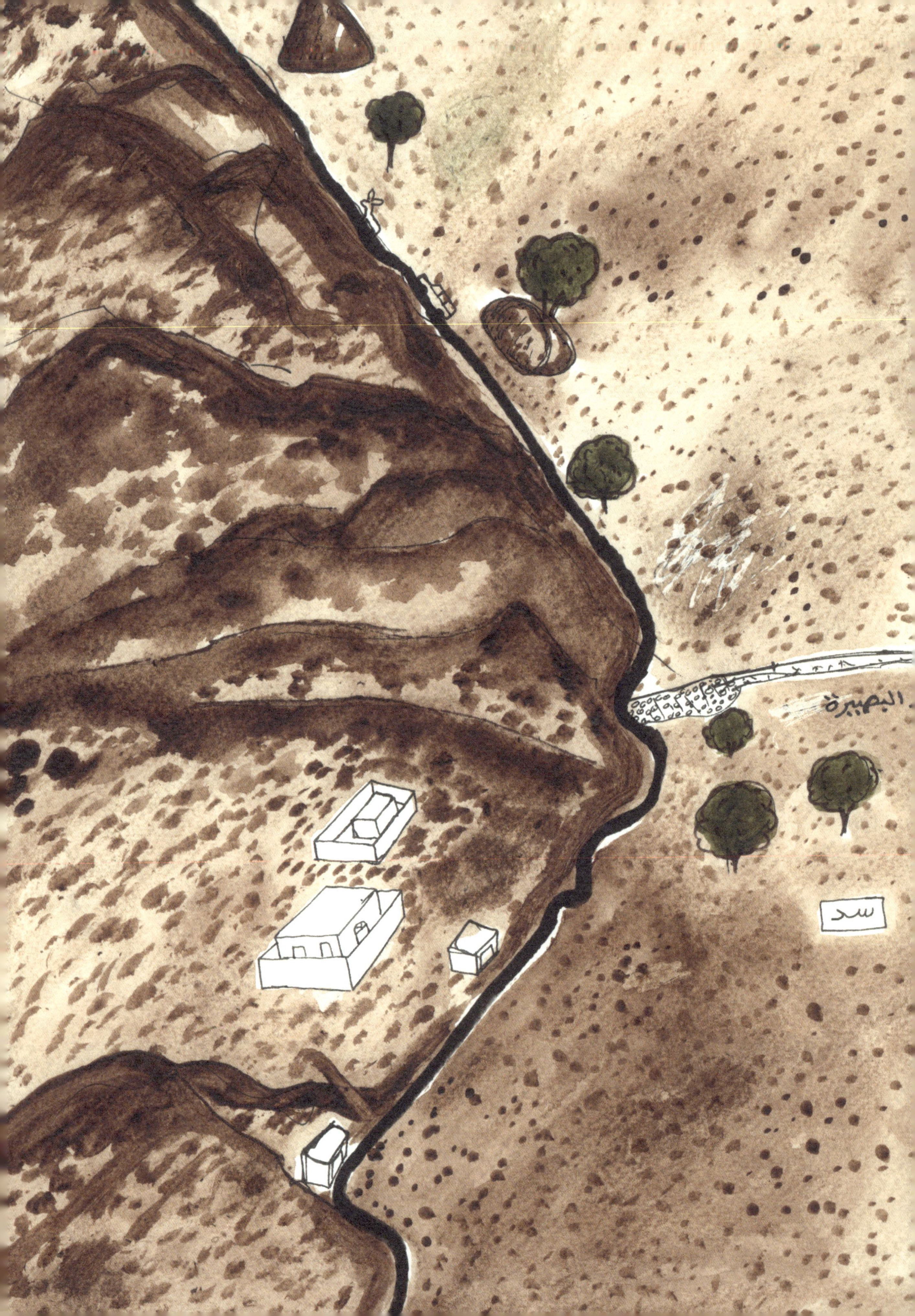

البصيرة
سد

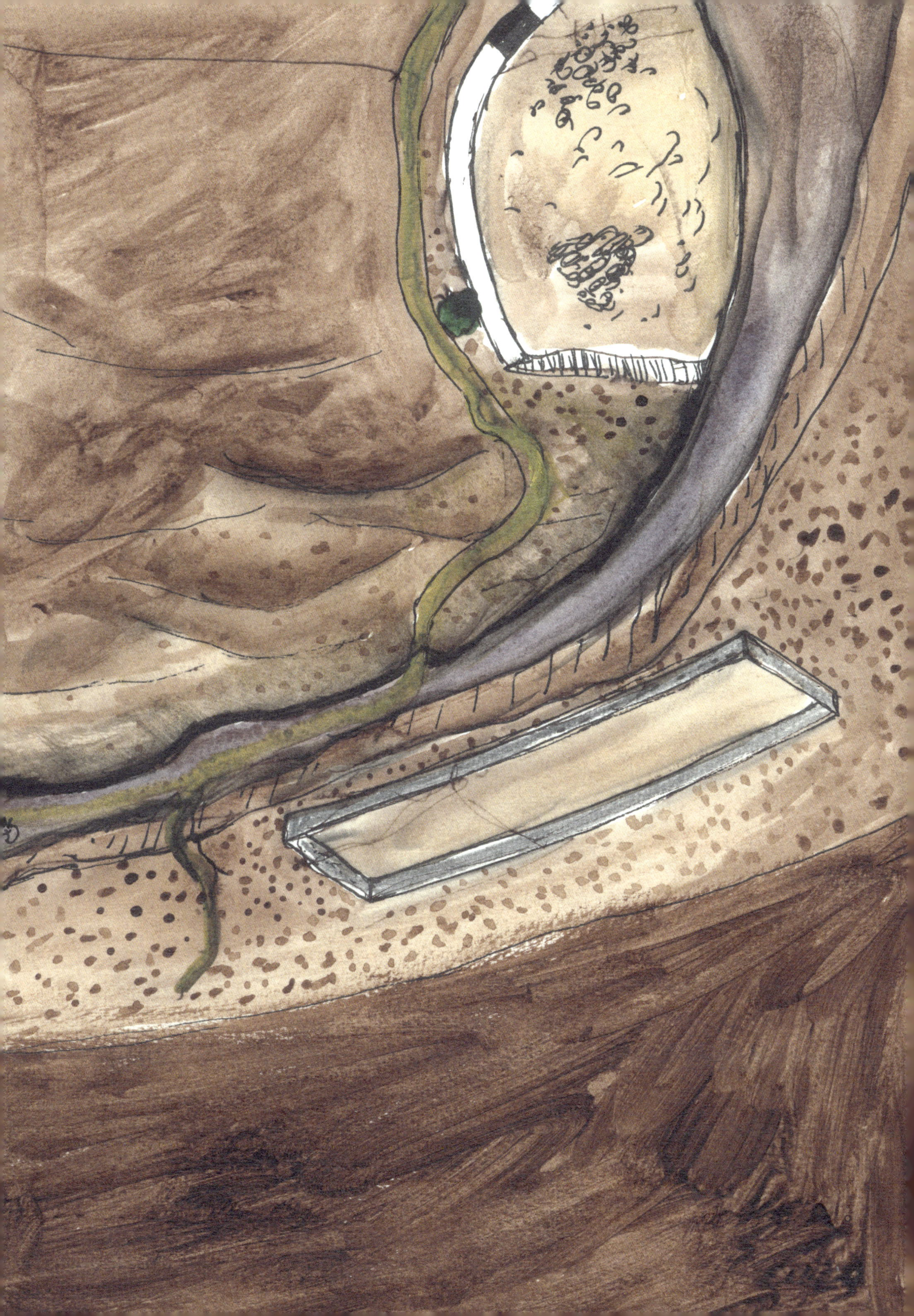

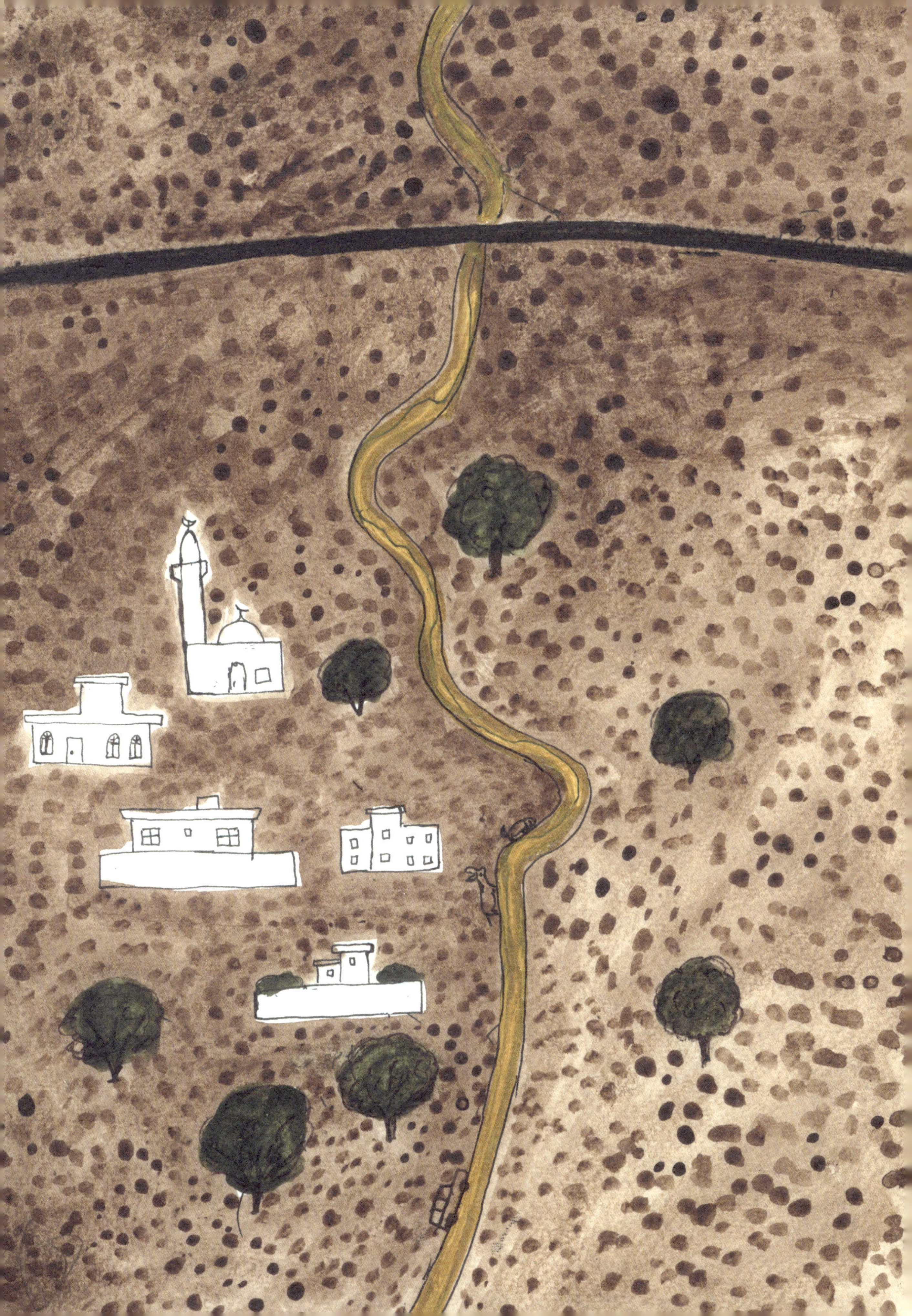

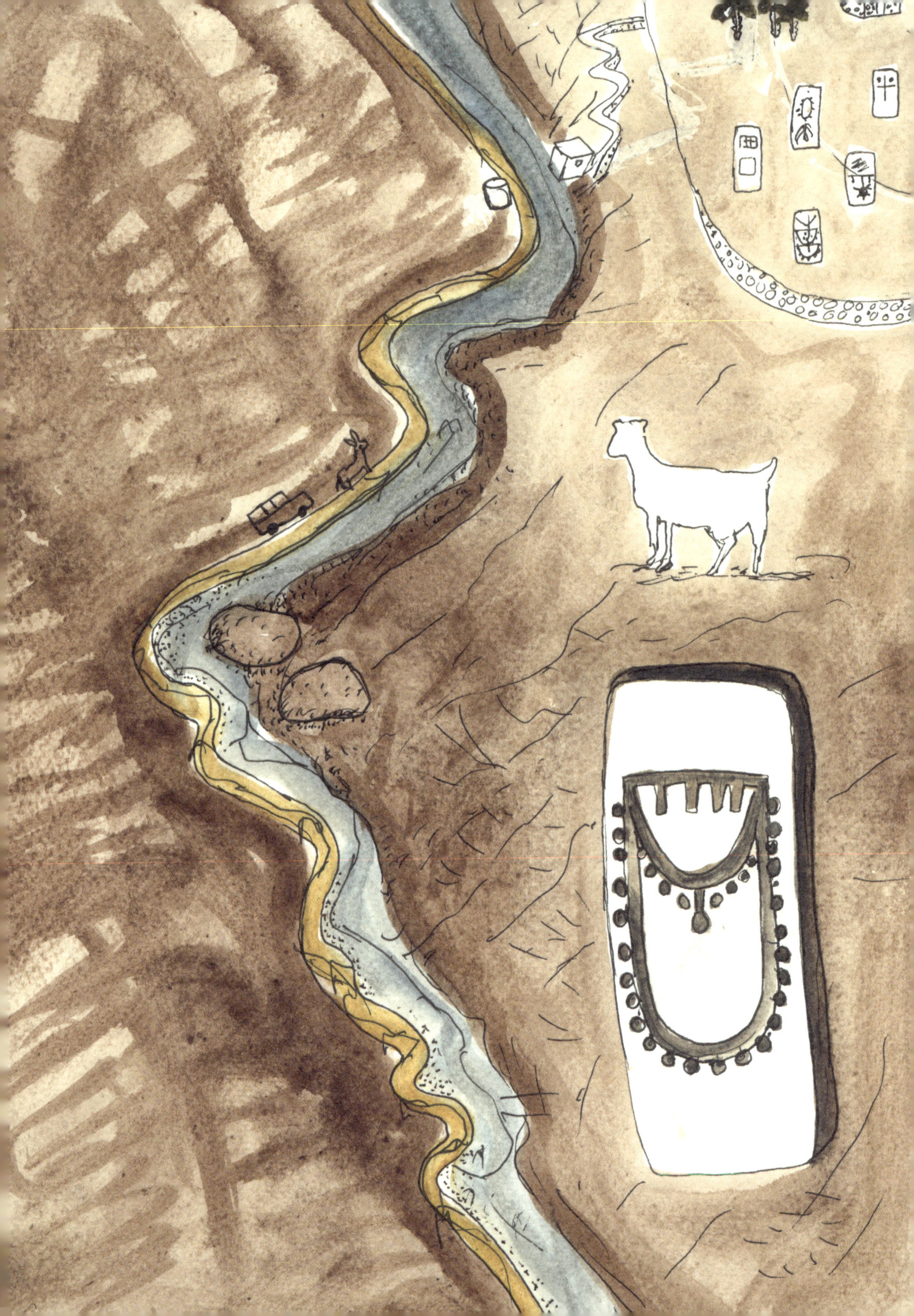

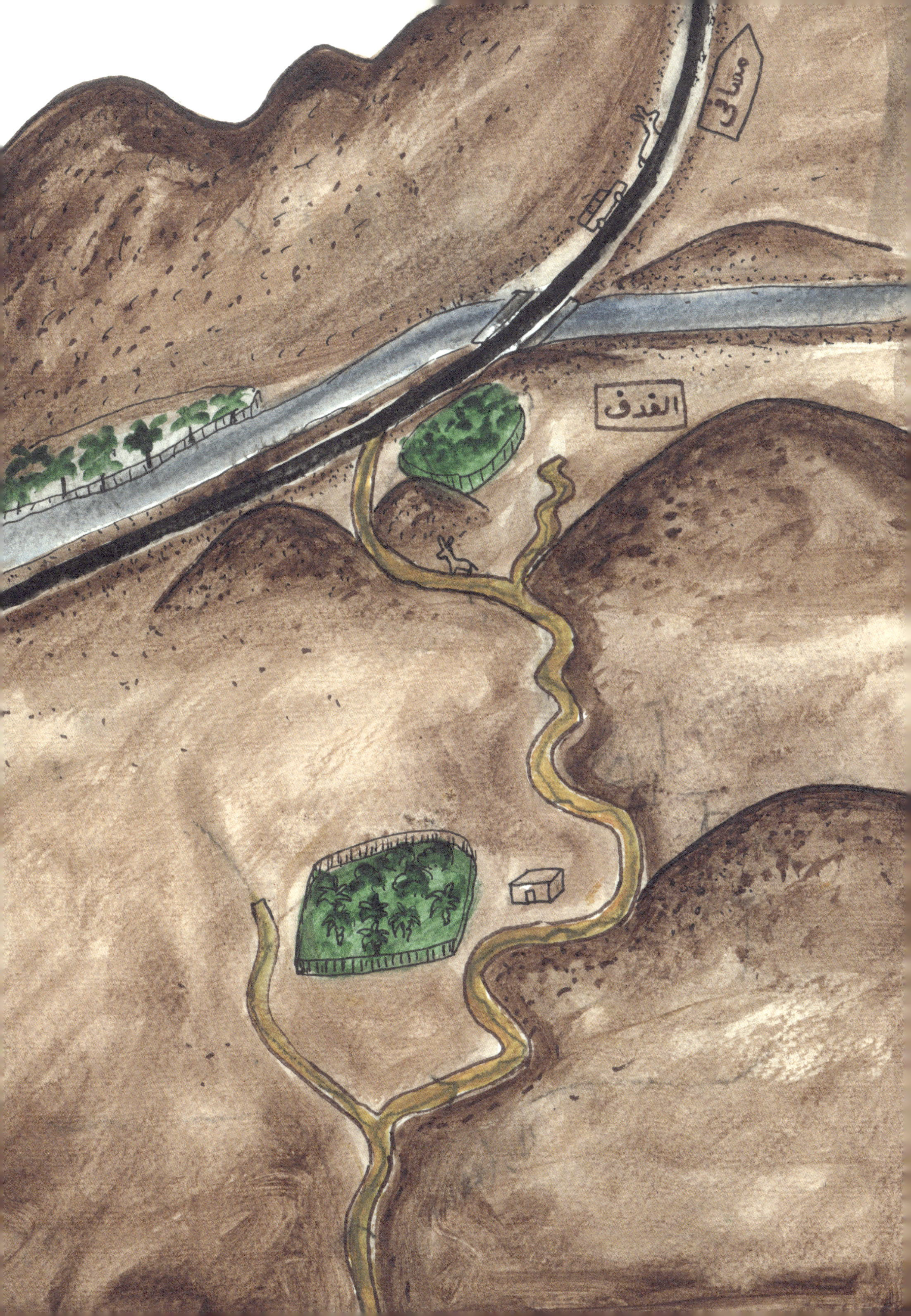

مساق
الهدف

Antarctic
Biennial

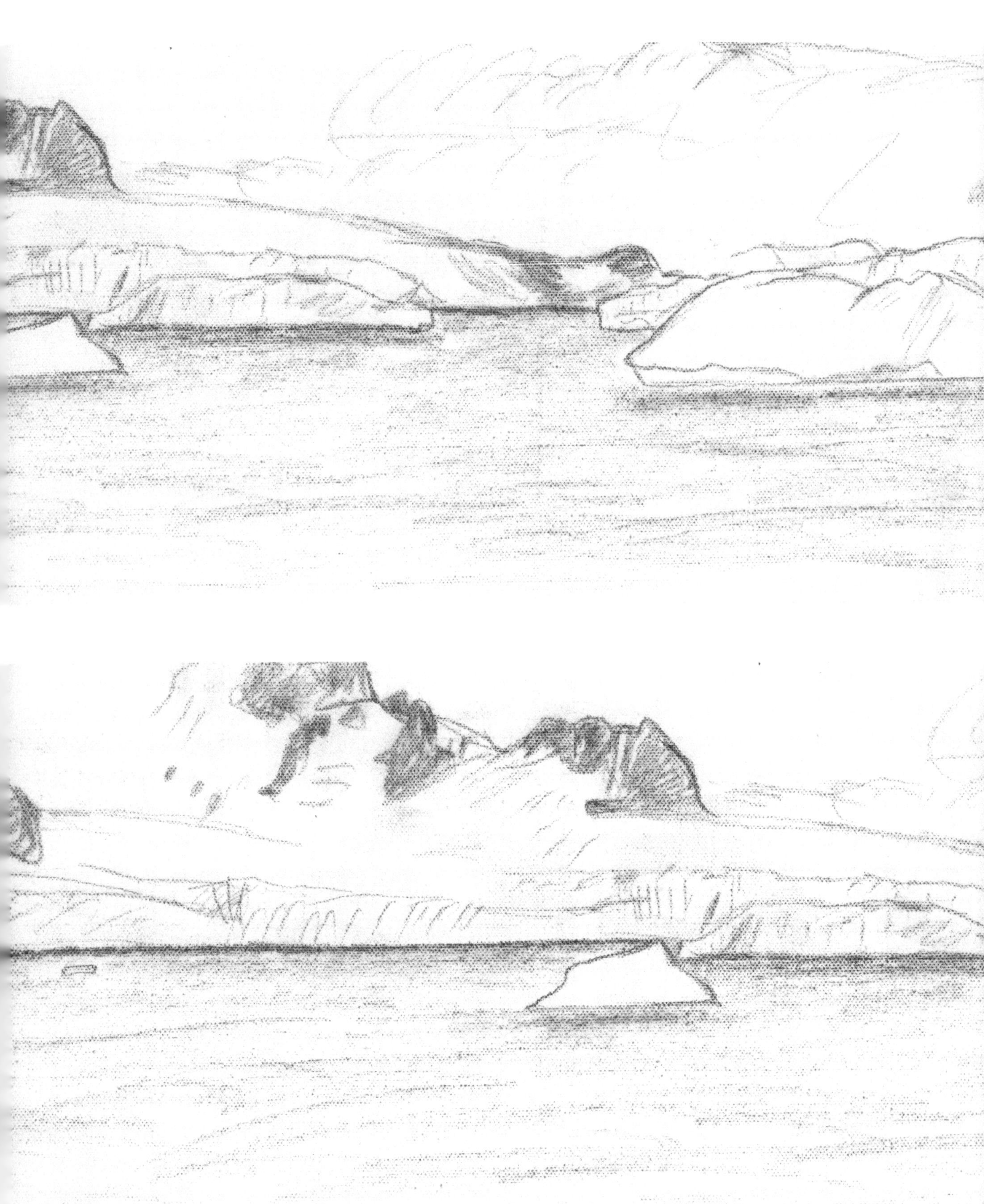

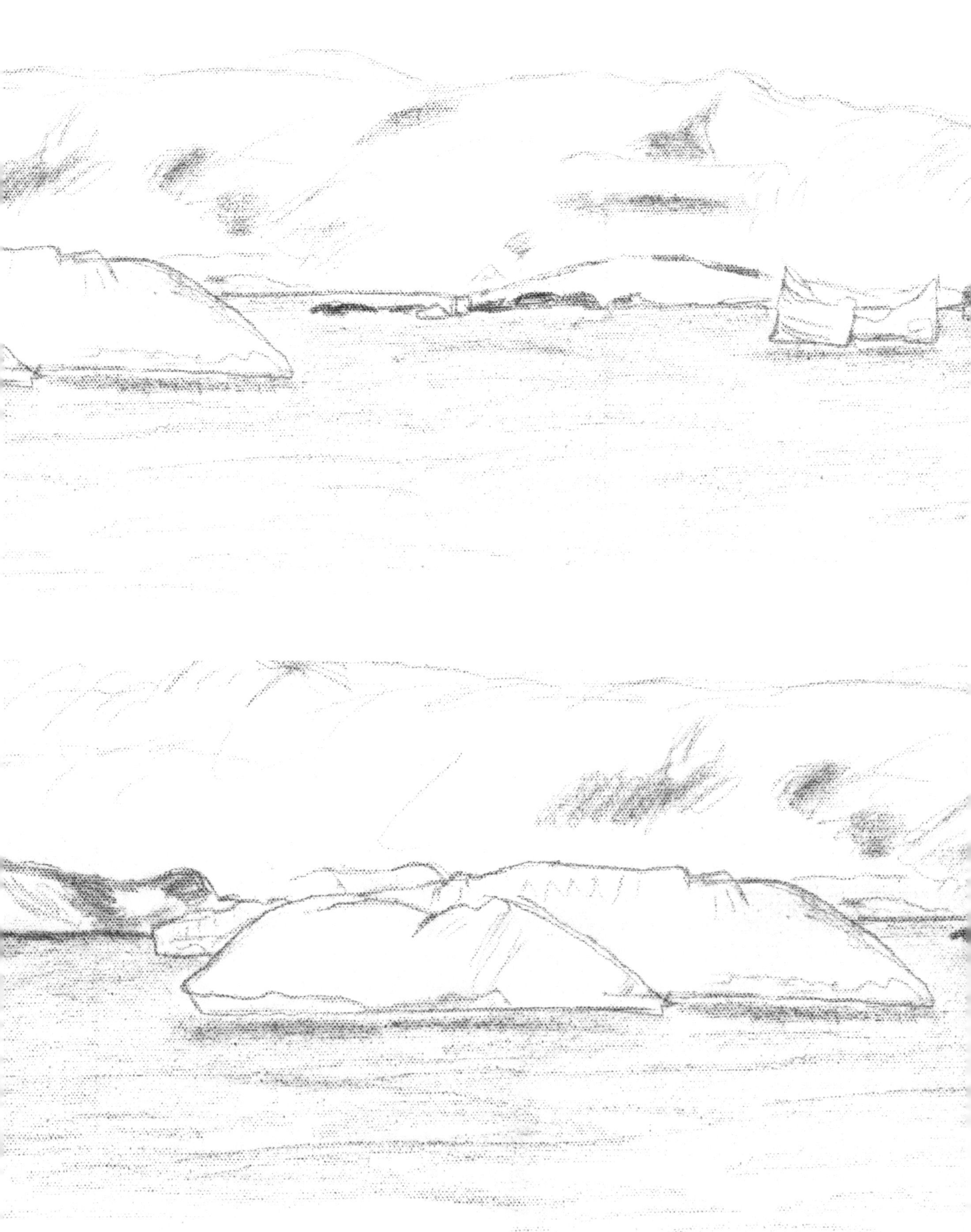

التي تنتمي إلى قبيلة واحدة ونوع واحد ، لكن
منقار أحمر وعلامة بيضاء ، أما الأنواع الأخرى
لم أراها ، مثل مثل القبائل البشرية التي تستوطن
مكان ما .

على الجزيرة يوجد مسكن بشري
عبارة عن غرفة أقامتها إحدى
البعثات لدراسة البطاريق
والحياة الطبيعية ، ولاحقاً
تخلت عنه بعد انتهاء المهمة
وأصبحت من آثار المنطقة
لا يسمح العبث بل ونقل أي
شيء من الجزيرة أو إدخال أي
عنصر طبيعي وإحضاره إلى المنطقة . بعض
الأماكن على الجزيرة الصخرية ، تغطيها ألوان
مختلفة ، الأخضر الفستقي إلى اللون الزهري
واللون السماوي ، الأزرق الفاتح واللون البني
وهو لون الصخور واللون الأبيض الذي يغطي
المنطقة .

حتى لا نقع نتحرك بمصباح نتعكز عليه للمشي بل
والتنقل ، وخلف تلك الهضبة ، منحدر سحيق
منع المشاركون بالتأكيد من الاقتراب منه وهناك
حدود حتى لا تقع مشاكل وإصابات ، من يقع خلف
تلك المنطقة لا يعود .

أحد المشاركين قدم عمل
فني ، وضع رأسه حتى صدره
في حفرة وهو عاري تماماً
رافعاً رجليه إلى أعلى
يحركها مشكلاً بها صور مختلفة للبحرة .

هناك بعض التجارب قام بها البعض ، أحضروا معهم
جرذ ليجروا حركته على الثلج وله أرجل تساعده
على الحركة أماماً لكن لم أتابع مشاهدته ، إذا كان
بمقدور الجرذ التحرك يميناً ويساراً أم إنه فقط
قادر على السير مستقيماً فقط .

إحدى المشاركات حاول إجراء بعض
التجارب وهي لتسجيل صوت الماء ،
وآخرين لديهم الفضول لاكتشاف
ما حولهم ومن حولهم وأكثر مهووس
بالتقاط الكثير من الصور وهذا شيء إيجابي
لإرسال الصور إلى عائلاتهم وأصدقائهم
وللذكرة ، بالنسبة لي ، سأستطيع إرسال بعض الصور

تحركت بنا السفينة حتى وصلنا إلى مكان يعج بالحيتان لا يقل عن 50 حوت في هذه المنطقة ، كان الجو مناسباً للنزول بالقوارب ، فأخذنا في جولة اقتربنا أكثر فأكثر من الحيتان التي تمرّ من تحتنا أو على بُعد أمتار ترفع مقدمة رأسها أو ذيلها ، وتتخاطب بصوت فيما بينها ، ومن الفينة والأخرى تمر بعض البطاريق تسبح بحرية و رأينا بعض الفقمات أو كلاب البحر تستريح فوق بعض الكتل الثلجية العائمة ، الطقس يتغير سريعاً ، بدأت الرياح تهب وارتفع الموج ، وقد تساقط الثلج هذا اليوم وأصبح الجو أكثر برودة من ذي قبل ، عادت بنا القوارب إلى السفينة ، وبعض القوارب ذهبت لزيارة إحدى الجزر .

19:30 تناولنا العشاء ، كالعادة جلس كلنا معاً على طاولات ، تكثر الحكي والحديث وتطول مراسم العشاء والغداء ، أولاً أكل سلطة ثم الطبق الرئيسي وأخيراً أكل الحلويات ، وهنا المشروب والعصائر تقدم بالطلب والدفع لاحقاً .
بالنسبة لعملي الفني ، فقد رسمت على بعض قطع القماش ولم يتبقَّ لي الإجمالي 7 قطع أريد الاحتفاظ بها لكتابة اليوميات المتبقية عليّ خلال الأيام القادمة، لذا بدأت بالرسم على دفتر ورقي بعض المشاهد ، أما ما يخص مشروعي الفني على السفينة ، فقد اهتمّ بنية ، وهي عبارة عن قطع فنية أراها تعوم بحرية لذلك فكرت برسم بعض وإعطاء كل واحدة حرفاً معيناً لتكون في النهاية حروف أبجدية أنتاركتيكا.

Antarctic Alphabet.

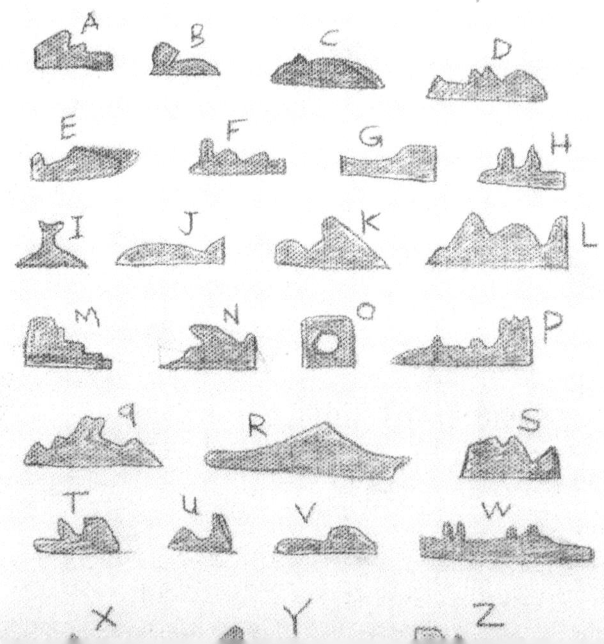

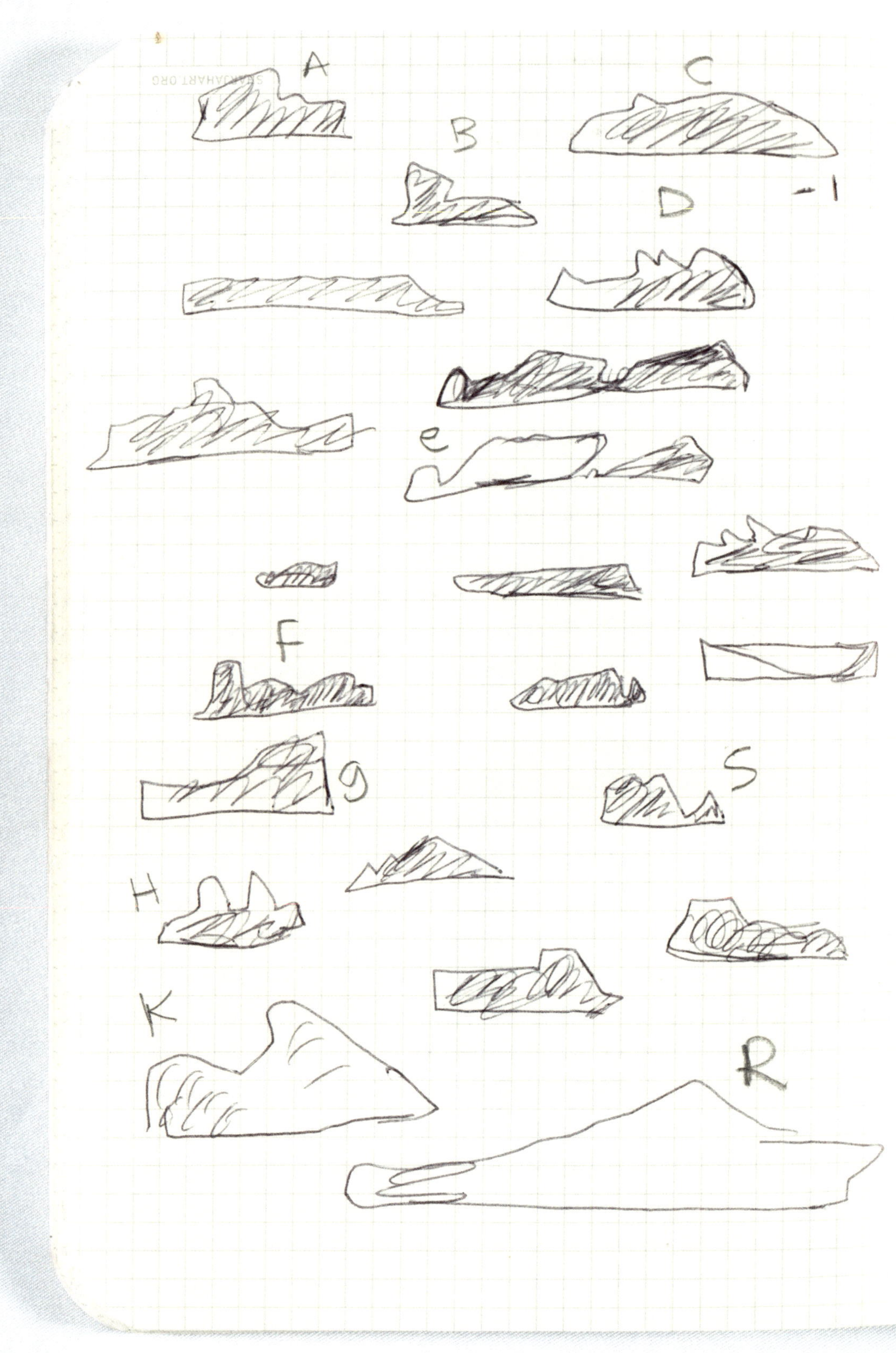
A
B
C
D
I
e
F
g
S
H
K
R

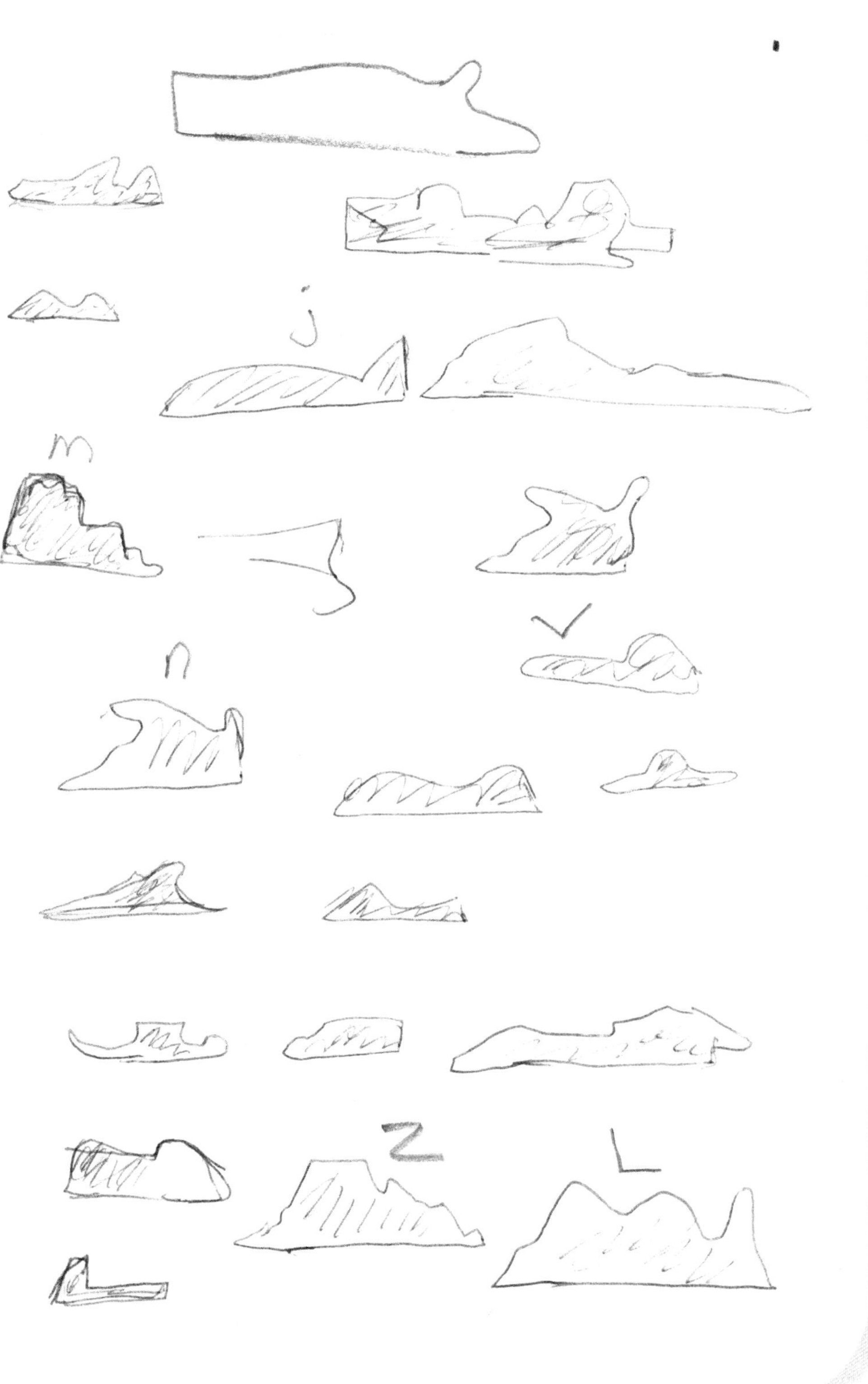

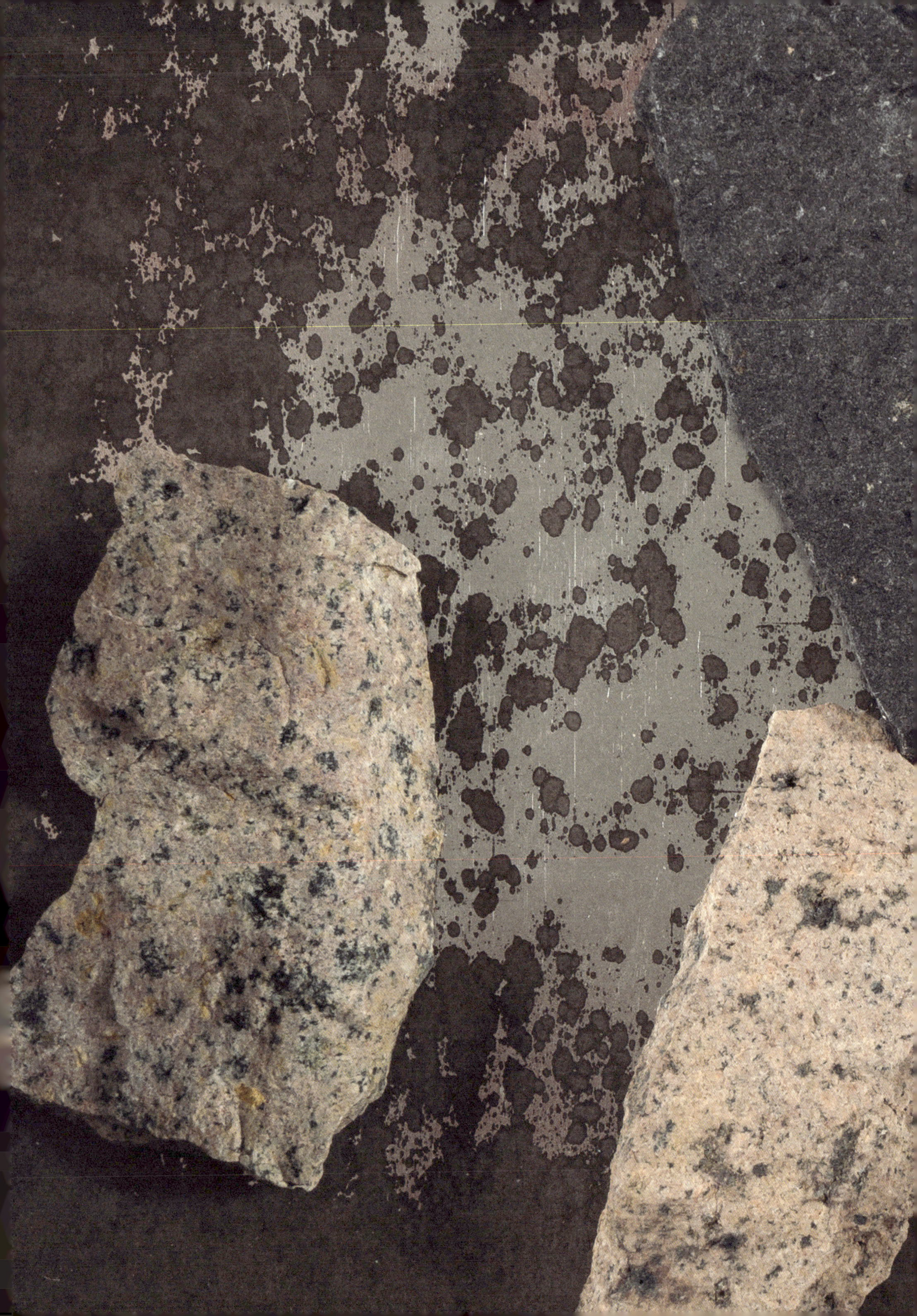

In 1959, Antarctica was declared a demilitarised zone. Under the Antarctic Treaty, about 14 million square kilometres of arid land, nearly double the size of Australia, were designated for scientific investigation and environmental preservation. This put an end to a series of dubious territorial claims in the 20th century from the United Kingdom, Norway, France, Argentina and other Western nations. No military bases or weapons testing, no mining and no waste disposal.

This uninhabited continent, despite being as far from the equator as a land mass can possibly be, sees less annual rainfall than any part of the world. Its lack of precipitation and exceeding dryness officially qualifies it as the world's largest desert.

What is old to Antarctica is new to us. As global temperatures rise, fossilised flora and fauna, along with latent microbiomes and bacteria, have resurfaced to join the scientific record. Here the ozone layer was first discovered, the area's ice core records occasioning a new understanding of both natural and human-induced climate change.

In 2017, 25 years removed from his last major sea excursion aboard the *Nippon Maru*, Abdullah Al Saadi found himself cutting through nautical miles of springtime Antarctic waters alongside 100 passengers, including artists, scientists and academics. Spearheaded by Russian artist and former submariner Alexander Ponomarev, this journey marked the inaugural Antarctic Biennale – an ambitious and short-lived interdisciplinary platform that attempted to leverage the unique status of the continent for research and creative activity.

The vessel, *Akademik Ioffe*, departed on 17 March 2017 from Ushuaia, Argentina, South America's southernmost port, beginning its 12-day voyage towards the Antarctic Archipelago.

Amidst the journey and its expected confluence of sperm whales, emperor penguins and elephant seals encountered across the Falkland Islands, Drake Passage and other key stopping points, what truly captivated Al Saadi was the sculptural nature of passing icebergs, which reminded him of his own more familiar context of Roos Al Jibal. Conceiving of them as mountains, Al Saadi viewed these organic structures, each unique and in constant phase change, as an opportunity to add another entry to his *Abjadiya* series: the *Antarctic Alphabet* (2017). Similar to Al Saadi's previous work,

My Mother's Letters (1998–2013), this 26-letter alphabet began as a series of sketches, with each letter attributed to an English counterpart.

While many of the installations and performances staged throughout this mobile biennale attempted to bring greater nuance to Ponomarev's somewhat utopic vision of the Antarctic as a pure, enigmatic stage for creative and environmental dialogue, Al Saadi chose to mine the oceanscape for fleeting, symbolic meaning – a methodology that by then had become a hallmark of his practice.

هناك بعض التجارب قام بها البعض، أحضروا معهم
جهاز ليجروا حركته على الثلج وله أرجل تساعده
على الحركة تماماً لكن لم () تابع مشاهدته، إذا كان
بمقدور الجهاز التحرك يميناً ويساراً أم، إنه فقط
قادر على السير مستقيماً فقط.

JOAQUIN
FARGAS

إحدى المشاركات تحاول إجراء بعض
التجارب وهي لتسجيل صوت الماء
وآخرين لديهم الفضول لاكتشاف
ما حولهم ومن حولهم والكثير مهووس
بالتقاط الكثير من الصور وهذا شيء
لإرسال الصور إلى عائلاتهم وأصدقائهم
والذكرة، بالنسبة لي، ...، إرسال بعض الصور

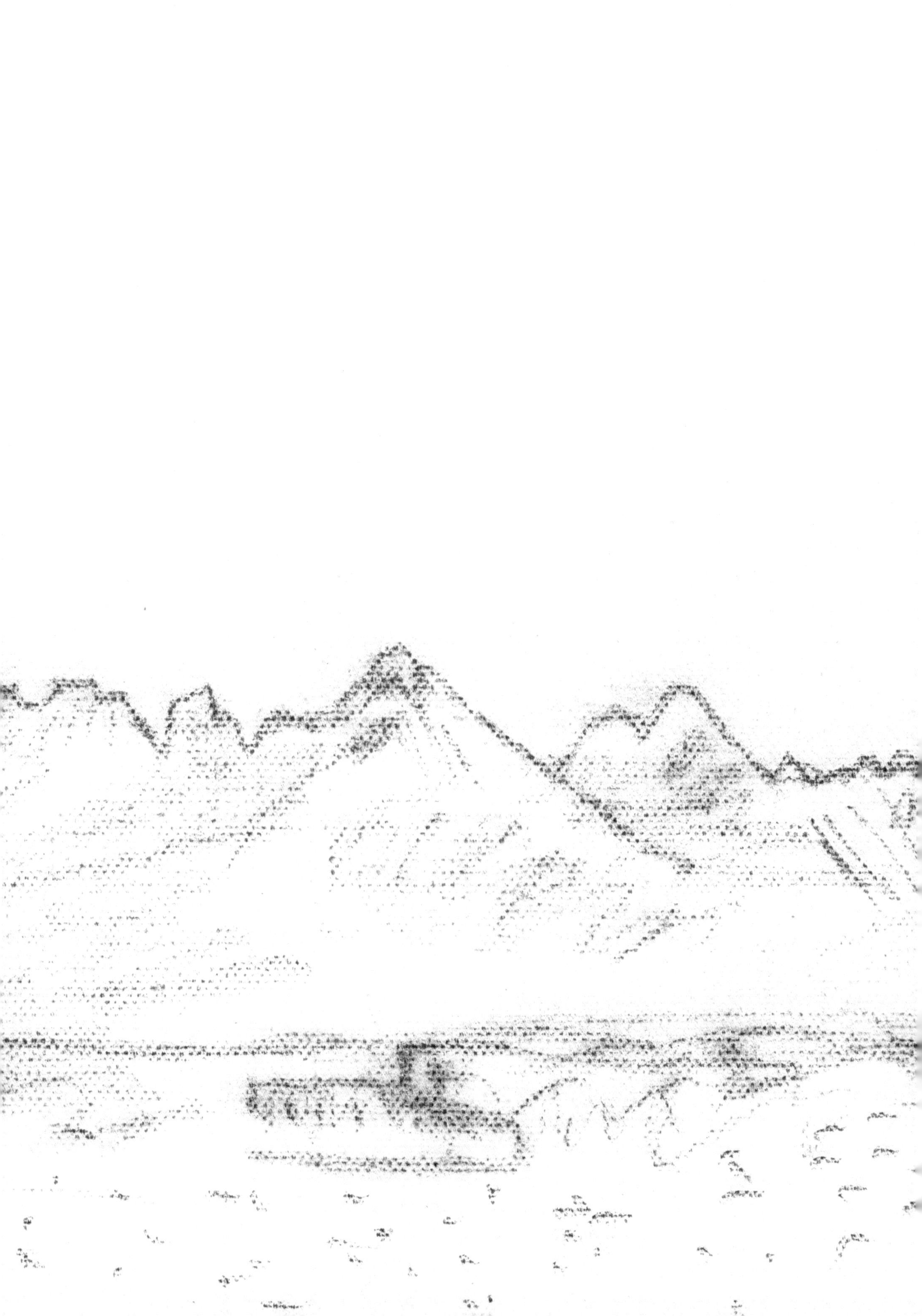

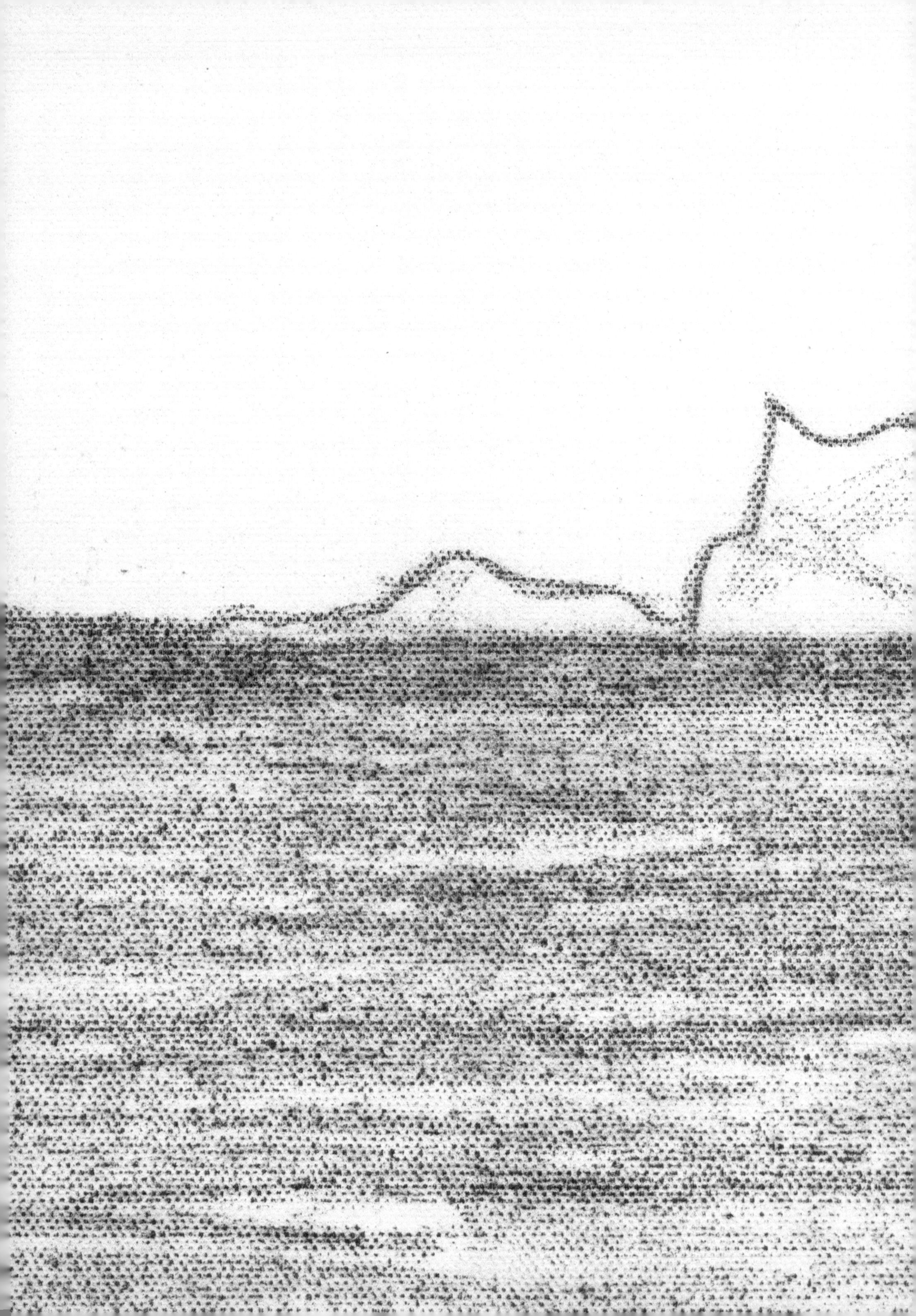

but all the hot countries you
see nature full of name elements
  trees, moun, rocks ~~~
in the south pole the artist
   sometimes find himself cant
draw any thing, he can draw
because what he sees a canvas
and if he tries to draw he draws
the canvas itself.

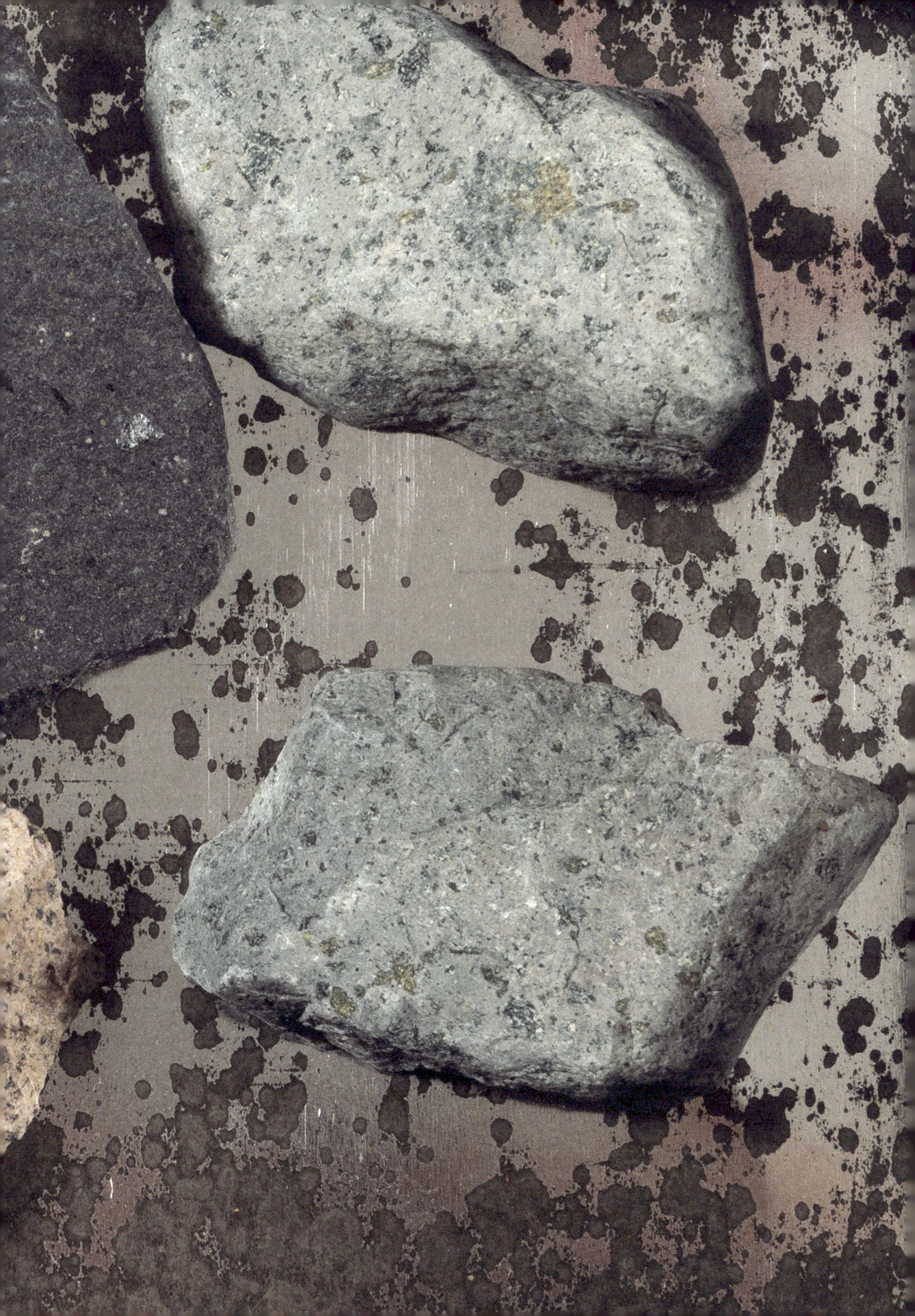

20/3/2019
عبدالله السعدي
القطب الجنوبي

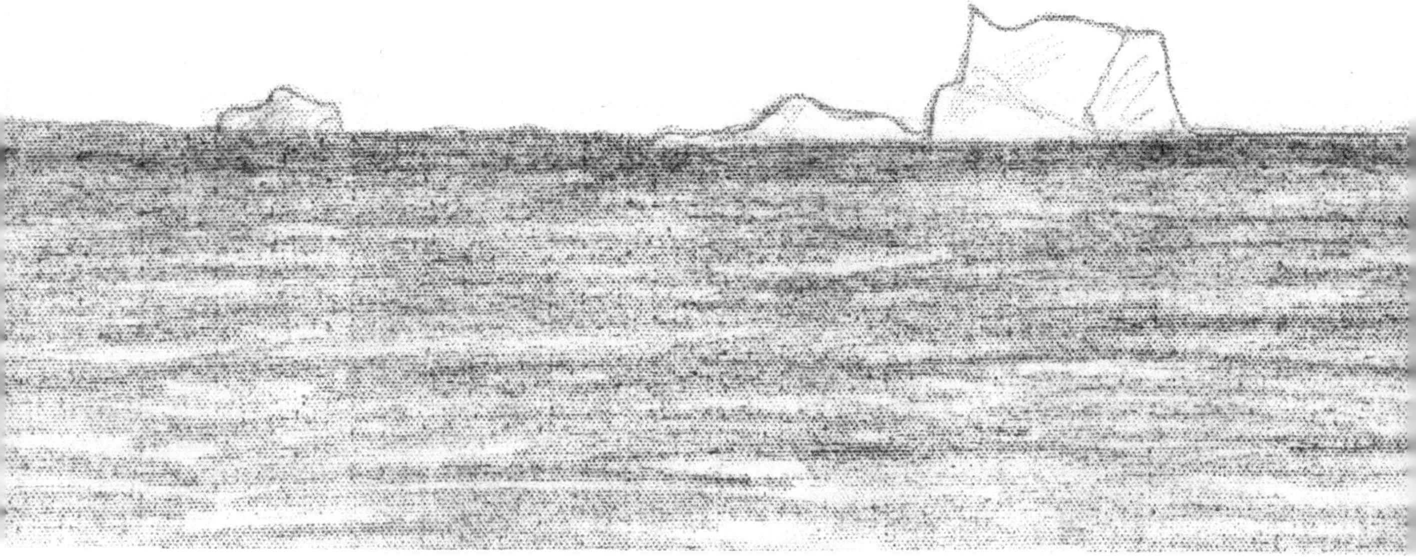

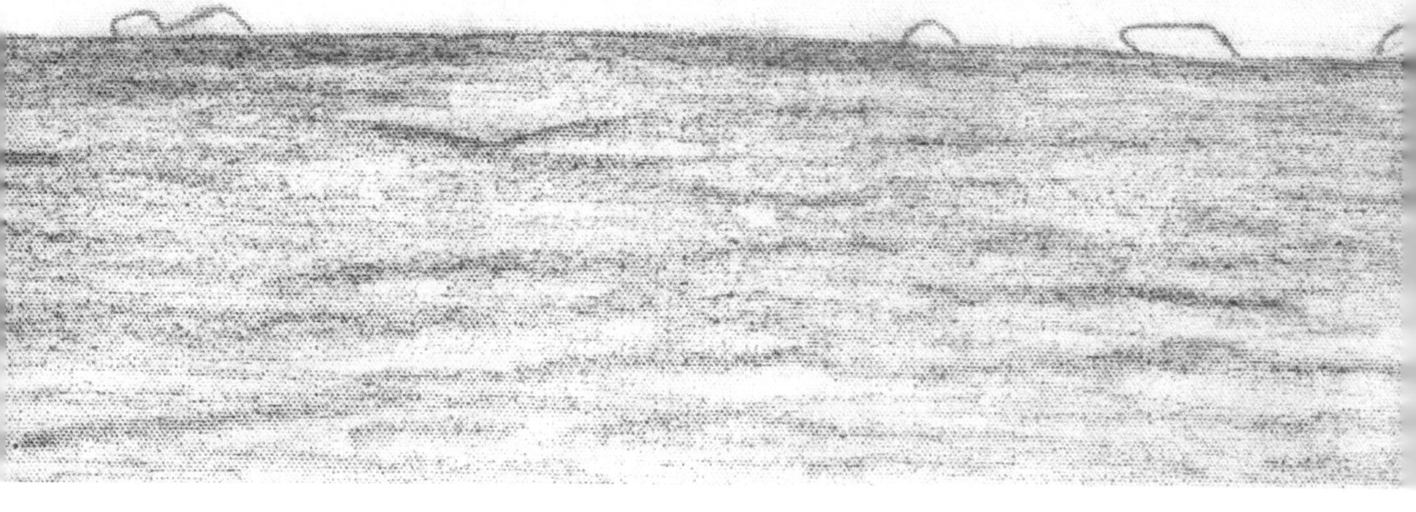

Findale 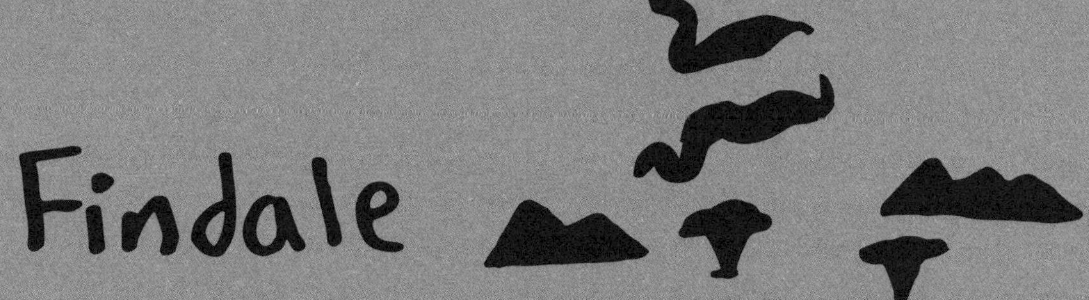

173

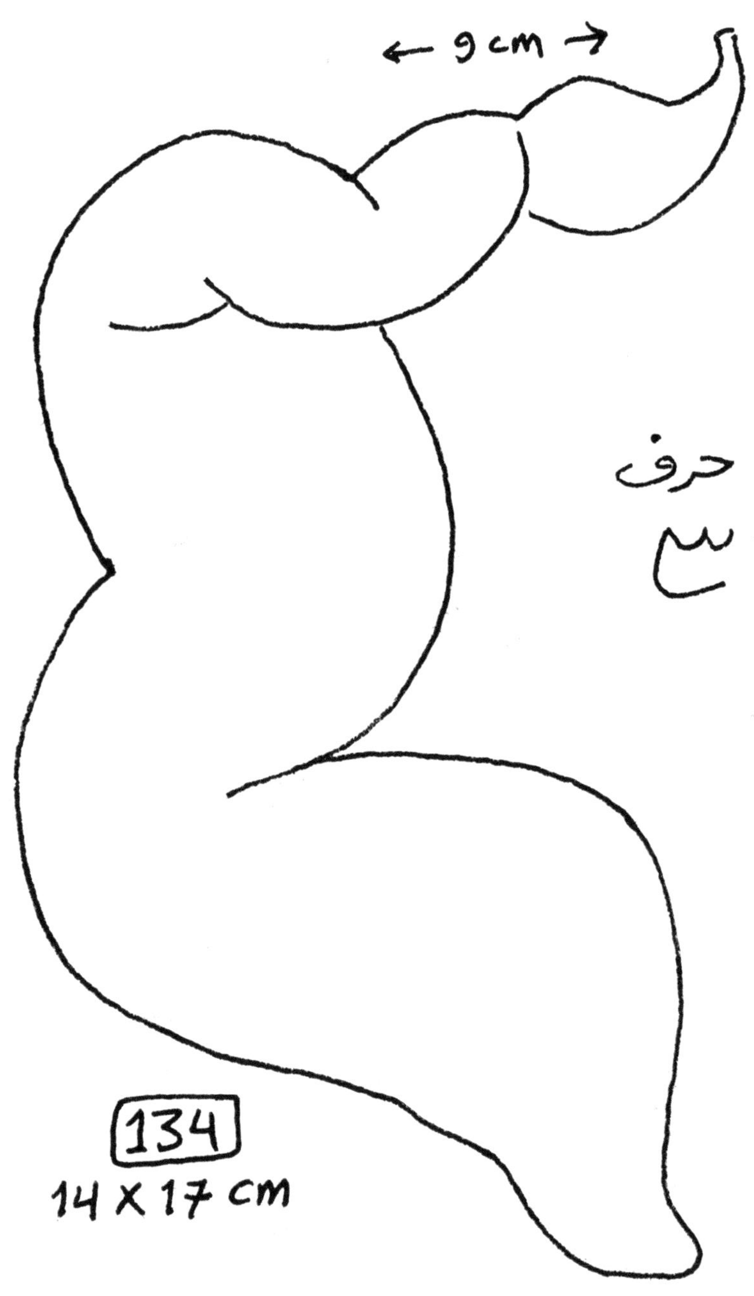

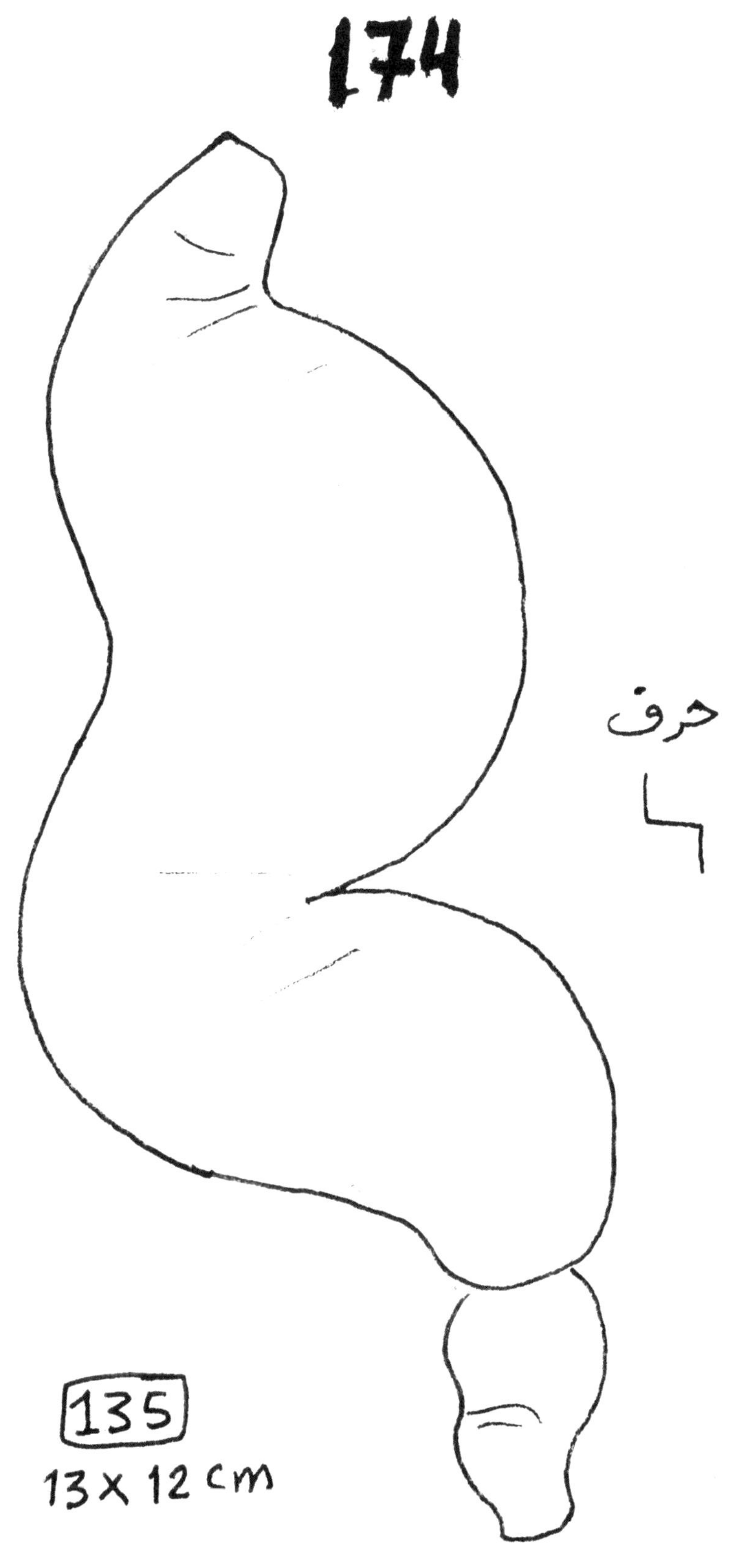
174
حرف
135
13 x 12 cm

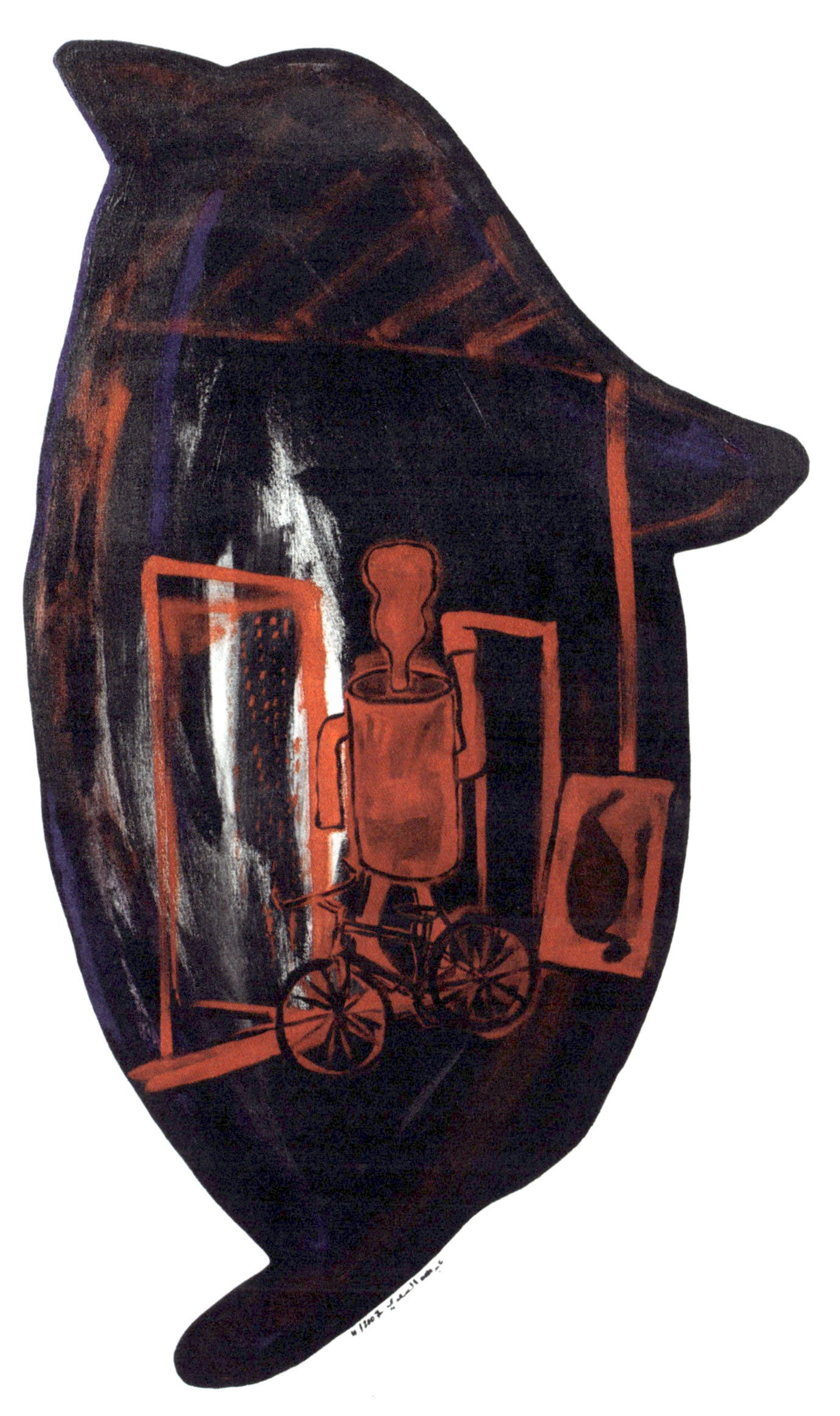

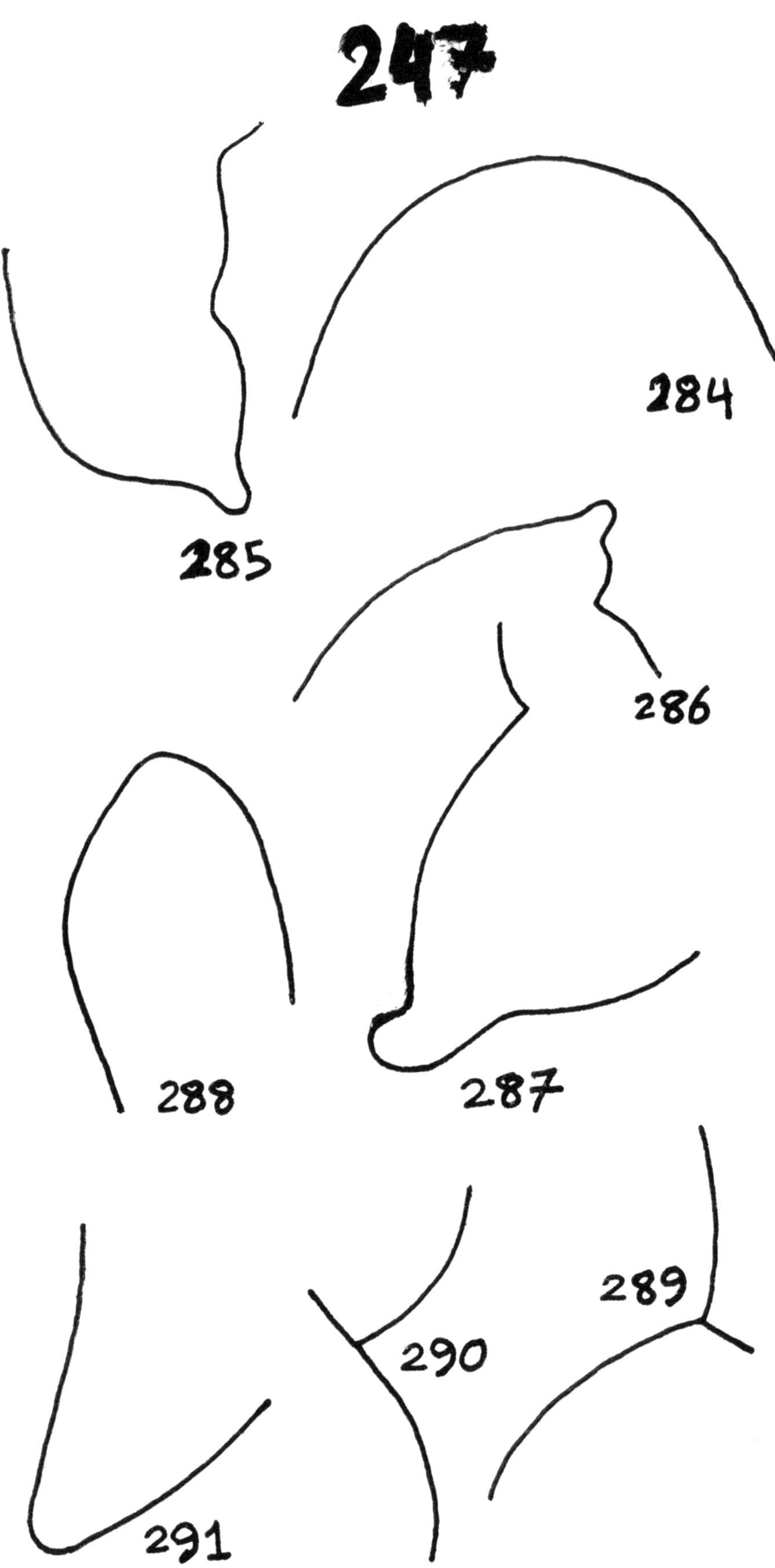
247
284
285
286
288
287
289
290
291

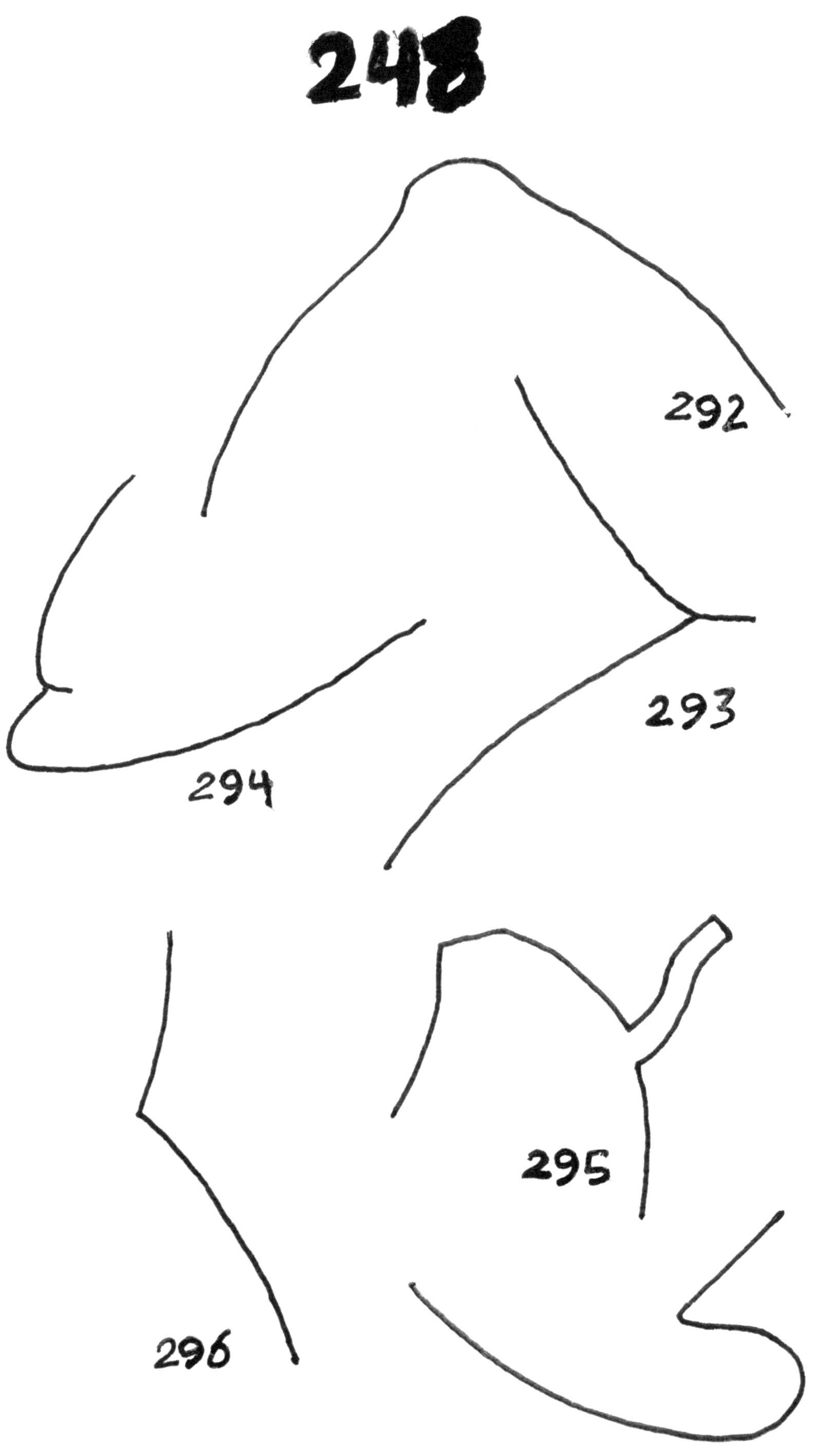
248
292
293
294
295
296

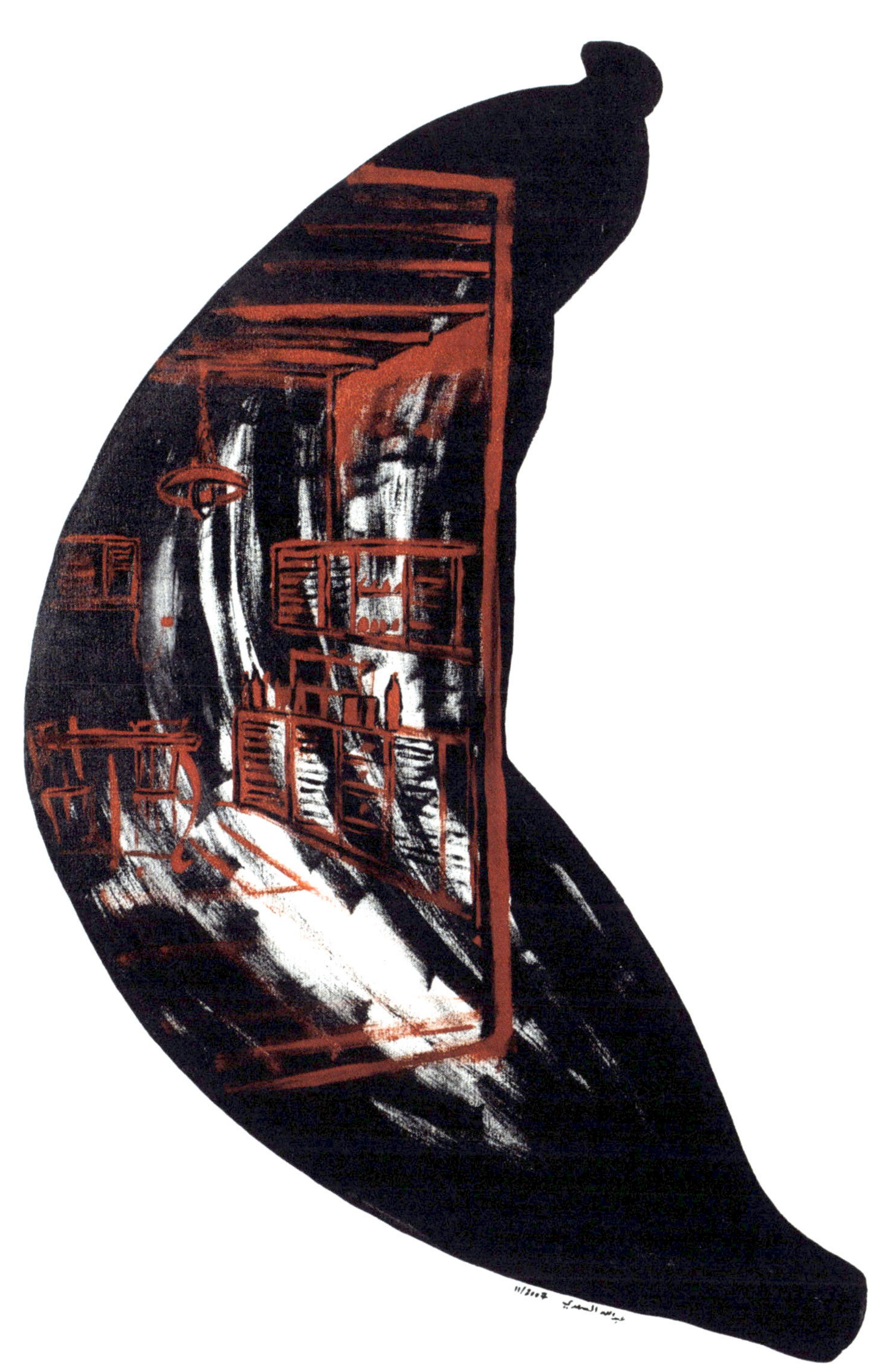

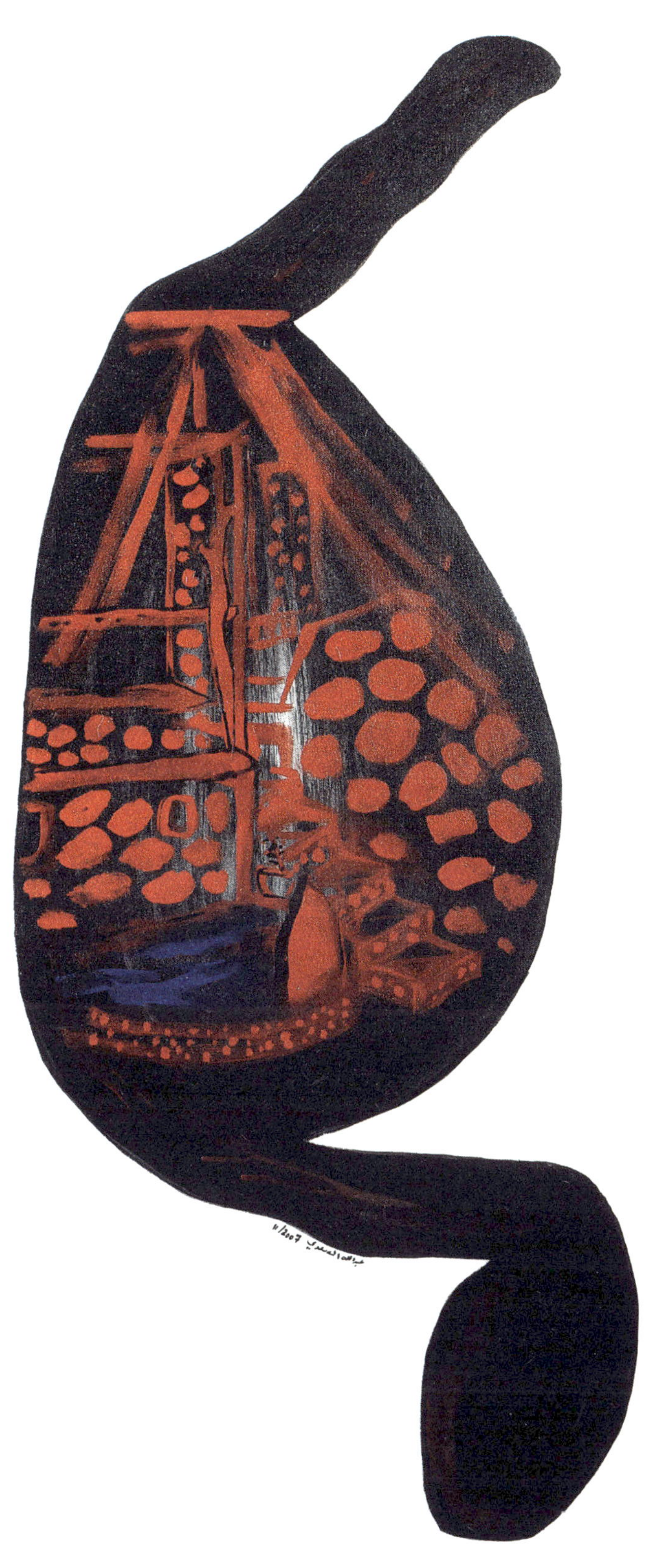

عبدالله المصري ٢٠٠٧/٤

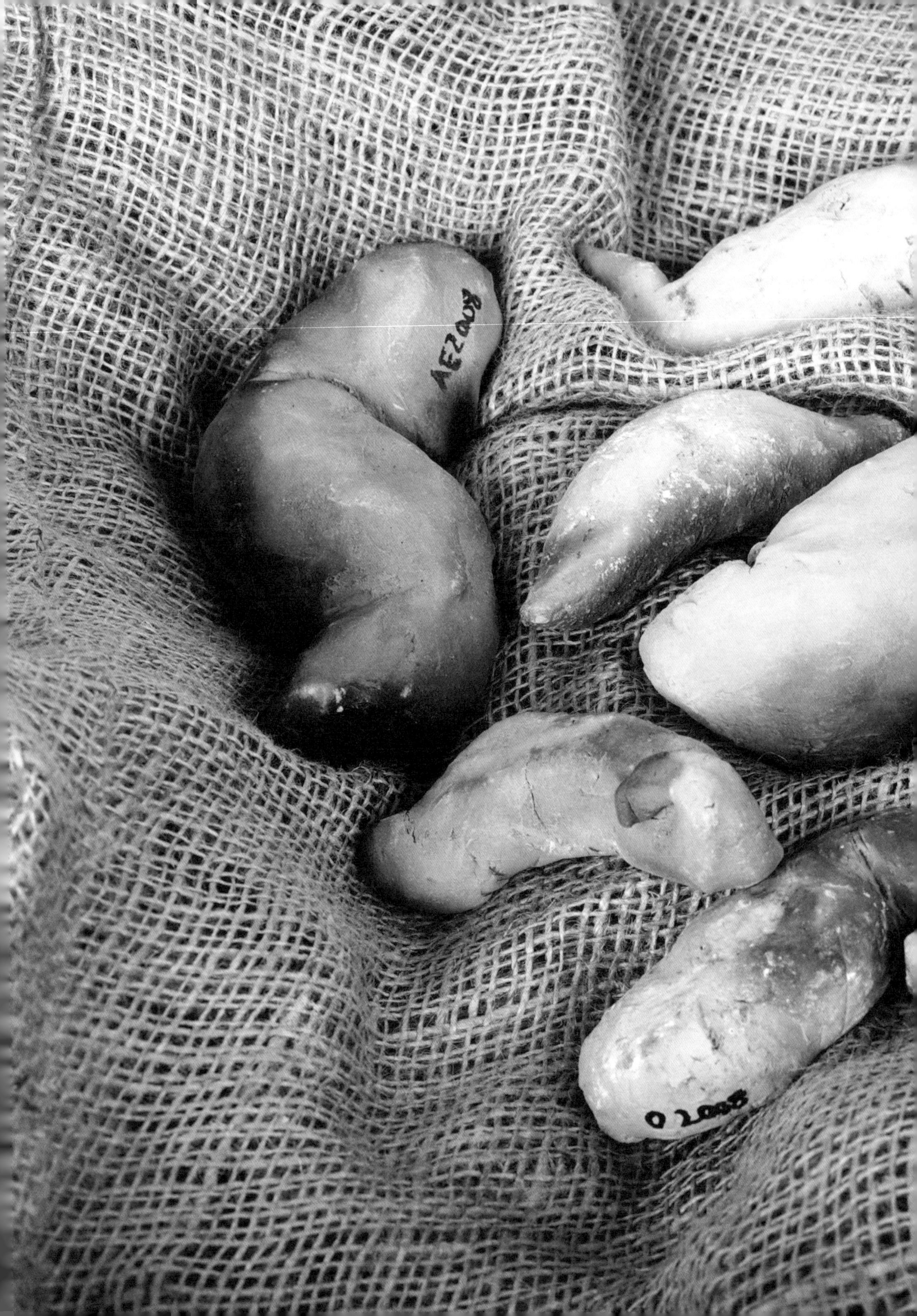

The earliest evidence of sweet potato cultivation was found in the caverns of Chilca Canyon, in what is now coastal Peru. A staple food for its Neolithic Period inhabitants, the crop appeared in tapestries and pottery unearthed in tombs and burial sites by late-20th-century archaeological digs. Its representation in artefacts of the era, alongside other crops such as maize, peanuts and squash, tells us that the sweet potato's roots run even deeper than the ancient Peruvian cultures that venerated it, to the dawn of agriculture in South and Central America.

The spread of the sweet potato beyond the Americas has long been attributed to the Columbian exchange. Beginning with Christopher Columbus' arrival on Caribbean soil in 1492, mainstream historical accounts ascribe the widespread proliferation of crops, livestock, culture and technology, as well as disease, of course, between the Americas and Europe, Africa and Asia to this period of colonisation and trade.

As far as the sweet potato is concerned, recent research suggests that it may have begun its journey much earlier, through naturally occurring dispersal or even sea trade, both hypotheses for its presence in the Polynesian Islands, for example, well before any European intervention.

Linguistic misattributions among the sweet potato, the yam (indigenous to Africa and parts of Asia) and other root vegetables, such as the Southeast Asian taro and the Japanese satoimo, have complicated the search for a definitive answer to both its origins and spread.

The word *batata* and consequently *batata halwa* entered the Arabic language through the Spanish *patata*, which was itself ironically a combination of the Indigenous Caribbean *batata* and *papa* from the Quechua people of the Peruvian Andes. In Abdullah Al Saadi's own milieu, he came to know and experiment with it through its local variety, known as findale (potentially loaned from Hindi). His father would grow findale between January and September, shaded in manure-rich soil typical of the mountainous areas of Madha. Watering was gradually scaled back once they began to take root, ceasing entirely for a month to allow the potato skins to thicken before harvest.

To Al Saadi, these tubers represent strength and resilience similar to the appearance of masculinity when they initially emerge from the soil, only to soften and yield once boiled or baked. This gendering of the potato, explored in *Studies of a Male and Female Sweet Potato* (2004), also extends to different varieties, mapping male and female dimorphisms and features onto the white, elongated Arabic findale and other more elliptical red varieties.

His attributions mirror a theory originating from Greek antiquity. According to the doctrine of signatures, the medicinal value of a plant could be inferred based on its physical similarities to organs of the human body. This theory suggested that nature was rich with allegory and that providence sought to give mankind clear signs towards healing. While Al Saadi makes no such claims, he does recognise the persistence of such beliefs in the agricultural folklore of his forefathers, incorporating these archaic, even erotic dimensions into his own corpus.

His personification of the sweet potato stems from this ingrained belief in correspondence between humans and land. Each variety is shaped by the farmer's ministrations. They divert precious resources into their fields, giving and taking in the form of selective irrigation, engineering thirst and want until the appropriate conditions are met. Every uprooted sweet potato then signifies a small death, promising new life for those above ground – a process of equal exchange that renews itself across harvests and generations.

Known in Al Saadi's works as the Sweet Potato Project, the findale works first debuted at the 2008 Emirates Fine Arts Society exhibition *Findale* and later at the UAE's pavilion at the 2011 Venice Biennale. Today, it is probably his most well-known work, as multifarious as its subject matter, spanning the mediums of oil on canvas, sculpture, stone engraving and video as well as another ideogrammatic alphabet in the same vein as *My Mother's Letters*. These works emphasise the findale as an evocative, transitional form that triggers as many personal, cultural and historical associations as a Rorschach test.

His production of 24 gold findale jewellery pieces, exhibited as part of *Emirati Expressions* (2013) at Manarat Al Saadiyat in Abu Dhabi, marked a high point in a project driven by a shared belief with the Neolithic Peruvians: that which sustains us is worthy of exaltation.

The sweet potato is as essential and versatile as a dietary staple as it is a denomination of creative currency, embedded deep within Al Saadi's imaginary. Through his explorations of its complex origins and amorphous, polyphonic nature, he once again broadens the scope of his cartographic practice.

Coming to terms with the limitations of his own body early in his career, Al Saadi has devoted considerable time and energy to divesting himself from anthropocentric art making and its aesthetic notions. By recognising the autonomy of the sweet potato, the beverage can and particularly, members of the animal world, whose capacity for travel in some ways far exceeds his own, he gains access to the silent, imperceptible migrations and movements that shape the world around him.

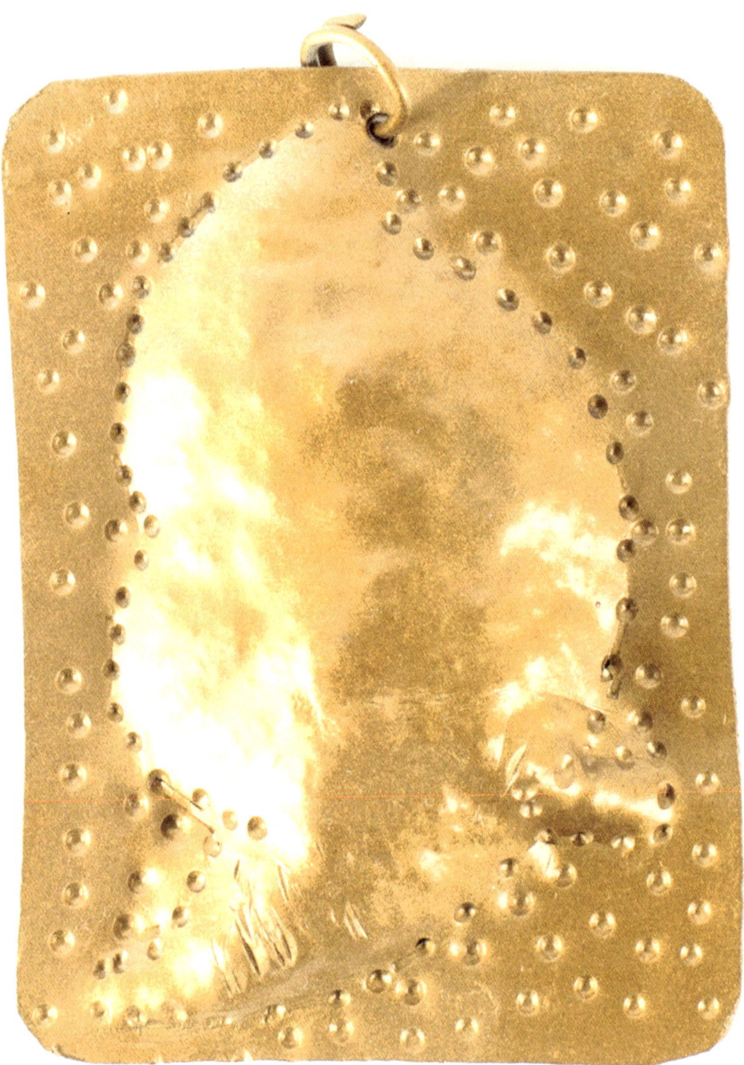

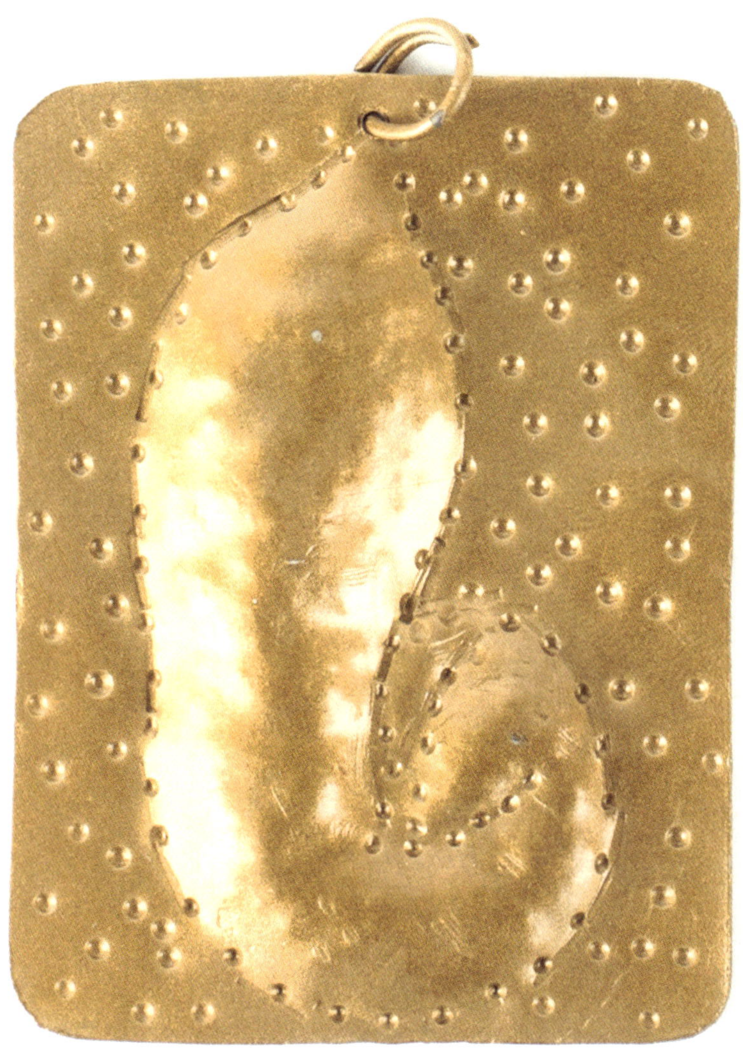

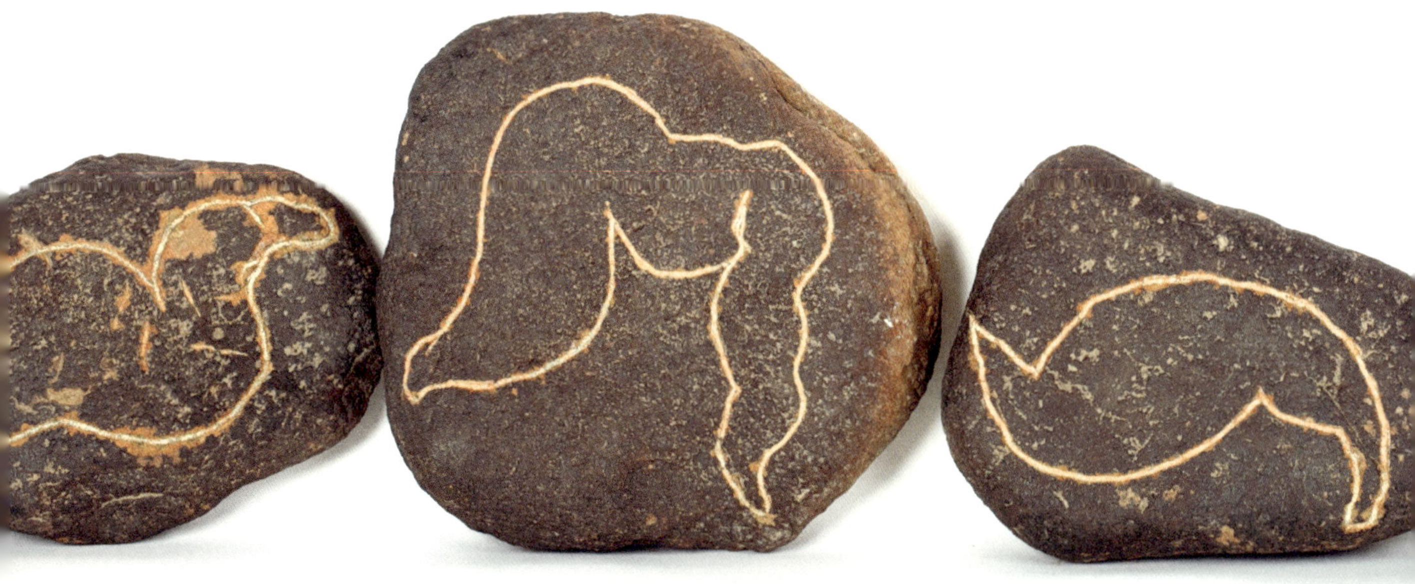

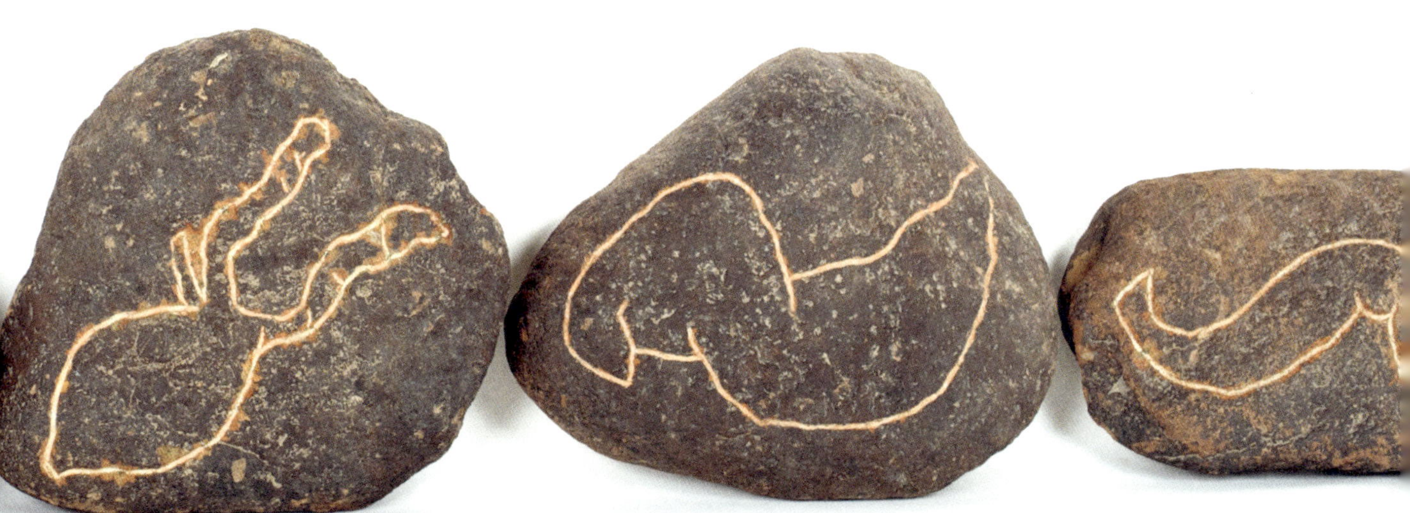

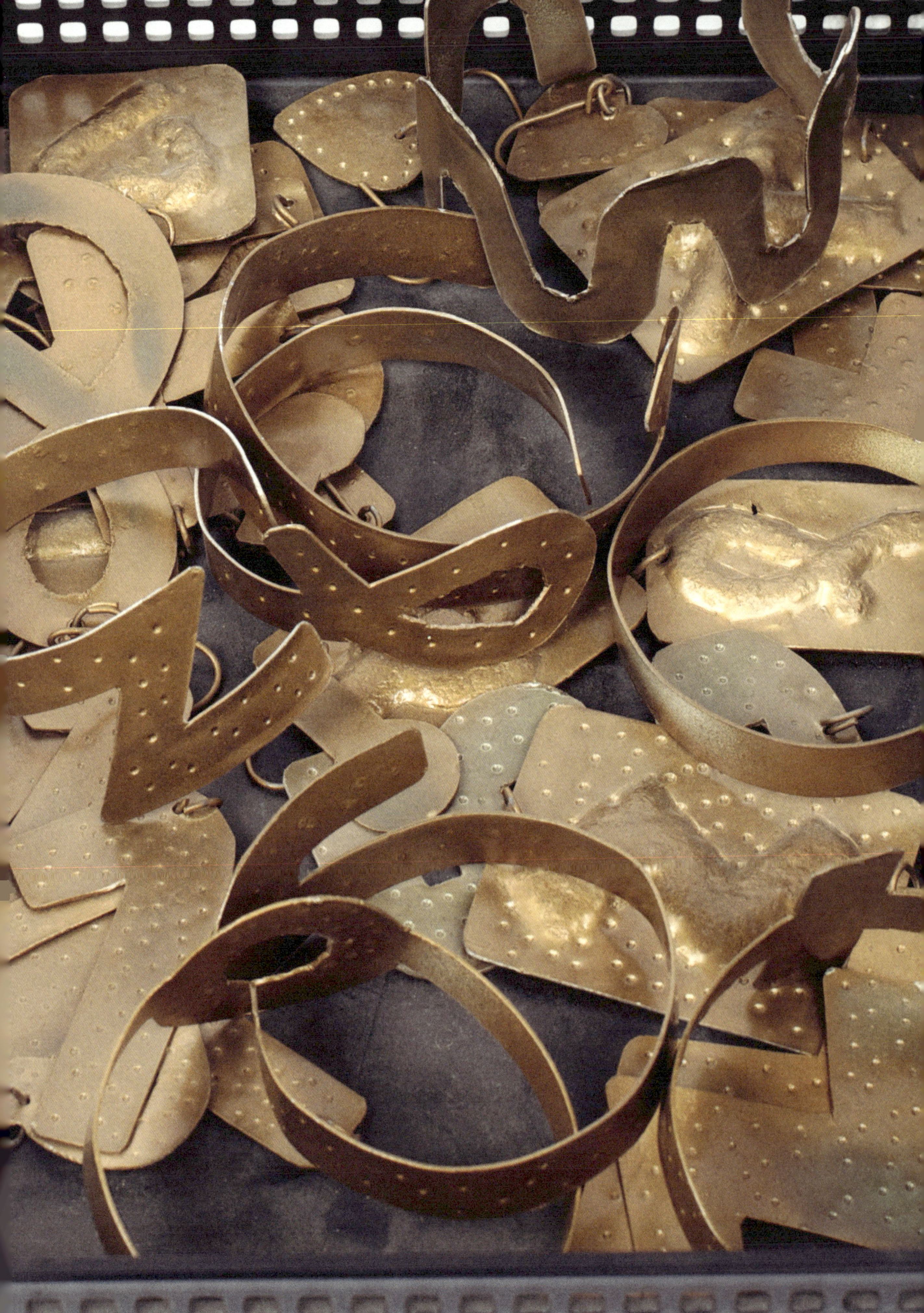

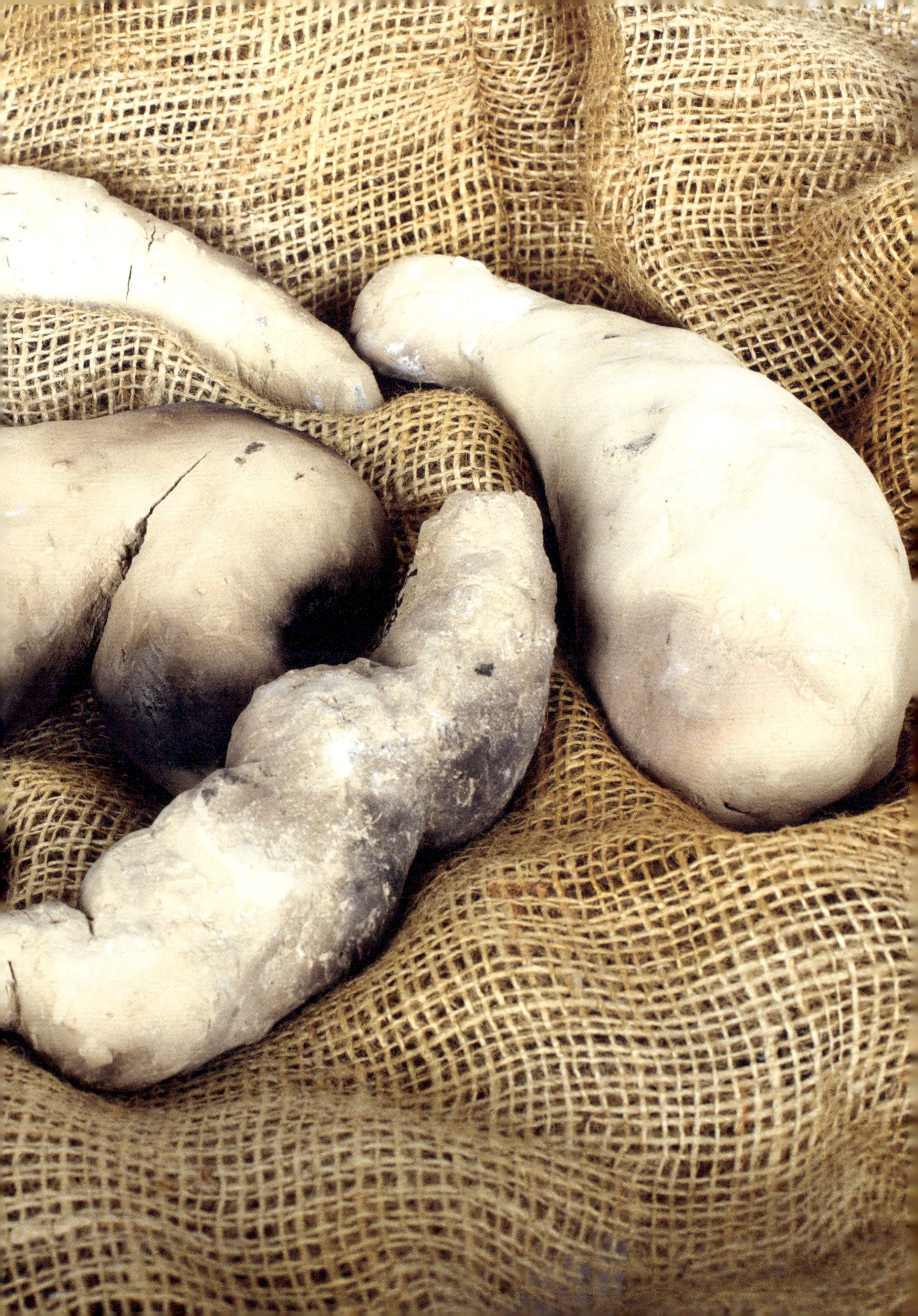

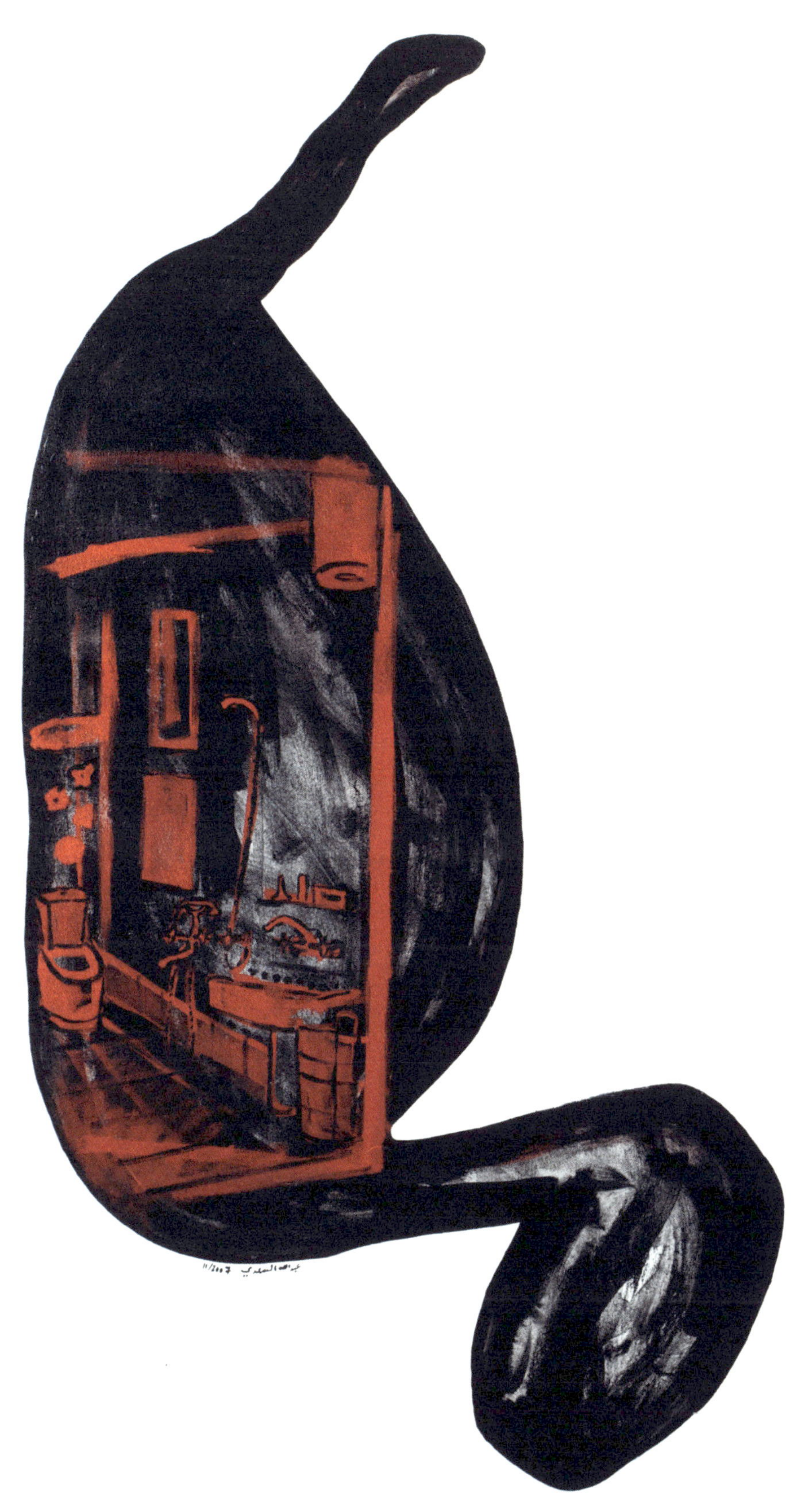

11/2007

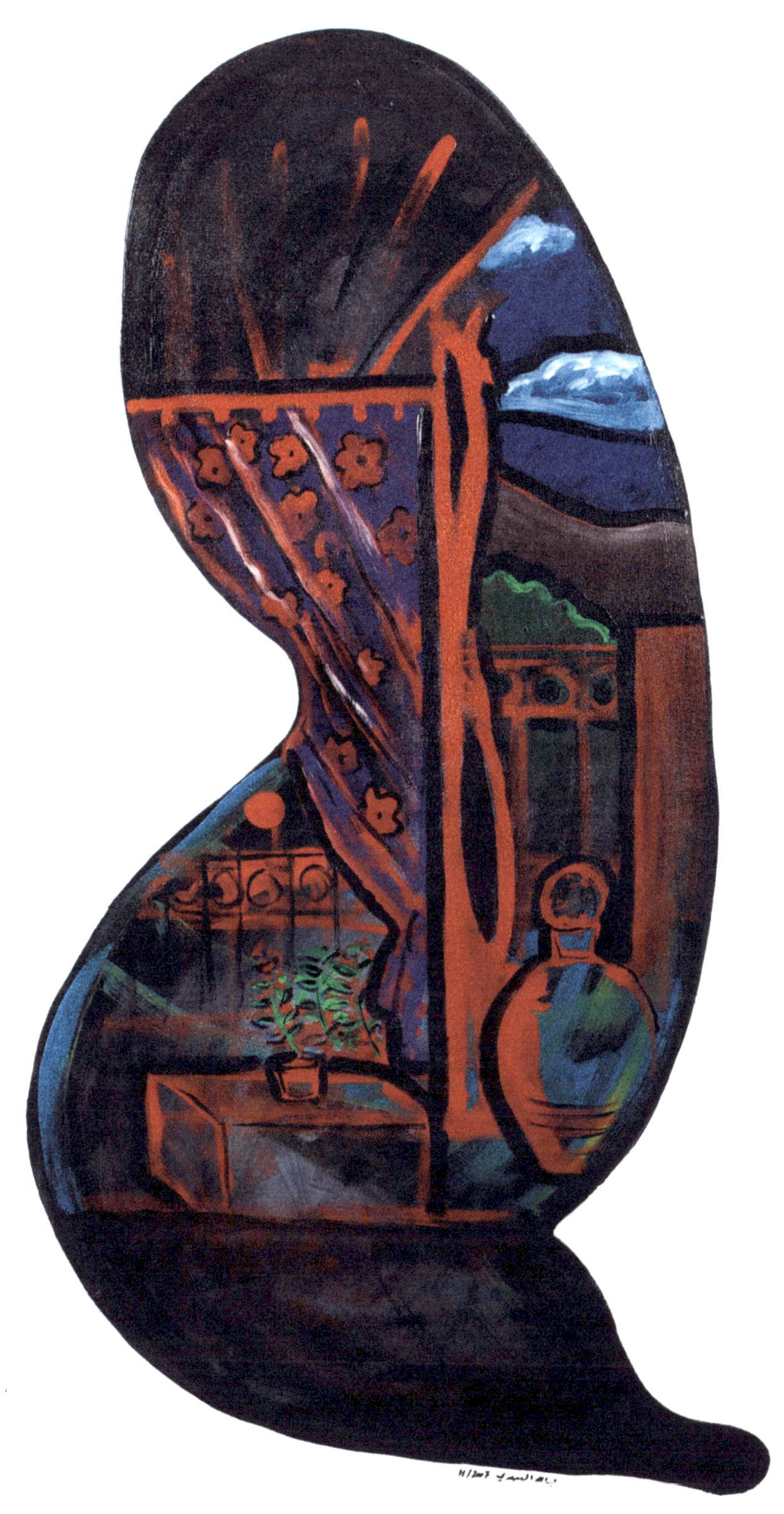

11/2007

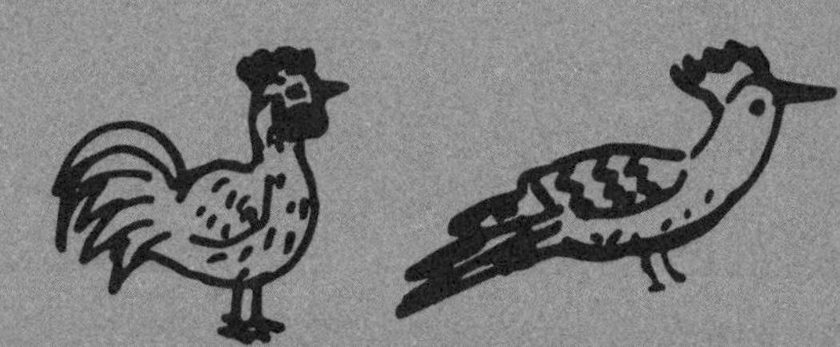

Recording all
Living Things

As a person, Abdullah Al Saadi is someone who could easily disappear in the landscape he diligently captures, chronicles, and archives. Al Saadi isn't tethered to his base in Madha, an exclave on the eastern coast of the Emirates, but operates from the broader land, moving from Fujairah, Khorfakkan and other town settlements in between. Before my first meeting with Al Saadi, I had been familiar with the flat, zoomed-out map drawings of his travels across the eastern coastal regions mentioned. What I wasn't prepared for was how comprehensively he cataloged so many of the everyday details of the living things contained within that larger landscape through carefully labeled drawings and paintings.

From his studio in Madha, set on his family's ancestral lands near the coastal town of Khorfakkan, Al Saadi would pull out stacks of drawings of fruits of various kinds, the insects that feed off them, vegetables and other lifeforms. His precision was almost encyclopaedic, yet the images were striking in their imperfect naturalness, instantly exposing the exaggerated uniformity and plasticity of produce as it is commonly marketed. For instance, dates, plant branches, and the local mango pop off the page with their maroon bruises, frizzy hairs and imperfect shapes – an ugliness that often gets lost in depictions of nature. The drawings bend popular conceptions of what is 'real' and 'imaginary,' forcing viewers to contend with what has become idealised and naturalised in society. Perhaps we are so used to the imaginary being real that our eyes have forgotten that the natural world and what it produces is inherently inconsistent and varied, mirroring human experiences. This is echoed in Al Saadi's ability to impartially capture the idiosyncrasies of the living things he encounters without imposing himself on them.

Al Saadi can achieve this because of his capacity to remain an embodied witness to the land and world that hosts him. On the few occasions I met with him, I was struck by how few words were said despite the environmental wisdom that he retained. I caught glimpses of not only the hundreds of iterations of sweet potato charcoal drawings that Al Saadi is well-known for but so much more. His series of drawings of sun melons spanning seven years (2013–2020) grew on his cousin, Ahmad Saif Al Saadi's farm. The sweet dates, also from Ahmad's farm, that Al Saadi drew individually, always meticulously recording the dimensions of each date. He also captured a variety of local mangos in colour, each painted from various angles. Every fruit in his artwork is measured and labelled in a precise, almost obsessive manner. Noting down the dimensions and origins of the species, not as a taxonomist, nor for a search in order, as in not with the intention of placing and classifying within a more extensive system, but as a means to understand how the species revealed themselves and their relationship to one another. These drawings, and others like them, do not claim to relay a holistic understanding of the coastal region where he's always lived. Yet, there is a magnitude to Al Saadi's body of work that surfaces from his reverence for every living creature he encounters and draws. It is as though he is deeply in touch with the unique singularity of each fruit, not only of each fruit but also of each fruit that grows on the same tree.

In this sense, Al Saadi's drawings act as a records of the ever-changing subtleties of the everyday fruits that can be easily over-looked. He doesn't consume his environment unconsciously. Al Saadi is an observer, a chronicler, and a witness to the incremental changes in the natural world. He is not an artist interested in chron-icling a static moment in nature. Instead, his practice is part of, not separate from, the wadi, and, naturally, visiting there awakens an antenna that jolts you back into seeing nature in the micro as mag-nificent.

During one visit at the height of the date season, I noticed a pile of fresh dates lying in the sun by his sculptures. When I asked, he told me he had collected them from the neighboring palm grove. Once they ripened, he would take them indoors to be pressed and stored for the season. Al Saadi's attunement to the subtle transfor-mations of his environment is thus not conceptual or theoretical. It is encompassed in every aspect of his daily life. Although these dates were meant for consumption, they're still part of his broad-er pursuit of collecting living things, arranging them, and storing them in his studio alongside taxidermied insects, plants, and rocks in his archive, where the anxiety of overlooking something when visiting his archive is everpresent. Perhaps as a window to read Al Saadi's amalgamation of seemingly unrelated objects and entities that are presumably perishable and, therefore, sit outside his archive is the term 'Apophenia', and Al Saadi as a person who cultivates apo-phenia. A word that Susan Lepselter uses to refer to the:

experience of perceiving connections between random or unrelated objects. This definition, though, already contains within it a specific point of view, an assumption of power. Who decides what is really related or unrelated? Who denies whether the relations between objects – or between events, or between spectacles of dominance across various contexts – are random and arbitrary? … But the people I write about here cultivate

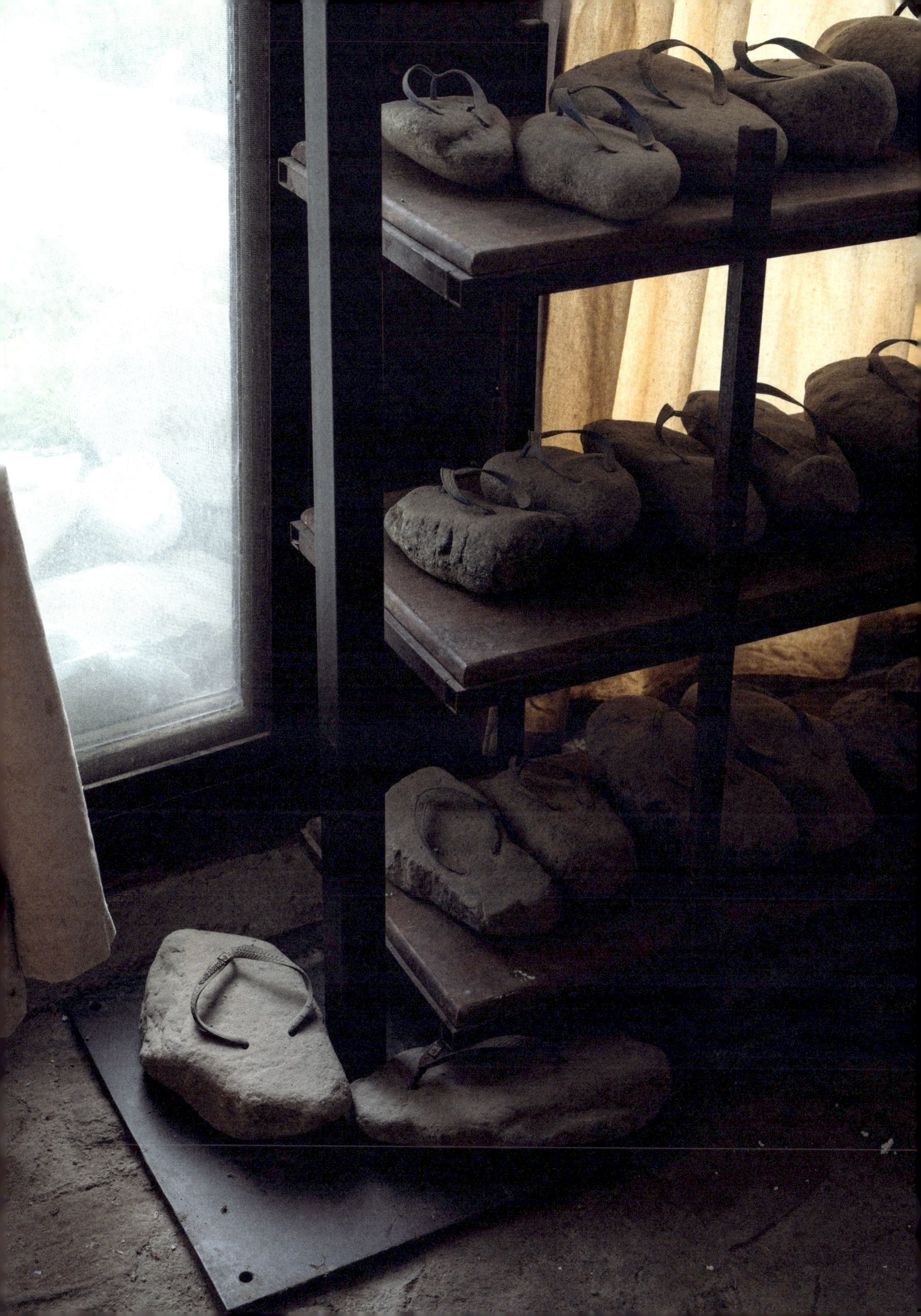

apophenia, not as an 'error,' but instead as a way to begin seeing those things that have become invisible. They foreground the naturalized patterns that normally go without saying.[1]

The space between the materials Al Saadi collects and inevitably records as part of his work are intertwined and could be read as part of his extensive sensitivity to archiving his micro-worlds.

Al Saadi's keen eye for his surroundings began at a young age when he recalls his early childhood memories of playing between the mountains of Khorfakkan: 'I used to look for the nests of the wild birds every day and follow the beehives and other insects... I also had Kalba to myself, a friend whom I hadn't heard from for years now... I once saw my brother draw two ducks using oil paint on our neighbor's walls, and ever since, the beauty of the two ducks has been embedded in my memory.'[2]

This quote illustrates how Al Saadi compiles knowledge about the environment that can't be read or understood from conventional historical archives. As an example, the earliest form of documentation that points towards the region's periphery is a report consolidated by a political agent appointed by the British Government in 1955 to oversee the slicing of the Trucial States, or in the terms of the document, 'proposals for coastal boundaries.' CM Pirie-Gordon describes Wadi Madha in quantifiable terms in his report: 'a village of 50 houses of Madhahana with some Beni Sa'ad, Dhawahir, and Naqbiyin, with about 900 palms at the mouth of the Wadi Madha, which reaches the sea near Murbah.'[3] The intention of the report was to justify how the boundaries of Wadi Madha came to be allocated as an extensive land area dedicated to the Musandam Governance. Pirie-Gordon frames that the pursuing land disputes had to be resolved swiftly as international oil companies were eager to obtain clear delineation of the boundaries from the British in the 50s. The slicing of the Madha/Sharjah land is referred to as a definitive line, 'The Frontier with Sharjah From Kharr al Najm in Wadi Hasanah. The line runs through Ras Salwa to Ras Hattatah above Wadi Shis, crossing that wadi at Ghubbat al Sallum. Thence the line runs north along the summits of the mountains, leaving Shis and Wadi Shis and all its tributaries to Sharjah and Wadis Bada' and Haurah and all their tributaries to Madha.'[4]

Al Saadi's body of work, however, occupies a unique space that allows us to learn about Madha's environment from a resident's perspective from their synthesis of the topography and from intergen-

1. Susan Claudia Lepselter, *The Resonance of Unseen Things*, (University of Michigan Press, 2016) 3-4.

2. Qasim Sultan, الخمسة قراءة في تجارب خمسة فنانين من دولة الإمارات العربية المتحدة، (Sharjah, Sharjah Cultural and Media Office, 2003) 39.

3. Outgoing Political Agent in the Trucial States C M Pirie-Gordon's impending final report, which will contain definite proposals for coastal boundaries, 1955. *Land and sea boundaries of Trucial Sheikhdoms in Persian Gulf*, 136.

4. Idib.

erational land-based practices. His varied method of recording all the living things he encounters in Madha contrasts the quantifiable language concerning Madha that is authored and circulated in traditional archives. Labelled as 'surveys,' this term conveys the content of the documents as a generalised, flattened and digestible form of conveying knowledge, specifically to those with little understanding of the place. What Al Saadi offers is that the environment can't be read, measured, or understood as quantifiable and that the species he comes across can't be lumped into digestible groups, even when recording the same plant group. Al Saadi's extensive body of work exposes the limitations of archives and their language of recording nature. In this way, he gives us a lens that helps us articulate how we can problematise the knowledge available in colonial archives. Looking at Madha and the coastal region through the lens of Al Saadi's work helps us identify what is missing in the colonial archive, precisely what is deemed significant to record and prioritise to the people of the land versus the extractors of the land.

Al Saadi is the antithesis of that in his role as an archiver and follower of bird and animal paths. Al Saadi's role as an archivist appears not in the singularity of each drawing or each document kept within his boxes but in their totality. He is an artist who takes himself out of the way – an archiver who has dedicated himself to the process of archiving. The archive is manifest. The archiver is hidden. Al Saadi is one of those artists who can be seen in all of his work, and yet his work doesn't encompass him because his character and his way of being is so subtle. It is always possible to take a step closer and see greater detail. My impression is that Al Saadi delicately reveals his work incrementally and isn't someone who will lay it all out. Most of his work is stored in tin boxes, which he will carefully draw materials from in response to particular inquisitions. And based on the level of curiosity and reaction, he will reveal parallel works.

There is no limitation to the surface that Al Saadi will use for his expression. He painted the car parked outside his studio with landscapes. He sets up exhibitions spontaneously in the natural environments he crosses through, and it appears as though the audience is not other humans but the environment. The environment itself is both his muse and his audience.

–Meitha Almazrooei

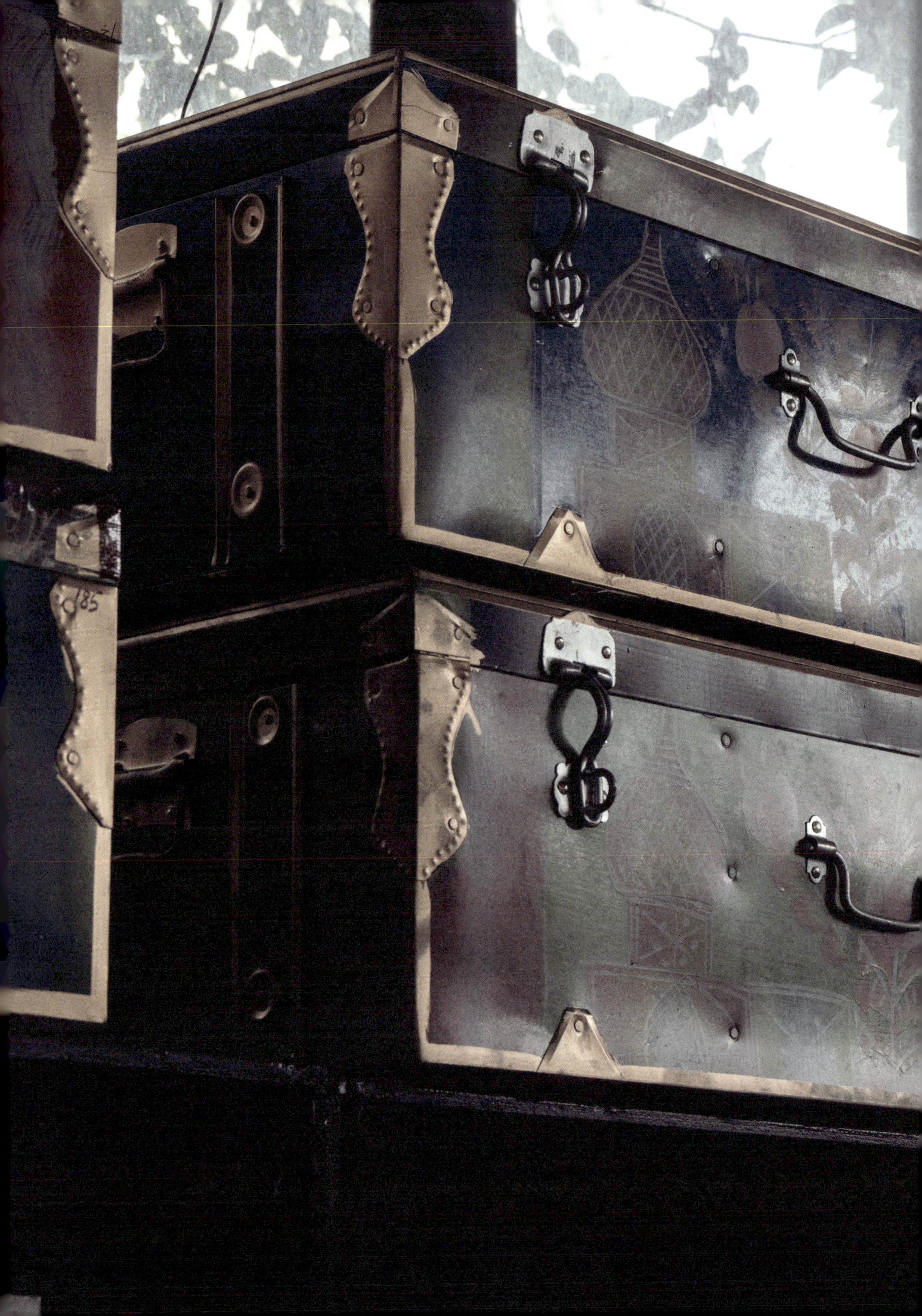

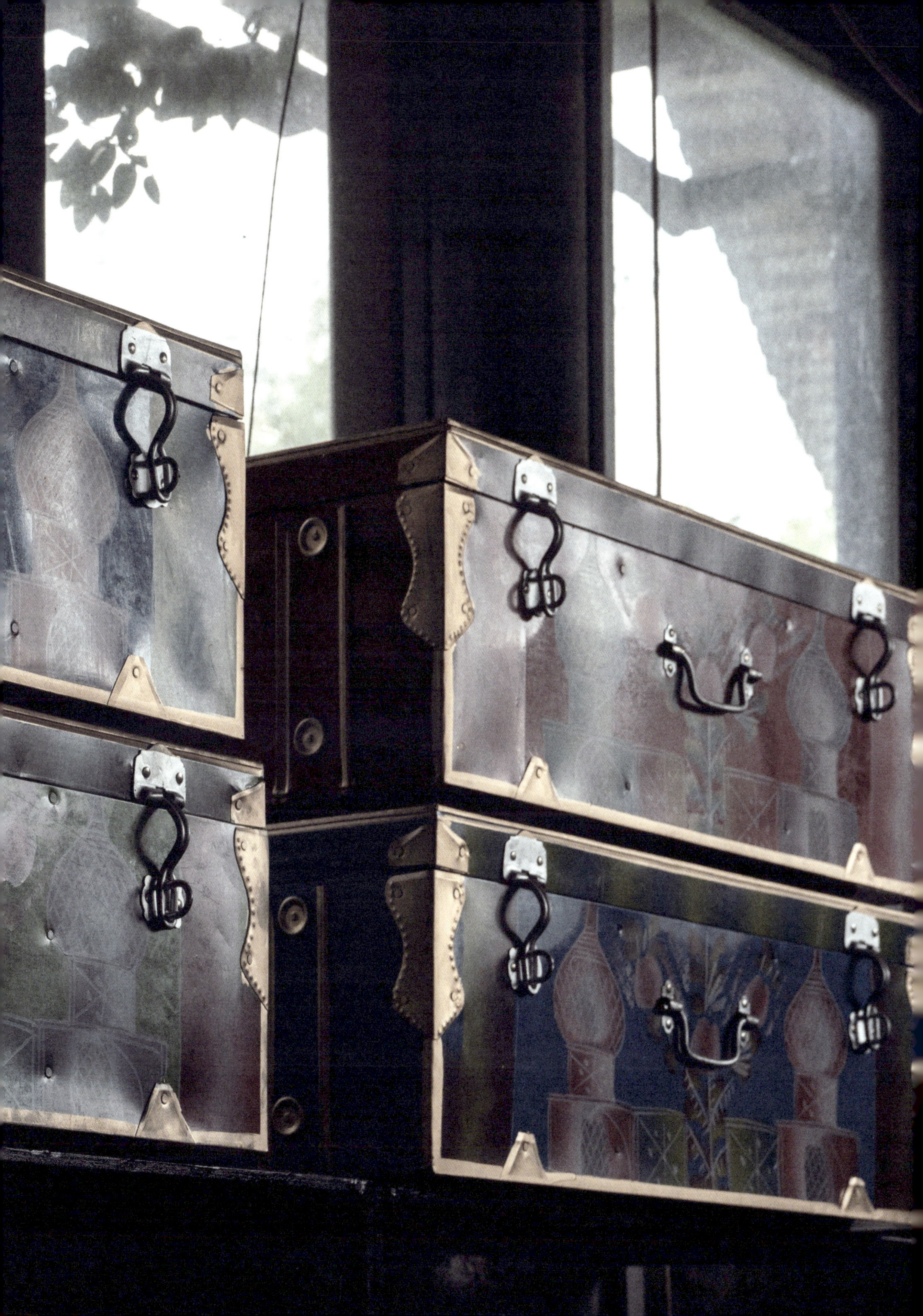

EXHIBITION HISTORY

-1989 : The first Solo Exhibition , UAE University. Alain .

-1994 : The Second Solo Exhibition , Emirates Fine Arts Society . Sharjah . 27 Jan to 1 Feb . Sharjah

-1997 : The Solo Exhibition " Iam In Japan ". Emirates Fine Arts Society . Sharjah . UAE .

-1999 : The Fourth Solo Exhibition . "Sharm Cafe" , Sharm Fujairah . UAE .

-1999 : The two artists Exhibition , Husain Sharif And Abdallah Alsaadi , Emirates Fine Arts Society , Sharjah . UAE . 04 to 13 December .

-2003 : The mobile Exhibition by Car , Fujairah .

-2004 : The mobile Exhibition by car . Khor Fakkan , Sharjah , UAE .

-2008 : The Seventh Solo Exhibition , Findale / Sweet Potato . Emirates Fine Arts Society . Sharjah . UAE .

-2014 : The Solo Exhibition " Al toubay " Sharjah Arts Foundation

-2002 : " The Fifth " From the Emirates . Ludwig Forum , Aachen , Germany .

- 2004 : The 26th Sao Paulo Biennale . Brazil .
- 2005 : The Fine Arts Museum . Buenas Aires , Argentine .
- 2005 : The Languages of the Desert , Kunst Museum , Bonn , Germany .
- 2007 : The Sharjah Arts Biennale . Sharjah . UAE .
- 2009 : A Dach platform at the Art Exhibition Of the venice Biennale , Venice , Italy .
- 2011 : The Sharjah Biennale . Sharjah , UAE .
- 2011 ; The UAE Pavilion at the 54 the International Exhibition of the venice Biennale , Italy .
- 2013 : Mind / Body , body art and performance In the Gulf Area , Centre Barsha , Dubai , UAE .
- 2013 : Emirati Expressions realised at Manarat Alsadiyat , Abu Dhabi , U AE .
- 2013 : 16 artists at New York University , AbuDhabi , U AE .
- 2014 : Here And Elsewhere , New Museum , New York , USA .

-2015 ; The Sharjah Arts Biennale (12) sharjah . UAE.

-2016 : Aichi Triennale , Nagoya , Japan .

-2017 : The Sharjah Arts Biennale , Sharjah . UAE.

-2017 : The Venice Biennale , Arsenale , Italy .

-2017 : The Antarctic Biennale , the South pole .

-2020 : Lahore Biennale . Pakistan .

-2022 : The Papers tales , Louvre Museum , Abu Dhabi , UAE .

-2022 : Expo Dubai , dubai UAE .

-2023 : Thinking Art . Maraya Gallery , Sharjah , UAE . 11 sep 2023 to Jan 2024 .

residences

-1990 : Cavilam , Vichy , France .
-1994 - 1996 : Kyoto , Japan .
-1998 :   University . Scotland .
-2008 ; Austria .
-2009 : Rio de Janiero , Brazil .

BOOKS BY AL SAADI

Sharm Coffee Shop. Abu Dhabi: Abu Dhabi Authority for Culture & Heritage Cultural Foundation. 2009.

Marende. Sharjah: Department of Culture and Information, 2008.

My Mother's Letters. Sharjah: Department of Culture and Information, 2003.

Circle and Line. Sharjah: Department of Culture and Information, 2003.

SELECTED WRITINGS ABOUT AL SAADI

Abou El Fetouh, Tarek and Younis, Ala. *On the Book of Sceneries: EXPO 2020 Dubai Public Art Programme*. Berlin: Hatje Cantz Verlag, 2022.

Abou El Fetouh, Tarek and Salti, Rasha. *Sites of Memory, Sites of Amnesia*. Abu Dhabi: National Pavilion UAE – La Biennale di Venezia and Kaph Books, 2024.

Aidabi, Yousif. *Al Fan Al Jadeed* [New Arts]. Sharjah: Department of Culture and Information, 1995.

Al Mueini, Abdul Rahman. *Window 2006: 16 UAE Artists*. Dubai: Total Arts Gallery, 2006.

Al Qasimi, Hoor. *1980 – Today: Exhibitions in the United Arab Emirates*. Abu Dhabi: National Pavilion UAE – La Biennale di Venezia, 2015.

Allison, Maya. *The NYU Abu Dhabi Art Gallery: 2014-2020*. Abu Dhabi: Akkadia Press, 2021.

Allison, Maya and Kattan, Bana. *But We Cannot See Them: Tracing a UAE Art Community 1988–2008*. Abu Dhabi: New York University Art Gallery, 2017.

De Marchi, Cristiana and Ali, Muhannad. *Is Old Gold?*. Dubai: DUCTAC, 2017.

Fadda, Reem. *Six Visions to be Unveiled for Emirati Expressions: Realised*. Abu Dhabi: Abu Dhabi Department Of Culture And Tourism, 2013.

Joo, Eungie. Sharjah Biennial 12: *The past, the present, the possible*. Sharjah: Sharjah Art Foundation, 2015.

Khozam, Adel. 'In the light and the shadow and life between them'. Sharjah: Department of Culture and Information, 2002.

Lagler, Annette. *5/UAE*. Aachen: Ludwig Forum for International Art, 2002.

Seaman, Anna. 'Abdullah Al Saadi: A National Treasure'. *Al Tashkeel Magazine*, 2016.

Sharif, Hassan. *Al Khamsa* [The Five]. Sharjah: Department of Culture and Information, 2003.

Sharif, Hassan. 'Abdullah Al Saadi.' *Al Ittihad Al Thaqafi*. 9 January 1997.

Tabbarah, Faysal, Almazrooei, Meitha and Srouji, Dima. *On Foraging*. Abu Dhabi: 421 and Kaph Books, 2023.

Thani, Ahmed Rashid. 'Abdullah Al Saadi wal Findale' [Abdullah Al Saadi and the Sweet Potato]. *Al Khaleej*, 12 April 2008.

Vali, Murtaza. *Accented*. Sharjah: Maraya Art Centre, 2015.

Vali, Murtaza. 'Object at/of Play'. In *Rock, Paper, Scissors: Positions in Play*. Abu Dhabi: National Pavilion UAE – La Biennale di Venezia, 2017.

Yousif, Mohamed. *Art in the Emirates: From the Translation of Heritage to Post-Modernism, 1970-2020*. Sharjah: Sharjah Institute for Heritage, 2021.

LIST OF ILLUSTRATIONS

All images are courtesy of the artist
Illustrations on the cover and table of contents as well as lettering
(back cover, spine, exhibition history) are by Abdullah Al Saadi.

P. 9
Black-and-white portrait of Abdullah
Al Saadi, 1979.

PP. 10-11; 26-27
Bicycle journey to Ras Al Khaimah,
1995. Photos by Abdullah Al Saadi.

PP. 16-17; 22-23; 28-29
Series of hand-drawn maps. Mixed-
media collages, 2000s 18.5 x 26.2 cm
each.

P. 33
Kharaj walam ya'ud [Left and never
returned], 1984. 46 x 65 cm. Oil on
wood. Photo by Danko Stjepanovic.

P. 35
Travelling, 1992. 50 x 75 cm. Oil on
canvas. Photo by Danko Stjepanovic.

PP. 36-37
Untitled, 1991. 75 x 50 cm. Oil on
canvas. Photo by Danko Stjepanovic.

P. 39
Self-portrait, 1992. 50 x 75 cm. Oil on
canvas.

P. 41
Untitled, 1991. 50 x 75 cm. Oil on
canvas. Photo by Danko Stjepanovic.

PP. 42-43
Shepherd, 1984. 93 x 74 cm. Oil on
canvas. Photo by Danko Stjepanovic.

PP. 44-45
Separation, 1987. 75 x 93 cm. Oil on
canvas. Photo by Danko Stjepanovic.

P. 47
Church of the Holy Family in Spain,
1992. 76 x 100 cm. Oil on canvas.
Photo by Danko Stjepanovic.

P. 48; 58
Collage of drawings and illustrations
from Abdullah Al Saadi's university
sketchbook (late 1980s-early 1990s).

P. 53
Untitled, 1991. 76 x 50 cm. Oil on
canvas.

PP. 54-55
Jebel Hafeet - Al Ain, 1992. 34 x 50 cm.
Charcoal on paper.

P. 56
Self-portrait, 1992. 50 x 75. Oil on
canvas.

PP. 58-59
Untitled, 1984. 52 x 72 cm. Oil on
wood. Photo by Danko Stjepanovic.

PP. 64-65
Preserved insect specimens in tin
cans from the early 2000s. Photo by
Abdullah Al Saadi.

PP. 68-69; 74-75
Manipulated scans of *Bones* and *The
Cavity Room*, 1991. From Abdullah
Al Saadi's catalogue *The 2nd One
Man Exhibition*, 1994. 14.5 x 21 cm.
Published by Emirates Fine Arts
Society.

PP. 70-71
Documentation from performance
work *Bones*, 1991.

PP. 72-73
Scan of news article 'Between
Collecting and Travelling' by Ahmed
Rashid Thani. Published in *Al Khaleej*,
26 September 1994.

PP. 79-103
Sketches, drawings and illustrations
from Abdullah Al Saadi's sketchbooks
from Japan and Scotland, 1995-1997.

P. 88; 97
Cover of Abdullah Al Saadi's
sketchbook from his time in Japan.
1995-1996.

P. 104; 121
Cover of Abdullah Al Saadi's
sketchbook from his time in Japan.
1995-1996.

PP. 106-119
I am in Japan, 1996. 12 x 207 cm. Pen
on paper (scroll).

PP. 124-136; 146-159
Illustrations from Abdullah Al
Saadi's artist book *Circle and Line*.
2003. 8 x 12 cm. Published by
Sharjah Department of Culture and
Information.

P. 136, 144; 145
Details of Abdullah Al Saadi's
mixed-media collages for *The Mobile
Exhibition* and *Sharm Coffee Shop
Exhibition*, 1999-2003.

PP. 140-141
Documentation from *The Mobile
Exhibition*, 2003. Photos by Abdullah
Al Saadi.

PP. 130-131; 142-143
Documentation from *Sharm Coffee
Shop Exhibition*, 1999. Photos by
Abdullah Al Saadi.

PP. 152-169
Manipulated scans of *Sharm Coffee
Shop Exhibition*, 1999. From Abdullah
Al Saadi's catalogue *The 4th One Man
Exhibition*, 1999. 14.5 x 21 cm. Self-
published.

PP. 172-173
Abjadiya, 2009. From 'Rio, Brazil.'
83 x 160 cm. Oil on canvas. Photo by
Danko Stjepanovic.

PP. 174-175
Abjadiya, 2009. From 'Rio, Brazil.'
83 x 161 cm. Oil on canvas. Photo by
Danko Stjepanovic.

PP. 176-177
Abjadiya, 2009. From 'Rio, Brazil.'
84.5 x 164.5 cm. Oil on canvas. Photo
by Danko Stjepanovic.

P. 179; 192
Sketches from Rio, 2009. Photo by
Danko Stjepanovic.

PP. 180-181
Huroof, 2009. From 'Rio, Brazil.'
80 x 116.5 cm. Oil on canvas. Photo
by Danko Stjepanovic.

PP. 182-183
Huroof, 2009. From 'Rio, Brazil.'
80 x 116.5 cm. Oil on canvas. Photo
by Danko Stjepanovic.

PP. 188-189; P. 184; 193
Extracts from Abdullah Al Saadi's
100th journal developed during his
residency in Brazil, 2009. Photos by
Danko Stjepanovic.

PP. 190-191
Painting of Abdullah Al Saadi's studio
in Madha, 2020. 86 x 164 cm. Oil on
canvas.

PP. 195-205
My Mother's Letters, 2008-2013
(details). Installation, assembled
objects, mixed media and a
publication.

PP. 208-213; P. 223
Diptych landscape scroll drawings of
Innsbruck (details), 2008. 14 x 166
cm. Pen on paper. Photos by Danko
Stjepanovic.

PP. 214-215
Diptych landscape scroll drawings
of Bolzano (details), 2008. 9 x 187
cm. Pen on paper. Photo by Danko
Stjepanovic.

P. 216; PP. 224-243
Scans from Abdullah Al Saadi's artist
book *Marende*, 2008. 11 x 16 cm.
Published by Sharjah Department of
Culture and Information.

P. 248
Photo of Abdullah Al Saadi in Japan,
1995.

P. 249
Photo of Abdullah Al Saadi in his
studio in Madha, 2024. Photo by
Danko Stjepanovic.

P. 255
Portrait of Abdullah Al Saadi, 2003.
Photo by Valsalan Kanara.

PP. 258-259
Documentation from Abdullah Al
Saadi's participation in the Ship for
World Youth, 1992.

PP. 262-271; 282-287
Camar Cande's Journey, 2010-2011.
Installation, video, 151 watercolour
paintings. Dimensions variable.
Commissioned by Sharjah Art
Foundation for Sharjah Biennial 10.
Sharjah Art Foundation Collection.

P. 272; PP. 276-277; 279-281
Documentation from *Camar Cande's
Journey*, 2010-2011. Photos by
Abdullah Al Saadi and Abdulrahman
Al Muaini.

PP. 290-307
Collected works and drawings from
a commissioned trip to Antarctica,
2017. 8 scrolls - charcoal on canvas;
sketching notebooks - pen on paper;
abjadiya [alphabets]; assembled
objects; found rocks. Dimensions
variable. Photos by Danko
Stjepanovic.

PP. 310-333
Naked Sweet Potato, 2008-ongoing.
Clay sculptures in metal coffers;
engraved rocks; drawings (ink on
paper); paintings (oil on canvas);
found object assemblage; handmade
jewellery; book; and video
performance. Dimensions variable.
Image courtesy of the National
Pavilion UAE – La Biennale di
Venezia. Photos by Mohamed Somji.
Some parts of the work belong to the
Guggenheim Abu Dhabi.

P. 339; 342-343
Documentation of Abdullah Al Saadi's
studio in Madha, 2024. Photos by
Danko Stjepanovic.

PP. 352-353
Documentation of Abdullah Al Saadi
drawing the surrounding desert
landscape, 1992. Photo by Abdullah
Al Saadi.

PP. 356-357
Untitled, 2014 (detail). 83 parts,
dimensions variable. Acrylic on
stones. Commissioned by Sharjah Art
Foundation for Sharjah Biennial 12.

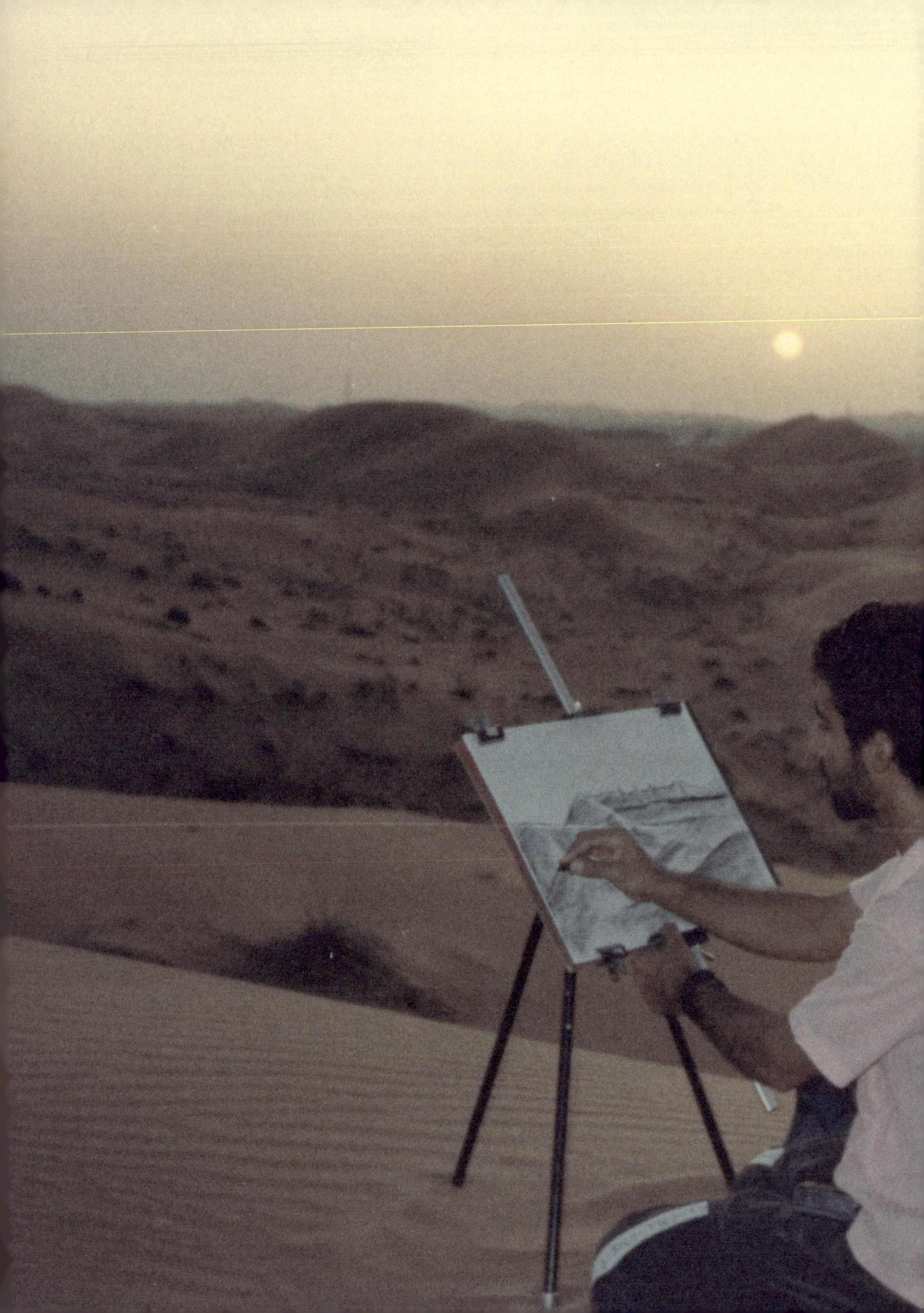

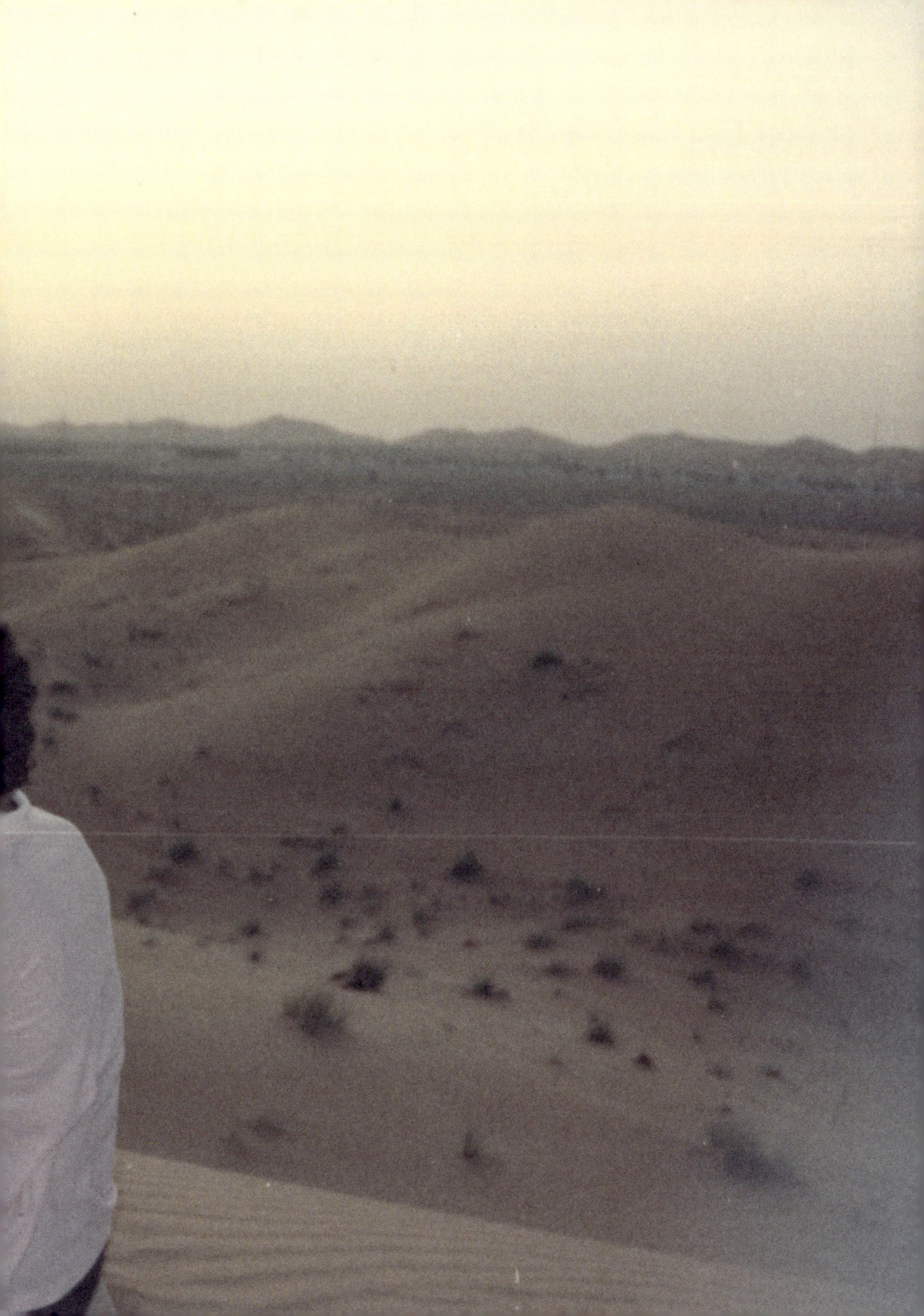

CONTRIBUTORS

Hoor Al Qasimi

Hoor Al Qasimi is President and Director of Sharjah Art Foundation, an independent public arts organisation which she established in 2009 as a catalyst and advocate for the arts, not only in Sharjah but also in the region and around the world. She has curated major exhibitions for the foundation and other international institutions, including the critically acclaimed Sharjah Biennial 15: *Thinking Historically in the Present* (2023). In addition to her role at the foundation, Al Qasimi also serves as President of the International Biennial Association, President of The Africa Institute and President and Director of the Sharjah Architecture Triennial.

Ahmad Makia

Ahmad Makia is a geographer, author and editor. His work spans the fields of spatial studies and human geography, gender and identity, Arab and Islamic history and material philosophy. He is founder and creative director of HYPERHOUSE, a boutique publisher and editorial practice; head of publications at Sharjah Art Foundation; and architecture and design editor at Kaph Books. He has published essays in academic journals, magazines, artist books, zines and online. Makia was also founding editor and contributor to the publishing projects THE STATE, ZIGG and Dubailand.

Ahmed Rashid Thani

Ahmed Rashid Thani (1962–2012) was part of the generation of thinkers who shaped the UAE's New Arts Movement. Venerated as the UAE's 'Father of Existentialism', he is especially known for pioneering modernism and publishing his poems in vernacular Emirati Arabic. Originally from Khor Fakkan and later residing in Abu Dhabi, Thani published numerous plays, poems, treatises, travelogues and short stories, as well as many essays in local newspapers.

Meitha Almazrooei

Meitha Almazrooei is an architect, editor and PhD candidate in History, Theory and Criticism of Architecture at the Massachusetts Institute of Technology. She received her MS in Critical, Curatorial & Conceptual Practices in Architecture from Columbia University's Graduate School of Architecture, Planning and Preservation. Her curatorial and editorial work has encompassed public programming for Guggenheim Abu Dhabi, publications for The National Pavilion of the UAE at La Biennale di Venezia, and the founding of *WTD Magazine*, an architecture and design platform which published urban narratives from the Gulf, the Eastern Mediterranean and North Africa.

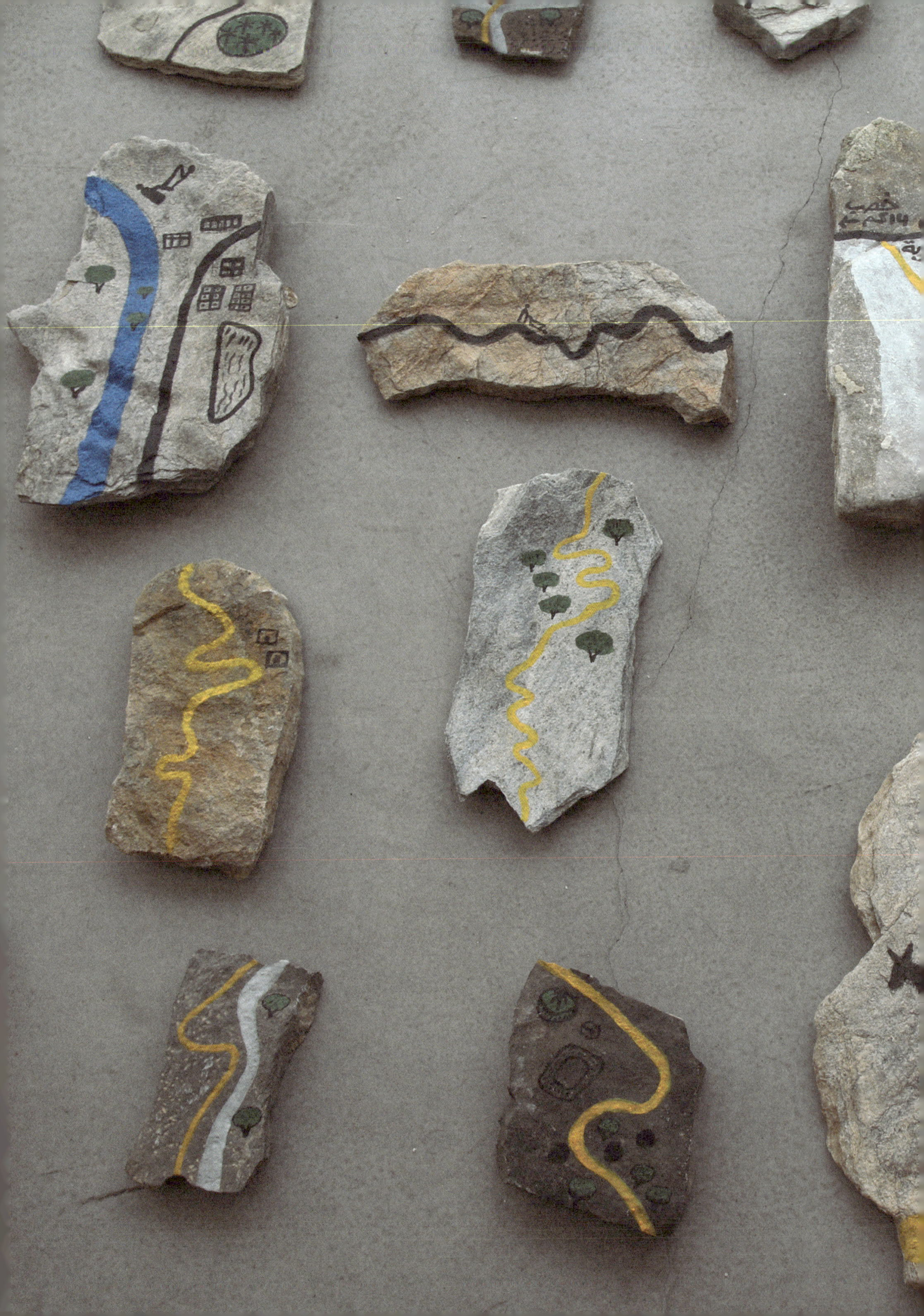

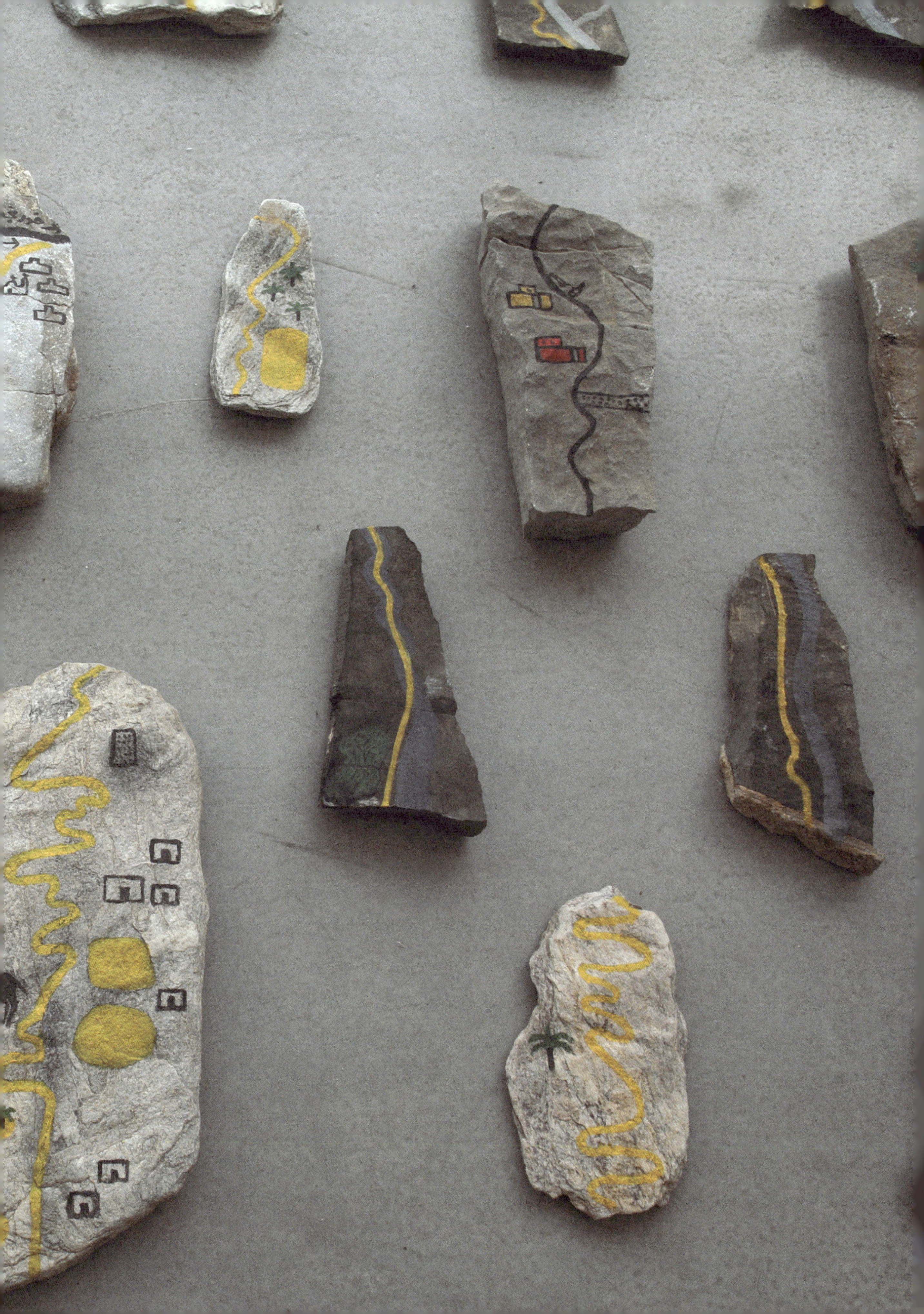

ABDULLAH AL SAADI

اخرج ولم يعد /

Sometimes You Have To Go a Long Way to
Come Back a Short Distance

PUBLISHED BY
Sharjah Art Foundation
PO Box 19989, Sharjah
United Arab Emirates
www.sharjahart.org

President and Director
Hoor Al Qasimi

Vice President
Nawar Al Qassimi

Director of Learning and Research
Noora Al Mualla

SHARJAH ART FOUNDATION

PUBLICATION

Commissioning Editor
Hoor Al Qasimi

Editor
Ahmad Makia

Managing Editor
Maria Mumtaz

Designer
Moez Akkari (Bao Books)

Editorial and Research Assistant
Mahmoud Mamdouh

Copy Editor and Editorial Assistance
Henry Ace Knight

Proofreader
Zeina Assaf

ISBN 978-614-8035-67-8

Publication © 2024, Sharjah Art Foundation

All artworks © Abdullah Al Saadi
All texts © 2024, the authors

First edition, 2024
Sharjah Art Foundation, 2024
Kaph Books, 2024

Printed on Arena Natural Rough 120 gr
and Gmund Heidi Soft Kraft 530 gr

Typeset in Bradford LL
and Gerstner Programm

Printed in March 2024 by Graphius,
Belgium

DISTRIBUTED BY

KAPH
ART BOOKS FROM THE MIDDLE EAST

Gouraud Street, Gemmayze
Immeuble Renno, 3rd floor
Beirut, Lebanon
www.kaphbooks.com

NORTH AMERICA - LATIN AMERICA
ASIA - AUSTRALIA
ARTBOOK | D.A.P.
75 Broad Street, Suite 630
New York, NY 10004
www.artbook.com

FRANCE - SWITZERLAND - BELGIUM
- LUXEMBOURG
Les Presses du Réel
35 rue Colson,
21000 Dijon, France
www.lespressesdureel.com

REST OF EUROPE
Idea Books
Nieuwe Herengracht 11
1011 RK Amsterdam, The Netherlands
www.ideabooks.nl

MIDDLE EAST
Sharjah Art Foundation
PO Box 19989, Sharjah
United Arab Emirates
publications@sharjahart.org

CIEL BOOK DISTRIBUTION
Al Manara Road, Al Quoz 1
PO BOX 282005, Dubai
United Arab Emirates
www.ciel.me